THE BIRTH OF INDIAN PSYCHOLOGY AND ITS DEVELOPMENT IN BUDDHISM

THE BIRTH OF INDIAN PSYCHOLOGY AND ITS DEVELOPMENT IN BUDDHISM

A Rewritten and Enlarged Edition of " Buddhist Psychology," published in "The quest" Series, London, 1914, republished 1924

BY

Mrs. RHYS DAVIDS, D.LITT., M. A.

PRESIDENT OF THE PALI TEXT SOCIETY

GYAN

Published by

Gyan Publishing House
5, Ansari Road
Daryaganj, New Delhi-110002
Phone: 011-47034999, 9811692060
E-mail: books@gyanbooks.com

Distribution Network
gyanbooks.com
India, USA, Canada, UK, Australia, France

ISBN : 978-81-212-2604-2 (HB)
First Published, 1936

2nd Impression 2021

Printed at: Gyan Press, Delhi.

The Birth of
Indian Psychology and its Development in Buddhism
Author: Mrs. Rhys Davids

THE BIRTH OF INDIAN PSYCHOLOGY AND ITS DEVELOPMENT IN BUDDHISM

A Rewritten and Enlarged Edition of "Buddhist Psychology," published in "The Quest" Series, London, 1914; republished 1924

BY

MRS. RHYS DAVIDS, D.LITT., M.A.

PRESIDENT OF THE PALI TEXT SOCIETY

LONDON

LUZAC & CO.

46 GREAT RUSSELL STREET

1936

NOTE BY THE EDITOR OF "THE QUEST" SERIES

ONE of the most marked signs of the times is the close attention that is being paid to psychological research, the results of which are being followed with the greatest interest by an intelligent public, and the continued advance of which promises to be one of the most hopeful activities of modern science. The observation, analysis, and classification of mental phenomena are being pursued with untiring energy, and the problems of mind attacked on all sides with refreshing vigour. In brief, the new science of psychology seems to promise at no distant date to become one of the most fruitful, if not the most fruitful, field of human tillage. But turn where we will to our manuals or special studies, we find no reference to the patient work of many centuries accomplished by the introspective genius of the East. In this field none have laboured with greater industry and acumen than the Buddhist thinkers, whose whole philosophy and therewith also their religion rests on a psychological basis. Not only so, but some of their main contentions are very similar to the later views advanced by the dominant schools of modern research. The work of these profound analysts of the nature of mind should, therefore, by no means be neglected by modern psychologists and those who are interested in their instructive labours—and who that desires to know himself can fail to be so interested? It must, however, be admitted that there is some excuse for previous neglect owing to the lack of books designed to smooth the way for those unacquainted with Oriental studies. It is with the hope of making a start in this direction that the present valuable Introduction has been secured from the pen of one who is acknowledged to be the most competent student of the subject in the West.

PREFACE TO THE FIRST EDITION

My book is an attempt to envisage faithfully something true in the history of a very interesting current in human ideas. This 'something true' is the analysis and theory of mind in the movement and culture we understand by Early Buddhism, as well as in that of its direct descendant still thriving in Burma, Ceylon and Siam, called Theravāda, or the Doctrine of the Elders. This also is called Buddhism—some call it Hīna-Yāna, some Southern Buddhism.

As to the book's quests and goals, two of the more proximate may suffice. While scholars are beginning to get at and decipher the long-buried treasure of Buddhist writings brought from Mid-Asia, the general reader is being told that the group of other descendants from Early Buddhism called Mahā-Yānism, is not only evolved from the earlier doctrine, but is its completion and apotheosis. The reader cannot judge in this matter, unless he has an all-round knowledge of what the developed system started from. Such a knowledge is not always present in those who are fluent about the complete descendant. Hence he is placed in the position of one who learns of Neo-Platonism and not of Plato, of Aquinas and not of Aristotle. My book's quest is to present summarily some of the thought contained in the mother-doctrine and her first-born child, much of which is still inaccessible to him.

The second object is to bring nearer the day when the historical treatment of psychology will find it impossible to pretend that the observation and analysis of mind began with the Pre-Socratics. Psychologists are, some of them, curiously unhistorical, even with regard to the European field with its high fence of ignorance and prejudice. Theories are sometimes put forward as new that have been anticipated in both Europe and Asia. I say 'curiously,' because the history of ideas about the mind is both fascinating and suggestive. Would Professor Bergson say of his brother thinkers, too, especially of the more constructive among them (I dare to include himself), that the past of psychological thought also *est là, continuellement*, but that so intent is their forward gaze that they 'cannot and must not look back'? Yet how much more impressive might they not make the present for us if they would, if they felt compelled to look back a little more! Let us hope that monographs in psychological history may eventually succeed in making it unnecessary for drowning, or other catastrophes, to bring flooding in upon them the ignored past of ideas in Indian philosophy.

With so large an object in so small a book, it has been impossible to compare the line of descent I have chosen with other lines, even with that of the Mādhyamika school, in which Professor de la Vallée Poussin has revealed much interesting psychological matter. I have also to apologize for bringing in several terms in the original. This was as inevitable, for clearness and unambiguity, as would be the use of corresponding Greek words in writing on Greek psychology. But we are more used to Greek words. Finally, if I have repeated statements made in previous writings, it was to avoid irritating the reader by too many references, as if suggesting that he might as well be reading not one book, but three or four.

C. A. F. RHYS DAVIDS.

February, 1914.

CONTENTS

THE BIRTH OF INDIAN PSYCHOLOGY AND ITS DEVELOPMENT IN BUDDHISM

CHAPTER I

INTRODUCTORY

In 1914 I published, at the request of the late G. R. S. Mead, a manual of Buddhist Psychology for "The Quest" Series of Manuals (G. Bell and Sons). In 1924 I published a new impression of this, adding in a supplement a few new impressions and corrected convictions. After yet another ten years the leaders of The Buddhist Lodge, London, consulted me whether a résumé might be made of the book for their organ, or whether I preferred it should be put aside and that I should give a fresh outline of the subject.

Of course, I preferred the latter. I have a mother's weakness for a ten-year-old child. But whereas a child grows, a book does not. Its mother it is who can grow. I do not pretend that my knowledge of Buddhist records has in those ten years become really adequate. But my knowledge both of the earliest Buddhist records we yet have, the Pali Tipiṭaka and of preceding and contemporary Indian literature, is better than it was. If I have altered much in what I now write about Buddhism, it is because I know it better, it is because I see it better in perspective. It is not because I am reading purely subjective experience into it, or finding just what I want to find, as is the criticism of some. I write of fresh discoveries I make as the days pass—things I had not expected to find, things that make certain conclusions of past and present writers on Buddhism untenable, but which have apparently been wholly overlooked.

My fancies have played no part herein. But reconstructive imagination has been busy. No historian can get along safely where this is not the case. We have to make alive a dead past. We have to show that past as in a state of becoming, of passing from older to newer values. And more: we need that desideratum of the historian, the man of science, the explorer in any field, an hypothesis of our subject in its most general aspect, which must be tested as we go. And in the field of Buddhism and its history we walk along a new road, where fresh materials have been, within half a century at least, coming to hand every year.

In this field we are as yet historically very weak. Our task is of immense difficulty, largely because India has never kept even the contemporary annals and chronicles such as we tried to do in Europe. "When I think," that fine scholar the late Francis Burkitt wrote to me, "of the confused history of Gospel criticism, of the 150 years of struggle to attain an historical view of the first announcement of the Gospel, I feel that your task is enormous." But our weakness lies partly in our unwillingness to discern, to admit that, in every literary composition which has come down to us, we have a history-in-little. More especially in such as were for a long time oral, not written. And this is the story of all Buddhist "books" compiled previous to B.C. 200, or even B.C. 100. Still is it being said that certain doctrines are certainly fundamental in Buddhist teaching of the sixth century B.C., *because* they happen to be endorsed with emphasis in books compiled orally centuries later, and scripturally centuries later still.

And if we of Europe are historically weak, the Indian scholar as yet among newer writers is, as historically alive, hardly to be found. I have not a few books on matters philosophical, religious and psychological sent for review, and as yet I fail to note, in this respect, any healthy growth. There is, on the contrary, a tendency to avoid historical survey of values as newly emerging, as gaining strength, as dying out. There is talk about systematic exposition, synthesis, and logical development—which is not the same thing as historical treatment—and we get juxtapositions of teachers separated centuries the one from the other, but no procession of thinkers, no relays of torchbearers. Thus certain interesting and important phases in the life of Indian culture, as being 'life-in-becoming,' and not a promiscuous jumble of men and ideas, are lost to us. I need hardly say, I am not here alluding to certain outstanding works by sons of India on her philosophy (not its psychology)—those, for instance, by Radhakrishnan and Das Gupta. It is progress in the men of tomorrow that I seek.

When in the older Pali Books, the Piṭakas I and II, we come across an amazing preoccupation with man, less as man and more as a quincunx of visible and invisible components—come across it for the first time in Indian thought—we naturally ask, Who was responsible for this new feature? Was it the founders? Was it the result of later compilation and editing? Was it orally taught at all? It is profoundly unsatisfying to hear in sole response: "The Buddhists recognize. . . . The Buddhists do not hold that. . . ."

Here is a cult or culture, existing from the sixth century B.C. till some six centuries A.D. in India. Now did that cult *always* "recognize" this? *When* did it come to reject that?

No merely systematic or logical treatment of Hindu thought will answer these questions. We must see that 'thought' as in a state of growth. We see it, in its Vedic, pre-Upaniṣadic stage as what Ernest Renan called syncretic, seeing all culture or religion or thinking as vaguely one and indivisible. In the Upaniṣadic age, we see it beginning to emerge into the analytic stage, which was preoccupied mainly with seeing things as manifold. The Indian teacher was beginning to look at the man in a new way: not as just what was seen (*rūpa*), and as the 'more' that was unseen (*nāma*), symbolized by his name, but as one who had, on the one hand, the instrument of body, on the other hand a subtler invisible instrument, hitherto accepted unanalytically as *manas*, the mind, with sight, hearing, breath. Historically to investigate all this, we do not put ourselves at the right perspective, if we group our subject as 'perception and inference,' a division of a late day emerging when India was beginning to cultivate what we call logic, and needed a division between names and argument.

Here then is how I come to the problem of Buddhist analysis of mind: in the Piṭakas is an incessant and pedantic persistence in referring to man as a fivefold plurality or manifold. Whence its origin? Is there anything like it elsewhere in Indian culture preceding or accompanying the birth of Buddhism? To speak generally: Can we trace in Indian thought, as we can in our own philosophy, the birth and rise of an analysis of mind, mind as distinguishable from the man or self, such as we now call by the name of psychology?

As yet I have found little help in this matter from any writers European or Indian. My effort of twenty years ago was a good baby and toddled a little way. What I judge was good is reproduced here. But here I hope to have shown I have wayfared a good deal further, albeit the lack of more erudite helpers will make this further effort also very provisional.

It is with reluctance that I use in my title the word 'psychology.' This is a term of this new world of ours, and of that only. And as to that, in my youth we never heard of it. Thirty years ago Guido Villa could begin his *Contemporary Psychology* with the words: "The word Psychology is nowadays on everyone's lips." Half a century ago we were speaking of 'Mental Science,' 'Philosophy of the Mind,' and even 'Mental Physiology.' The newer term indicated at once a greater divorce from philosophy or metaphysic, and a halt called to too much identifying the range and values in things of the 'psyche' with the range and values in things of body. But we have been swift adaptors as compared with India. India, which gave birth to a psychological culture centuries before Britain was known to Cæsar, never, to the best of my belief, made any such conscious segregation of the study of mental phenomena, as to feel the need of a name for it. She neither felt it then, nor has she felt it since. She has ever been, I repeat, too syncretic for the evolution in her culture.

It is to be confessed that, in adapting from Germany through France our term for this study, we have come to make it a pretty bad misfit. The translation of Blancard's *Physical Dictionary* (1693) was 'intituled' a 'description or doctrin' of Man, under 'Anatomy and Psycology' [*sic*]. Hartley, seeing in 'psyche' mind rather than man, called his Psychology "theory of the human mind, with that of the intellectual principles of Brute Animals," thus reducing the 'Man' to adjectival rank. As meaning, for Sokrates, the man, 'psyche' has come to be left out save in language, where she is ineradicable. 'Mentology' had been a juster word. But since neither Germany nor France had a word equal in scope to our 'mind'—do readers remember how Fechner worried over the two half-terms *Geist*, *Seele*?—our neighbours retained the Greek term when they emerged from writing treatises in Latin, avoiding at least a hybrid compound.

In India we have the twofold picture (to go no further) of psychology on the one hand beginning and persisting with the man or self as a *sine qua non* in the analysis; on the other hand, in the Buddhist development, gradually lowering the man in value and then totally rejecting him—save in language.

It is to make the first part of the diptych clearer as the historical, that is, the true, introduction to the second part, that I have here tried, much more fully than I tried twenty years ago, to trace the dawn in analytic outlook in early Indian culture. It is only in this way that we can begin to account for the distinctive trend taken in its estimate of man and his mind by Buddhism. I am fully aware, that the tithe of attention bestowed as yet on what I have said in recent years in the latter subject will not be extended, save yet more grudgingly, to what I have here put forward about Vedic mental analysis. But it was necessary to get at the historical perspective, and, as I say, I could find no work adequate to supply what

Siebeck called "the desiderated pre-studies."[1] Such, in the study of Oriental psychology, he left, not without much perspicacious sketching of his own, to the field of "the yet to be expected." If, in showing in some detail the psychological background of early Buddhism, I have set out matter suggestive for better work by younger experts, I am content.

If I have refrained from making inquiry into the Mahābhārata, beyond occasional glances at its Bhagavadgītā, I may be forgiven for not seeking in it those birth features which it, as having accepted Sānkhya and Yoga as already adolescent features, could not be expected to reveal.

[1] *Geschichte der Psychologie*, Vorwort. I acknowledge with pleasure the reference, kindly sent me by Dr. C. G. Jung, to his own 'pre-studies' in early Indian psychology, namely, in his *Psychological Types*. See below, Chap. VII.

CHAPTER II

MAN AND HIS MIND IN VEDIC LITERATURE

In asserting that preoccupation with mind was a new phenomenon for the thought of India generally, I am not referring to mind taken *en bloc*, or to mention of mind in idioms of speech. I mean a new sort of attention paid to mind. I mean an analytic attention. I mean a distinguishing of mind from man. I mean a breaking up of mind into parts, features, phases.

In the Vedas (the hymns and applied utterances [*saṃhitas*]), the idioms referring to mind—this is nearly always *manas*, much more rarely *citta*—are not strikingly archaic; they are much like our own analogous phrases. Here are some:

" Sun travels quick as mind," . . . " we know what thy mind was " . . . " approving thy mind " . . . " this praise has been offered by the mind " . . . " what a man reaches with mind, that he expresses by speech " . . . " by what great mind may we arrest the storm gods ?" . . . " wise in mind . . . trembling in mind . . . pleased in mind " . . . " a woman mindful of the gods " . . . " we must consult the thought (*citta*) of another . . . beyond our thoughts (*cittāni*) " . . . " which prayer is to be the choice of thy mind ?"[1]

Mind (or thought) is here reckoned as a phase of activity in the life of man. If mind is therein qualified,

[1] From the Rig-Veda Hymns. May I here remind the reader unversed in Indian transliteration, that the *c* is in every case pronounced like *ch* in church ?

interest is not felt in the quality *as* a feature of mind, such as wisdom, trembling, pleasure. Mind is plastic self-expression of man by man. It is *man who is alone interesting*, whether he be human or divine. As to his ways of activity, mental, vocal, or other, we are at a pre-analytic stage of growth.

Again and indefinitely later: when we look at the Vedic collections of ritual sayings known as Brāhmaṇas, there is much mention of mind (*manas*). But here too it is the *self* who is the sole centre of interest: the *man* who with body and mind is busy planning, measuring ('mind' is literally measuring) his altar, the concrete picture and symbol of his constraining will, the man who is, at the centre of his being, however vaguely and syncretically conceived, a More than any modes of his activity, the valuer or worth-er of it all.

But in the Brāhmaṇa reckoned as latest: that of 'the hundred paths' (*Śatapatha*), and in its final portions, we seem to see how mind was already being given a spurious importance as a pseudo-man—an importance against which the founder of Buddhism is seen, at the outset of his career, warning his followers. We find mind, namely, usurping supreme value as the sole ultimate pre-existent and creator, in terms almost identical with those applied in the early Upaniṣads to the Ātmā, or Self, where the latter term is made to serve to express the syncretic whole of the man. Let these hundred paths, *i.e.* talks, however, not be taken as more than quasi-poetic flights, since, in the same portion, we find the sole ultimate existent named death, who is 'creator (!) of mind.' In the Brāhmaṇas, as in every other body of compilations, born and handed on as oral expression, it is as an epitome of changing values that they must be read, values changing, different both in time and in place. The accretion of this and that portion into the several 'books,' as which they now survive, will have been a gradual and lengthy process, but a process which we tend to forget. They, with the Āraññyakas,[1] bridge over an indefinite interval from Vedas to early Upaniṣads, yet are they nearer to the former in this, that they too are in the pre-analytic stage with respect to mind. Nowhere have I found any attempt made to resolve mind or thought into constituent parts. Nowhere *in them* (I say it with the diffidence of imperfect knowledge) do I see any attempt made to see in mind something in parts and functions analogous to those of body.

It may here be said that I am assuming the way in Indian culture was bound to be along the same lines as was that of European culture; that just as with us psychology emerged from the development in physiology, even as the latter grew out of biology, biology from chemistry, chemistry and so on from physics, so must it have been in other lands at other times. That I am assuming, that progress in reasoned bodies of knowledge must everywhere be that of the study of life intervening or supervening on matter, and of mind intervening or supervening on life.

Nay, I am not assuming anything so cramped in vision. I am, it is true, inclined to conclude, that human culture, here and there, then and now, will emerge from a relatively unanalytic (Renan called it a syncretic) stage to one of analytic, discretic thought. But I am so far from imagining, that the subjects, on which that adolescent thought exercises itself, are taken in the *same order*, no matter when or where, that Indian thought-procedure reminds me of Bergson's

[1] 'Forest Sayings,' supplements to the Brāhmaṇas.

musing over the history of culture. It may be remembered how, in his sagacious reflections to the Society for Psychical Research (1913), he "asked himself what would have happened in modern science, if it had started the reverse way: with the consideration of mind (*esprit*), instead of matter; if Kepler, Galileo, Newton, for instance, had been psychologists." This reverse way did, if to a limited extent, take place in India. Analysis of mind apparently preceded that of life in matter. The cataloguing and discussing of bodily parts and functions first appears in Brahmanic and Buddhistic literature as emergent in a culture, which was already much occupied with analytic treatment of the mind. And we cannot trace the existence, previous to this emergence, of any growing incorporated results of analysis in matter so affecting and influencing Indian culture as to deserve to be called 'sciences.' But we do find mental analysis emerging and profoundly affecting that culture.

Further than this I cannot apply Bergson's musing. He felt sure (*certainement*), that such an inverted evolution would have produced by this time a psychology transcending anything we yet dream of, one in which man would look upon our present psychological achievement as in our physics he looks upon the physics of Aristotle. We, familiar with the general laws of spiritual activity, as we now by no means are, would, he thought, be finding our main difficulties lying in the way of understanding those of matter and motion. A ship proceeding against the wind head on would be to most "an apparition."

Well, no one will accuse India of having produced a Newton, an Einstein in psychology, or a Kepler in psychic research. An intermondial culture in ethics, in politics, in sociology is yet uncharted for her as it still is for us. India is still a home for mysteries of *ṛddhi* or psychic will-force, but she is far from being a home for an intelligent investigation of it. It were unwise to predict that she will long so remain. But as yet the scientific way of Western culture has proved to be of more active growth. Limitations that growth still has, and these are well shown by the address I cite. It is possible that these limitations are due to the same cause as the shortcomings in the growth hitherto of Indian psychology and psychic research: in both there has come to be an excessive tendency to value the man in and as mind, in and as thought.

To revert to what I was saying, before this digression: it is true that when, in Indian literature, an early attempt is met with, to distinguish man from mind, we find it citing, as an aid, the bodily parts and functions as a parallel. But it is done by way of a simile, drawn from the better-known: the seen, the tangible in *popular* knowledge, to illustrate the unknown, the unseen, the intangible. We never move far from the parable in India's speech; it were unnecessary here to infer the existence of any established physiological lore. I return to this later.

It is in the early Upaniṣads that we come upon the new note, and uttered in a way that reveals the note as new, as a more in teaching. Here we find (*A*) the mind spoken of in a manifold of terms as a 'more' (*bhūyas*) in that whole, which was not included under the word *rūpa*, the seen shape of man. The word for this residual whole was 'name' (*nāma*). Here also we find (*B*) the mind spoken of as a wherewithal to act upon the body. I take each of these in more detail.

(*A*) It is not clear when Indian culture began to use the term *nāmarūpa:* name and shape. I believe we first meet with it in one passage of the Taittirīya Brāhmaṇa. In the early Upaniṣads it is connected with the primitive expression of analytic interest in distinguishing the man as a duality, proceeding from the primal unity of the divine self, but split into body and name in the process. Grappling with the wording of the ineffable, the teachers use this and that simile and parable. Thus Deity enters heat, water, food and, with *ātmā* (? breath), separates out name and shape. Or, separates out man and woman, or a cosmic egg is hatched, and so forth. Where it is the first-named result, 'name and shape,' we must avoid the error of identifying *nāma* with mind. *Nāma* stood for everything, in the word 'man' (*puruṣa*), which was a more than the seen shape. It is at a much later stage that we come upon the attempt, in the elaborated Suttas of the Majjhima (or mid-length) Collection, to describe *nāma* as the several parts into which 'mind' had by that time come to be analyzed.[1] *Nāma* was very much all that we ourselves understand under name *as well as* the yet more inner world of mind. Mind we find explicitly brought within the concept *nāma*.

Again, whereas the teacher's attitude shows an incipient tendency towards analysis, we must be careful not to see it as too much so. Readers of translations may be misled, in Dr. Hume's mainly excellent renderings, by his use of a term so new even among us as 'differentiated':—

"Verily at that time the world was undifferentiated. . . . became differentiated by just name and form, as the saying is: He has such a name and form. Even

[1] Sutta No. 9.

today this world is differentiated just by name and form, as the saying is. . . ."[1]

Here other translators had rendered by 'unmanifested,' 'undeveloped,' 'unentfaltet,' any one of which is a more suitable rendering for *avyākṛta*. Śankarâcariya the commentator, centuries later, sees nothing here of analytic interest as such. He is solely preoccupied with the causality in the process. I repeat, I do see the dawn here of an analytic outlook, but it is no more. 'Differentiate,' a verb unknown to old Johnson, who would have put 'to difference,' is for us still too near mathematical refinements to fit well in the vague breadth of those early teachers. I am not venturing to say, it is etymologically wrong to have selected 'differentiate'; it is for me an historical error. It is a failure in historic imagination.

Whichever term is selected, we cannot fail to see that, in conceiving the man as having become a duality, a manifold out of unity, the Indian mind is valuing, in a way, the coming into its awareness of a 'more.' Indian teachers did not stop there. They show no great interest in the bodily 'more' within *rūpa*. But in the more to be found in *nāma*, a very lively interest is shown. In the following passage, we see the student's attention being diverted from *nāma* as this or that concrete worthing and *naming* of anything, to what could be opened up out of *nāma* itself as a worded *value*. In the Chāndogya Upaniṣad, 7, 1, the student admits a knowledge of many mantras in groups known by the name of this or that: vedas, purāṇas, vidyās, but begs that he may learn to know about the 'ātmā,' since, it would appear, that herein lies transcendence of

[1] *Thirteen Principal Upanishads*, p. 82 (Bṛh. 1. 4. 7); *cf.* p. 423.

troubles. The teacher, to whom is assigned the purely symbolical name of Eternal Youth, Sanat-kumāra, the name of a Brahmā divinity, tells him: "Verily whatever you have here learned is just[1] name (*nāmaṃ*). Heed it (as such). He who values the name as Brahman, he so far is a rover in the worlds where he wishes." The student Nārada then asks: "Sir (*bhagavaḥ*), is there more (*bhūyas*) than *nāma*?" The answer is: "Verily there is more than *nāma*." And Nārada: "Sir, tell me that."

We then get a number of things valued and worded as making up a 'more' in *nāma* than the one meaning of name or designation. Each is declared to be a 'more' than the preceding one. "Speech," *e.g.*, is more than *nāma*; mind (*manas*) is more than speech; purpose is more than mind, thought than purpose, musing than thought (musing is *dhyāna*, a word not easy to equate, but of high psychic import. We shall come again to it. To continue): "awareness-in-surviving is more than musing" (here a gloss: "and knowledge," is added). Awareness-in-surviving is *vijñāna*, *i.e.*, it had this meaning in the seventh century B.C.; in exegesis it had become merely understanding of Vedas, etc. We shall come again to it. Power, food, water, fire and space follow as other developments; we then revert suddenly to things mental:

Memory is more than space, hope (*āsā*) than memory, spirit, literally, breath (*prāṇā*), than hope. "For as the spokes of a wheel hold to the nave,

[1] Translators here render the word *iva*: the identifying particle 'just (that),' by 'only,' or 'mere.' A similar mistake is oftenmade in the Pali *eva*. Again, the following injunction, to attend to? or meditate upon? (*upâste*) is inconsistent with their choice. On this word see J. Przyluski, 'Bouddhisme et Upaniṣad,' *Bn. Éc. Franç. d'Ext. Orient*, 1932, fasc. I.

so does all this (more) hold to breath. For breath goes on with breath, breath gives breath to breath; breath is father, mother, brother, sister, teacher, brahman. A reviler of any of these is upbraided as parricide . . . and the rest, but if the corpse of any of them be burnt, the breath having departed, none would say to the ashes: You are a parricide (or matricide, etc.). Breath is all this, and he who perceives it becomes a superspeaker (*ativādin*)."

In other words he has drawn out the more that is in *nāma*. We have here, as it were, man in the New. We cannot say, in spite of the graduated progress, that we have anything fit to be called a psychological series. A term in use is shown, in this new learning of turning-inside-out, to have veiled a great wealth of things, known by names both new and old. We are reminded of a child who has found the key to a box and is pulling out the contents *as he finds them*. Mind is pulled out as a more in the *nāma*. So are, with no attempt at subduction, at classification, many states or faculties which *we* should bring within mind. It is a new thing in values; it is a worth in the man *as a manifold*, and to that extent, in man as having a 'more' in his nature. The more is both in the contents of *rūpa*: heat, water, etc., and of *nāma*. A richness in the content of both is being revealed to the student's attention. But that the twofold wealth is to be grouped by the one instrument, the mind, under the two heads severally, is not here brought out.

It is *nāma* that is being looked into as including all the 'more' that it is. And beyond the new note struck of this 'more,' three ideas about *nāma* and *rūpa* together are chiefly interesting. Namely, (*a*) "*nāma-rūpa* is effected," or accomplished, or sundered off (*nirvahita* is variously rendered) "by space."[1] An incurious exegesis here identifies space (*ākāsha*) with Deity. I would not go to an opposite extreme and read the new into the old. But I am inclined to see, in this mantra, the poet's vision dimly feeling after a truth in advance of his age—that man's varied movements 'in' space build up his notion of himself as having a body and mind within a 'world' conceived as in space. (I should add, as one of the worlds in that space.)

Next (β) whereas "*nāma-rūpa* is the real (*satyaṃ*), breath (*prāṇā*), in other words, life, "is by them veiled."[2] Here is wisdom acknowledging what was, as for us it still is, mystery. The very man-in-man, life, 'the immortal' is veiled in his instruments. *Prāṇā* was to be worshipped, for it hid Brahman.

Lastly (γ), man as worthing himself in *nāma-rūpa*, reveals himself thereby as potentially creative. "He knows this—I verily am this creation. I created all this. Hence is creation. Truly he who thus knows becomes in this 'creating' like him."[3]

"He projects (from the self) . . . yea, maker is he (*sa hi karttā*)."[4]

"He who has found, has awakened to the Self . . . he is of everything maker, creator of all. The world is his; he is just the world."[5]

Here we have three notable mantras on a 'more' in the man: man's environment as *requiring* a manifold in him, man's name-and-shape as shrouding the central mystery, man as valuing creation from *being himself* of creative potency. These deserve to rank high in any stage of culture, and reveal an increase of vision into the Many in the One.

[1] *Chānd.*, 8, 14, 1. [2] *Bṛhad.*, 1, 6, 3. [3] *Ibid.*, 1, 4, 5.
[4] *Ibid.*, 4, 3, 10. [5] *Ibid.*, 4, 4, 13.

But there occurs yet a fourth mantra, wherein the Manifold, in *nāma-rūpa,* is seen as tending forward and yet as back again to the One:

"As flowing rivers tending toward the ocean . . lose *nāma-rūpa* and are called just thus: ocean, even so of this spectator all sixteen parts tending towards the person (*puruṣa*) disappear, name and shape broken up, and are called just thus: person. That one becomes without parts, without dying. Hereon this verse:

> As are the spokes in nave of wheel,
> Wherein the parts are firmly set,
> That who must be known I know,
> So be you not perturbed by death.[1]

Here is insight of synthesis after analysis. Both body and mind, which are implicit in the wider concept of name, are ultimately resolved into that Unity whence they came.

(*B*) The other new thing, I suggested, is the distinguishing of mind as intermediary between man and his body. Not only, as in the Vedas, do we see mind spoken of incidentally in words expressing man as agent thus or thus; the mind in the Upaniṣads is spoken of in a more pointed way as a wherewithal to act upon the body. I say 'spoken of,' meaning that the allusions are incidental, not adduced in a set teaching about the nature and functions of mind. Analytic treatment, I repeat, was but nascent. Thus in a lesson on the production of food by Prajāpati Father we read:

"Three (kinds) he made for himself: mind, speech, breath. It is said: 'My mind was elsewhere, I did not see. My mind was elsewhere, I did not hear. It is with the mind truly that one sees . . . hears.'

[1] *Praśna,* 6, 5 f. The citation is from a middle (later) Upaniṣad, but both the similes are in the Bṛhadāraṇyaka.

"Whatever is to be known is a form of mind. . . . Mind having become this helps him."[1] Mind here, as instrument to man, is called a food (*anna*). *We* should have said instrument or tool or organ; here we are, relatively speaking, in an instrumentless world. I do not meet with any one of those three terms in early Indian or early Buddhist literature.[2] Dr. Barnett uses "senses' instruments" for *mātrā* (measurers), in his Gītā translation, II, 14, but in these earlier Upaniṣads the word *mātrā* is used only for material, or piece of matter. And it is curious, seeing the growing need of a term for the 'helping thing,' how old Indian vocabularies, if here I err not, are to seek for such a general designation for it.

But that *manas* is ever shown as being an intermediary in sense on its own behalf, as the recipient and enjoyer (*bhōktar*): this, I repeat, is a decadence from owner to instrument that I only find in Buddhist Suttas. Here there had come to be omitted the ultimate enjoyer as figured in the Upaniṣads, *e.g.*, in the midway Kaṭha:

> Know thou the self as riding in a chariot,
> The body as the chariot. Know thou *buddhi*
> As the driver, *manas* as the reins.
> The senses, say they, are the horses,
> Objects of sense, where they range over;
> The self, combined (*yukta*) with senses and with mind,
> Enjoyer has he been by wise men called.

It was only in earlier Buddhism that *manas* was also seen as just a combining strap, linking yoke to beast.[3]

Not only in body but also in mind, we have a some-

[1] *Bṛhad.*, I, 5.

[2] In a Commentary only (*ap. Majjhima*, No. 39) do I find *upakaraṇāni*: 'helping things.'

[3] *Saṃyutta*, i. 172 (*mano yottaṃ*).

thing which is not the very man or *puruṣa*, but is that which " helps him " to use for his purposes the messages of his senses. Man " seizes hold of " and animates the body " with the mind (*manasā*) "; " with mind " he sees, hears, feels, etc. " People say: ' The mind was elsewhere; I did not see. The mind was elsewhere; I did not hear. It is with the mind truly that one sees . . . that one hears. . . . Therefore even if one is touched on the back, he discerns it with mind " (Bṛh. i, 5, 3). I shall later come back to this passage.

It is, in passing, of interest to note how the senses, at least those of sight and hearing, are looked upon, not as passive recipients, but as active, as having, to recall my teacher's insistent refrain, a coefficient of energy. They, with speech, " and the others," presumably mind is one, are called actions (*karmāṇi*), functions intending to act. " I am going to speak,' the voice began; ' I am going to see,' said eye . . . ' to hear ' said ear, each according to its function (or ordered procedure: *vrata*) " (*ibid.*, 21). We shall see this again in *citta*.

Even where the three ' intellectual ' senses are said to be overgrasped by their respective objects, it is they who are, not only grasped, but themselves graspers (*graha*, *atigraha*). As very young psychology, the notion deserves quoting. " How many graspers are there ? How many overgraspers ? Eight and eight. Which are they ? . . . (The eight are breath, speech, tongue, eye, ear, mind, hands, skin. It is not clear why smell is omitted.) Eye verily is grasper. It is seized by thing-seen (*rūpa*) as overgrasper, for by the eye one sees things-seen."[1] Mind is here grasped bv desire (*kāma*), for by mind one desires desires. So

[1] *Bṛhad.*, 3, 2.

hands are grasped by overgrasper action, and skin by overgrasper touch.

If it be said, that there is more to be said about the archaic psychology of the older Upaniṣads than these two features:—that, in 'mind,' is shown an unfolding of *nāma* as revealing a 'more' (*bhūyas*) in man's nature, and an instrumental mediary between man and his body, I am the foremost to admit this is so, and shall presently deal with the 'more' that is to be said. One brief and incidental analysis of mind I have already quoted in the reference to mind as a more in touch.[1] And it is not the only manifold in mind that we find. Moreover, there are other terms, almost as in our diction, nearly coincident in meaning with mind. There is the word *citta*; there is *vijñāna*; there are also the relatively late terms: *cetas*, *cetana*, *buddhi*. But all of these are, as compared with *manas*, very infrequently used. Here, thanks to Jacob's invaluable Concordance, is the measure of infrequency in the 13 'principal,' *i.e.*, Early and Middle Upaniṣads:[2]—

Manas :	173	references
Citta :	18	,,
Vijñāna :	29	,,
Buddhi :	12	,,
Cetas :	3	,,
Cetana :	3	,,

Each and all of these five are mental terms of very general import, nevertheless only one is found used with this general import as very much preferred, both early and late. It is clear that, in the word *manas*, mind, the early Upaniṣadic teachers found this venerable traditional term, with its active implication of

[1] Above, p. 20.
[2] For names of these 13 see below, p. 32, and Chapter VIII.

'minding with purpose,' the most suitable for their audiences.

But at this early stage, I am not concerned with early attempts to unfold a more in mind itself. It is with the early attempt to distinguish in 'mind' something that came under *nāma*, as all of man that was not visible, yet was, in itself, 'not-man,' and with the early attempt to distinguish in 'mind' something used by man in wielding body through sense, that I am here concerned. It is the man himself, not mind, wherein I see this twofold archaic attempt at analysis, and see it as a New Word. And now the question arises: Did the new word find origin within the world of brahman teachers, or was it imported from without? This I shall try to answer in a later chapter.

CHAPTER III

MAN OR SELF IN THE EARLY UPANIṢADS

In accord with what I said above, it is with the man or self, spirit or soul, with the ' I ' that we must begin a more methodical inquiry; we must not begin with the psycho-physical, with the senses. I note with concern, that Indian writers are beginning to follow us in beginning with the latter. *We* take them first because we started our psychology on a basis of physiology, as a sort of parallel to our physical mechanism. This, as I pointed out, was not the Indian way. And I do not think it is the right way in psychology for us. Buddhists came to place the senses, as *rūpa*, foremost, long before we did. But that was because they had worsened the idea of the man, the subject, and had made mind, as a sort of sense, into a dummy-man.[1] They were as a-psychological as are we. They clung long to a fivefold analysis of body-cum-mind, a defective one and not original, on the negatively worded plea, that it was made to eliminate the man or self.[2] They got a little further when, centuries later, they refashioned their analysis, so as to make the ' dummy ' man into a mind (*citta*) having constant and contingent factors, like our genus and species.[3] But like us they were cultivating still their blind spot to the inexpugnable ' man,' and in

[1] This will be dealt with in Chapters X, XI.

[2] *Visuddhi-magga*, P.T.S. ed., pp. 478 ff.

[3] *Abhidhammattha-sangaha*, trs. as *Compendium of Philosophy* (P.T.S. ed., 1910).

consequence they did not give us a true picture of inner experience.

We made, in James Ward, one great attempt to give a true picture. In it[1] he sketched a self, or 'subject,' *by whom* all experience was experienced as "presentations to a self," who "in consequence was affected" this way and that by it, and underwent what he thought fit to term "innervation producing changes in the motor-continuum, or conation." It was a bold and a needed attack. In so far as it failed, he aided failure in two ways: he made the *impressed* self the most essential feature; he defended his position as not confusing the "pure" with the empirical, "biotic" ego. It is true, that he calls his scheme one of three distinct irreducible facts: attention, feeling, presentations, but actually we leave him with the presentation and the recipient self as predominant. Again, I make bold to say, that had he confused, had he identified the pure with the empirical self, he would not only not have given away his case in his attack, he would have taken up a sounder position. He should have defended his self bowing to presentees as that who is, for us, for us as yet, the real, the metaphysical, the epistemological, the essential, the absolute self. He should not have made this impressed self the mere proxy of the very, the spiritual man.

I should have been a heretic in the eyes of my teacher Croom Robertson, had I said this to him when he was discussing Ward's then new essay to us in the 1880's. How, he would say, does Ward's definition of presentations as to a self "help us in his psychology, however intelligible that definition may be in his philosophy? It had been better had he limited his psychological

[1] *Ency. Brit.*, 1885: art. 'Psychology.'

inquiry to the manifestations of mental facts as they are found." My belief is, that my dear teacher now knows better. We do not help either our psychology or our philosophy by splitting up the self into (*a*) the winged steed of an as yet inconceivable reality and (*b*) a useful 'biotic' hack, indispensable to the language of psychology, and thereby to the mental procedure in psychology. I cannot yet know what I really am, as I shall know, when in the far future I shall come to the culmination of life. But to say that the empirical self is not the very 'I,' is to worsen the matter without proof. The self I know in experience, as the mind-er, the valuer, the will-er, is the one self whom I now know in part, and shall know whole. Very children are we yet, but the child knows the real in the degree *in which he can know it.* "Quum essem infans, ut infans sapiebam . . . nunc cognosco ex parte, tunc vero cognoscam prout cognitus fuero" (1 Corinthians xiv).

Now I do not find that the teaching in the earliest Upaniṣads made the distinction (*a*) and (*b*). There was a distinguishing between the self who taught or listened and the self who was said to be Brahman, Deity, a distinction as of non-attainment and attainment. But there was no distinction between 'myself' as transcendental and 'myself' as empirical. And it was just here that the Indian had his safeguard in what may look like an accident of language. He did not use that possessive pronoun to make the self a mere appanage of the man, or, to use our new slogan, of the 'personality.' He never said myself, yourself, himself. For him self was just 'self' (*ātman*). If he did anything 'himself' or by himself, he called it 'of self,' or 'by self.' He had no possessive pronoun, when distinctively claiming anything as his own. He called it 'for me the *x*' (or 'of me'; the inflection is the same). And he only called *x* so when he used emphasis.

Here he was usually more indefinite than the Greek. Where we get, in the Gospels, "dash thy foot (*ton poda sou*) against a stone," he would have said just 'dash foot.' It was only when he was speaking with great and novel emphasis that we find him saying "the self of, or for, me." In being able linguistically to avoid our excessive emphasis of appropriation, the Indian escaped much of the mistiness which hovers about our thinking. We cannot rid ourselves of muddle in our idiom: 'my self, my soul, my spirit.' Everywhere this darkens our vision. We do not see, that self, soul, spirit is not 'of me,' 'mine,' but is just I. We do not see that the self, soul, spirit is the one and only reality. Contrast with this the way in which, in the Pali Jātaka or 'birth' stories, the "Blessed One" is made to wind up some reminiscence of his former lives. He does not say: 'X was myself' (much less: 'X was a previous complex of what is now I'). He is made to say 'X was just *I* (*aham eva*).'

The Greek was a little less hampered than we, almost as little as was the Indian. In the Gethsemane utterances, 'My soul is exceeding sorrowful . . .' the text has *hē psychē mou.* Here the reference to *psyche* as 'of me' is perhaps less possessive than in the English, yet is it still 'mine.' How much more fitting is not the pronoun when applied, not to the *psyche,* the very man, but to an attribute of the man as in that other utterance: "that joy, my joy might remain with you" . . . *hina hē chara, hē emē* . . . "the joy that is of my nature, my life, my becoming," an aspect of Me, a feature of Me. But *psyche* is not aspect nor part of Me; it is I, just I. And so had Sokrates said four hundred years earlier than when Jesus was speaking Aramaic. Or at least was made to say, in the dialogue known as Alcibiades I.: "either man has no real existence, or the *psyche* is man . . . surely there is nothing which may be called more properly ourselves than the soul?"[1]

The European translator, unable to be thus undistinctive, gives to his reader an exaggerated impression of appropriation, or at least of allocation—and be it noted that I write mainly for such a reader. Let the latter take up such a passage as Kauṣītaki 2, 11, where a father welcomes his returning son:

> From every limb of mine you come!
> Right from my heart you are born forth!
> You are myself indeed, my son!

So Dr. Hume.[2] This literally rendered will read thus:

> From limb (and) limb you are produced (*sambhavasi*),
> From heart you are born forth,
> Self indeed, son, are you!

Thus in *three* lines we have to eject *four possessive pronouns* to get the Indian balance of emphasis. I am not saying that the translator has thrust in wrongly that which is implicit in the Vedic. But by using our possessive pronouns he has imputed to the religiously minded Indian parent all the possessive sentiment of an average English or American father. The Indian father had been taught to see in 'heart' and 'self' (*ātman*) a MORE than the latter parent would see. For heart and self implied an innermost essence that was very God. And this, in the translation we overlook.

[1] 130, C.
[2] *Thirteen Principal Upanishads.*

But here comes a reader who checks his translation with the original:—What then, he may say, do you make of these renderings of the following:

esa ma ātmântar-hṛdaye (Chāndogya, 3, 14, 3, and 4):
He is myself within the heart (Max Müller);
Dieser ist meine Seele im inneren Herzen (Deussen);
This Soul of mine within the heart (Hume);
Dieses mein Selbst im Innern des Herzens (Böthlingk)?

I should prefer to see this rendered 'He is for me the self. . . .' So also in this:

sa ma ātmeti vidyat, sa ma ātmeti vidyat (Kauṣ., 3, 8):
he (is) for me the self—this one should know (*bis*).

And compare this:

bhūtasya bhūtasya tvam ātmâsi (*ibid.* i. 6):
of each being thou the self art.

Well, here again the translators are not verbally incorrect. But that which they render explicit is not just what is in the Indian view implicit. The European proprietary emphasis suggests the self as goods owned by the man or 'being.' For the Indian the man or being is, in 'self,' *i.e.* in soul, spirit, referred to a More than he, the visible live man, is. If there be a question of property at all, it is the visible live man: the beminded body, *which is the property of the self*, the *ātman*, the *puruṣa*, and not the other way round, no less than is any tool or apparatus the property of its owner, the user. *We* make the user the property of the tools. And in the Indian way we come more clearly at the 'more' in the man expressed by 'self' or 'soul,' than when, by the possessive pronoun, we make the very inmost reality of him appear as a part, an appanage.

How little this is evident to European writers appears in the very work which has done more to bring home to us the real gospel of Sokrates than perhaps anything else: John Burnet's 'Socratic Doctrine of the Soul.'[1] He renders Sokrates' own account of his mission at his trial as being a "caring and taking thought for 'your' soul," *tēs psychēs*, more carefully rendered by Jowett as "for the soul." Burnet confessed elsewhere to a contempt for Oriental philosophy.[2] Well, the loss was his, that he spoke not out of knowledge. Thus he mixes up mind or consciousness with the man, when he wrote: "Sokrates was the first to say, that "the normal consciousness was the true self." Sokrates never said this; at least he is not made to say so in the two works included in the *Dialogues* from which I quote.[3] He would have explicitly distinguished mind from the man, as he did in the case of the body and the man, had the Athens of his day paid attention to the relation between mind (*phrēn, noûs*) and the man (*psychē*). He was very analytical, but just this he did not analyze, as India had begun to do.

Again, Burnet rates the *body* as the 'I,' calling it "our personality" . . . that misleading word! Thus, he imputes to the Orphics the idea, that for them "the soul was not the normal personality; it was a stranger from another world that dwelt in us for a time." Note the 'in us.' This could only mean: dwelt in our bodies with our mind-ways. This perverse seeing the man or person as the 'seen' is a very willow-the-wisp for Western writers. They see the man or person as the corpse discarded by man or person, every time they word dying or funerals. The Poet, the Press, and the Churches are especially eloquent in flaunting

[1] *Transactions of the Brit. Acad.*, 1916.
[2] *Early Greek Philosophy*, p. 17.
[3] μηδεν ἄλλο τον ἄνθρωπον συμβαίνειν ἢ ψυχήν.

this error[1] every week, nay, every day. It may be, as I get reminded, that 'we know what we mean' when we read or utter this wretched perversion of the true for either X or Y, who is certainly not the crumbling body or ashes, is living on elsewhere, *or* is persisting only in idea, our ideas or his or both. But we are not yet at a stage *when we can afford* to speak in this slovenly way, confounding, as Sokrates would remind us, the instrument with the user, tools with the shoemaker, harp with harpist.[2] And it would be well if, I will not say journalists but, churchmen took a vow for the duration of life to avoid speaking of some dear or respected departed as here and now "laid to rest," or of the place where he or she "lies." Let them see to it that it is not they who, in another sense, "lie"! It is too much to hope, that we shall ever cast out our thievish pronouns here, and speak with Oriental truth. But we can do much more than we do to foster the true in outlook, by not using words which we should be ready to admit were in meaning false.

Once more India had here the advantage over us. From very early days of her civilization, the word 'man' (*puruṣa*) had meant for her mainly the more than the visible physical man. For us 'man' is mainly the less:—the vitally animated body, or again the inanimate body. The unseen is relatively less real. For India the unseen man was relatively the more real. Name and shape he was, as we saw. But *nāma* covered the "More," the *bhūyas*, that he in very truth

[1] I have but just seen this combination, in which we are exhorted by a priest in a daily journal, in Tennyson's words, having 'buried the great duke'—not his body—to "leave him"—not his body—"in the vast cathedral" (Sept., 1935).

[2] *Op. cit.*

was. Here I think we might, where pronouns are too stubbornly ingrained for reform, succeed in making language more true. We might use our great little word 'man' for spirit, soul or self, rather than for the visible bodily instrument, including the instrumental ways we call mind.

Herein we might win a double benefit in the true. Our emphasis, our perspective would be sounder, for we should see the real 'less' in the clothes, the real 'more' in the clothes-wearer. And we should get less mixed up in the many meanings of soul and spirit, and with the degradation of 'self.' We have won to the care, in our ethics, of the fellow-man at the heavy cost of debasing the ethical and religious meaning of 'self' to our 'worse self.' And either soul, spirit, tends to mean for us little if anything more than the fluttering *kēr* of the Greek, or the term suggests many uses of 'soul' where the meaning is, if not the body or physical life (as in the S.O.S. signal), just a phase or faculty of man or men:—'a soul for music,' 'the iron entered into his soul,' 'the Soul of a People' and the like. Were we German, we could speak of the man in the useful common name of *Mensch,* for which we have no parallel better than human being, or the newer 'human.' As things are, the word 'man' does not necessarily mean male sex only:

Of man's first disobedience and the fruit . . .

very certainly involves Eve the woman. In a work I published seven years ago[1] I used the term 'man-in-man' for man as spirit or soul or self, and I still think, we might do much worse than adopt it. In a recent book by an American physician, A. B. Jamison, 'spiritman,' 'Godman,' 'Godself' are used indis-

[1] *Gotama the Man,* p. 66.

criminately in the effort to find a worthy term for the very or spiritual 'me.' But we must wait till mankind *feels the need* of naming worthily the More that he is, above and beyond body and mind. I do no more here than open up the beginnings of India's analysis of mind with this start:—that India accepted the user of mind as self or soul in the highest sense, and did not, in the word 'man,' admit, that the self or soul *belonged to* a something more ultimate, or on the other hand to a something more material.

Just what do we find about the nature of the man deemed as knowable in the Upaniṣads reckoned earliest, namely, in Bṛhadārañyaka, Chāndogya, Kauṣītaki, Taittirīya, Aitareya? We find the man (*puruṣa*) spoken of as "in the heart," "in the eye" (or, less directly, in water, or in a mirror). We also find the man described as being *-maya* in many things, *e.g.* mind-*maya*, breath-*maya*, purpose-*maya* (*kratu-*); and again as *rasa* (essence, lit. taste) of this or that, *e.g.*, he is the essence of plants, as speech is the essence of him, and again he is *aṇima*,[1] the fine, the subtle or sublimate.

We need not, in these verbal attempts, see the man imagined as 'made of,' or as 'consisting of,' or as commensurate with this or that. Translators are here again very misleading. These are but so many *aspects* under which the teacher was seeking to express that whom he knew only 'in part,' that for whom words, befitting a world of space mainly, were not coined. We have a similar affix in *-vidha*, having the form of, or of the kind of. The renderings used are suitable when we are speaking of material things, *e.g. lohamaya*, 'made of copper';[2] it is different when we are on

[1] *Chānd.*, 6, 8, 7, etc., etc. [2] *Ibid.*, 1, 6, 5.

matters immaterial. And these teachers had not our convenient term 'aspect':—way of considering. When we say God is love, is light, we do but mean an aspect under which we are fain to make shift in wording the ineffable.

It was the *man as manifold* that we find brought in these old sayings to the front. They show awareness that man manifests himself in divers ways. And herein is shown awareness of the man, as thus and thus, as a More than is to be expressed in any one term or phrase. Thus, in his being 'in heart,' or 'in eye' we have an attempt to express the inwardness, the centrality of the 'man-in-man.'

This aspect of man the manifold as essentially a unity we shall consider presently. But even when we come across such bold sayings as that of Chāndogya 4, 15, 1: "That man who is seen in the eye . . . the self: *that* is immortal fearless Brahman," this should be taken as meaning that man is, in a sense, divine in that he is more than were he man in the sense of being just body and mind, or rather body and name. India was not so irrational, so absurdly irrational as to be seeing more than this in the man—as to be seeing the Most in the man. The famous mantra in the sixth portion of the cited context: "That art *thou*" (*tat tvam asi*) is but the seeing in the man just a More, namely, the divine promise in his nature, the divine *potentiality*, as *we* can say, but as India could not, as Europe could not before Aristotle. Had India found this fitting word, her teachers might conceivably have used it as finely as we see our Bentley doing, a generation before Samuel Johnson quoted his Sermons: "The true notion of a soul's eternity is this, that the future moments of its duration can never be all past and present, but still there will be a futurity and potentiality of MORE for ever and ever."[1]

Yes, even as divine, even as immortal, even as made perfect, even as no longer potentially but as actually Brahman. This concept India was finding she could express, if not by 'potency,' by the term 'becoming' (*bhava*). She in these oldest Upaniṣads worded man as in a state of becoming.

This has brought us to the man under the aspect by which, in the Upaniṣads, early and later, he is mainly taught:—as *ātman*.

This word is but little used in the Vedas; according to Bloomfield's Concordance some 14 times only in the Rig-Veda. It is there rendered as either 'breath':— "(Agni) has become dear like vital breath and worthy to be searched for" (so Oldenberg)—or as "self or soul of what moves and stands" (so Bloomfield). To what extent *ātman* then actually meant 'breath' for the hymn-utterers I know not. But it can hardly have meant this still to the Upaniṣad teachers, since they are constantly using another term: *prāṇa*, for breath, which to some extent served to mean both life and lives. *Ātman* apparently meant for them the very innermost of the man, the 'I' the 'me,' as being a something more than the visible man, or than that which was understood by *nāma*, a more which was one in nature even with the Most, the Highest, with that which, since the time of the Vedic poets, had come to be called Brahman, the essence common to all 'gods,' or manifestations of Deity.

We know not who was the messenger in Northern

[1] Dictionary, 'Potentiality.'

India of this that we now call Immanence, but we see that it was being taught in all the Upaniṣads as an accepted belief. And to say that the man was *ātman*, or *ātmavant*: 'besouled,' was to see, in the self that was 'he,' the potency of the divine nature. The 'he,' the *ātman*, the man-in-man, as 'in the heart' or 'in the eye,' "in Brahma-town, a little place, a little lotus-flower," meant just that centrality of being which for man has a significance deeper than any sweep of outward expansion. We have lately learnt this significance in the material atom, a speck of radiant power. The Indian felt after its truth in the man-in-man, a focus of radiant energy, and tried to express it by calling the man (*puruṣa*), or self (*ātman*) not only "Brahman," but also "mano-maya," the nearest word he had to our finer word 'will.'

For this divine potency, I repeat, he had no fitting word. Neither had he learnt worthy terms of value rather than mass, of quality rather than quantity. He sought to express these by pouring forth words for the infinitely small coupled with the infinitely great: small as "a grain of rice, barley, millet"[1] yet as be-minded, like the light, transcending all space, lord of all that is. Systematic exposition is not to be looked for; the new immanence was somewhat blinding and not yet in perspective; it was a bookless world and the teacher could not as now draw up neat 'handbooks' for his classes, or refer them to the new 'manuals.' He was growing in this mandate, no less than were the students; he was stumbling along seeking fit words, bringing perhaps with each new day a fresh aspect of

[1] Rhys Davids, who was fairly hagridden with the notion of *ātman* as a 'mannikin,' scarcely discerns the nature of the quest here. *Cf.* his 'Theory of Soul in the Upanishads,' J.R.A.S., 1899.

that *Ātman*, who, he said, "is what should be searched out; assuredly is what one should desire to understand." Could That "be here found and true desires therewith, then could one in departing become a farer as he desires" (Chānd., 8, 1, 6). Let the reader note the puzzled inquiries by householders, fathers of students, made to teachers: "Who is 'self'? What is Brahman? Whom do you revere as 'self'? (*ibid.*, 5, 11, 1 *f.*). Could anything more clearly show us, that the thoughtful Indian was up against a new word or mandate? And more: that a new way in words was needed to make truly rational a new teaching?"

The religion of his day had been honestly seeking after the *satya*: the real or true, or what we may call 'most worth while.' Now what was truly this? Not only was the teacher in a process of evolution; he so far felt this, that he saw man generally in such a process; he taught his pupils to cultivate this; he even beheld Deity in it. He could not, or did not say it in so many words: 'all is evolving'; nor again could he say that, in his searching for the true, man was willing to grow. But he had one fine word; on that he laid hold and made a very extended enlarged use of it—the word 'become': *bhavati*: to change into what you were not before.

To say that 'you, the self-for-you, is the Highest' is on the surface entirely irrational. But already there was the belief, that by observing this and that in pious ritual man could 'become' immortal, nay, could become divine. Surely the constraining force in the new uplift of teaching about not only the future but the present nature inherent in man could only be by making it clear, that he in *being* was more truly to be called *becoming*.

Now in my *Manual of Buddhism* (S.P.C.K., 1932), in Chapter IV: 'The New word: (A) Whence it came,' I have gone to the best of my ability into the increased use of, the increased emphasis on, this verb *bhavati*.[1] The literary difficulty lies mainly in our uncertainty how far this verb had sunk to a mere auxiliary of the verb *as*, to be, how far it had retained the implication of growth, or 'coming to be.' Our own verb 'to be' has entirely lost this implication; it is a mere auxiliary of 'is.' Yet it is derived from the Aryan root *bhū*, the root of *bhavati*, and that pregnant root is the parent of such words as, in Greek, the growing living thing: *phusis* or *physis*, and our own word 'to build,' to say nothing of the Latin *fui*, *futurus*. In the future tense of *bhavati*, the more vigorous auxiliary has superseded the more rigid *as*; 'will be' is 'will become' (*bhaviṣyati*), not without scathe to the latter verb. An unfolding of the new, it has sunk to mean a mere repetition in occurrence, like the tickings of a clock: the sun has arisen, is rising, will rise. But if, for the early Upaniṣad teachers it meant, in any verbal inflection, merely a shadow of 'to be,' *why do we find them making so increased and pronounced a use of it*, especially where mere repetition is clearly not meant?

Where growth, development, evolution, and not mere recurrence is meant, we, who have let die our own peculiar word for this: 'to worth' (*weorthan*, *wairthan*), can best express this by 'become,' a word which has its own curious history. Meaning in the Middle Ages 'to come to, to get to,' as well as 'to

[1] This chapter was partly modelled on an article I wrote for the Gift-volume presented in 1931 to Sir George Grierson, presented alas! only in MS., since the funds of the Lahore Linguistic Society were not found sufficient for the printing of it till a few years later.

come to be,' we find it toned down in "The Merchant of Venice" to 'to fit,' 'agree with.'[1] Yet not to this alone:—"the stone that the builders rejected is become the headstone of the corner"[2] had not been duly expressed by the verb "is" alone, nor the saying "gave power to become the sons of God"[3] by the word "be." Process past and future is indicated, and 'to be' is *now* powerless to do that. In article and book, I have put this forward, that it was a new insight into the dynamic implications of process, past, present, future, in the notion of 'being' that was inspiring those teachers. Else had there been no larger use of forms of the verb *bhū* than we find in Vedas and Brāhmaṇas.

There has been, so I seem to find, a curious insensitiveness to this feature in the Upaniṣads among exponents. In Indian writers there is the traditional stand taken on Being (*sat*) as static, and all change in being as illusion (*māyā*), an attitude which grew out of the reaction against this emphasis on 'becoming,' such as we find had come to pass in certain Upaniṣads and their commentary. Becoming, in nature, in things material, is necessarily followed by decay; and this was materialistically applied to the becoming of the spiritual man; either a very gross error, or indicative of a worsened *meaning* in the word. In European writers, at least in English writers, there has been almost as it were a conspiracy to avoid using the word in translations, or to notice any significance in these *Bhū*-forms. Either it may have been felt as not good literary English, a hybrid in meaning; or the

[1] "Stillness and the night become the tutches of sweet harmonie." *Cf. Oxford Dictionary*, art: 'Become.'

[2] *Matthew*, xxi. 42, etc.

[3] *John*, i. 12.

writer may share the Indian prejudice, as Deussen did, who in conviction was, as he betrayed to me, a thorough Parmenidean: holding that being as such is the only reality. "*One path only is left for us to speak of, namely that It is . . . immovable, without end. Nor was it ever, nor will it be, for now it is all at once, a continuous one. . . . How can what 'is' be 'going to be' in the future?*"[1] In the works cited I have given instances of the perversity of the translator (and of one relative exception) and I could add to them. An influence at their elbow has been the mediæval Commentator, for whom the original meaning has faded out because of an historic change in values, and who is only concerned to be orthodox and to edify.

The collective result has been a quasi-conspiracy of silence, Indian and European, about this increased use and emphasis in forms of the verb *bhū* in Upaniṣadic literature. The 'exception,' Dr. R. E. Hume, uses[2] 'become' for every half-dozen evasions of it by others, yet even he shows himself insensitive to it in his Introduction, in which is no word about 'becoming.' He can render the prayer in Taitt. Up. (I., 4):

amṛtasya deva dhāraṇo bhūyāsam .

by "O God, may I *become* bearer of the immortal!" yet, just after this, he renders the teacher's injunction (not to himself but to the pupil): *mâtṛ-devo bhava, pitṛ-devo bhava*, etc., by, not 'become,' but 'be'! Yet surely, both in the prayer (or inward self-aspiration) and in the injunction also, there is the wish to see brought about a 'coming to be' of what is not as yet

[1] From fragments preserved by Simplicius. Burnet, *Early Greek Philosophy*.

[2] *Thirteen Principal Upanishads*.

sufficiently realized! Why the inconsistency? Here, I imagine, simply the finding it less elegant to say, "Become (one who has) mother-as-God!" than "Be one. . . ." Meanwhile the reader who is dependent on translations reads and goes his way unimpressed by the insistence in the Upaniṣadic idiom. Deussen even rejects 'becoming'—in spite of having his own fine word *werden*—in the cited prayer, with "Möge ich sein!" (may I be!) To such a conscience all things in translation are possible!

If only I could persuade readers no more to go their way 'unimpressed'! Dr. Hume has helped them much; it is a pity he did not help as much as he might consistently have done. Not only does he, here and there, render the *bhū*-inflections by 'is,' not 'become,' he renders *Bhava* as an epithet for Deity Itself by 'Existence,'[1] as if the Vedic word were *sattva*! This epithet occurs, it is true, in a later Upaniṣad, yet it is one where 'becoming' is *still* imputed to Deity: "This One became threefold, eightfold . . ."[2] thus handing on the earlier teaching of our first four Upaniṣads. In these, 'becoming' is seen as an attribute of Deity-in-action, in creation. Here we do not find just the fiat uttered: Let there be, or become! This has grown, in that later Upaniṣad, into the sayings: "He brooded upon himself (or mused)"; "He thought, Let me enter"; "He uttered."[3] In the earlier sayings it is the *divine Artist Himself who is becoming.* Oneness is felt as unsufficing. "He sought from being one to become many." Till then *na vyabhavat*: "he did not, or had not, become apart," or manifold.[4]

Not because imperfection was becoming perfection.

[1] *Maitri Up.*, 6, 8.
[2] *Ibid.*, 5, 2.
[3] *Ibid.*, 2, 6; 6, 6.
[4] *Bṛh.* 1, 4, 11.

This is one of the two cramped ways in which readers of Eastern literature regard 'becoming.' Either they see in it mere change, mere impermanence, or they regard it as merely steps from the undeveloped till perfection is attained. Yet they have before them instances of a becoming, where change with purpose, yet without the purpose to improve and amend, is the motive, namely, in the constructive work of a consummate artist or composer. This the Indian of a later date recognized, as when Rāmānuja dedicated his Commentary to that "highest Brahman . . . who in play (*līlā*) produces, sustains and reabsorbs the entire universe."

And the man, the self, as inherently divine, partakes in this creative potency as belonging to his 'becoming,' even if it be not creating in the kingdom of art. There are many other ways, as we know, of making the new to come about. A new outlook had come to Indian religion, and it was this, this great More in the man in it, that the teacher sought to 'make become':

> He who has found and is wakened-to the self,
> who this conglomerate abode is come into,
> creator he in sooth, maker of all the world,
> yea, very world is he. (*Bṛh.* 4, 4, 13.)

The very word 'wakened' (*pratibuddha*) is here of significance. Here alone, in these earlier teachings, is it met with in other than a physical sense. The new outlook was calling for the new meaning, a meaning in which it was to have a great future in the coming message of Buddhism.

As if significant of the light that greets the morning-waker on earth to new life, to fresh activity, to release from darkness, the new outlook on the *ātman* who is the man, the *puruṣa*, is often referred to under the aspect of light (*jyoti, bhāsa*). We find the 'man' called self-lighting (*svayaṃ jyotir bhavati*: he *becomes* self-light).[1] The *ātman*, we read, "is light"; *ātman* is light in the heart of the *puruṣa*. He prays: "from darkness lead me to light (*tamaso mā jyotir gamaya*)."[2] For in light he saw a symbol of immortality (*jyotir amṛtaṃ*), as his fellow-men elsewhere have seen, a light "beyond that of the sky (*paro divo jyotir*)," a light within the man (*antah puruṣe jyotis-*),[3] the light more intimately his, or he, than the evanescent light of sun, moon, fire, or the uttered word. And that the man is "self-lit" is bound up with his creative potency. Self-lit he creates his own world, this world or that, selecting, building, constructing (*nirmaya*), projecting from himself (*sṛjate*), "for he is creator" (*sa hi karttā*).[4]

Possessed with this idea of radiant essence, we see, in one context, the *puruṣa* pictured as the sheen of various bright things: "a saffron-coloured robe, like white wool, a flame, the gloss of the lotus-petal, lightning, the gleam of an iridescent beetle,"[5] as it were playing with the subject. Nowhere insisted upon, these fancies emerge in a Pali dialogue between Gotama and a 'wandering student.'

The showing that the nature of the man, as depicted in the difficult gropings of the older Upaniṣadic teachers, is that he is essentially divine, essentially a being who is more truly a 'becoming': these two affirmations have taken many words in the saying. But there is vice and danger in being over-concise. There is more yet to be said.

[1] *Bṛh.* 4, 3, 9; *Ch.* 3, 18, 3.
[2] *Bṛh.* 1, 3, 28.
[3] *Ch.* 3, 13, 7.
[4] *Bṛh.* 4, 3, 9 ff.
[5] *Bṛh.* 2, 3, 6; *cf. Majjhima*, Sutta 79.

Whether it was held as a corollary of the divine nature or not, the man was certainly held to be imperishable (*akśiti*, *akśara*: we should say immortal). As such he had the right-of-way of all the worlds. And not at death of the earth-body only; in deep sleep (and presumably also in swoon) he is shown as leaving that body, to a certain degree independent of it. That 'he' is still of necessity in a body is not clearly admitted; the term for this other or 'subtle' body: *linga*, is a word not met with in the early Upaniṣads. 'He' is called "lonely bird" (*ekahaṃsa*), yet is he by no means alone save when emerging and re-entering; he hastens to join his other-world kin.

As 'man' also we meet with him coming to guide the fellow-man just come over from his deathbed: as *puruṣa*, but not now of earth (*a-mānava*), he leads that man onward.[1] And the final attainment which he makes from having been embodied man, namely, the becoming Brahman in more than potency, in actuality, may be said to involve or imply the essential quality of imperishableness. The teachers would have used 'corollary,' if the word had been there.

Thus the one man as in many lives, many worlds began to find utterance, man, to quote Edmond Holmes, "as needing an infinity of time for the pursuit of the ideal."[2] But to develop this corollary was not their mandate; they touch on it as an accepted belief, but without clear vision. Development came only with the rise of the Sakyan, or original 'Buddhist' teaching. And the decadence of this teaching at a later stage, coupled with its preoccupation with animal rebirth, finds, I think, reverberation through late editorial hands in the three allusions to such rebirth in the early Upaniṣads. It is

[1] *Chānd.*, 4, 15, 5 f. [2] *Headquarters of Reality.*

not in the least integral to the teaching of their Immanence, nay, it is, for me, out of tune with it.

The phrase I use: 'right of way' is in part textually justified by the words in which the eminent teacher Yājñavalkya teaches the progress of man towards the Highest, towards realization of That Who he essentially is. Brushing aside, as it were, the Vedic distinction of a twofold way leading to Gods or to Fathers (*devayāna pitṛyāna sṛti*), a teaching represented in other contexts as traditional, he speaks of just one way (*panthā*):

> " An ancient narrow way stretched out,
> Touched by me, yea, and found by me,
> Whereby the worthy, Brahma-knowers, go
> Upwards to heavenworld at liberty " (*Bṛh.*, 4, 4, 8),

a way of progress the variety in which, for each man, is pictured by divers colours—a figure quaintly interpreted by exegesis. The word he uses is not the *magga* or *paṭipadā* (or *añjasa*) of such central importance in the gospel of Gotama Buddha. In Pali literature *pantha* is oftener used for byway or junglepath. For these early Upaniṣads it supersedes any substantival force there may have been in the word *yāna* (lit. that which makes to go). And if for these teachers too it meant a way of often perilous adventure no less than of hope and faith, it was, for that, no less a true epithet.

That the 'way' was not one of a drifting along, a being driven along by a law of *ṛta*, or cosmos, or necessity, but one of man's choice, striving as he fared on in his 'becoming':—here India had to wait for Gotama. It is true that the life of man as a whole, he shedding the desires (*kāmā*) that are less worth while and seeking just the self, the God within, was a dynamic process of growth, not in body or mind, but in soul, in the real man, *is all there*. But to express it as 'way of growth,' so as to make the idea of practical use for the student, for any listener, was not the mandate of the earlier teacher. He sowed the seed.

Another great Helper fostered the plant. But how much Yājñavalkya heralded 'the way' is not recognized as it should be. Listen to this earlier John the Baptizer teaching the man as in a way of becoming: "As he acts, as he behaves, so becomes he. Doer of good becomes good; doer of evil, evil. He becomes virtuous by virtuous action, bad by bad action (*karma*). They say, The man is made of desire (*kāma*). (I say) As is his desire, such his purpose (*kratu*); as is his purpose, such the deed he does; the deed that he does, of that he gets the fruit."[1] Then after a verse on rebirth, he goes on: "He who is desireless (*akāmo*), who is desirer of Ātman, disdesired, desire-won, life (*prāṇa*) leaves him not; being God he goes to God (*Brahman*);" or again. "he *becomes* verily the fearless Brahman (*abhayaṃ hi vai Brahman bhavati*)."[2] In other words, he no longer desires as he once desired; he has lost those desires; he seeks the Divine Self, therein and thereby having won his (better) desire. Here we are not yet in the world of an inflated monastic vogue, which saw in the word *kāma* only a lower meaning, the desires of the sensuous man. *Kāma* then amounted virtually to our 'will,' taken in that broader sense in which I use it, the term *kratu* (alas ! to be let die) being the bridge between will and act, between *kāma* and *karma*. And in a dynamic gospel such as this was, the figure of the Road was beginning to serve for its right expression.

I have suggested man's imperishableness as being a corollary of the new teaching of 'Immanence,' but the teachers had not such a term, nor do they reveal aware-

[1] *Bṛhad.*, 4, 4, 5. [2] *Ibid.*, 4, 4, 25.

ness of the attribute as being such. Neither is there felt a corollary when they set forth another aspect of the God-man, namely, fearlessness and loving emotion as to the Self sought in and by the self. The man, the Divine Self, is repeatedly called "without fear (*abhaya*)," as just cited, another term which finds frequent reverberation in Buddhist sayings (*e.g. akutobhaya*: the no-whence-fear). "The man," says one Upaniṣad, "seen in the eye, the self: *that* is immortal, fearless."[1] But the fearlessness lies in the man-as-seeker: "If one perceives him clearly as self, as God, one does not shrink away from That (*tato na vijugupsate*),"[2] that is, from the Man-as-sought. Nor is the new glory of this More in the man expressed negatively only. 'That,' the Man-sought, is declared to be the one thing supremely and uniquely dear (*priya*). The perfect, the ideal self —the adjectives are *not Indian*—is that Beloved, in and through whom all else that is held dear deserves to be so. "Lo! verily not for desire (*kāmāya*) of husband, wife, son, the gods . . . are these dear; for desire of the Ātman are they dear."[3]

There is, perhaps, no nobler basis for the moral life than this corollary of Immanence: that the fellow-man, man, woman, child, is precious to me because the self that each is and that I am is fundamentally God. And I have repeatedly said so. But the lovely word is never pressed home, either in the Upaniṣads or in the Buddhist Suttas, where Gotama is shown standing with Yājñavalkya, as it were, at the open door of it. The development of the sinister doctrine of 'not-self' barred the way in Buddhism to any building on a basis of the self as real. In the Bhagavad-Gītā we do find that basis admitted, but no real superstructure. "He who

[1] *Chānd.*, 4, 15, 1. [2] *Bṛhad.*, 4, 4, 15. [3] *Ibid.*, 4, 5.

. . . looking alike on everything sees the self abiding in all beings and all beings in the self . . . who worships me as dwelling in all beings . . . ";[1] this is all. No inference, no corollary follows, yet how near the poet came !

I come finally to a dual attribute of the man or self, which is more pertinent perhaps than any of the foregoing to a consideration of him as the psychological ' subject ' of mental experience. I mean, to the man as valuer and as user.

That we are at the very early stage of analysis of such experience is betrayed by the absence of any word for the man as either valuer or user, or, for that matter, for anything as used, as valued (save as ' dear ' and the like), *e.g.* any word for ' instrument.' There were then relatively so few ! But implicitly there are interesting beginnings.

In respect of man as valuer I do not mean any valuation of the Divine he saw himself as being. That was declared to be ultimately in-valuable:—" not thus, not thus," or, in reply, " no ! no ! (*na-iti, na-iti*) is the *ātman*; unseizable . . . indestructible . . . unattached . . . unbound . . . unwavering . . . immune . . . there is nothing higher than this." That he ' is thus and thus ' —why ! " you could not see the see-er of seeing . . . hear the hearer of hearing, . . . think the thinker of thinking . . . be aware of him who is aware: This is of thee the self; all else is woeful."[2] I mean the man as valuing this, that, anything, as measuring, as computing, and admitting, in so doing, that there were limits to his power of estimating.

It is a little curious, that this attribute, as made explicit in the early Upaniṣads, has not been better recognized.

[1] *Gītā*, vi, 29-31; *Saṃy.*, i, 75. [2] *Bṛh.*, 3, 9, etc.; 2, 6; 4, 3.

For it is an essential ground of that faith and hope in the 'man' or self which is their main theme, that the man, as valuer, is ever revealing a More in his nature, without which he could never win, or even aspire to win, to the Highest. We cannot conceive man as inherently divine who is incapable of judging " This is better, is worse than that. In this I believe; as to that I doubt, I deny." Nor, as to that, can we rightly conceive any valuing as being such without the man's reality, the reality of the man who is not body, sense or mind, but who 'has' all these, uses them, values by them. Not one of these exists or functions on its own behalf. " Everything disowns him who in this or that class of life knows anything else than the man (*ātman*). All these are what the man is." . . . " We do not grasp, lay hold, perceive " (*grahaṇena*) the sound of an instrument—drum, conch-shell, lyre—" till we have grasped both instrument and player." And, concludes Yājñavalkya, so is this great being—we should say 'life'—" a mass of awareness (*vijñāna-ghana*)."[1] Not, as some have imagined, a cosmic mass of consciousness, but the God-in-man. " For all is led by, based on awareness, and that is intelligence (*prajñā*) and that is Brahman; . . . that is the *ātman* by whom one sees, . . . hears . . . speaks, discriminates . . . that which is purpose, desire, will (*vaśa*)."[2] And this who the man is, This " should be seen, should be hearkened to, should be thought on, should be pondered on . . . so is all known."[3] Herein, in words often repeated, is shown the man as valuing in all that is ultimately most worth while, the man as seeker. But in no term for 'using' or 'valuing' is there yet revealed any analytic awareness.

To him thus seeking there came the new outlook of

[1] *Bṛh.*, 4, 5, 9. [2] *Aitareya*, 3. [3] *Bṛh.*, 2, 4, 5.

a twofold order of instruments: *manas*, or mind as actively measuring, as valuing, mediating between the self and the body. Of this more presently. For the man the activity did not end with measuring, else had it been, as valuing, more limited. There was of the measure taken application to conduct. Not measurer alone was he, but director of what he should do and not do. The self is finely called *antaryāmin*: "who makes to go within," and to know the self as thus active is declared to be virtually the 'thread' to all knowledge.[1] Declared to be a power in all nature, this inner controlling is also said to "inhabit" the sensuous and mental being of the man, "other than any sense, other than mind," or "awareness, whom these" do not know, but "the body of whom the mind is, who controls as indweller:—this is of thee, the *ātman, antaryāmin*, immortal."[2]

In this way did the Indian teacher account for what we in our age have called 'conscience,' a tremendous fact which in early Buddhism found utterance not as *antaryāmin*, but as *dharma*, the "great self who is to be revered."[3] In neither mandate was discernment that, in the inner urge to act thus or otherwise, man was shown as essentially 'willer.' The *latter* strove to teach this in the repeated and strong commending of effort or energy (*vāyāma, viriya*) to be stirred up. In the *former* this is not the case, and such words are all but lacking. Ardour (*tejas*) and *vīryya* occur here and there, but in relation to creation and sacrifice, not to duty and conduct.

I have here striven to mention the more essential things about the 'self' which so preoccupied India's

[1] *Bṛh.*, 3, 7, 1 ff. [2] *Ibid.*, 3, 8, 20.
[3] *Saṃyutta*, i, 140; *Anguttara*, ii, 21.

efforts in early analysis of man and his mind—things for which she found utterance. There are things for which she found no *adequate* utterance: among these I have named 'will.' There is yet another matter about which she was then not so conscious in any detached way as to give it a name. I refer to our terms holy and holiness. I cannot quote any word, any passage for these.

When, for instance, the Hebrew seer 'sees' Deity enthroned, about Him winged messengers, faces covered, and hears the cry Holy! *kadesh!* is He! the whole world is filled with His glory! and feels the temple tremble to its foundations at the voices, he is confounded that he 'of unclean lips' should see and live. Not till a messenger touches those lips with 'live coal' comes the upsurge of the inspired will: 'Here am I! Send me!' When the Indian Kauṣītaki pictures the impersonal Brahman made personal as seated in the Hall that is Wide, so that the man entering feels the glory of Brahman enter into him, he makes the Deity made visible say: 'Who art thou?' and the man to reply forthwith 'What Thou art, That am I!' In the one vision we feel awe and wonder, the emotion, as our manuals say, of the sublime. In the other, we do not. The relativity essential in the emotion[1] is nowhere. Emotion, if present, lies in the identity. It is as if the child Samuel had in his night vision said: 'Speak, Lord! for it is thou who hearest,' not 'thy servant heareth!'

I am not here discussing whether the Hebrew *kadesh* or *qadosh*, the Greek *hagios* (of Jude) or the *hosios* of the Apocalypse rightly coincides with the Latin *sanctus* or with our 'holy,' or whether they may

[1] Bain, *Mental Science*, 'Emotion of Wonder.'

not lack in some degree the segregating, the almost *tabu* force of the Hebrew word, or whether again our own word has not suffered, in retaining the sense of awe and the sublime only, while it has lost its original meaning of 'well' (hale), 'whole.' The point is, that both these meanings seem unworded in this early literature. Neither awe, nor the sense of ineffable content seems to be testified to by silence. Silence took on interesting recorded development in Buddhism. In that, it is stated as supervening due either to the confusion felt at the merited reproof, or to the felt sympathy in comradeship needing no words.[1] But the Indian was more likely to express the numinal sense *in utterance*. And this may well have been by some ecstatic syllable or name, such as OM, or AUM; or by BRAHM!—this perhaps in later times. For not in any way does his sense of the supreme worth in the Divine appear to have suffered degradation by the transformation of That from the external to the immanent.

We have now surveyed the older Upaniṣads for the picture they draw of what, in psychology, we should call the self or subject of the presentations of experience. We have seen that he was reckoned as essentially divine: in other words, as capable, in his nature as a 'being-in-becoming,' of seeking out and following on to an actual, not merely a potential union with Deity; that as such he was creative; a seeker of that whom he needed not to fear, must rather supremely love; that he was valuer and user and enjoyer of such

[1] Gotama and his grouped and seated disciples seem to have been noted for the 'Ariyan silence.' Probably exegesis does not explain it as I have done.

attributes as were his, but in any essential sense were not he; that in valuing, he mandated himself inwardly as to conduct; finally, that whereas he was under this or that aspect, perceptible, he was, ultimately, inconceivable.

And I trust that they, be they of East or West, who will, in days to come, handle more worthily than I can the subject of this book, will recreate more sympathetically than is yet the case the outlook of those early Upaniṣadic teachers. We have tended to look at these old sayings as conveying truths already old and well-established, truths which were but an expansion of an all-inclusive wisdom with which the Vedas are overmuch credited. For my part, I seem to feel the utterers as being under a *new* preoccupation, somewhat resembling that of Paul of Tarsus, of John the Elder, of the author of the Epistle to the Hebrews, realizing with a glowing wonder the fulfilment of old sayings in their prophets: "It shall come to pass that in the place where it was said unto them, Ye are not my people, it shall be said unto them, Ye are the sons of the living God." As we read of "power to become the children of God" (*tekna genesthai*: the Upaniṣadic 'become'); "led by the spirit of God *are* sons of God" (*eisin uioi theou*); "waiteth for the manifestation of the sons of God"; "be unsullied, the sons of God"; "God dealeth with you as with sons"; "that we might receive the adoption of sons"; "because ye are sons God hath sent forth his spirit into your hearts crying Father"; "what love . . . that we should be called the sons of God"; "Dearests, *now* are we the sons of God," do we not feel here uprush of elation in a newly realized mandate? And is it likely there would be less when the mandate was not "sons" of God, but Deity Himself taking man's heart as his city: Brahmapura ?—That art *thou* ?

That the Vedas have their earlier and later periods we at least acknowledge. And this is but to say, in other words, that the utterers of the hymns were, both collectively and personally, in a state of spiritual growth or at least of change. That the Upaniṣads have their earlier and later periods we also acknowledge, but it seems to me that each Upaniṣad is too much rated as a house built in a day, or, where a succession in parts is admitted, that each part represents the product of one man's mind. Coming late to a more careful study of them, I find each of these early Upaniṣads a motley, a welter of ideas and sentiments that were charged with a new call to "search out, to utter, to grow up to" a fresh point of view, varied, often ill-digested, often ill-expressed, often even disorderly, often, probably, of both earlier and later dates, to exploit the mystery of immanence, of God in man, of God as man. The typical mantra: *tat tvam asi*: 'That art *thou*,' was one of identification between two entities apparently terribly unlike. "What," said Job, "is man that Thou art mindful of him ?" To make the affirmation plausible something had to be done with the copula 'art' (*asi*). The teacher had no words to say, the 'art' is only true *potentially*, not actually. But he could put this into his thought: '*As*' (being) is also '*Bhū*' (becoming); everywhere around us we see being in process of becoming; in the future, *as* and *bhū* are one and the same: 'will be' (*bhaviṣyati*) is 'will become' (*bhaviṣyati*). 'That art *thou*' is really, actually, 'that thou art becoming.' Becoming is what thou needest. Study to become one who is becoming that. Pray to become actually That.

This is where I see the occasion for this new vogue of wording man's nature, man's doing, man's quest as *a becoming thus and thus*. This is where I see the need of doing literal justice to this new effort of wording, if we would reconstruct the outlook of the Upaniṣadic teacher, both the brahman and the kshatriyan. That he put it into such words as I have used will not be found. Men, especially men of old, cannot clothe in fit words the process of becoming going on in them. They have not the process in perspective, as we can have. They say what they feel, in such terms, along such thought-ways as they have. But if, now and again, they break out of the rut with new idioms, it is for us to seize on these as guides to the new values that were dawning upon them.

CHAPTER IV

MIND IN THE EARLY UPANIṢADS

FROM the early-Upaniṣadic treatment of the self or real man, as the inexpugnable first datum or subject of experience, I come to examine how, in that treatment, we find the mind dealt with. And first, as what does 'mind' emerge?

In saying 'mind' I have made it clear that in this literature we have a fairly equivalent term in *manas* (or *mano*), the Aryan parallel to our own word, with the root-idea in it of 'measuring' (*mā* and *mī*). But, as in our own vocabulary, so here we find other words, both nouns and verbs, more or less parallel in connotation, such as *vijñāna* and its verb, *dhyāyan* and verb, *citta* and verb, *mati* and *saṃkalpa* and their verbs:—terms for awareness, thought, reflection, purpose. None of them has a scope equal to that of *manas*; how far they differ and fall short I will try to indicate later. In *manas*, as often used in these Upaniṣads, we hear a reverberation of certain attributes of the self or man often listed in the earlier Brāhmaṇa Sayings: thus, "mind and speech when yoked together convey the offerings to the gods."[1] Again: "Mind when created wished to become speech, speech to become breath, breath to become eye (sight), eye to become ear (hearing), ear to become work, work to become

[1] *Satapatha-brāhmaṇa* (S.B.E. ed.), I. 124.
[2] *Ibid.*, IV. 376 *ff.*

fire, viz., in the sacrifice"; all but the last "sought after the self." It was a very natural effort to muster in array the real man, the man who is more than the visible body, the man who has 'name' as well as 'form.'[1]

That these attributes, called in the Brāhmaṇas 'vital airs' (*prāṇā*, breathings, and practically a makeshift for the needed term 'life'), are represented as "seeking the self," viz., as that on which they were 'established' (*pratiṣṭha*), should not be overlooked. It may be said, the self here means merely 'body,' as we find occasionally in the Upaniṣads. But by that a material body is not meant, but just a word for man's totality; we use the word ourselves in this meaning of sum or entirety or collection.[2] And my point is that, in Indian psychology, man's attributes are not conceived as going to produce, as complex, a self as product, but that in the self they have their basis and *raison d'être*.

I am not wishing to underworth the position ascribed to body. I may here refer to the *hita*'s; arteries, veins, 72,000 in number (literally: fit things) said to radiate from the heart.[3] It was by the *hita* proceeding up to the head, that the self was believed to emerge and re-enter (doubtless in the 'finer body'), the *hita*'s being "for departing in various directions." But no further use of a spiritual kind is shown in this suggestion of anatomic research. The main thing was, in

[1] It is interesting to see the early attempt here to express 'form' as genus, the notion of wider extension than name. "Form is 'greater,' *i.e.* wider, than name, for whatever is name is verily form" (*Śatap.*, V. 28).

[2] *Cf.* the 'body of Christ' (1 Cor. x. 16) for the Christian community.

[3] *Bṛh.* 2, 1, 19.

associating the self with body, to dissociate him therefrom. Emphatically he was not body.

> Man of thumb-measure is the self within,
> Sitter in heart of creatures shrined;
> Him from one's own body should one draw,
> Firmly like pith from reed.[1]

Here is relative simplicity in the mystery. But where in this figure was mind to fit in? Did it belong to pith or to reed?

We see this problem exercising the early Buddhists in a Suttanta which is one of the only two mentioned by name in the chronicle of the congress held just after the passing of the Founder.[2] In the second of seven subjects of study, the student is to construct mentally a complex (*kāya*) of a mental sort (*manomaya*), constructing (or creating) it from this body (his own body) with form and parts complete. " Just as if a man were to pull a reed from its sheath, when he would know: This is reed, that is sheath. Reed and sheath are different. From the sheath the reed has been drawn forth. Just too as if one were to draw a snake from its slough, . . . just too as if one were to draw a sword from the scabbard."

For the exegetist there is here no question of a new problem. Was it not said by the enlightened allwise one? How should he be wrestling with a new 'more'? The comment suggests there is supernormal vision, but is mainly irrelevant. I may see too much in the passage, namely, that we have a crude attempt to see in man's subtler instrument, the mind, a functioning complex, which is in a way parallel to the living body in the symmetry and order of its functioning, a tool

[1] *Kaṭha*, 6, 16 f.

[2] *Dīgha*, No. 2.

which was somehow nearer to the man, as his thinking is nearer to him than brain, as the wielding of his creative thought is nearer to him than hand and foot. But it was precisely this uniformity in procedure of our mindways, akin to the uniformities in bodily processes, that stimulated our own young psychology, growing up in the inverse way to that of India, in the train of physical science.

I have been a little 'previous' in associating this fragment of probably very early Buddhist teaching with the somewhat similar way in which the Kaṭha Upaniṣad presents a simpler problem. I hope to return to the former in a later chapter. In alluding to it here, I have wished to show how, under the same metaphor of drawing out, used to express the work of introspective analysis at its outset, the early Buddhist went a step further than his Upaniṣadic predecessor—predecessor by no great interval of time—and sought to distinguish, not man from his body, but mind from body, as an inner, subtler instrument than body, yet as an instrument allied to it, in a way, in 'form.' If the Buddhist had then got far enough in analysis to distinguish process from form, it is probable that there would have been talk of that, more than of parts or limbs. But the Sānkhyan use of process (*vṛtti*, lit. turning or rolling on) had not yet given stimulus to analysis. The Pali *pavatti* had not yet come into the philosophic usage so prominent in later exegesis. As occurrence or going on, it was just popular—*e.g.*, "Well, Hatthaka, do things go on (for you in another world) just as they used to on earth?"[1] That which we have to concentrate on just now is the novelty, in both Upaniṣad and Sutta, of seeing in the older, un-

[1] *Anguttara*, i. 278 ('go on': *pavattino*).

analyzed *manas*-attribute an adjunct or instrument of the man, as both (*a*) analyzable and (*b*) somehow co-worker with body in the service of man the 'enjoyer.' This is such very wonted food for us, that we are slow to see it as new food, fallen like manna in the wilderness, to be assimilated for the first time.

So far we have the old handed on as what was still being generally taught, and best represented in the Chāndogya. Mind is still grouped with other attributes as a form of 'life' (*prāṇa*). It is also catalogued as fifth and last sentence in a Vedic Sāma, or chant, called *nidhana*, or placing, a sort of 'Amen!' In these the man is enjoined to revere the sacred hymn with each of his faculties.

A further old outlook on mind, namely, as spatially referred, is to call it 'abode' (*āyatana*), a view strongly reverberating in Buddhism. This again with ritual significance, speech being offered to as 'best,' eye as basis, ear as attainment (Chānd., 5, 1, 3-6). That this localization of mind was an attempt to figure its 'inwardness' can be seen from the following. "As to the self one should attend to Brahman as 'mind'; as to devas one should attend to Brahman as 'space'" (*ib.*, 3, 18, 1). Here there is no intention of seeing Deity *as* either mind or space; the idea is to combine what is most inward with what is most outward for an all-embracing concept. Again, Kauṣītaki tries to get at a relative inwardness by saying, that "off behind speech sight is enclosed, off behind sight hearing is enclosed, off behind hearing mind is enclosed, and off behind that the *prajñātman*, the living self" (2, 2).

Thus conceived as relatively central among man's attributes, it follows naturally, that mind was also looked upon as relatively a point of unity, whether of afference or efference is not clearly made out. Thus: "as of all waters the uniting-point," or confluence "(*ekâyana*) is the sea, of all touches the *ekâyana* is the skin, of tastes . . . the tongue . . . of smells the nostrils, of forms the eye, of sounds the ear, so of all intentions the *ekâyana* is mind (*manas*), of all knowledges (*vidyāna*) the heart, of all acts the hands . . . of all Vedas the *ekāyana* is speech."[1]

This sounds more like a notion of afference only, not efference. But I would point out, that the later Buddhist notion of perception, figured as a clash between organ and object, or sense-impression, comparable to that of cymbals, or of two rams butting, is as much efferent as afferent. And this tradition may possibly be not exclusively Buddhist. Again, that the selecting purposes, intentions (*saṃkalpa*), centre in mind, is much more suggestive of an outgoing, efferent activity than the opposite. Equally so is the phrase: "with mind (as grasper) one desires desires,"[2] where activity is more radiant than receptive. Our own tendency has been so much that of the ancient way of seeing in the man-as-intelligent the receiver more than the goer-forth-to-receive, that any old anticipation of this radiating view of him deserves attention.

We may also note that the teacher just takes mind in his stride, as he also takes the heart and 'knowledges,' seeing in each a quite limited centrality among many others. He does not attempt, as some centuries later the Buddhist editors attempted, to show mind as a unifier of sensations into percepts, using the term *paṭisaraṇa*, 'resort' or 'referee.' Sensations are referred each to its own organ and no more. And it was a point, in the later intervening

[1] *Bṛhad.*, 2, 4, 11; *cf. Kāuṣ.*, 3, 3. [2] *Bṛhad.*, 3, 2, 7.

Sānkhya Sūtras, that "the man or self *is*," because the eye does not serve any purpose of its own, or the ear, etc.[1]

I may have overlooked, but all I can find to achieve here anything approaching a perceptional consensus is this passage: "the great unborn self who is This under the aspect of (*-maya*) knowledge in living attributes (*prāṇesu*), ruler, lord, king of all . . . they who know . . . the seeing of eye, hearing of ear, thinking of mind, they have recognized (*nicikyur*) God; *just by mind* is (This) to be perceived."[2] Here the referee is taken to a higher power than mind, which is limited, aptly limited to a capacity to 'perceive' the perceiver. And it is interesting to note, that when Buddhism made mind the sole referee, the Commentary takes the older way, illustrating by a 'ruler, lord, king' who enjoys tribute from five villages, viz., the five senses.

Speaking of figures brings us to those of light (*jyoti*) and of music, or at least of the chanted speech, as an aspect of mind. It is characteristic of the yet unclouded sky of the culture of that day, unclouded by the vogue of monasticism, that the teacher saw mind in such figures as revealed it as a More in the man, as an instrument for learning and putting into action this More, and less as something to be deprecated and held up in terms of the Less in man. We meet neither with the abusive terms poured out on the fourfold mental complex in the Piṭakas, nor with the valuing man's inner world—'heart' for mind—as a source of all evil promptings, such as darken[3] the words of Jesus to his disciples. "Mind (*manas*)," we read, "is the light of man," even as earth is his abode, fire his world,

[1] *Sānkhyakārikā*, No. 17. [2] *Bṛhad.*, 4, 4, 18 f.
[3] *E.g. Matt.* xv.

he the goal of all that is self (*sarvasyâtmānam parâyanaṃ*),"[1] and so in other contexts.

And as to music, we find mind, once more in its Brāhmaṇa-setting of five attributes, 'chanting' to aid the powers of good against those of evil. Herein mind chanted what was useful (*bhogastaṃ*) for the former, but what was lovely (*kalyāṇa*) in its purpose it chanted for the self (*ātmane*). The powers of evil, the allegory goes on, divining defeat for themselves in these chantings, "rushed upon the singer, and pierced him with evil; and that evil is the bad that one purposes (*saṃkalpayate*)."[2]

Once more, the swiftness of mind, echoing in these Upaniṣads from the Rig-Veda, shows us how much the Indian outlook sets a 'more' in the man-as-having-mind, a more for potential good. Swiftest it conceived the self to be, who

> "Past others running, goes standing,"

standing (*tiṣṭhat*) meaning equally 'persisting.' It, 'the one,' is swifter than mind (*manaso javiyo*):—so the later Īśā Upaniṣad.[3] In the earlier Chāndogya I find, if I am to believe two of five translators, that mind is as in our "as quick as thought," the type of swiftness. The other three read from a recension which must have *kśiya* (perishes) for *java* (swift). The sense of the context is on the side of the two, since the man at the highest or most (*ātman*) must have mind at the most. The passage, referring to the man or self as surviving death, says: "as swift as mind he wins to the sun," or, granting the reading *kśiyate*, "while mind fails he wins," etc. The latter can only be valid if we see in it a limited connotation of mind, as a function only of the

[1] *Bṛhad.*, 3, 9, 10. [2] *Ibid.*, 1, 3, 6. [3] *Īśā*, 4.

body, a limiting which I do not find in these Upaniṣads.

There *is* at first sight a limiting in the fine saying, the second Valli in the Taittirīya, where the way of man in his quest to attain the Highest is described. The self is considered first under the aspect of life (*prāṇa-maya*); then under that of mind as an "other and within" the living man; then under that of understanding (*vijñānamaya*), as "other and within" the man *plus* life, *plus* mind; lastly under that of bliss (*ānandamaya*), as "other and within" the man *plus* those two. And of the man having mind it is said:

> That wherefrom words turn back,
> Together with mind, not having attained,
> The bliss of Brahman he who knows
> Fears not at any time at all.

Here it is fairly plain, that mind is not superseded, any more than is life, but is wrought up into and with the further evolution, just as man purposing, seeking, striving evolves into man at a higher power. I incline therefore to vote for the reading above of 'swift' as typical of mind, and not for its 'perishing' as the man fares further in the worlds.

The typical swiftness of mental action emerges in a curious way in mediæval Hīnayāna Buddhism. Cited as typical in the *Questions of King Milinda*, we find it in mediæval exegesis from Buddhaghosa to Anuruddha,[1] an interval of some 700 years, used, in the word *javana*, lit. swiftness, to mean 'moment of full perception,' or 'apperception,' the original meaning of the word *having become totally lost*.[2]

[1] His classic manual is translated (P.T.S. ed.) as *Compendium of Philosophy*.

[2] *Ibid.*, pp. 126, 245 ff.

We have now surveyed the Upaniṣadic nature of mind (*manas*) in the picturing it as (*a*) referred to the self in that it was a seeking in the self a basis, (*b*) as spatially referred to what is inner, central, to activities of mind, (*c*) herein with efferent suggestion, (*d*) as light, (*e*) as singing, (*f*) as type of swiftness in movement, (*g*) as other than (in the sense of evolving from) life, and evolving into ' understanding.'

I now come to a more detailed treatment of what, in Chapter II, I called ' the new note ' uttered in a way that reveals the note as new, as a ' more ' in teaching:—mind-concepts treated as a ' more ' (*bhūyas*) in the invisible man or self (*nāma*), and mind spoken of as a wherewithal to act upon the body. Here is shown a clear awakening to the notion of analyzing mind as a ' more ' (*bhūyas*) in the hitherto undifferentiated worth of the man as just ' name and form.' And I would ask the reader to turn back and consult what is there cited from the Chāndogya (Prapāthaka 7). The section is said to be the teaching of one Sanatkumāra (" the ancient youth ") to one Nārada, and consists of eighteen sections unfolding a ' more ' in the man as *nāma*, *plus* eight. These eight have the appearance of an insertion, a last section being a summary of, and inferences from, those sections only which precede this insertion.

This summary declares that, for the intelligent, each element in ' the More ' is " from the self." But there is no attempt to affirm any progressive evolution in the More. It is misleading to call each item with Max Müller " better," or with Deussen " grösser," or with the Tatya ed. " even greater," or with Boethlingk " mächtiger," or with Dr. Hume to speak collectively of the summary as a " progressive worship of Brahma up to the universal soul." There is no such order in the method. There is simply an outpouring of now this, now that attribute or function discernible under the term *nāma*. In spiritual value the order is as retrogressive as progressive. Thus, the 'more' that man (as *nāma*) has in speech and mind, mind-ways of divers kinds, is succeeded by the more that he has in strength, food, water, heat and space. And in the summary, the sole link binding this manifold of the *nāma* is the referring of the items, not one to the other, but each independently to the self, like spokes in a wheel to the hub—to use an Upaniṣadic simile. The wording introducing each 'spoke': *x* "is assuredly more than" *y*, expresses no *plus* in value, but only that there is in *nāma* a 'more' than the last-named item. It is like a child pulling fresh treasures out of its Christmas stocking. We are at too new a stage in analytic art to find a logical grouping of the *nāma*-manifold, based on introspective habit.

To revert to the mental items: these are five. The term *nāma* having disclosed the 'more' that is speech—and the Indian value in speech would demand a separate essay—the next in the more are mind (*manas*), purpose (*saṃkalpa*), thought (*citta*), musing (*dhyāna*), understanding (*vijñāna*). Firstly, the feature to be noted here is that 'mind' is understood, not in the inclusive sense of our use of the word, but as *worded wish alone*. Here is the text.

"*Manas* is surely a more than speech; verily as the fist enjoys (lit. becomes because of: *anubhavati*) two acorns, two berries, two nuts, so *manas* enjoys both *nāma* and speech. When by mind he minds (*manasyati*): 'I want to learn mantras . . . I want to do karmas,' then he learns, he does; when he wishes for

3

sons, cattle . . . this world and that (world), then he wishes. Truly mind is self, is world, is God (Brahman)."

Here the cognitive aspect of mind is not so much described as is the *volitional* aspect. *Manas* here is virtually 'will.' Cognition as worded thought is but a coefficient; as is also the emotional coefficient of desire. And we can now the better understand why there is more of an intellectual kind yet to come out of the name-stocking; why also 'purpose' comes next: purpose is called the 'coming into one' (*ekâyana*) of name, speech, mind, as if it were, in a way, their self: "have *saṃkalpa* as *ātman*." They are supported in purpose (*pratiṣṭha*); even so heaven and earth are a continuous purposing (*saṃakalpetām*), wind too and space, water, too, and heat. Through the purposing of them, rain is purposed, etc.

If here I have rendered a little differently from my five translators, it is not because I forget the ambiguity of *saṃkalpa* as a 'fitting together' in time and space, and as expressing the man 'minding' this and that way, coming into ordered action in 'purpose.' For that matter, it is the perennial difficulty of psychology, that she is compelled to use words of spatial reference for non-spatial experience. And in *saṃkalpa* translators are ever at sixes and sevens. Where I have 'continuous purposing,' the two Germans have *zu Stande kommen* or *kamen*, Hume, 'were formed,' Max Müller, just 'willed,' with a useful footnote. I incline to agree with the last, in that he keeps the psychological bearing to the front, this being pertinent. I would only add, that there seems no need to impute 'will' or purpose to the material conditions. The Upaniṣadic teachers were clear as to divine design, if not clear in anything else. And I see no need to see more than poetic licence in the text.

That which psychologically interests me is that, between the terms *manas* and *saṃkalpa*, we have a very earnest effort to express the essential attribute in man of 'will,' for which a parallel Aryan form did not emerge in India so forcefully as it did with Western Aryans. It was there, not as $\sqrt{val}$, but as $\sqrt{var}$, but *var* expanded only in the negative way of prohibitive will, thus *saṃvar-*, to control, restrain, suppress, so too *nivar-*.[1] Buddhism, starting with a forceful message of will, a mandate of choosing and becoming, did not expand *var* in a positive way, nor develop the later *śakti*, *i.e.* ability-to, but exploited makeshift terms for effort, energy, endeavour, initiative.

A little more on *manas*, before I take the other four 'more's.'

I have referred above to the almost startling way in which a beginning in psychological analysis appears in the old, the Bṛhadārañyaka Upaniṣad. Namely, on mind being described as intermediary between body and the man, who is thus shown as the owner of two instruments. Mind in the instrumental case, *manasā*, is ever recurring in these sayings. But it is exceptional to find mind emphatically 'seen' as the instrument mediating between the man and each sense. This mediation is not applied to the senses of smell and taste, but only to the senses more urgently connected with man's spiritual education: sight, hearing, touch.

I am not reading into the primitive discernment here any later ideas of the building up our sight-picture of the external world on a basis of touches. I do not find this felt after till the day of Buddhist exegesis.

[1] More on p. 108, below.

What we have here is, that sight and hearing (these in the Vedic are just 'eye' and 'ear') bring about a number of results, not physical, but mental: "desire, purpose, doubt" . . . and so forth. Here the mind is not the sense-function but a coefficient in the function. No less is it so with touch. If the object touching be not seen, let alone heard, the mental coefficient supplies an image of what is touching. The fact that the text describes the experience as naïvely as it does, as compared with the technical terms which I have used to deal with it, shows the passage as a threshold-feature.

The Upaniṣadic terms for this instrumental agency in both sense and mind were to call them messengers, procurers and servants, so far away was the needed term tool, instrument. Thus Kauṣītaki would say: "Of the same life (*prāṇa*) as Brahman, mind is messenger (*dūta*); eye, watchman; ear, announcer; speech, handmaid. He who knows that mind is of the living Brahman a messenger becomes bemessengered (*dūtavant*)."[1] Another teacher spoke of mind (and other attributes) as a procurer: as such "may this divinity, mind, procure this thing for me from so and so."[2]

I come now to the *bhūyas* recognized by the term *citta*.

In this word was nothing new, but as we saw, it was never the favoured term as was *manas*. In its root we have man's awareness worded as perceiving, observing. The result is as a manifold or motley, *cit-* meaning also this, but the active agency in the process is not so strongly implicit as is the 'measuring,' planning,

[1] *Kauṣ.* 2, 1. [2] *Ibid.*, 2, 3.

willing, in *manas*. The double meaning of observing and of ' motley ' is expressed in a verse by the exegetist (on the Māṇdukya Upaniṣad), Gaudapada, thus:

> *Cit* is, of man's inmost, knife-in-time,
> Of man's external (world), diversity;
> Only herein lies any difference;
> As a perceiving, this the same as that.[1]

Gaudapada's date is associated with that of his more famous pupil Śankara, that is, round about A.D. 700. The Māṇḍūkya Upaniṣad he is dealing with is far later than our few early Upaniṣads, and in it we are also in a different cultural layer from these, even if it be not yet that of Gaudapada. Yet the Māṇḍūkya resembles, in this at least, those early Upaniṣads, in that it goes even further, and makes no use of *citta* whatever. The one exception to their lack of interest in this word, which in Pali literature plays a fairly large part, is the remarkable, the unique allusion made to *citta* as a *bhūyas* in man's *nāma*. Here it is:

" *Citta* is surely more than purpose. Surely when one thinks, one purposes, one minds, one utters speech, one utters it in name . . . all these things (are) going-to-one in thought, are thought-beselved (*cittâtmāni*), founded in thought. Hence even if a man knowing much becomes without thought, they say, he is nothing, whatever he knows. Surely if he knew, he would not be so without thought. On the other hand, if one who knows little but becomes thoughtful, they listen to him. . . . Have respect to thought."[2] The refrain follows as in other items of the ' bhūyas.'

We must here see, in the word ' know ' (*vid-*) something corresponding to our estimate of learning acquired

[1] *Cf.* Deussen, *op. cit.*

[2] *Chānd.*, Prap. 7.

superficially, without that process of mental digestion and assimilation to which alone *we* should give the name of thought. That being so, it is very singular that the general stage of intelligence here assigned to *citta* has not been taken up in contemporary and later Upaniṣads. Sanatkumāra must have been a highly original teacher, sufficiently respected to have his teaching handed down with those of Uddālaka and others named in the Chāndogya, but who failed to found a psychology in which *citta* is assigned the high place our psychology has assigned to thought or intellect. Actually, judging by the Pali Suttas, *citta* for a long period meant no more than our more popular and very general use of thought and thinking, *e.g.*, in the saying: 'A penny for your thoughts!' Its revenge came, if not earlier, certainly in mediæval Hīnayāna Buddhism. Here, as I have said, it appears having ousted *manas* and *vijñāna*, as the generic *sine qua non* of intelligent activity, the whole of mental procedure being looked on as constant or contingent factors (*cetasika*'s) in an act of *citta*.[1]

The position generally of the term in Buddhism belongs to a later chapter. In the middle Upaniṣads, it is only the Maitri which, as in other features, so here, reflects the early Chāndogya teaching, and, in just one context, uses the term *citta* in its general import:

> That non-thought standing in thought (*acittaṃ cittama-dhyasthaṃ*),
> Unthinkable supreme mystery (*acintyaṃ guhyam uttamaṃ*),

namely, the very Man. The passage is in the later portion of a work which, even in its opening, betrays a fellow-feeling with the monastic pessimism that

[1] *Abhidhammattha-sangaha* ('Compendium of Philosophy').

spread over early Buddhism. This does not explain the passing revival of the word *cittaṃ* in religious teaching; it may however be a hint that, with this spreading vogue, the word *citta* was, for some reason, coming into religious teaching once more.

Cetasika finds no mention in the Upaniṣads, early or late, but *cetas* we find, if rarely, and only on the threshold of the newer values. This is in the late sixth book of the Maitri (6, 34), where we find both *cetas* and *citta* exalted to mean nothing less than the *prajñā* of the early Upaniṣads: " who abiding in his own *cetas* meditates thereon " and the like: passages hard for the English reader to follow because of the confused renderings by translators.

But the verbal noun *cetana* appears already in the Kaṭha, used in the effort to express the oneness of the very man, among either men, or the manifold of the man's own thoughts:

> who is the intelligent among intelligences (*cetanas cetanānaṃ*), .
> The one among many . . . who so perceive him have eternal peace.[1]

Nevertheless neither *cetas* nor *cetana* won its way to being an asset meeting a felt need in Upaniṣadic culture. The appearance of both is just meteoric, unlike the gradual growth elsewhere of the use of *citta*, or the stand-by, early and late, felt to lie in the word *manas*.

I come to the *bhūyas* shown in the term *dhyāna*, a term to which the first Buddhist teachers gave a new expansion. To this the Chāndogya description sounds like a prelude, if a faint one. Translators are divided as to the rendering. The English have used 'reflection,'

[1] *Kaṭha*, 1, 17; 5, 13; *cf. Śvet.* 4, 11.

the newer vogue prefers 'meditation'; the Germans, with a better word to hand, use *Sinnen*: musing. This is for me much the truest equivalent. Here is the description of the 'More' in it: "*Dhyāna* is surely a more than *citta*. The earth is as if musing (*dhyāyati*); the firmament, the sky, the water, the mountain muses as it were (*va iva*); devas muse, men muse; hence among men they who win greatness become recipients of the gifts of musing, not small men who are quarrellers, talebearers, slanderers, but they who are eminent, they become recipients. . . ." The refrain follows.

Here whereas reflection and meditation are admissible, as suggesting an outwardly reposeful if inwardly active concentration, they may possibly lead astray in implying any concentration whatever. They savour too much of the Western or modern notion, that the still and silent one is turning over some object in intellectual activity. I venture to think that we are nearer to the meaning of *dhyāna*, as here used, in the remark of the solitary villager familiar to many of us, when it was said how much he must be thinking about as he sat alone: "Well, sometimes I sits and thinks; sometimes I just sits." When once we can persuade ourselves that, even to the solitary, the matter of perception and of thought are not limited to the seen and to the inner store, but may come (as Aristotle would have said), *thurathen*, from without, but not therefore necessarily from this external 'world,' there arises a new possibility in the fruitful results that *dhyāna* or musing may bring.

That this possibility was definitely looked for in *dhyāna* by early Buddhism we shall see later. I am not of opinion that *dhyāna* conveyed this meaning to the early Upaniṣadic teachers, in spite of the suggestion of a patient brooding in nature, as if dumbly expectant, conveyed by the cited description. This would certainly have touched upon it, and not on the somewhat obscure distinction drawn between men of nobler and men of petty nature. The Chāndogya makes no further allusions to *dhyāna*. The Kauṣītaki uses the term repeatedly as a concomitant of *manas*: "*manas* knows *dhyāna*," as if the latter were meaning idea or concept; again, "*manas* with all *dhyāna*'s goes into unity in life (*prāṇa*)"; again, "*manas* pours all *dhyāna*'s in it (*prāṇa*); with *manas* it obtains all *dhyāna*'s" and again: "wisdom (*prajñā*) having mounted on *manas*, with *manas* one obtains all *dhyāna*'s." Here the root-meaning of *dhyāna*: brooding, musing, is scarcely applicable. Deussen leaves his *Sinnen* in the lurch and falls back on *denken*, *Gedanken*. The word seems indeed to have been used in a quite general way, much as *citta* was, *pace* Sanatkumāra, for any inner unit of mental activity considered as object, and not, as *manas* was, as of the subject.

It is not till the middle Upaniṣads that *dhyāna* begins to emerge as a mental state which it is now the vogue to call mystic. Thus:

> By making one's own body the lower friction-stick,
> And *Om* the upper stick,
> By practising the friction of *dhyāna*,
> One may see God (or, 'a god': *deva*) as it were hidden.

And in the later Maitri No. 6, we come upon the full-blown practice of "sixfold Yoga," where *dhyāna* is placed between "withdrawal of sense," and concentration (*dhāraṇā*).

We have now to consider, in Sanatkumāra's 'More,' the word *vijñāna*. There is none that is more interesting, for it is a word with a curious, all but buried history. In the early Upaniṣads we find it, *with one exception*, used to mean, in a quite general way, the work of cognition or intellection, without special reference to messages of sense as such, as we often find is the case with *manas*. Thus, in Kauṣītaki:[1] "This is the view thereof, this the *vijñāna*, namely . . ."; in Chāndogya:[2] "Verily when one understands (*vijānāti*), one speaks the true (and *vice versa*); only he who understands speaks the true; but one must desire to understand understanding (*vijñānaṃ vijijñāse*)." In the Bṛhadārañyaka,[3] it is equated with "seeing, hearing, thinking of, musing over" the self, the which if done "all is known." Again,[4] "where all has become just the self . . . whereby, and on whom would one think (*manvīta*)? Whereby and whom would one understand? Whereby would one understand him by whom one understands this all? By whom is one to understand the understander?" Again,[5] it is seen as an item, as is *manas*, in the manifold of the man-complex, and referred to in the same terms: "Ātman, inner urger, immortal, dwelling in *vijñāna*, yet other than it, whom *vijñāna* does not know, whose body *vijñāna* is, who urges it from within (*antaro yamāyati*)." Elsewhere *vijñāna* is ranked with bliss (*ānanda*) as a supremely divine attribute:

> *Vijñāna* directs sacrifice and also deeds;
> *Vijñāna* all devas worship as Brahman, chief;
> If one know Brahman as *vijñāna* . . . then . . .[6]
>
> Brahman is *vijñāna*, bliss . . .[7]

---

[1] *Kau.*, 3. 3.
[2] *Ch.* 7, 17, 1.
[3] *Bṛh.*, 4, 4, 5.
[4] *Ibid.*, 2, 4, 14.
[5] *Ibid.*, 3, 7, 1.
[6] *Taittirīya*, 2, 5, 1.
[7] *Bṛh.*, 3, 9, 28.

Again, the whole mental world is viewed as *vijñāna*, *not-vijñāna*, and what may be *vijñāna*.[1]

In the middle Upaniṣads, the importance of *vijñāna* is not lessened. The (probably) later muster of divine, *i.e.* spiritual attributes appended to the Aitareya classes the term as one of four variants of *jñāna*, knowing: *saṃjñāna*, *ājñāna*, *vijñāna*, *prajñāna*. The Maitri, as is its general tendency, sees a twofold, a dual *vijñāna* (again in the later No. 6), as the alternative between an active all-understanding self and a self without *vijñāna* —possibly a protest against the impassive self of Sānkhya. The Kaṭha allusion has its special interest. Namely, *vijñāna* is the special attribute of man under the aspect of life viewed as wayfaring in a chariot.[2] In this famous context, quoted above, the driver (*i.e.* *buddhi*) directed of course by the warrior, the man of the chariot, must have *vijñāna* in the control of his horses the senses, 'mind' being the reins; mindful and pure he may win the goal. *Vijñāna* here is ranked as subordinate to *buddhi*.

I need not say, that the 'goal,' lit. 'that place' (*tat padaṃ*),[3] is no earthly objective; we are here concerned with life as a whole, and with Man consummate or Brahman as the final goal, the *parâyana*, or 'going beyond.'[4] And it is of interest to note, that it is as such that the older Bṛhadārañyaka speaks of Deity as *vijñāna*:

> *Vijñāna*, bliss, is Brahman ! goal of the giver of offerings,
> Yea, and of him who stands and knows.

This is of interest in view of the specific association there came somehow to pass between man as having

[1] *Bṛh.*, 1, 5, 8. [2] *Kaṭha*, 3, 3 ff. [3] *Ibid.* [4] *Bṛh.*, 3, 9, 28.

the attribute of *vijñana* and man as one whose life transcended the span lived on earth. However much the Bṛhadārañyaka uses the term, as we have seen, for general cognition, it looks, in one context, as if *vijñāna* were associated with this bigger destiny of man. Listen to this:[1] A Brahman teacher and a prince are discussing how one may most truly conceive Deity. The latter listens to the former's many analogies and rejects them as known and inadequate. The former begs he may in turn be taught. The prince takes him to a sleeping man and wakes him; he then asks: "While this was sleeping here, where was the *man considered as vijñāna* (*vijñānamayah puruṣah*) ? Whence has he come back ?" The Brahman confesses ignorance. The other: "When he had thus fallen asleep, the man considered as *vijñāna* having by *vijñāna* taken to himself the living organs' (*prāṇa*'s) *vijñāna*, he being in inner space in the heart, he holds the organs bound and is said to be asleep. (Meanwhile) he then enters his worlds, taking his *prāṇa*'s with him as a king his attendants . . ." or comes back to rest.

Now it may have been accidental that the man of the sleeping body is here called, not *manomaya*, but *vijñānamaya*; or again it may have been purposely done, because the *implication* in the latter term was more pointedly that of man as survivor, having a right of way in the worlds, than was the implication in the term *manomaya*. The evidence so far, in support of the former alternative, seems weak, and no translator of the Bṛhadārañyaka or Chāndogya has stopped to consider the choice here of *vijñāna*. But then no translator as yet has been aware of that which gives real significance to the choice, namely, the fact, quite

[1] *Bṛh.*, 2, 1, 15 ff.

evident in the Pali Suttas, that, as and when surviving death, a man is called just *viññāṇa, i.e.* 'the being aware,' and further, that whether it was the very *same* man who survived is, in one Sutta,[1] very hotly contested, the tendency, at least in the edited version that we now have, being to show, that *viññāṇa* was, no man, but a product of antecedent mental conditions.

But that *vijñāṇa* meant once, not attribute, but the man himself, as much as *urvan* meant this in ancient Persia, and 'soul' means this for the Christian world, is clear. The body, instrumented (*-mātra*) by death, is the locus or station (*adhiṣṭhāna*) of the self (the Pali term is *ṭhiti*), but the inmate of the locus is the self disguised in the ambiguous term (*vijñāṇa*). His ingress, his egress was figured as by the sutre (*vidṛti*) of the cranium, and it only becomes of interest to the earlier teachers, when the departure of the self in either deep sleep or death is considered. With the leaving, temporal or eternal, the self is held to attain to a power of self-disposal called by the, to us of this day familiar, term *svarājya*: self-government. That it was only relatively so I find nowhere brought out. The *rājya* is described as fivefold: of mind (here put first, not as elsewhere second), "of voice, eye, ear and understanding: this and more he becomes.'[2]

Attainment as fivefold is further developed as over the external world (*adhibhūta*), namely, earth, intervening space, sky, quarters, interquarters, and over his person (*adhyātma*), namely, sight, hearing, mind, speech, skin, flesh, muscle, bone, marrow: all as modes of life (*prāṇa*). And this is as far as the early men go into their anatomy, in an attempted category. When the later men were declining on to a teaching of man as a less, they

[1] See below, chap. XII. [2] *Taitt.*, I, 6 f.

paid more attention to the body and its parts. We are at present in a mandate of the man as a More, a spiritual More; in such a teaching man is relatively unheeding of the body.

The solitary occurrence of *vijñāna* in this connection in the early Upaniṣads hereby becomes, I repeat, of much interest; clearly, however, it does not appear to have been a usage current in Sanatkumāra's school. And the problem for me is, not that prince Ajātaśatru used the term when and as he did, but what Sanatkumāra meant to convey, in his contrasting eminent and mean men on a basis of the presence or absence of *vijñāna*. It is not what we should have looked for, judging by its use in the other Upaniṣads.

Apart from Sanatkumāra's recorded teaching, there is one other point of interest in the use made, in the same Upaniṣad and in the Taittirīya, by others of the *vijñā*-group of terms. This is in the use, in the verb, of the causative and the desiderative to an extent I do not meet with in the verbs belonging to *manas* and to *citta* respectively. Thus, in the former: the student is found not merely learning, but begging "Do you, bhagavat, (sir), cause me to understand more (*bhūya eva ma vijñāpāyatviti*)," and in the latter, the teacher is not simply imparting, but is urging the pupil in a fivefold repeated injunction: "*that* it is to be desired to understand; *that* is God (*tad vijijñāsasya; tad brahmeti*)." The difficulty of the gerund is coped with by 'try to know,' 'suche zu erkennen,' 'desire to know,' 'be desirous of understanding.' It is possible that the verb lent itself better to expressing not merely intellectual effort, but also to an earnest will to know, to an emotional fervour in the holy quest, such as was so essential in a teaching of Immanence, where the knowing 'who thou art' could only be gradually won by a persistent "following on to know," of which Hosea spoke, and in so following on, to become That Who thou art in more than affirmation and belief. But I do not stress this use of *vijñā-;* we find it also, at least in the desiderative, used with other verbs: "Lo, verily, it is the self that should be seen, . . . be heard . . . be thought (*mantavyo*), be mused on (*nividhyāsitavyo*), Maitreyī"; it is merely that *vijñā-* is more usually selected.

The one thing to be borne in mind, in a nascent psychology where will and feeling found scarcely any conscious expression, is the breaking out into speech of this new fervour of desire, desire wherein will and feeling are blended, in the quest to realize what the Immanence view of man meant for its exponents. We are so forgetful, as I have said, of the newness in the view, that we overlook the fervour, and see only a number of bearded pundits talking old saws. And that the ferment of the still new teaching found echo in the opening injunction of Gotama of the Sakyas: "Were it not better that you sought after the self?"—this we overlook alas! still more completely.[1] Yet his choice of words was that of the Upaniṣadic teachers, earlier and later, Chāndogya and Maitri:—*they*: "*ya ātmā . . . vijijñāstaitavyah anveṣtavyah*: 'the self who is to be understood, to be continuously sought'; *he*: *varaṃ attānam ga-veyyesātha*; 'better that you thoroughly sought after the self?'" The *ga-* here, in place of the prefix *anu-*, does not occur in the Upaniṣads, and may possibly have been a more colloquial term, suitable for popular, non-academic address, to ex-

[1] Professor Radhakrishnan has now recognised this in print (*Hibbert Jl.*, Oct., 1933).

press preponderant importance, as the hunt for cattle in a land and culture of the cow (*ga-*) might typify.

There are in our items of the More two other terms of psychological interest; terms rendered by memory (*smara*) and hope (*āsā*). Our (mental) 'retention' comes nearer to *smara*. The former occurs only once elsewhere in these Upaniṣads (*Kauṣ.*, 2, 4), where it means just having in mind. Sanatkumāra's description is as follows: "even if many without-memory be assembled, they would not hear anyone at all, would not think (*manvīr-*), would not understand (*vijāniran*). But surely if they remembered, then they would hear . . . think . . . understand. Through memory surely one discerns his children, . . . his cattle. Heed *smara*."

The more usual term is not *smara* but *smṛti*, and this form is used just below: "in a pure nature *smṛti* becomes firmly fixed."[1] Here, whether at the bidding of the exegetist, or because he judged the traditional meaning of 'sacred tradition' needed it, Dr. Hume has not 'memory,' but 'traditional doctrines.' My other four translators are content to use 'memory' for both contexts. The only other passages in early and middle Upaniṣads where *smṛti* occurs[2] use it as just 'memory.' And while I do not profess to understand why, in one and the same 'lesson,' *smara* and *smṛti* were used, I do not see that it is necessary to load the word *smṛti* with doctrinal implication just there and then.

More interesting to me is the 'more' in 'hearing' lent to the act by memory. The word is clearly used to mean, not just reaction to any sound, but the reaction

[1] *Chānd.* 7, 26, 2. [2] *Ait.* 5, 2; *Mait.* 6, 31.

plus a coefficient of retention of past experience, whereby a sound, unless it be entirely new to experience, is recognized as sound (or group of sounds) (*a*), not sound (*b*) or (*c*). This is a little touch of psychological insight, unmated by anything similar in these early Sayings, like a song long long before sunrise, but quite smothered if, with Deussen's heavy hand, we try to make it depend in any way on what has gone just before as to 'space.' None of the translators associates hearing in this passage with the other classic term *śruti*: 'traditional revelation,' possibly because the word occurs only in the verb, in a conditional mood. Anyway I follow them, for *śruti* with this laden meaning is absent from these Upaniṣads, its rare occurrences in them meaning obviously just the sense of hearing.

Then there is *āśā*, hope, which is brought in, as a coefficient, whereby inflamed, memory and deeds prove efficient, and whereby not only earthly treasures seem possible to be won, but also those of other worlds. There is a consensus among translators here, yet one would have thought, that this word, which means 'expectation' and 'strong desire,' at least as much as it means 'hope,' called for comment. Its occurrence in the early Upaniṣads is very rare, for all its implications. The only other Chāndogya context is among the Sayings on the Chanting: "Let him sing to win *āśā* for men, grass and water for cattle, a deva-world for the sacrificer, food for himself."[1] Similarly in three Bṛhadārañyaka contexts and one Kaṭha.[2] In the last two of these, *āśā* is strengthened by *parâkāsa*, expectation, lit. distance, a twin phrase repeated from the

[1] *Chān.*, 2, 22, 2.

[2] *Bṛhad.*, 1, 3, 28; 2, 4, 2; 6, 4, 12; *Kaṭha*, 1, 8.

Śatapaṭha-Brāhmaṇa. There is nothing in these Sayings of the interesting emphasis given to 'expectation' in the Buddhist Suttas (*pāṭikankhā*), wherein expectancy *takes the place* of hope, while the word *āsā* is maintained as the worthy attitude of man as striving to advance.[1] It is the more interesting, that Sanatkumāra should have selected the term for his *bhūyas* items.

The seven items of the *inserted* clauses (above, p. iv, 7) are all of psychological interest. They are *satya*, *vijñāna* again, *mati*, *śraddhā*, *niḥṣṭhā*, *sukha* and *bhūman*. Of these, *vijñāna* here does but help to show the seven as having been thrust in later. The *bhūya* formula is not used here, but we have (*a*) the pupil's response: "Sir, I desire to understand *x*" (*vijijñāsa*), (*b*) each item made to be a result of the preceding item, *e.g.* "when one thinks (*manute*), one understands." This usually does duty for description; not always. Thus the first item follows from the fourteenth of the *bhūya* items: *prāṇa*, that is the man, as alive, not body or attributes only, but the man. He who sees him as this is a beyond-speaker (*ativādin*), one, that is, in whose words is a 'More.' Now he who speaks with this 'more' speaks what is *satya*, *i.e.* real or true: the word means both.

To follow this profound saying, it must be recollected that, in *prāṇa*, we have a word meaning at once breath-and-spirit (lit. breath) and life (or vitality), a word not so closely linked with this present body as it is for us. The man retained his *prāṇa*, even when exercise of it through the earthly body ceased (*cf.* p. 16).

[1] *Anguttara-Nikāya*, i. 107 f. Elsewhere *āsā* is one of the 'black sheep' of desire.

Next, truth-speaking involves understanding, and understanding involves *mati*, or cognition, or intellection. Then, thinking (*mati*) involves faith (*śraddhā*): " one who has not faith does not think. It is just he who has faith who thinks. But one must desire to understand faith."

This is a much more original statement about faith than is to be found elsewhere in these early Sayings. There are besides this some eight references to the word, linking it with sacrifice, with gifts to the brahmans, *i.e.*, teachers and priests, with austerity, truth, chastity and rule for the forest-recluse, with the way out of the dying body. And faith is called the head of the man (*puruṣa*), as cosmic law (*ṛta*) and truth are his right and left sides, and *ātman* the whole self of him. Psychologically interesting are (*a*) faith referred to as " entering a youth," (*b*) as based on the heart, since it 'knows' faith, and (*c*) as combining with knowledge (*vidyā*) and teaching (*upaniṣad*) to make action more energetic (*vīryavattaraṃ*).[1]

But the making faith (or belief) a condition of thought is to show the value of the New in the True, the More in the New. Had Sanatkumāra said but just this, he would merit a high place in India's seers. Of the translators only Deussen makes passing comment, viz. " *credo ut intelligam.*" Like our 'faith,' *śraddhā* in Indian literature, here and elsewhere, is much pre-empted by rite and ritual, but not wholly. We see, emerging in (*a*) and (*b*), the 'forward view' in the disposition to worth and make become the new, which is present with all constructive effort. And it is this meaning in faith that reverberates in the Pali *saddhā*, which is the characteristic of the genuine, singleminded

[1] *Chānd.*, I, I, 10.

convert: "who left the world out of faith," whether to become lay-disciple or monk.

The next three stages are also of psychologically religious interest. Thus, because of having faith, the man "grows forth"; as a result he effects or achieves; in so doing he "gets pleasure or happiness." There could not be, for the listening pupil, a more apt or more stimulating chain of ideas.

There is, it is true, some ambiguity in the term *niḥṣṭhā*, which I, following Dr. Hume, render "growing forth." We may dismiss Max Müller's renderings, "attend" (*i.e.* on a tutor), and "performs sacred duties," as savouring over-much of the contracted orthodox outlook of Sanskrit exegesis, whence it was probably derived. *Niḥṣṭhā* can mean either 'basis,' lit. 'placing down,' or 'standing out from,' *i.e.* distinction, eminence, as in the consummation of effort. In these early Upaniṣads, the former meaning occurs only once in a purely physical meaning. In the meaning here chosen, it occurs only in that context.

In the later Tejobindu Upaniṣad, *niḥṣṭhā*, in the phrase: "that is *niḥṣṭhā*, that is *parāyana*," means, if we may judge by the accompanying phrases on the all-embracing nature of Deity, basis as the *opposite* of consummation, Alpha and Omega. In the Gītā, we have, in the three occurrences, both meanings apparently meant, as Garbe shows, albeit Dr. Barnet cleaves to 'foundation' throughout. In the Pali Suttas the dual meaning is there too, but the sense of achievement is the more usual one, the term usually referring to the arahan status: "gone to, or going to *niṭṭha*: *niṭṭhaṃgato*.[1] Ambiguity has been inevitable with a prefix so ambiguous as *ni*(*r*) or *ni*(*s*). It

[1] *E.g., Anguttara*, iii. 450; *Saṃyutta*, iii. 99.

means equally down on to, as in a river current (*ninna*), or mental concentration, and 'out from,' as in a way of salvation being 'out from' (*nissaraṇa*). My own choice has been determined by our context:—'growing forth' conduces to performance (*kṛti*, lit. doing), just as *this* induces happiness.

The last stage is of even greater religio-psychological interest. The pupil-refrain: "I desire to understand," namely, happiness, being said, the next and last term is given: "That which is *bhūmā*, that is happiness. In the little is no *bhūmā*. Just in *bhūmā* is happiness. But *bhūmā* one must desire to understand." The pupil responds accordingly. Then: "Where one sees naught else, hears naught else, understands (is aware of) naught else, that is *bhūmā*. Where one sees aught else, hears, . . . is aware of aught else, that is little. *Bhūmā* is verily that which is undying; that which is little is mortal." "On what, sir, is *bhūmā* established?" "On its own greatness, or (if you will) not on greatness. That which people here call greatness: cows, horses, elephants, gold, slaves, wives, fields, abodes—*I* say not so, said he; for (here) one is established upon another. *That* verily is below . . . above, . . . west . . . east . . . south . . . north. Yea, it is indeed this all. . . . *I* verily am below, *I* above, *I* . . . even all this. *Ātman* verily is below, above, to west . . . yea, is indeed this all. Verily he who sees this, who thinks this, who is aware of this, who loves the self, has delight in, intercourse with the self, bliss in the self, he becomes *svarāj*, he becomes wayfarer at will in all worlds. But they who know differently from this, are *añya-rāj* (other-ruled), they become they who have perishing worlds, they become they who fare not at will in any world."

Here I have let the word *bhūmā* stand. My translators have found it a hard nut to get a fit word. Choosing, in the only other context, 'multitude,' 'Vielheit,' 'Fülle,' 'manifold,' they *here* have 'plenum,' 'Unbeschränkte,' 'Vielheit,' 'the infinite' and 'infinity,' 'immensity' (*ib.* 1, 5, 4). Verily in the multitude of counsellors there is not always safety. For me *bhūmā* is just 'becoming,' the root being unquestionably *bhū*, the *-ma* signifying what it signifies in *karma*, *dharma*, etc.

But I have no hope that such a rendering will commend itself, so contracted, so undeveloped is, for us, all that 'becoming,' that 'werden' does and should mean. If ever we come to see that, in man's nature, the one supreme essential is a sempiternal coming-to-be, best shown in his will; that this coming-to-be is not commensurate only with his imperfect state, but is in range divinely infinite, then and then only shall we be willing to see, in this great peroration of Sanatkumāra, a fit culmination in *bhūmā* as 'becoming.' In any case the passage is an asset in the ancient psychology of religious aspiration. But how is it not strengthened if, instead of dissipating its splendid energy in just the apprehending of a Many, we let it concentrate on the central process of which the Many is only one aspect, namely, on the process, anticipated in the word on 'life' (*prāṇa*), and expressed in the verbal root *bhū*, the Greek root *phu*, the Gothic *bauan*, to live, the Anglo-Saxon *byldan*, to build. It is true, that for the Indian speaker, the word *bhūmā* may have come to mean no longer anything more than a manifold, just as the kindred word *bhūmi*, earth, may have become dumb for him save as just the thing he stood on. We cannot know for certain; but as uncertain, shall we help to confirm him in his loss, by using the merely external meaning of 'manifold,' and not the deeper one of 'becoming'?

We have now surveyed the More found in man's *nāma*, or name-complex. Let us now briefly discuss the More these old Sayings found to lie in one item of *nāma*: in the 'mind' itself.

One of these More-lists I have kept till now. This was in the passage averring, that mind (*manas*) was necessary as intermediary between the man and his sensations, *i.e.* his body, mind is said to have a content of, as we have wrongly called them, 'states,' they being more truly processes. There was no word for such as yet; *vṛtti* was to come in with Sānkhya. We read (Bṛ. 1, 5, 3): "desire, doubt, faith, unfaith, steadfastness (*dhṛti*), shame (*hiri*), musing, fear:—all this is truly *manas*." This is all; the teacher, whose name is not given, could doubtless have added more; he was but giving instances. He was, I repeat, but showing how, into a sense-process, work of mind, work that British psychology has called re-presentative, enters into that process to aid it. If you do not see who touched your arm from behind, you get busy inferring, supposing. The little list is only worth quoting, first, because it is a solitary instance of classifying inner processes as mind; secondly, because it is a harbinger of the way in which sense-perception (in the term *pratyakśa*) and inference were to be linked long after in the psychological matter going to make up what was known as Nyāya or Logic.

A longer, more important list of mental factors is in the last section of the Aitareya Upaniṣad. More important, because it is clearly intended to give a full description of that whereby the very man or self may be recognized. This very brief Upaniṣad, which is not an appendix to, but a middle portion of the Forest Sayings called Aitareya Arañyaka, may, on a superficial reading, seem to amount to little more than the play of the teacher's fancy over the mystery of creation and the threefold birth of man: as embryo, as human of earth, as man of other worlds. Actually it has a psychological interest of its own. We see the new manifold in creation, expressed elsewhere as "made separate" (*vyakṛta*), here called a separating, a splitting asunder, a bursting. We see the creating mother called "she who is making become" (rendered by 'nourish'): *sā bhāvayitrī bhāvayitavya bhavati* :— "she (as) one-who-makes-become becomes that-who-is-to-be-made-to-become,"[1] so strongly is the notion of life as a coming-to-be possessing the speaker. We see the work of life presented as process, wherein if there be no proceeder rationalizing it all, it has no real 'name.' "If all this goes on (without *me*), speech being uttered . . . mind being thought, who then am I?" As *we* should say: 'Where then do I come in?' We have the acts of creation preceded by that ancient word for thought: *īkś* : looking, a verb so indispensable to the Indian mind, that it has no fewer than fifty-one prefixes:—"The ātman looked (*īkśata*)." I find it a pity to resolve this term into purely cognitive terms, as do the translators: ('bethought, *erwog*, reflected').

And now the 'list' I spoke of: this is in the final section. In it *we are in a different world* from the rest of the Upaniṣad. We have come away from the utterances breathing an afflatus of the creative urge,

[1] This is camouflaged by all translators, who for *bhāv-* use 'nourish, *pflegt*.'

the drive to become, pervading the foregoing. The one link with this is the coda of the apotheosis of the Rig-Veda-seer, Vāmadeva (given, with a difference, in the preceding coda). Now this may well have been appended to a later addition, made at a time when the analysis of mind-content, as a more in the self, was in a much more advanced stage than it appears to have been when the preceding Sayings of the Aitareya were uttered. No translator has apparently had this impression; for me it is a conviction. Here is the 'list':

"'Who is this?' 'As self we regard him.' 'Which (is) that self? Whereby one sees, or hears, or whereby one smells odours, or declares (*vyākaroti*) or is ware of sweet and unsweet?"[1] 'That which (is) this heart, and this mind (*manas*): this knowing again (*samjñāna*), coming-to-know (*ājñāna*), knowing-apart (*vijñāna*), knowing-more (*prajñāna*); sagacity (*medhas*), insight (*dṛṣṭi*), decision (*dhṛti*), thinking (*mati*), considering (*manīśa*), urge (*jūti*), memory (*smṛti*), purpose (*saṃkalpa*), intention (*kratu*), long-life (*asu*), desire (*kāma*), will (*vaśa*): just all these become names of wisdom (*prajñāna*). He Brahman, he Indra, he Prajāpati, he even all these devas; and these five great become-things: earth, wind, space, water, light: these and those which are as it were small and mixed, seeds of this kind and that, eggborn, matrixborn, sweatborn, sproutborn; horses, kine, men (*puruṣā*), elephants: everything that lives, moving, flying, standing still: all this is guided by wisdom, based on wisdom. The world is guided by wisdom. Basis is wisdom. Brahman is wisdom.'"

[1] The translators are not unanimous if any or all here is query. I follow Deussen.

I give the whole context that the reader may better judge of the outlook as a whole: the culmination in a self, a man, who is essentially one with the very Highest. As to the 'more' that is here unfolded in the man in terms of mind, the only list that I know of which resembles it, and resembles in some detail, is the list of the factors constituting the same notion: *prajñāna* = *paññā*, in the opening section of the Pali Abhidhamma-Piṭaka, in reply to the question: *not* "Who is this, namely, this who is the outcome of the whole process of creation and becoming?" but "*What* in this connection is *paññā*?" That is, What, in the 'more' to be analyzed in a typical "good thought (*citta*)" is the wisdom which analysis reveals, among other factors, in it? We even get in the two lists similar triads of terms: a threefold *vicaya*, a threefold *-lakkhaṇa*. The Pali list is fuller, and perhaps the analysis is more advanced. *Saṃjñāna* (*saññā*) is ruled out, as belonging to a special description of less advanced intelligence; *ājñāna* is lacking, which is curious, since it belongs to the Sutta and Vinaya vocabulary (*ājān-*); on the other hand, we get *sampajañña*. (In passing, I have rendered *prajñāna* in two ways, for an obvious reason.)[1]

Now the period elapsing between the *preceding* Aitareya Sayings and this Abhidhamma compilation is perhaps some four centuries: say, B.C. 650-250. I am not pretending that the Aitareya *list* is four centuries later than the preceding three sections. But when we compare the two lists, I find that the stage reached in analysis in the former *is nearer* to that reached in the latter, the Pali, than it is to these preceding three sections. If none of my translators has noticed this, I would suggest it is because they have not made that

[1] I return to this list in Chapters XIV, XVIII.

intimate acquaintance with Pali Abhidhamma, let alone psychology, which has been my lot.

The really impressive feature in the Upaniṣad section is not its approach to Abhidhamma, but the fact, that the sparse glimpses of mind, as what I would call a more-worth in the man, which we find in the early Upaniṣads, has here culminated in a peroration which sees, in man's conception of the Highest, something only meant to be described in terms of mind: *prajñāna*. This betrays, with no uncertain voice, the spreading preoccupation of a later day with the nature and worth of this instrument, mind; in other words, with the growth of the teaching which was coming to be known as Sānkhya.

I do not mean, that the value assigned herein to *prajñā* was late; on the contrary, Kauṣītaki and Bṛhadārañyaka leave us in no doubt about this. It is in the whole picture of the self as exercise of mind, *beginning with* and passing beyond *sense-values* to the implication of will in the term *vaśa*, the whole as resumed in wisdom, literally 'forward-knowledge,' that I see this advance in study and analysis of mind, not elsewhere so worded in the Upaniṣads.

What then have those two Upaniṣads to say about *prajñāna* or *prajñā* ?

In the Bṛhadārañyaka, "Brahman," Yājnavalkya says, "is to be regarded as *prajñā*." To the question: "What is *prajñatā* (wisdomness)?" he answers: "Just speech . . . . an ally is made wise (or known) (*prajñayata*) by speech . . ." then follows a list of the collections of Sayings: Vedas down to Commentaries, "oblations, food and drink, this world and that beyond, and all beings, all are by speech made known." Here is no definition in terms of mind as such. The Sayings are not referred to *as* work of mind.

Further, Yājñavalkya is reputed to have said: "By just knowing It a wise brahman gets *prajñā;* let him not aim at many words,[1] bringing endless talk." Here, on the other hand, the link between *prajñā* and speech is rudely brushed aside. In these two contexts alone is the word used.

The Kauṣītaki uses it oftener. One teacher, describing a vision of man's wayfaring by the way (*yāna*) of the devas, brings him to a materialized glory of God, a hall wherein "*prajñā* is Brahman's throne." Again, in that man is and has, virtually, whatever Brahman is and has, we read that, of these attributes both "thoughts (*dhīyo*), and what-is-to-be-understood and also desires: these are acquired by *prajñā*." Again, *now* we find *prajñā* just listed with other five attributes: speech, life *prājna*), eye, ear, mind, *then* we see *prajñā* made a sort of chief among these and others, as it were a dummy-*ātman*, in that all other attributes are so many 'mounts' for *prajñā*, mounted on each of which, the man becomes obtainer and enjoyer of what they bring. To rationalize this position, the speaker at times uses the compound *prajñātman*.[2]

I say 'he,' assuming that this section 3 gives us more or less the actual teaching of the man after whom the Upaniṣad is named. When Kauṣītaki was this brahman teacher in India, it is impossible to say exactly, but I venture to see him as a near predecessor of the first Sakyan (Buddhist) teachers. It is true that it is not in 'his' Upaniṣad that any use appears of 'sānkhya' terms. But in two points he suggests nearness to the birth of the Buddhist movement: these are, importance he attaches to *prajñā*; and the

[1] *Bṛhad.*, 4, 4, 21.
[2] *Kauṣ.*, 2, 14; 3, 2, etc.; *Ait.*, 5; 2, 3.

warning note he utters against losing the man or *ātman* in the study of his attributes.

Now for the founders of Sakya, *paññā* was highly valued—an appreciation which lasted till the compilation of the first collection of the Third Piṭaka. To the description there of *paññā* I have referred, and I add this:—not one of the many terms revealed by introspection, which are there defined, is treated of at anything like the length bestowed on *paññā*. And throughout the Suttas it is by *paññā*, now called *ariyā*, now called *sammā* (noble and right), that a man achieves advance in his spiritual growth. Like the central teaching of the Way itself, it is connected with the process of " making become " (*i.e.* spiritual growth): " *viññāṇa* is to be understood, *paññā* is to be made-become."

Again, there was, when Sakya began, a great preoccupation already abroad with the study of 'mind' as distinct from both man and body: this I have commented upon. The danger in this new 'psychological' attraction began soon to work disastrously in the young Sakya, probably even before the Founder had passed away. The 'man,' the 'self' was even then beginning to fade out. But even if the Founder, like Kauṣītaki, uttered his warning note about it, the note would by the afterman have been let die. By a quasi-miracle his injunctions to seek the 'man' or 'self,' and walk by That as by a lamp have survived (if with a distorted meaning), so also has a warning against seeing the very man in his instrument, mind. There survive, besides, only phrases of Upaniṣadic wording about the man as using his mind; nothing more. The rest is hyper-preoccupation with body and mind, rather than with the user of them.

Kauṣītaki's warning is, even in the Upaniṣads, unique and points to a present danger not existing in the days when Yājñavalkya and Sanatkumāra were on earth:—" One should desire to understand (*jijñāsa*) not speech, but the speaker; . . . and so on for the sensations of smell, sight, hearing, taste;" touch is a curious omission; then . . . " one should desire to understand not the act, but the agent; nor pleasure and pain but the discerner (*vijñātāraṃ*) of them; nor love, but the lover, nor going, but the goer, nor mind (*manas*), but the minder (*mantāraṃ*)" (3, 8). How forceful is not the warning shown when we look at what grew up in the spreading world of Buddhist culture soon after! Yet no translator has, in my opinion, rightly applied the warning, so old have they made Kauṣītaki, so little heed have they given to Buddhism. Śankara's exegesis, it is true, chatters on all unheeding of what had taken place (after all) some thousand to seven hundred years before his day, and in no way gives the translators to think. But who would look to an Indian Commentator for historic facts? The only translator who here pauses to think (Deussen) loses himself in a metaphysic which is for me beside the point.

The portion after the 'warning' has for me a suspicious likeness to an appended commentary on the foregoing. But it serves to show, in the words, " life is verily the *prajñātman*; it is joy, ever young, immortal," that we have, in the man or self who exercises *prajñā*, one much occupied with the growth, not so much of sensuous exercise, or the growth of *manas* or *vijñāna*, as with the growth, the becoming, of that More in the *very self*, so essential if he would be That-Who-he-was in more than potency and promise.

We may almost, in these Kauṣītaki Sayings, look

on *prajñā* and 'mind' as a Janus-faced intermediary. In both terms we have man's instrument, but in sense and act, it is with *manas* that man faces these; with *prajñā*, man faces, *in himself*, that potential Most towards Whom he has turned. It is only thus, I think, that we can follow the thought in the passage preceding the warning:—" For truly apart from *prajñā* speech makes known no name whatever; the mind of me, he says, was absent; I did not become wise as to the name." Mind is made to function in the same way in smell, sight, hearing, taste, hands in action, feet in going, body in pleasures or pain . . . and in thought itself (*dhī*). Śankara's comment here is merely talk about words; it reveals from a psychological point of view no advance on Kauṣītaki's original 'song before sunrise.' Our translators have approached the sayings from the point of view of philology, or philosophy, or religious literature, not of psychology; hence it is perhaps that they seem to me to miss that which was exercising the mind of the ancient teacher.

Let us now revert to the Aitareya list of mind-terms. Of the tetrad of strictly cognitional compounds: *saṃjñāna ājñāna*, *vijñāna*, *prajñāna*, have the earliest Upaniṣads anything approaching analytical interest to say about the first two? The answer is: about *ājñāna*, nothing; it occurs here only, nor do later Upaniṣads use it. Yet it is a term frequently used in the Pali Suttas. It is also an old, a Vedic word, and has, I learn, the connotation, though not this only, of attending to, as used for the inception of awareness, such as we mean in saying, one learnt it, of some new thing. About the other term, this is used, in the form *saṃjñā*, once only in any Upaniṣad, albeit it too is frequent in the Pali Canon. Here its more distinctive use is somewhat that of our (sense-)perception: a becoming aware of some *thing*, with an element of recognition. Or, as Buddhist exegesis puts it: as having a name. It may be said to be used in this sense in the Bṛhadārañyaka,[1] where, in a repeated context, Yājnavalkya shocks his wife Maitreyī by saying: "After passing on there is no *saṃjñā*" (*na pretya saṃjñâ 'sti*). He has led up to this by commenting on how, in order to search into the nature of 'the man' (*ātman*), one must see everything as evanescent beside *that*, everything as but flowing into, and culminating in *that* who is One, so that, in wayfaring further, it is the essential oneness that persists, and not the particular accidents of an experience which we apprehend as a 'twoness' (*dvaita*). Yājñavalkya was certainly not so shortsighted as to see, in the man, a non-survivor; nor so muddled as to see, in the survivor, a mere complex of body and mind; nor yet so contracted in his outlook as to see, in the survivor, were he never so holy, one who on leaving earth achieved the end of that way (*panthā*), of which he spoke.[2] Not yet was "the understander to be understood." But it would be the *understander* who would come gradually to outweigh in importance the *things understood*—so I understand his somewhat confused and difficult searchings. Whether my sister Maitreyī came to see it thus is not told. "After speaking thus Yājñavalkya departed."

Of residual terms of cognition, the word *dhī*, occurring among the terms illustrating the content of mind in the Bṛhadārañyaka list, but, curiously, not occurring in the fuller Aitareya-list, is rare in the older Upaniṣads, and is not used with any more distinctive meaning than we give to 'thought,' in our own 'thought, word

[1] *Bṛhad.*, 4, 5, 13 f. [2] See above, p. 44.

and deed.' The triplet, in their usage, is '*dhī*,' in the plural (*dhīyo*), 'what is to be understood' (or noticed, *vijñātavyaṃ*) and 'desires' (*kāmāni*).

We find also a non-distinctive use of it in the injunction *dhīyā dhīyā*, 'by repeated thinking,' as that wherewith man produces food. This is in a curious, interesting review of the divine and human task of producing food, to wit, nutriment of all kinds: man's bodily food (*anna*), deva-food, animal-food (milk), and the less material food: mind, speech and life (breath).

With the much more distinctive derivative of *dhī*, namely *dhyāna*, I have more to say presently, in connection with the emergence of Yoga.

Another cognitive term *medhas*, *medhā*, meaning literally fat, juicy essence, sap, *Saft*, occurs but twice, beside figuring in our Aitareya-list. Yet it is a long-lived word, dating from the Rig-Veda, and used in Pali Suttas. It is with *medhas* and *tapas* (heat, ardour) that the Father, Prajāpati, creates his foods.[1] The god who may be prayed to is described as a sheath of Brahman covered with *medhas*.[2] It is instructive as showing how, in his notions of man as intelligent, the Indian tended, in them, to be not calmly static, but vigorously dynamic.

Manīśa, finally, is not so longlived, but is apparently not older than our Aitareya list, nor have I found it in Pali. It is but a convenient 'more' in the vocabulary of mind, an outcrop probably of the increasing preoccupation with the mind as such.

Perhaps the most noteworthy difference in this literature from corresponding features in our own is, with the exception of *smara*, *smṛti* (memory), the absence of terms for what we call the representational work of

[1] *Bṛhad.*, 2, 5, 1. [2] *Taitt.*, 1, 4, 1.

mind. Thus I find no mention of 'image' or 'idea,' of 'imagination' or 'ideation' *as such*, nor for our 'conception,' 'judgment' or 'reasoning.' As to the last, *tarka* does not occur till the Kaṭha: "Not by reasoning is this thought to be attained." We only find it again in the late chapters of the Maitri.

'Thought' here is not *dhī*, but *mati*, a term also occurring in our Aitareya-list. As word it is a co-derivative with *manas*, but it never rivalled the popularity, the felt need, of the other term. We found it in the inserted portion of the *Bhūyas*-analysis:—*vijñāna* emerges, supervenes where *mati* is.[1] The Chāndogya does not use it again. In the Bṛhadārañyaka it occurs thrice: and always as a sister-term with other mind-words to give fuller expression. Thus: "with seeing, hearing, thinking of (*matyā*), understanding (*vijñānena*) the self, is this 'all' known."[2] Again . . . "you could not see the see-er of seeing, hear the hearer of hearing, think the thinker of thinking (*na mante-r-mantāraṃ manvītha*), understand the understander of understanding. He is the self of (*or* for) thee (*eśa ta ātmā*), in all; aught else (is) ill (*ārttaṃ*)."[3] "Once more: as the thinker (*mantar*), the knower, etc., one ceases not to be, when in deep sleep one is active, since thinker, knower, is imperishable."[4] Nothing more till the Kaṭha, when, as we saw, *mati* is contrasted with *tarka*. The Kaṭha is a poem and fitly leaves it at that.

In the earlier years of the oldest Upaniṣads we are clearly not yet at a stage in which the 'More' that is in mind had already been subjected to what we should now call analysis. We are, I repeat, but at the threshold of it. But we are at the threshold, not wholly outside.

[1] *Chānd.*, 7, 18, 1. [2] *Bṛhad.*, 2, 4, 5.
[3] *Ibid.*, 3, 4, 2. [4] *Ibid.*, 4, 3, 28, 30.

Language was already rich enough for analytic beginnings, but, like our own vocabulary up to less than a century ago, it was not used with scientific precision. We too have wavered in our use, for instance, of such terms as perception, intuition and thought. If the reader would see the headway made in analytic procedure in Indian culture, some six centuries after this date, let him consult the *Questions of King Milinda* on the term *sati* (*smṛti*) and its modes, anticipating our own eighteenth-century psychology on 'association of ideas.'[1] Or the attempts made in Buddhist exegesis to expound the 'representational' activity of mind. None of it goes far—as to that *we* are still without any satisfactory theory of memory—but it has got a little further than our early brahman teachers.

[1] *S.B.E.* xxxv., p. 122 f. Below, Chap. XIX.

CHAPTER V

MIND IN THE EARLY UPANIṢADS (*continued*)

EMOTIONAL AND VOLITIONAL ASPECTS

I WOULD like now to summarize the ways in which those other phases of mind, which we call emotional and volitional, emerge in these sayings.

Of the former, we turn naturally in the first place to those two central terms: pleasure, pain; happiness, sorrow, or 'ill.' And here, if coming from a pre-occupation with Buddhist sayings, one cannot but be struck with the difference, in emphasis on the two, between these and the early Upaniṣads. In the former no subject is more dwelt upon than are they[1]; moreover they are defined, described and elsewise brought into such relief, that the real message of the founders is thereby greatly obscured. In the early Upaniṣads, with the exception of the Kauṣītaki, the two scarcely find mention. The Chāndogya re ers once only to *sukha*, never to *dukhha*; the Bṛhadārañyaka refers once only to *dukhha*, never to *sukha*, and in one context only to the kindred word: *artta*, afflicted. The Kauṣītaki mentions them four times in conjunction: *sukha-dukhha*, but only as one among the several attributes of the man: thus, they are "acquired by the body," as if to segregate them from being attributes of mind. (In Buddhism we find a distinct pair of terms for the

[1] See below, Chap. XV.

latter.)[1] As externally relegated, they are called the body's measure-of-becoming (or being, *bhūtamātrā*). And as we saw, the student is enjoined to consider not pleasure or pain so much as the discerner of them.

In the first of these contexts, and in this Upaniṣad repeatedly, the two terms of a hedonic meaning: *ānanda*, *rati*: bliss, delight, are inquired about separately, and given sexual association.[2] But elsewhere, *ānanda*[3] is used (*a*) in a general sense of blissful rest after achievement, (*b*) as contrasted with evil (*pāpman*), (*c*) as referring to the whole personality:—this is when the self is considered as *ānandamaya*: under the aspect of *ānanda*—(*d*) as a mental affect:—here we should say there is a coefficient of thought in intense happiness:—(*e*) as peculiarly an attribute of Deity: "Brahman is understanding (*vijñāna*), is bliss, the goal. . . ."[4] Thus much from the Bṛhadārañyaka; the Chāndogya never mentions the word; the Taittirīya has much to say of *ānanda*, and, in common with the Bṛhadārañyaka, draws up a comparative scale of 'blisses' beginning with human efficiency and wealth, and culminating in either 'Brahman' or 'the world of Brahman,' but in which, in both lists, each stage of divine bliss, even the highest, is equalled by that of the man who is Veda-versed and is 'straight' and 'not smitten by desire.' The scale is of interest just here, since this rare comparison of values reveals a tendency to think analytically.

The Kauṣītaki alone has any use for the word *rati*, but only in conjunction with *ānanda* in sex-matters.

[1] *E.g.*, *Abhidhamma-Piṭaka*, Book I. and Commentary: *Kāyika*, *cetasika*.

[2] *Bṛhad.*, 2, 4, 11; *Tait.*, 3, 9.

[3] *Bṛhad.*, 2, 1, 20; 4, 3, 9.

[4] *Ibid.*, 3, 9, 28.

In later works and in Pali poems it is lent a more spiritual meaning. Other adjuncts of *ānanda* are *muda*, and *pramuda*, which appear also in Buddhism with spiritual implication. The verb *mud-*, to enjoy, occurs but once in the two chief old Upaniṣads, and quite generally.

In more specific emotional terms the Upaniṣads are extremely barren, with perhaps the one exception of fear, nor is this inquired into as such. Of love in any but a sexual sense, the one very notable instance is the justification of it, under the term 'dear,' *priya*, solely, if the loved person be recognized as identical essentially with the divine self. But of amity, of sympathy, as between man and man I find no mention. Anger (*krodha*) is equally absent. Doubt (*vicikitsā*) we have seen once; there is but one other occurrence: "if one would believe this—the indwelling of Deity—he would have no more doubt." Wonder seems to be totally absent;[1] novelty no less. No attention is drawn to anything as being beautiful. Or as being ludicrous.

The emotion of liberation, on the other hand, is there from the first, albeit the distinctive term for it, when the release is of a religious kind, emerges later. *Mokṣa*, release, is *first found* in the Śvetâsvatara, and then in the Maitri Appendixes. But the verb 'being set free from' (*pramuc-*) is in both Chānd. and Bṛhad. Upaniṣads, and is echoed in the Kaṭha. Either it is the body from which release is seen as an advance, or from dying itself, or it is from desires (*kāmāni*). In every case, there is no seeing, in the being set free, a living in a Less; it is the winning to a More that liberty brings. Similarly for St. Paul there lay in the emotion a looking

[1] Into the emotion of 'the holy' I have gone on p. 50.

forward "to the glory of the liberty of the children of God." For the Indian teacher the man here was as a wayfarer with eyes bandaged seeking a country, having the bandage 'released' and *so* coming to arrive; "even so, where there is a teacher (*ācāriya*), one knows: 'Of this (I am) only so long as I am not released (*vimokṣe*), but then (there) is to be an arriving.' "[1] The arriving is the seeing 'That art *thou*'! In this saying: "Shaking off evil as a horse its hairs; shaking off the body, as the moon releases itself from Rāhu's mouth (I), the made self, pass into the unmade Brahmaworld."[2] So again: "When the man frees himself from these limbs just as a mango, or fig, or berry releases itself from its bond (*bandhanāt*), and he hastens again according to the entrance and place of origin back to life (*prāṇāy'eva*)."[3] Finally, in Yājñavalkya's 'way-song' we get: "When all desires are unloosed (*pramucyante*) nestling in the heart, then immortal the mortal becomes; therein he reaches Brahman . . . by it (the ancient Way) the wise go hence to the bright world, upwards released (*vimuktah*)."[4] These are all the references; nowhere is there any inquiry into the notion of freedom as being thus or thus. The emotion is implicit only, though we feel it is there. Or do I speak too much as a child of the West in linking too closely profound emotion with the word freedom, liberty:

liberté, liberté chérie?

It matters perhaps little to us whether the liberty be, as sung in the Marseillaise, political, or whether—if we be women—it mean domestic, social freedom, or whether it mean personal wander-whither-you-will

[1] *Chānd.*, 6, 14.
[2] *Ibid.*, 8, 13, 1.
[3] *Bṛhad.*, 4, 3, 36.
[4] *Ibid.*, 4, 7, 8.

freedom, or whether it mean religious liberty from shackles of dogma and church, these words have a power to stir and make throb possessed by few other words. I do not seek, save perhaps in the Buddhist nuns' Anthology, such a multiple aura in the Indian contexts. The aura is none the less multiple, as I have there shown by citing.[1] And I judge we shall misjudge the contexts, if we read them as the dispassioned statements of a theory, uttered in the cool accents of an exegetical pundit. That the speaker often breaks in them into verse of itself suggests emotion, afflatus. That he often so speaks is not, *usually*, to cite an utterance, nor to aid mnemonically (when it would have been resorted to at a conclusion).[2] He will say: "Here this verse comes to be"[3] as if it were a New, a More occurring to him. Even where recourse is not had to verse, the prose at times has the impressiveness of poetry. And nowhere perhaps is this more strongly suggested than in the section where Yājñavalkya responds to his royal pupil's request for teaching with the question, the central of all questions: *Quo vadis ?*[4]

"Equipped as thou art with the trappings of a king, with the Hymns, with our teachings, thence, when thou art being released, whither wilt thou go ? (*ito vimucyamānat kva gamiṣyati ?*). Thou art as one about to go on a great journey (*mahantam adhvānaṃ*) preparing a chariot or a ship, so art thou in an equipped self . . . now whither ?" "I know not, sir; whither shall I go ?"

The answer is in terms of Immanence, a teaching in which the 'whither' is ultimately not in terms of

[1] I return to this topic in Chapter XV.
[2] *Cf.* the verses in *Compendium of Philosophy*, P.T.S., 1910.
[3] *E.g., Bṛhad.*, 4, 4, 8, etc., etc.
[4] *Ibid.*, 4, 2.

where or whither, that is, of space; not in terms of worlds or of spans of life in such. Yājñavalkya had taken the measure of his eager pupil, and directs him to the Highest in the figure of utmost withinness, and then to a Within which embraces All, and then: "the Ātman is not this, not that! Ungraspable . . . indestructible . . . unattached . . . unbound, untrembling, unharmed—verily, Janaka, by thee Not-fear has been reached!" "Not-fear be also with thee, Yājñavalkya, who hast taught not-fear. . . . My people and I are (with thee)."

The little scene vibrates with emotion. Release was as the spark to the outburst, but it is not the final word. Its power is after all, at all times, but a negation of hindrance to be, to do, to become. Nor is the other term final: the absence of fear. It too is but a negation of the undesirable. Both terms are so clothed about with the borrowed vestments of the yet greater good: the open way to become That Who thou art, that man has often suffered vision to be dimmed as to this. It is not always so in these Sayings. It is true enough that the ultimate uttermost 'Well' is "ungraspable," is that "wherefrom words turn back together with mind, not having attained."[1] But the speaker of these words has faith that the Highest is not therefore a Void, but is so far conceivable and expressible that "bliss is bound up with Brahman," has faith too that the constantly enjoined effort "to seek out, to come to know" will culminate in a "becoming Brahman," and that to the Highest it is worth while to pray:[2]

From the unreal (*a-sat*) to the real make me go!
from darkness make me go to light!
from death make me go to the undying!

---

[1] *Taitt.*, 2, 4.

[2] *Bṛhad.*, 1, 3, 28.

And in this aspiration, for the seeker 'to know' was to 'become,' to know Brahman was to become Brahman, both now as a new and a more, opening up in this life, and at some time hereafter as a final becoming. Here indeed there may be found an acid test to the adequacy of Being (*sat*) to stand for the Indian as attribute of Deity. The man is told: "That art *thou*," yet he has to become That, that is, to come to be what he was not before. "He who knows the chiefest and best," we read, "becomes the chiefest and best."[1] "He who knows this—that the self is Brahman—becomes Brahman the No-Fear (*Brahmâbhayaṃ*),"[2] We surely cannot rightly understand this appreciation of 'being' in Indian religion unless we read into Being the More, the New, for which both it and we need the stronger word 'becoming.' It is but to be expected, that we should find the realization of this great expansion or deepening—however it be conceived—in one saying opening up with the words *hāvu*, *hāvu*, *hāvu*, literally Oh joy![3]

I have said thus much to make clear what writers have, for me, not made clear, and that is the strong element of living emotion often palpable in the early Upaniṣads. That there is also any tendency to *dwell* on an emotion, with a view to distinguish it from other phases of mind, *quâ* phase, this—I repeat,—I do not find. Analysis of emotion is, in a nascent psychology, a later arrival than that of cognition.

That the teachers preserved emotional reticence in their Sayings is to be expected. The Buddhist Suttas, dry as they tend to be, are yet more concerned with the emotions and sentiments than are these. The

[1] *Bṛhad.*, 6, 1, 1. [2] *Ibid.*, 4, 4, 25; *cf. Ka ha* 6, 2.
[3] *Taittirīya*, 3, 10, 5.

difference is perfectly natural, if we recollect that, in the Upaniṣads, we are in the world of the Academy, in the Suttas we are in the world of the home and the market. The main point of interest for me here is, that reticence is nowhere overcome in order to distinguish and to classify, as is the case, up to a point, with the cognitional side of man's activity. We are, in these Sayings, in a world of the Apologia and the New Mandate; not yet in a field of more detached, critical survey.

I now come to inquire whether, in contexts where volition is expressed, we find the early teachers at all interested in volition as such. Here, as I have repeatedly said elsewhere, we are handicapped from the start by not finding any word, noun or verb, which we may equate with 'will' and 'to will.' Nowhere, I have said, that is, nowhere in Buddhist Sayings can we match, in so many words, the acid test supplied in such a sentence as that of Jesus: "*Savena!* I will! Be thou clean (or whole)!" And the case is not altered in the Upaniṣads. How absent (with just one important exception[1]) is any emphasis on will-terms—terms either of conation, or of decision, of choice—is suggested at least by the total omission of references to such in the Indexes of translators. And yet how overwhelmingly important is the subject of man as willer in any religious utterances, let alone any sayings of psychological insight! It is only in terms of mixed intension, terms where the coefficients of thought and feeling are markedly blended with volition, that we can see, that the man as *kārī* and *cārī*, as doer and behaver, was by no means omitted from the teachers'

[1] Below, p. 111.

values. And hence I will go exhaustively into the utterances about such mixed terms.

But first a word on any terms which come nearest to being pure will-terms. We find none in our little illustrative list about the contents of *manas*.[1] But in the (later) Aitareya supplement[2] occur two terms which may be called purely volitional: *jūti* and *vaśa*. The one gives the dynamic urge of will, and, very much later, emerges in Buddhist psychology as *javana*, or apperception. The other gives the power or control in volition, and it too has an important, if non-academic part to play in the Buddhist Sayings long before the former term appears. But whereas these words are both Veda-terms, no cultural use is made of them in the earliest Upaniṣads. Save for one mention of *vaśa* in the Bṛhadārañyaka (where "the self, knower among senses, lies in the heart, ruler of all—*sarvasya vaśī, sarvasyeśānah*," 4, 4, 22), neither term is met with till the Kaṭha, Śvetâsvatara and Maitri.

I come then with empty hands to the mixed terms, such as purpose, choice, resolve, intention, desire. Here, as our teachers say (or used to say), we have, in varying preponderance, the coefficient of cognition, or of emotion (or feeling), or of both. Putting purpose, intention (and design) apart for the moment, we turn to the several instances of a case chosen, with the word for alternatives, things chosen, 'boons.' In these is matter of peculiar interest to us European Aryans, since it is here that we meet with the Indo-Aryan equivalent of our own words: *Wille* and *uolo*; the √*val*, in India, shifted to √*var*, or if it be preferred the *var*, in Europe, shifted to *val*. The *var* appears in the verb *vṛ*, *vara-*, the noun, in the words

[1] Above, p. 87. [2] Above, p. 89.

vara, better (*i.e.* selected, chosen out) and *vara*, boon, or (with Deussen) wish.

We have but few instances of these words in the earliest Upaniṣads, *e.g.*, Bṛhadārañyaka (1, 3, 28) and Kauṣītaki (3, 1), another following in Kaṭha, where the choice may be called the *Leitmotif* of the whole fantasy. In Kauṣītaki we find the meanings of *vara* mixed up in a word-play in which the Indian speaker delighted. " Indra: Choose thou a boon (*varaṃ vṛṇīṣveti*). Pratardana: Do thou choose for me . . . (*tvam eva me vṛṇīṣva*). Indra: Not verily doth a better choose for a not-better; do thou choose (*na varo avarasmai vṛṇīte; tvam eva vṛṇīṣva*). Pratardana: No boon verily (is it) then to me (*avaro vai khila me*)." We have here discrepant recensions, and hence variants in translation, but the choice-words and the pun are clear enough. Another earliest instance is—a case of ancient lore—in which man placed high value in the chant as a vehicle of super-will to effect. Namely, that if a brahman, in chanting a *stotra*, or hymn of praise, wish a wish, he may win his desire, gain his boon. Another is where the teacher is granter of choice of questions to his pupil, a prince.

This is all; nowhere do I find any notion moving in these Sayings as to the religious importance of considering 'the man,' the self, as not merely desiring, but as choosing, as willing this rather than that, nor any awareness that, in his power to choose, lay a mighty '*bhūyas*' or 'more' in that *nāma* or invisible personality which had begun so to intrigue the teachers. It is barely suggested in the little mind-list of the Bṛhadārañyaka by the term 'doubt': the something in 'mind' debarring from assent.

As to that, it is chiefly in meaning 'to debar,' repress,

restrain, hinder, that the *var*-root took on development in India. The dictionary reveals more than double the number of cases where *var*-cum-prefix means this negative sense, as compared with those in which the volitional meaning is positive. In later days, the Buddhists saw, in the teaching of the Jain Founder, mainly a gospel of restraint or *saṃvara*. They themselves, in falling away from their own gospel, went far in the same direction. That gospel had placed the man as chooser in the forefront; it had shown him his potential identity with Godhead as a way of not being but becoming, a way leading to That whom he needed and sought (*attha*). I refer to it here to show what a new expansion of this idea of choice, left latent in earlier thought, it actually was. Manhandling of the words in which it has come down to us, first of the oral, then of the documentary form, has caused it to be unduly overlooked.

Then as to the mixed terms, *dhṛti* and *kratu*: steadiness and intention—the renderings do not pretend to be adequate for either, at any time and in every context. Both are old terms, the latter especially, a Rig-Veda term, but only the former survives in Pali Sayings as *dhiti*. In the former we have the cognitive coefficient strong; in the latter we have the nearest approach perhaps made in India to 'will,' so near are we in the form to *kar-*, to do or make. Curiously this fine word did not survive to find entry into the Pali at all, and many were the makeshifts doing duty for it. Together with 'action' (where we see *kar-* expanded into *karma*), and with 'desire' (*kāma*, of different descent), it goes to compose one of the rare psychological dicta of the early Upaniṣads, a dictum which shows how essentially the Immanence they accepted was ***driving them to take up a dynamic view of man.*** This is in a lesson, where Yājñavalkya is speaking on the matter, to him of imminent importance:—the man's birthright in, not earth only, but in worlds. "According as one acts, according as one behaves, so becomes he. Doer of good becomes good; doer of evil, evil. One becomes virtuous by virtuous action, bad by bad action. But some say: Man is just of the form of desires. (*I* say:) As the desirer become, so intention becomes; so the action he does; the act which he does, that is (in him) accomplished" (*yathā kāmo bhavati tat-kratur bhavati, tat-karma kurute, yat-karma kurute tad-abhisampadyate*).[1]

In repeating this striking utterance (which, had it been developed in frequency and treatment in these Sayings would have shown the speakers as actually the first Buddhists), I have tried to present a closer translation of the original than any we yet have. Deussen is here especially wide of the mark, both in depreciating *kāma* to 'craving' (*Begierde*)—the word, as we shall see, had not then so worsened—and in calling *kratu* insight (*Einsicht*). In *kratu*, we have here the man midway between desire, stated elsewhere as being in and of mind, and action. Or, as I would say, man, as willing in the process called desire, develops desire into the willing we discern as planning—a living the act in anticipation—and then acts. And by all this he becomes what he was not before, he 'being' not simply a 'being,' but essentially 'one-who-is-becoming.'

The Chāndogya is equally insistent on the factor of *kratu* as being of utmost importance to the man in view of his right of way in the worlds—a context ascribed to the teacher Śāndīlya,[2] and either an echo,

[1] *Bṛhad.*, 4, 4, 5; above, p. 45.

[2] *Ch.*, 3, 14, 1.

or else an anticipant of a passage in the (late) Śatapaṭha Brāhmaṇa[1]—"Now verily the man is *kratu-maya* (has the form of will). As the man in this world becomes purposed, so he having passed on becomes. Let him form a purpose." Or intention. (In 'purposed' I have used *kratur-* as adjective; it may be rendered 'purpose,' but for these teachers 'man' was 'man,' and we mislead if we see, in their effort to impress, any notion of resolving the man into that wherewith he expressed himself.) The Bṛhadārañyaka version, bringing in desire and the act, suggests a later, more definitely conscious judgment.

The dying out of *kratu* after the day of the greater Upaniṣads was a serious loss to the vehicle in which the early Buddhists had to give their message. It lingers on, a rare visitor, in the middle Upaniṣads, and comes once in the Gītā,[2] but only as meaning ritual procedure!

Nor do any fit words for resolve, decision, determination[3] seem to have taken its place. The word *adhiṭṭhāna*, which emerges as 'resolve' in later books of the Pali Piṭakas, and seldom at that, does not mean more in the early Upaniṣads than 'eminence' (*adhiṣṭhāna*), nor do I find that it took on later the volitional force it came to imply in the Pali. And I cannot find any other such terms. Where for instance we have cases of insistence in a thing willed, there seems to be as it were a way of trying to comment on this without the fit term. Thus when Pratardana insists on not naming a boon, Indra's counter-insistence is called "departed

[1] *Ś. B.*, x. 6, 3. [2] ix. 16.

[3] Where now and then they occur in translations, I find, in tracking them down, that they have no fit originals in the text.

not from the true (or real), for the deity was the true."[1] Again, when Naciketas insists on keeping to the boon he has asked of Yama (or death), Yama comments on his persistence merely with "I think you want to know, but you have not many things you wish for." As if he had wished to say: "You do stick to your point!" When at length the lad has gained his point, his perseverance elicits a more positive remark: but the one word characterizing his determination is *dhṛti*, steadfastness:

> The winning of desire, the world's broad base,
> The endlessness of will (*kratu*), the no-fear that's beyond,
> The magnitude of praise, the range, the base,
> Wise Naciketas having seen has waved aside.[2]

Kratu as "endless" is very impressive, and it may be is profoundly true.

I may in ignorance have overlooked other terms for decisive volition, but it is fairly certain, that words for firm persistent will *as such* are greatly to seek in these Sayings; and this, in a cult which is so firmly insistent on seeking out, inquiring into, where the world was content to let things slide, is a curious and interesting paradox. Namely, how far men may need fit words to express a serious want, where fit words are not, and how long it may be, if ever, before they frame fit words. We shall revert to this in Buddhist psychology.

We come finally to *kāma*, desire. The first things, perhaps, that may strike the reader of the Upaniṣads who approaches from the study of Pali are (1) the gradual growth in the term of a worsening which is not there, or much less there at first, (2) the absence of that useful coadjutor, the term *chanda*.

[1] Above, p. 109. [2] *Kaṭha*, 2, 11.

(1) I have already commented on the misfit in Deussen's craving or lust for *kāma* in the Bṛhadārañyaka passage. *Kāma* is practically the only term for desire. There is also *icchā*, but never is it lent the strong significance of *kāma*. When the teacher, to the view, that desires are the one thing in man's hereafter-prospects that count, rejoins, that desires are but the *conditions* of that intention (or will) and resultant acts, and that it is these latter which are the determinants of his fate, he is not proposing to strip the wise and good man of desire, and so undermine both intention and action. The crucifying of desire as craving came along sure enough, in the Buddhist monastic values, but the sky was not then darkened in that way. The very life of Immanence is the desire to "seek after the Lord if haply man might find Him" where He was to be sought, namely, within. We should not have felt it amiss, if this quest of what is often called "bliss" had been likened, as in the Hebrew poem, to the thirsty hart seeking the waterbrooks. The one way, in which desire is seen as less worthy than not-desire, is in the reaching that inmost divine: "He who is not-desire, disdesire, desire-won (*akāmo niśkāmo āptakāmo*) is he who is Self-desiring (*ātmakāmo*). . . ."

> When are set free all the desires that nestle in the heart,
> Then mortal immortal becomes; therein Brahman is gained.[1]

Similarly the man, in the later Maitri, who loses the self in the great self is called *nirātman*, not, heaven forbid! because he was not-self, but because he was relatively no longer 'a' self. It was part and parcel of the wave of monasticism that was just beginning to creep up after the day of the early Upaniṣads, to see in

[1] *Bṛhad.*, 4, 4, 7.

fulfilment of a desire, the cessation of all desire. That a truer value was to see, in fulfilment, the power to exercise perfectly the will which had its vents in desires, was felt after in those early sayings, but it was too big a view for their successors. And in the monasticism of these, depreciation crept over the meaning of *kāma*, and the man who desired became the man who turned back from the highest desires to re-exercise of lower desires on earth again.[1]

(2) The word *chandas* is only used, in these early Sayings, for metric speech. Associated therein with the spells and other utterances of sex-desire, it also brings a somewhat soiled face into Buddhist sayings, and tends to be condemned, or else to have the passport-prefix of *dhamma-* attached to it. The absence of it, as a word for sensuous desire only, may have hastened the downfall of *kāma*, but I cannot pretend to trace its progress in its diverted meaning.

To return to the latter term: and its undepreciated meaning: our translators hinder us much in the inconsistent way with which they drop the word 'desire' for *kāma*, when, had they persisted in its use, its high function would have been clear. In the well-known dialogue between Yājñavalkya and his wife Maitreyī, wherein all things most valued derive their true value from the embracing value by which all things are, as *we* might say, seen in God, or *sub specie æternitatis*, the word 'love' and 'lieb sein' and 'is dear' are put for *kāma*, thus: "Not through desire (*kāmāya*) of the husband becomes husband dear . . . not through desire of wife becomes wife dear; not through desire of children become children dear; but through desire of Self become husband, wife, children dear," and so on.

[1] *E.g.*, *Muṇḍaka*, 3, 2, 2; *cf. Mait.*, 4, 2.

Here we see desire not only hallowed when, in husband, wife, child is seen the precious counterpart of that most precious Thing within one's heart, but as also in itself reckoned worthy, witness the teacher's attitude towards his own wife: "Dear in sooth, lady, though you be to us, you have made your dearness grow," namely by your questioning me. Through the renderings as given above, we overlook this more-worth in *kāma* when *kāma* is honourably felt.

And I would go further. I would maintain that, rightly to estimate the Vedic, not the later monastic, meaning in *kāma*, we must use the word 'desire' in a special sense. Etymologically, our European 'desire' means longing with regret, as of something unattained or even lost; the Latin *desiderare*. Something of this, save when we speak in a quite formal way, clings to the meaning of desire. Besides this, there lurks always, in desire, sensuous feeling, if not sensual feeling. The word is thus too clogged to serve as a worthy expression of a spiritual urge. Yet it is just this spiritual urge working in the man, both towards the fellowman and towards the indwelling Deity, that is here meant. The only term which, for me, comes near to it is our 'good will,' the good will towards men, or towards men of good will of the Lucan angelic message. Will, in this sense, is man in a process of spiritual growth, such as those Indian teachers were trying to get at with their frequent use of 'becoming,' where our translators usually put 'being.' And it is less overweighted with the coefficient of feeling; the volitional power in the Vedic word *kāma* would become rightly predominant were we to make Yājñavalkya talk in terms of good will; the emotional factor is fitly toned down into 'good.' Maurice Bloomfield came near to ranking *kāma* with will in discussing Yājñavalkya's dictum on man's life as a process of *kāma, kratu* and *karma*. It is true he ties himself up, in quoting, by calling *kratu* insight, but just previously he has waved this unfit rendering aside: " Deed and the will, or ' desire,' as the Hindus call it, back of the deed, are essentially one and the same thing. On desire man's nature is founded; as his desires so are his endeavours, as his endeavours so are his deeds."[1] I would not go so far as to see in will and deed ' essentially the same thing.' I would say, that will, purpose (or endeavour) and deed are the serial expressions of man's essential nature, and that is a Becoming, a coming-to-be what he was not before.

I am not saying, that ' good will ' is here a perfect fit, but I maintain it does not permit us to overlook, in our ambiguous terms ' love ' and ' desire,' the very vital point of the Vedic *kāma* having in it *more of conation than of feeling*. That it became, in degenerate days, overweighted with sensuous feeling I am the last to deny. Craving, *taṇhā* (*i.e.* thirst), the word by which monastic Buddhism virtually ejected ' will ' from its gospel-mandate, is defined in one of its phases as *kāma*. But we do need, in Yājñavalkya's noble discourse, wherein he shows how Immanence gives man the true basis for ethics, some word like ' good will,' the word wherewith St. Paul almost repeats his teaching in his " with good will doing service, as to the Lord and not to men."[2] St. Paul, by the way, is compelled by the Greek idiom, weak also in will-terms, to use *eunoia* where, as in *eudoxia* in the angelic chorus, it is the cognitive coefficient that is too strong.

It is a tragic fate in his utterance that man here, man

[1] *Religion of the Veda*, p. 259. [2] *Ep. Ephesians*, vi. 5.

there, has to use the imperfect tools he finds to hand when it may be a New Thing he is struggling to reveal. I am not saying we can do better, in Englishing the Upaniṣads, than to render *kāmāni*, desire in the plural, as 'desires.' There is more dynamic force in 'desires' than in 'wishes'; more of such force in desire than in 'love.' The Indian is not lucky in tools in his words for 'love,' and I was compelled to resolve this word into several aspects when asked to write on 'Love in Buddhism.'[1] Was it possibly the unfit term which led the poet of the Bhagavad-Gītā to take but a timid tentative step toward expounding Yājñavalkya's great song before sunrise: " He who . . . looking alike on everything sees the Self abiding in all beings and all beings in the Self . . . who worships me as dwelling in all beings . . ." ?[2] So far he gets. Yet what a superstructure of the warding of the fellowman on this account could there not have been, had for that poet's predecessors the word *kāma* been maintained at the lofty height of 'good will,' and not been let lapse to mean desires of body and mind only!

" There are so many desires in man; I'm not wanting to eat," mutters a sick scholar in the Chāndogya.[3] " So far (goes) he who desires," murmurs the poet of creation in the Bṛhadārañyaka.[4] But they went no further in any attempt to analyze desire or to value it as this and not that. Man's analysis of himself as user of this and that began with himself as watching and receiving, that is, with himself as cognitive. Here, as Bergson reminds us, he could catch himself as relatively static; he became as the flying bird just while perching;

[1] *Ency. Religion and Ethics.* See below, p. 301.
[2] VI., ver. 29, 31.
[3] 4, 10, 3.
[4] 1, 4, 17.

but in feeling, in will (*i.e.*, in conation), he was in flight; he lived so strongly he could do no more than live, not watch his living. So the psychology of will and desire had to wait.

With the exception of the few striking words on *kāma* and *kratu*, noticed above, that which this early teaching had to say about both will and desire should be read into what it said about *manas* (mind) and *saṃkalpa*. We shall get much too intellectual an impression of it if we omit to do this. The German student has been well fore-armed by the sagacious way in which Herman Oldenberg pointed this out in one of his last works, that on the Brāhmaṇas,[1] but not all students have the advantage of knowing German. "If," he wrote, "we inquire into the specific functions assigned to *manas*, we find that already, in the Rig-Veda, thinking, feeling, willing are indiscriminately applied to it." Instances from Veda and Brāhmaṇa follow, including one from the Bṛhadārañyaka: namely, that *kāmā* is overgrasper of mind, "for by mind one desires desires" (*manasā hi kāman kāmayate*).[2] Of *saṃkalpa*, again, he wrote, that the conjunction between this and *manas*, developed in the later Sānkhya, already occupies the stage in the Upaniṣads, the literal meaning lying in "a placing in right order or place," either in idea or in practical intent, in fact "much what we understand by 'dispositions.'"[3]

Of no less interest is it to heed what an equally eminent French Indologist left in his notes, a little later, on *saṃkalpa* and *manas*. I refer to Émile Senart's post-humous annotated translation of the Chāndogya (pub-

[1] *Vorwissenschaftliche Wissenschaft:* Die Weltanschauung der Brāhmaṇa-texte, p. 69 ff.

[2] *Bṛh.*, 3, 2, 7.

[3] *Ibid.*, p. 71 f. *Cf.* the root=*klp*, to fit.

lished 1930). "*Saṃkalpa* is really untranslatable, and 'concept' renders it badly, for this does not include its various meanings of thought, concept, will . . . *saṃkalpa* in a way implies a play on words. *Saṃ-kalp* has the general meaning of *se constituer, se réaliser*. *Saṃkalpa* is the realization by way of mind, whether it be realization of thoughts, ideas (=conception, imagination), or of thoughts in facts (=resolution, will). But *saṃkalpa* may apply equally to the production of the voice, the word, etc., through the inner faculty of *saṃkalpa*, no less than to the production of external appearances. Hence the involving (*enchainement*) of ideas, not at first obvious."[1] In passing, be it noted, he renders the word, in the "*bhūyas*," by *pensée* (thought) and *manas* by *esprit*. The French have no more distinctive word for 'mind' than this, or *intelligence*.

Actually the early Upaniṣads make a very limited use of *saṃkalpa*, either as noun or as verb. Of the latter there are but three such occasions, and of these one is an echo of the other two. They are *Chānd.*, 1, 2, 6, and *Bṛh.*, 1, 3, 6, and *Chānd.*, 7, 4, 1. In the former parallel, mind is shown working as *saṃkalpa*; and since this, and not the more usual 'minding' is chosen, we may see in *saṃkalpa* a 'more' in the concept of mind. Thus, when "mind is afflicted with evil, one purposes (*saṃkalpayati*) both what should, and what should not be purposed (*a-saṃkalpanīyaṃ*)." The latter context is about *saṃkalpa* as a 'more' in *nāma*, which I have already examined.[2]

Of neither context is any further use made in the

[1] *Chāndogya-Upaniṣad* (Collection Émile Senart, Paris), ed. by A. Foucher.

[2] Above, p. 66 f.

Saṃkalp-.	M-Müller:	Deussen:	Tatya:	Boethlingk:	Senart:	Hume:
1. Ait. U., 5, 2 ...	conceiving	Vorstellung	determination	—	—	conception
2. Kauṣ. U., 3, 2	conception	Erkenntniss	resolve	—	—	conception
3. Kena U., 30 ...	imagination	vorstellen	ascertained	—	—	conception
4. Chānd. U., 7, 4, I.	will	Entschluss	will	Wille	pensée	conception
5. Chānd. U., 8, 2, I.	will	Wunsch	wishes	Wille	—	conception
6. Bṛh. U., 1, 5, 3	representation	Entscheidung	determination	—	—	imagination
7. Bṛh. U., 2, 4, 11.	percepts	Strebungen	determination	—	—	intentions
8. Kaṭha, 1, 10[1] ...	—	Gemüth	(appeased) in thought	—	—	intent (appeased)
9. Śvet. U., 5, 8 ...	pacified[2] thoughts	Vorstellung	determination	—	—	conception

[1] *Sakya*, p. 85. [2] *Sāntas* . . .

teachings; whence it is evident, that no very effective instrument was felt to lie in this term to express the great dynamic interest, running through these Upaniṣads of man as a seeker, of man as wayfarer in the worlds. It is a relatively weak term, and it may be for this reason, unfelt by themselves, that translators are ever trying to fit on to it now this rendering, now that. How true this is I have already shown by a comparative table, and here show once more with additions (p. 121):

It is the rare and often apparently indeterminate use which, as we here see, is made of the term, that goes to justify me in saying, in *saṃkalpa,* we cannot say forthright, as did Regnaud, that, "since *saṃkalpa* is shown as *manas* in action, we may take it to mean desire or volition,"[1] *i.e.*, will. We may humour alternatives to a certain point, but there is a limit to laxity, and some of these variants call for too much of it. I can only conclude, either that the translators were uncertain as to the meaning, or that precision in terms of mind was not part of their mental equipment. If so, they err in notable company. No one thrust the potency and basic quality of will upon dormant European philosophy as did Schopenhauer, yet how slovenly he is in psychology one needs not much reading of him to find out.

[1] *Matériaux.*

CHAPTER VI

THE OTHER-WORLD MIND

I COME finally to a 'more' in the *nāma* which is not included in the analysis or output of the waking *nāma* considered above, but which none the less formed a feature never lost to view in these collections of Sayings. I mean the unseen equipment belonging to the man when he was not waking but sleeping. The Sayers have each something to say here to their pupils, but the Sayer who enters most fully into the matter is Yājñavalkya, greatest of the Sayers. There is the man who sleeps and dreams; later this came to be called 'monkey-sleep,' as if it were a mock-man experiencing a mockery of reality, or else a state of unrest, "shifty as an ape." This state the Bṛhad. U. explains as the man imagining (*mañyate*)[1] through ignorance the very objects arousing fear, etc., which he sees when awake,[2] and which by implication are illusory.

Then there is the man in deep sleep, or, as the Sayer worded it—apparently without our word 'deep'—"where the sleeper desires no desire whatever and sees no dream whatever." Or, at least, where just the Self is his desire (*ātmakāma*), a state technically called *samprasāda* (satisfaction).

Now concerning this state the reader is faced by a double difficulty. On the one hand, the text is palpably confused. In the same chapter (*i.e.*, 'brāhmaṇa'), viz., Bṛhad. 4, 3, we get the man in dreamless sleep, described in the loftiest terms as "in the embrace of

[1] N.B., not *saṃkalpayati*. [2] *Bṛhad.*, 4, 3, 20.

the 'wisdom-self'" rid of sorrow, desiring only that Self, a state in which all earthly and other-world relations are merged: "there father becomes[1] not-father, mother not-mother, worlds not-worlds, Vedas not-Vedas, where social rank is naught, and *śramaṇa* not-*sramaṇa*, ascetic not-ascetic, where neither evil nor good follows him." Not that he has become insensitive or mentally unaware, the text goes on, since the man is imperishable, but because of the cessation of his awareness of things as separate objects. But we also get the man "in deep sleep" returning to his nest, namely, the sleeping body, "having had enjoyment in this *samprasāda*" of a very different kind—and here the teacher breaks into verse—

> Having by sleep prostrated what is bodily,
> sleepless he looks down on the sleeping (things),
> deriving light again he goes to the place (*ṣthāṇa*),
> the golden man, the lonely bird.
> Having with living breath the low nest guarded,
> he the immortal one fares thence at will,
> the golden man, the lonely bird.
> Within his sleep he goes both up and down,
> a deva he, he makes shapes manifold,
> now pleasantly with women jesting,
> now seeing things of fear and peril.
> His pleasure ground they see,
> but him sees no one.

It is fairly clear, that we have here a confusion between: (*a*) the man in dream-sleep; (*b*) the man in deep sleep, sleep from which it was held dangerous to wake him, that is, his visible body, suddenly, lest in the man's absence in his "pleasure ground (*ārāma*)," the wakened body behave like an idiot; (*c*) the man who has finally attained the Highest, after the death of his last body. On the other hand the refusal at present

[1] Note the verb, usually translated 'is'!

of Western writers (let alone many of the East) to take seriously the hypothesis of the 'other,' subtle, or astral body, so long and so widely hinted at in both West and East, together with the easy compliance shown by many in the hypothesis of man, quâ individual man, existing in a 'discarnate' disembodied state, tends to make the expositions of writers as confused as is this old text.

For me there is no reasonable doubt that Yājñavalkya agreed, that the man, when, in deep sleep, he quitted the body, did so in a second body, emerging in some way he does not clearly specify,[1] a body which in later Upaniṣads is alluded to as *linga*, or physical factor,[2] and in other literatures as the *lingaśarīra* or *sukṣuma-śarīra* (subtle body). To be travelling afoot or in 'chariot' or enjoying pleasant intercourse are matters needing a living body as instrument of expression and movement. And in the 'ārāma' of the co-present next world it is the subtle body which becomes the real, the tangible; it is the earth-body which becomes to its user as a wraith.

We have thus, I repeat, a double vagueness to hinder clarity. Discounting our own myopia, I feel convinced we have, in the Bṛhad. text, a confused result of later editors, first oral, then literary, touching up a matter in which their later day had lost the key. Were this not so, Śankara and other exegetists would very clearly have put us wise in the matter. There has clearly been an attempt at an analytic description both of light and of deep dreamless sleep in this lesson, in which the teacher sought to show his pupils man's close mondial interrelationship. Almost equally interesting is the Chāndogya lesson, where, in an allegory,

[1] Thus, 2, 1, 19. [2] *Śvetā*, 1, 13; *Mait.*, 6, 10.

the older god Prajāpati is teaching the younger, Indra, to win, in periods of time, ever a less unfit conception of the, to both of them, inconceivable Highest. Namely, that it is not in dream-sleep that man becomes Deity, nor in deep sleep; that body is but the platform of the deathless, bodiless self; and exists but 'for this' or that function (the word 'instrument' is here lacking). Yet here too is no clear word about the 'other' body, whom the aftermen had clearly lost sight of.

Some day, it may be, an editor, in the light of the subtle body hypothesis, will sift these two confused, and probably much edited passages, handling the Vedic Sanskrit with competent knowledge. Deussen might have done this, so far as possessing the conviction, that in both these passages we are facing a mass of mixed earlier and later material. But he is too mystical, just as Dr. Hume is too metaphysical, to pause and give heed to that which is for me just here the real burden of the teaching: namely, that Yājña-valkya and his worthiest colleagues were, not only men who had set their faces towards the Highest, whom they called Brahman or Ātman, but were also men who saw man as on the threshold of his next world, who saw him as *living*, now waking now sleeping, *in both worlds*, and who saw him as aware, if he were, as we say, psychic, that he did so live—live not as embodied here, disembodied there, but as the possessor of alternative bodies.

Of any anticipations in the unconscious and sub-conscious now so stimulating research I find in the early Upaniṣads no sign, nor any serious preoccupation with dreams. I may here be myopic. Under Bud-dhist developments there will be a little—a very little —to say.

One day they who are now engaged on research in early Indian thought may give expression, as now I do not find that they do, to the fact, how barren a field is that early thought in attention as occupied with the subconscious, the unconscious. I may here have overlooked, yet the makers of long indexes bear me out, e.g., Winternitz, Deussen, Thadani, etc. Dr. Hume (*op. cit.*, p. 46 f.) gives due attention to Upaniṣadic thought on the man-in-sleep, yet (1) the cited revelations about man's other-world mind are dubbed as 'supposititious,' (2) he makes no comparisons with modern research. Incidentally Dr. C. G. Jung does not appear to have found matter in this connection worthy of note in his own inquiry into early Indian thought. It is true that we have ourselves but taken yesterday to this field; but early Indian thought anticipated us in many things.

And further, workers in that field may come to find a sufficient reason for that incuriosity in the acceptance of the two bodies copresent in man on earth (I do not here inquire further), alternatively active, according as he is what *we* call conscious or unconscious, and calling thus for an alternative set of 'mind-ways,' ways which, in 'psychic' experience, are both active and co-operating. We are striving with immense patience to discover, by way of the earth-mind, the true nature of ourself as sub- or un-conscious. Indian thought saw (dimly enough) in that nature a possessor of more instruments than we credit ourselves withal. Herein he was dealing, not with an undeveloped field of 'mind,' not with a self groping in the dark, but with a different mind, a different body.

CHAPTER VII

INTRUSION OF SĀNKHYAN ANALYSIS AND EMERGENCE OF YOGA

THE appearance in Upaniṣads, reckoned as early, if not the earliest, of a wedge of new teaching, not altogether in harmony with that which they mainly emphasize, was much discussed, especially by German scholars, during the latter half of the nineteenth century: Weber, Max Müller, Gough, Oldenberg, Barth, Jacobi, Garbe. The last-named, in his *Die Sānkhya-Philosophie* (1894)—a book which should long ere now have found an English translator[1]—makes clear this 'first appearance' in his opening chapter (pp. 14-15). Weber had affirmed, and Barth also, that, *pace* yet older teachings, the ideas which came to belong to the "Sānkhya system" already appear in oldest Upaniṣads in a motley mixture with teachings of opposed views. Garbe rejoins: "I, as against Weber, must assert, that in Vedic literature, as far as this is pre-Buddhistic, no Sānkhya teachings are to be found." (We need not here find the term "pre-Buddhistic" a complication; it is merely a hypothetic milestone for dating certain Upaniṣads.) Under Sānkhya teachings, he goes on, "I understand of course the distinctive theses of this system, the content of which is formed by the following ideas:

[1] After forty years I would now express the hope, that a worthy *successor* to Garbe's pioneering may, if he be not English, find a translator, as Garbe did not.

"Absolute separateness of the spiritual and the non-spiritual principle,
Plurality of souls,
Independence and eternity of matter,
Constituents of matter as *sattva*, *rajas* and *tamas*,
Evolution of the world from primeval matter,
Therein psychical organs as evolving first, then external things,
The triad of psychical 'organs' (*karaṇa*),
The twenty-five 'principles,'
The fine elements (*tan-mātrā*),
The inner body (*linga-śarīra*),
The 'dispositions' (*saṃskārā*),
The psychical processes grasped as purely mechanical, only 'raised' into consciousness by the spiritual power of the soul (*i.e.* 'man'),
Denial of God,
Release alone possible by the dissociation of spirit from matter."

The Upaniṣads, in which Garbe first found one or more of these more or less jarring, or at least novel elements emerging, are the Kaṭha, Maitri, Śvetâsvatara, Praśnā "and similar Upaniṣads." I presume he may, by the last, have chiefly meant the Muṇḍaka, Īśā and Māṇḍukya, possibly also the Mahānarāyana. I write subject to correction.

He goes in detail into Weber's claim, that 'Sānkhya' ideas were to be found even in the earliest Upaniṣads, and shows that the claim is forced too far. Thus a term closely associated with Sānkhya is the second of the 'triad' listed above: *ahaṃ-kāra*, lit. 'I'-making. The theory was, that a threefold function (lit. procedure, *vṛtti*):—intellect (*mahat*, or *buddhi*), I-making and mind (*manas*)—fused and transmuted the manifold data of sense into the spiritual awareness we now, in our own way, call 'consciousness.' *We* might call this 'I-making' the relating of impressions to an agent and valuer. Now this term occurs once in an 'earliest' Upaniṣad: the Chāndogya (7, 25, 1), and, except that, only in those later Upaniṣads in which Sānkhyan ideas are clearly traceable. But Garbe contended, that this term is not, in the Chāndogya, used in the distinctive Sānkhyan sense, but refers to nothing less than the divine Self. Instruction (*deśa*) about the one and the other is given in identical words. Namely, that reference to an 'I' and, equally, the self means an omnipresent fact: 'I,' the self, am everywhere in every world.

I see the force in Garbe's contention, and would only add this: that for the earlier Brahman teachers, the 'I,' as a phase in the self-concept, was present, but they were *not yet interested in it as such.* There is for instance the episode of the supremacy of the breath-as-life (*prāṇa*) over other faculties, called 'I-betterness,' in three of the oldest Upaniṣads, but no *analysis* of the 'I' is there. The Sānkhyan vogue was not yet taking up their attention.

Nevertheless in one of these, the Kauṣītaki, it is, as I have said, beginning.[1] I cannot otherwise explain the warning note of that teacher, not found elsewhere, yet so significant of a change in thought which for him was dangerous (I condense it): "Speech, sight, sound, deed, pleasure and pain, going, mind, are not what one should wish to find out; one should know the speaker, the hearer, the see-er, the enjoyer, the goer, the mind-er." This is precisely the warning a

[1] Above, p. 94.

wise teacher 'of the right wing' as we might now say, would utter, who saw going on a growing interest in the instrument, the machine, so that interest in the user, whose growth was culture's main object, was slackening. And it is, as to that, precisely the warning a wise psychologist should utter today.

No less sagacious are Garbe's contentions, that the word *sattva* in the Chāndogya (7, 26, 2) is used in the general sense of nature, not in the specific Sānkhyan sense of 'goodness,' and that other terms in the Bṛhadārañyaka (*linga*, *avyākṛtam*, *sambhūti*) are similarly used in no technical way.

When, however, we come to the Kaṭha Upaniṣad, whereas the main teaching is true to the acceptance of Immanence, or identity of man-nature with God-nature, as accepted in the earlier Upaniṣads, we cannot, even if we read at the mercy of translators, fail to note new notions not met with before. The reader can find these enumerated in Dr. Hume's translation: *Thirteen Principal Upāniṣads*, p. 8. For my reader's convenience I give them here. They are given as three: (1) a non-spiritual principle, called in Sānkhyan Sūtras *prakṛti*, lit. what is made manifest, is 'described'; (2) a gradation of psychic principles in the order of their emanation from the *avyākrti* (lit. the not made discriminate); (3) the first appearance of the word for one such principle: *buddhi*:—intelligence (?), intellect (?), lit. awakeness.

Here it should be noted, that the Kaṭha does not use the term *prakṛti*. The assertion that the lines:

> *She who arises with life-breath,*
> *Aditi, maker of divinity,*
> *Who stands entered into the secret places,*
> *Who was born forth through beings—*

refer to that unspiritual principle is the work *of the exegetist only*, or, in Dr. Hume's words, is 'traditionally interpreted.' Further, that the gradation alluded to:

> Higher than senses are values-in-things (*artha*),
> Higher than values-in-things is mind,
> And higher than mind is intellect (*buddhi*);
> Higher than intellect is great self (*mahan ātmā*);
> Higher than the great is not-made-discriminate;
> Higher than not-made-discriminate is the man,
> All-pervading and without other body (*linga*),
> Higher than the man what is there?
> That is the goal, that is the highest bourn,

has been in a way anticipated by the 'more' that, in the earlier Chāndogya, was, as we saw, being drawn out from the content of the word 'name.' There, as we saw, no attempt was made at logical sequence in the matter of grouping. There *was* an attempt made at valuation. Thus, we read, "mind is more than speech," because "it compasses both speech and name." "Purpose is more than mind," because "in purposing one is minding, one utters speech, one intones this in name." But, I repeat, we must not see, in the valuing, the carefully graduated symmetry of the *later* Kaṭha, or we shall let the earlier author in for conclusions far from his intent. His interest lay, not in asserting that *M*. is 'greater' or 'better,' or even 'mightier'[1]—as translators wrongly render *bhūyas*—than *N*., but in showing up the 'more,' the rich, hitherto undiscerned manifold in the concept *nāma*. His object is mainly descriptive, not cumulative.

Lastly, with regard to the very interesting first, and fourfold occurrence of the new term *buddhi*, a word in the Sānkhya Sūtras interchangeable with *mahat* (great one), I would say: (*a*) it is curious that the other

[1] Boethlingk's translation.

practically new word of the mental triad:—'I'-making, does not first occur also in the Kaṭha. It does not appear till the day when were compiled Svetâsvatara, Maitri and Praśnā, and once only in each. In still later Upaniṣads it is noteworthy, that whereas *buddhi* became a fairly frequent term, *ahaṃ-kāra* may be found relatively little. It is indeed a little remarkable that this word ever found acceptance by Brahman compilers, so strongly does it suggest a *factitious* feature in man's finding 'the headquarters of reality'—to quote my friend Edmond Holmes—in the self, the soul, the very man. (*b*) The appearance of *buddhi* in a psychical sense is, in its own way, no less strange. The root *budh* and derivatives are not seldom used in the oldest Upaniṣads, usually but not always[1] with the merely physical meaning of awaking from sleep. The transition to mental awakening is sudden, and for this reason, and *yet more for another*, seems to betray it as the spearhead of exotic thought.

The other reason is, that had the new interest betrayed in the mind, of which *buddhi* is a symptom, arisen from an advance in the left wing of *Brahman* teaching, we should have expected to find a graduated value drawn not between mind (*manas*) and *buddhi*, but between mind and *prajñā*. Here is the faculty which would, by them, have been assigned to the place of intermediating between mind and the self, had they been in that day interested in a graduated estimate of mind. In the early Upaniṣads: Chāndogya, Bṛhadārañyaka, Kauṣītaki, Taittirīya, *prajñā* occurs nearly sixty times. And now and again it is expressly shown as the faculty which intermediates between man's instruments and the self or soul.

[1] See above, p. 41.

The Śvetâsvatara and Maitri Upaniṣads, the date of each of which, or rather the dates of each portion of which, cannot be said to be pre-Buddhistic, betray more markedly the growing influence of Sānkhyan analysis. In the former, we not only meet with both *buddhi* and *ahaṃkāra*, but with the compound *sānkhyayoga*, as if a definite way of study were implied:

> (By knowing) that cause, attainable by *analysis and valuing-effort* (*sānkhya-yoga*) . . .
> (That God), one is released from all fetters.

In the Maitri we have both *buddhi* and *ahaṃkāra*, and also the word *guṇa* used with its specific Sānkhyan aspect of the three 'constituents of matter.' *Prakṛti*, the manifest or material, appears in both Upaniṣads. And in both these and other Upaniṣads, presumed to be more or less contemporaneous, there is shown an increased tendency to use numbered sets of things material and spiritual, a tendency used, but less used, in the earlier Upaniṣads.

Later Brahman, *i.e.* Vedāntic, exegesis became busy in forcing identities, between Sānkhya and Vedānta, *e.g.* between the manifest (*prakṛti*) and illusion (*māyā*), where neither term is mentioned in the text. On the one hand there is allusion, in the Śvetâsvatara, to 'deluded' teachers; on the other, Cowell maintained that this Upaniṣad was "the most direct attempt to reconcile the Sānkhya and Vedānta."[1] That which remains clear is that the sayer, or sayer *and* editors, of this most interesting work were undergoing the impact of a New Word, a new way of looking at man and things, at life and Deity. And the evidence of the

[1] Edition and translation of the Maitri.

new terms used shows, that this new way was, in the main, a new view about the mind, such as is prominent in the Sānkhya Sūtras.

But this, which I am not alone in calling Proto-Sānkhya, was not the only new growth in a systematic view of man's self-expression that we find developing in the Upaniṣads. I refer to what is linked, in a passage cited above, with Sānkhya, namely Yoga. There can be no doubt about the growth, and the relatively stronger growth of this when we compare, *e.g.* in the columns of Jacob's invaluable Concordance, the few references to Sānkhya, most of which are *not* to the Upaniṣads, with the full columns of references to Yoga, one half of which *are* to the Upaniṣads, both to the word itself and to the number of compounds in which it appears.

The word 'yoga' is not to be found at all in the earliest Upaniṣads, that is, if, with Regnaud, we see in parts at least of the two: Aitareya and Taittirīya, a somewhat later tradition.[1] It *does* occur once in the latter, and then in a context which suggests it as an accepted technical term in religious culture. Thus, when the man is looked at under the aspect of *vijñāṇa*, he is compact of faith, order, truth, might and *yoga*, *yoga* being as it were the very body, *i.e.* totality (*ātmā*) of him. Here is of course no reference to a definite method or 'system,' any more than are the other features. But the fact that 'yoga' is mentioned at all, and not in the three Upaniṣads generally conceded as earliest: Chāndogya, Bṛhadārañyaka and Kauṣītaki, is possibly another straw of evidence endorsing Regnaud's guess, he overlooking it.

[1] *Matériaux.*

Unless indeed a later editorial hand has substituted *yoga* for *dhyāna*. It is *dhyāna*, not *yoga*, that we meet with in Chāndogya and Kauṣītaki. But there *dhyāna* means no special form of mental activity, as it does in the later Maitri, where *dhyāna* is assigned third place in a "sixfold yoga,"[1] the object of which is declared to be "the going to the oneness of the one": *ekasya hai ekatvam eti*. *Dhyāna* there (in Chānd. and Kauṣ.) would seem to have meant just a work or product of mind (*manas*), as when we say 'thinking a thought.' It occurs where we should have looked to see *citta*. This is not easy to explain, for *dhyāna* meant a brooding or musing; and in that unfolding of the content of *nāma*, alluded to above, *dhyāna*, called a 'more' than *citta*, has a special connotation assigned it very unlike that of *citta*.

We can see anyway, that *yoga*, emerging in the midway Kaṭha, appears later as a practice embracing both intellectual activity, in the term *tarka*, such as is indispensable in analytic thought, and also other ways of mind:—suppression of impressions of sense, musing, fixed attention (*dhāraṇa*) and concentration (*samādhi*). But that *tarka* counted for much in *yoga* was not true. The mental activity which we are tending today to call intuition, an attitude the reverse of intellectual, *i.e.* analytic activity, is more akin to *yoga*. We shall come back to this. My object in mentioning it here is to draw attention to a second growing, changing influence coming up in Indian culture, about which two things are to be said:—(*a*) it was in its own way a development of mind; (*b*) it was not, like Sānkhya, exoteric, but esoteric.

Now, whereas we may not have within reach the how

[1] 6, 28.

and why of the rise of an exoteric inroad of thought, we ought, when the new word is esoteric, to be able to trace somewhat of its how and why. On this I may venture a suggestion when I am looking more closely at the changing psychology in the middle Upaniṣads. For we should betray ourselves as overshadowed by our psychology of yesterday, the dominant psychology when I was working myself into Buddhism, if we were to find less of psychological interest in Yoga than we find in Sānkhya. In fact we need to break away from the European psychology both of yesterday and today to appreciate the nascent psychology of India. We need to put the man, the mind-er first, not last, or nowhere at all. With that goes this: that we must put first man as a seeker, and after that the man as reacting to impressions that come, whether he is consciously seeking them or not. We can follow neither the analytic disentangling of the man from mind of Sānkhya, nor the effort at unity of man with the more-that-is-in-man of Yoga, if we make our start in the traditional European way with sense-process.

Let not the student of psycho-analysis, especially as dealt with by Dr. C. G. Jung, misunderstand me here, when I speak of 'the rise' of an exoteric, or esoteric inroad of thought. I am not denying that these two tendencies are prehistorically human, or that pre-occupation with the one may seek to readjust poise by the other. In Chapter VI. of his *Psychological Types*, Dr. Jung has sought to trace the two in early Indian thought, not as I do here in *sānkhya* and *yoga*, but as (*a*) the expression of experience as in pairs (*dvandva*; the 'opposites' of translators is intrusive and exegetical), and as (*b*) the resentment at this as spiritually hindersome and a matter to be overcome. It is true that he has not taken into account the fact, that the many references he has been careful to give are from works covering a time-range of about a thousand years. In that interval, in any given realm, human values will have undergone much evolution. But it is also true, that references to generalized experience as being in contrasts are frequent, early and late. And the writer finds, that (for India as elsewhere) " the optimum of life recedes more and more from the opposing extremes, and seeks out a middle way, which must necessarily be irrational and unconscious, just because the opposites are rational and conscious " (I quote only from H. G. Baynes' translation.)

Hereon a brief word of comment: (1) What we deem rational, logical, depends on our premises; the 'irrational' becomes perhaps rational when we have come to substitute wider, deeper premises. This in passing. (2) The stating of impressions by way of pairs is indeed characteristic of the Upaniṣads, early as well as later. They occur in the talk about the " more " in " nāma " with which I have dealt twice (pp. 15, 64*f*). But they are there used, simply as part of the contents of 'speech' and not as either of interest in the new mind-analysis or in any way hindersome. " Speech is surely more than *nāma*; it makes known . . . Vedas, etc. . . . as well as heaven-earth, wind-space, water-heat, gods-men, beasts-birds . . . right-wrong, true-false, good-bad, pleasant-unpleasant. Verily were there no speech *the last four pairs would not be known.*" This is all, and it is worth keeping in the historical picture. (3) The awareness of coming to know pairwise is, it is true, seen evolving, under the growth of the ascetic or monastic ideal, into a spiritual hindrance in later works: the Gītā, the Māṇava-dharma-śāstra, etc. We see it marked by the emergence of the technical term *nirdvandva* for a man held to be spiritually released. (4) The rise of introversive practice or *yoga* in its quest of unity will have fostered that discontent with such duality.

The method I have followed here is to show the gradual growth of interest in the ways of mind as both aware of the manifold, whether pairwise or otherwise, and aware of a one, a unity, to which all should be referred.

Finally, as to both Sānkhya and Yoga, let my readers not imagine that, in considering either of these new influences on India's nascent psychology, I am seeing, in either influence, anything that we of today would call a 'system.' It took centuries to elaborate a system of Christian philosophy. It took no less time to elaborate the early teachings of Brahmans, of Kapila's school, of the Sākyans (Buddhists), into anything fit to be called a system. There was no word in early Indian culture for what would now be so called. 'Nyāya' may have later amounted to this, but it is, if I mistake not, for the early Upaniṣads an unknown word. 'Vidyā' was rather knowledge in general than a systematized form of knowledge; it was knowledge as the opposite of ignorance,[1] knowledge as that which the teacher taught, especially if it was about *amṛta*, for this was *vidyā* that brought man to the devas, made man 'become Brahman.' But it was not any logically connected system, such as was eventually elaborated as the Sānkhya system of our era, or that which Patañjali called the Yogânusāsana: connected

[1] "Far, diverse, opposed, these that are known as *avidyā* and *vidyā*" (*Kaṭha*, 2, 4).

instruction in Yoga, also of our era. I have quoted Garbe's list of Sānkhya 'principles,' but he is careful to call them merely distinctive "thoughts which go to form Sānkhya philosophy." And Dr. Hume makes due allowance for "a supposititious period when the terms of philosophy may have existed without distinction of systems."

To speak of teachings in terms of systems is, for Indian culture, too much the way of the man in a world of books, of the pen. In this volume I write of a bookless world. In that world it was not, as Garbe renders it, *schriftwidrig*, 'contrary to scripture,' to call a teaching *aśrabda*; it was contrary to 'what was heard,' to the utterances of accredited teachers. And whereas in these one got impressive mantras, and sequences of mantras, one did not get the logically connected world-view, which a culture of the written word rendered (alas!) so much more makeable. 'Philosophy' is solely the offspring of the writing Greek. The early Indian loved *sophia*, *i.e. prajñā*, no less, but he did not see it in systems of axioms and deductions. For that matter neither did the Greek of the period of which I speak. We cannot call up a true picture of the curriculum of the school of a Yājñavalkya or Kauṣītaki, but it is probable, since we find many subjects of a curriculum, but nowhere "a staff of masters," that men like those two had made all knowledge their kingdom, and that the Upaniṣads represent, of their teaching, their sayings, more or less detached, on the things that mattered most for the man, as man, to learn, reflect upon, if possible realize and, especially if the learner were an intending teacher, to learn by heart. Here we have philosophy in the making, here we have material for a system, but we have nothing more. Let no such words obtrude themselves on the reader of these inquiries.

Neither was there the word 'psychology.' It needs the long perspective we have, to discern the birth of what we mean by that. For the Indian parent the event was too new to be thus christened.

CHAPTER VIII

SĀNKHYA AND YOGA IN THE MIDDLE UPANIṢADS

I come to consider a little more closely the eight Upaniṣads usually assigned a position in time later than the five hitherto examined. Regnaud ranked them in four groups: No. 5, Īśā, Kena; No. 6, Kaṭha, Praśna, Muṇḍaka, Māṇḍūkya; No. 7, Śvetâsvatara; No. 8, Maitri (or Maitrāyana). It is possible that the Māṇdūkya has here too early a place, but, as the historically sensitive Deussen remarks, the data for a precise chronology do not exist, India having been the reverse of 'sensitive' in this respect. My object here is to bring into relief the way in which this eightfold group is revealing an interest in the New—a New in the procedure in man's inner world of mind—an interest due to a twofold stimulus: the growing influence of the analytic teaching, coming into the brahman academic world from the school traditionally ascribed to Kapila; the growth of a habit and practice of introspectional attention and discipline, resulting from the acceptance of Immanence, and coming to be called Yoga. And I have tried to trace the first note in this twofold interest as struck by the 'more' (*bhūyas*) in that inner world unfolded in the Chāndogya, and by the instrumental mediacy of mind between man and the messages of sense worded in the Bṛhadārañyaka.

The reader will better discern the degree of this twofold growth if he, on coming to study the Upaniṣads, confines himself, for a period, entirely to the former member of the "twofold stimulus," as considered in the last chapter. He will then the better see into what a relatively new world he comes when introduced by groups 5 and 6 to group 7, and yet more to group 8. He will perhaps be struck mainly by the new and richer psychological vocabulary, and by the awareness of this, that man's vision, as turned inward, finds terms unused before for 'introspection.' He will also be struck by the fact, in man's outward vision, that the sky has become overshadowed, to a degree unfelt before, by a clouded concept of life—of life as ill because of man's hampering bodily encasement, and because of all the social evils to which the dominance of this encasement led men. And he will see man seeking a refuge from ill, not only and not so much as heretofore in the glory of his inherent oneness with Deity, but rather in the world of the mind, namely, in a misty atmosphere of *ideas concerning* Deity, which the teachers pour forth in a new wealth of words.

Here it seems best to consider for a space what survives of the earliest sayings assigned to that school called of Kapila, and whence came the later 'system' called Sānkhya. I have already quoted a list of credal items in which Garbe drew up an outline of Sānkhya principles. But it will go much further to inform readers, if they have the patience, to glance through these sayings in the oldest wording in which they have come down to us. They are known as the aphorisms of the *Sānkhya-kārikā*, and are attributed to one Īśvarakṛśna, simply on the strength of the claim put forward in the penultimate verse of the seventy-two verses of Aryan metre in which the work consists. No attempt is made to name an author.

Īśvakraṛśna claims only to have compiled the verses, handing on in them " a mystic (*guhyaṃ*) lore for the needs of man by the supreme sage," who gave it over to Asuri, and he to Pañcasikha, who diffused it. No date can be assigned for their work on earth. Our only clues are to trace parallels between things said in these verses and other literature.

This is possible to quite a considerable degree, the parallels appearing to a marked extent—as Deussen pointed out—in the Maitri Upaniṣad. His work being inaccessible to some readers of English, I give his parallels here:[1]

Maitri.	*Sānkhyakārikā.*	*Translation.*
2, 7: prekśakavad avasthitaḥ svasthaśca.	Aph. 65: prekśakavad avasthitaḥ susthaḥ.	standing aside as spectator well placed.
3, 2: nibadhnāti ātmanā ātmānaṃ.	Aph. 63: badhnāti ātmanā . . . *prakṛti* ātmānaṃ prakṛtiḥ.	binds self by self.
5, 1: svârthe svābhāvike 'rthe.	Aph. 56: svārthe iva parârthe ārambhaḥ.	for ther own ends, for specific ends depending.
6, 10: mahādadyaṃ viśeṣa-antaṃ lingaṃ.	Aph. 40: mahādādi sūksmaparyantaṃ . . . lingam.	begins with intellect, ends with elements *or* extends to the subtle (body).
6, 19: lingam nirāśrayaṃ.	Aph. 41: nirāśrayaṃ lingaṃ.	the (subtle) body without support (or subject or attachment).

More of the like might be adduced. They do not suffice to make out one of the two works as a result of the pre-existence of the other, whether as oral or as written compilation. Deussen only claims that " a

[1] *Allgemeine Geschichte der Philosophie*, I., pt. 3, p. 410.

peculiar relation (*Verwandschaft*)" is apparent. He has also reminded us, that the editor of the Aphorisms states that both of these are a faithful reproduction of another (oral) compilation: the Śaṣṭitantraṃ, which has not survived. This permits a fairly plausible guess, that the compiler (-ers) of the Maitri, in view of the growing prestige of Sānkhyan analysis of mind, had listened to the expounders of its teaching and adopted many of its phrases.

Inferences from parallels would of course be much more effective, could a certain date be assigned to one of the set of parallels. To a certain extent the reflection, in the Maitri, of Buddhist parallels comes in to aid. But the aid is at best very negative. It is difficult to say, how much by it the Maitri is made out to be later, or the Buddhist influence earlier. So different indeed are the views about the 'man' or *ātman* in the Maitri from those which had come to prevail when the *Sakyan*[1] teaching became of importance in India, that we must seek some other, some common factor affecting both the one and the other, where lies any resemblance. This will have been the growing vogue in monasticism, a vogue which is not inherent in either the brahman academic world, or in original Buddhism (Sakya), however much the latter is made responsible for propagating it. This is the clouded sky—to repeat the figure—which overshadows both the Maitri and the Pali Suttas. And it was this, together with the growing effect of Sānkhyan analysis of mind, which led to the crumbling Immanence we see emerging in the Maitri, and to the crumbling belief in the reality of the *ātman* which is patent in the Suttas.

[1] I use the Pali spelling; the Sanskrit is Śākya.

Now to the *Kārikā* itself. We do not, in the first place, find in it all of those "distinctive theses" listed by Garbe, and cited above (p. 129). We must, for example, rule out at least two: plurality of souls and denial of God. Nor do we find the word *saṃskāras*; 'dispositions' are here called 'bhāvā' or 'states,' whether as of being or becoming.

I shall be called to task concerning the first ruling. There can be no doubt that exegetists took the eighteenth aphorism as affirming that 'souls were many.' But these wrote at a much later date when the plurality was accepted. Accepted elsewhere in the *Kārikā* it certainly is not. Had it been, we should have read, *e.g.*, in aphorism 17, "since (these things are so) *souls exist*," and not "soul (*puruṣa*) exists." We should have read in aphorism 19, not "soul (*puruṣa*) is proved to be witness, solitary, neutral perceiving, and inactive," but "souls are," etc. So in other aphorisms. A heresy so startling would have needed to be rubbed in, as it is not.[1] It is not even affirmed in Aph. 18. The compound *puruṣabahutvaṃ* 'manifoldness of the soul' is going no further than the *bahudhā*, 'in many ways' of the Upaniṣads: "one God in manifold forms" (*Chānd.* 4, 3, 6); "the inner soul who makes his one form manifold" (*Katha*, 5, 12); "the one Controller making manifold" (*Śvet.* 6, 12). The soul's manifoldness in the aphorism refers to the man's varied experiences in a series of many bodies, unequally 'gifted' "because birth, death and the organs are severally allotted, because procedure is not simultaneous, because *guṇas* are found unequally, the manifoldness of the soul is persistent." Thus the aphorism, so far from asserting the new, does but repeat a truth insisted on, since

[1] We find 'selves' already in *Kauṣ. Up.* 3, 6.

we found Sanatkumāra showing it in detail, in the Chāndogya.

In fact it is the very manifold presented by the soul, *i.e.*, the man (*puruṣa* or *ātman*), considered in his entirety, which is the outstanding feature in these aphorisms. Concerning 'souls,' 'men,' they are silent. The main topic is the 'man' in his dual aspect: soul in the midst of a cosmic 'manifest' of phenomena, called *prakṛti*: 'what is made out,' manifest, or *pradhāna*: 'what is put forward,' phenomenal. Soul as bound to, while being " the opposite to " this manifest. Soul as being " witness, solitary, neutral, perceiving, inactive," *sui generis*, *we* should say, and hence incomparable, not to be rated, valued. Soul as in a way 'having' about, around him forms of this Manifest, partly physical, partly non-physical, yet mechanical, forms which he has the appearance of exercising, yet which are truly to be called " in the final incontrovertible and pure knowledge :—I am not (that); not for me (is that); (it is) not I "[1]. It is with this insight, say the following aphorisms, that " the soul (*puruṣa*) stands aside, a spectator, steady " of the cosmic Manifest. " I have seen, says he unmoved. I have been seen, quoths She, and leaves him alone. Bound yet awhile, there remains no motive for creating "; " like the desisting potter's wheel," the man whirls on awhile; " then comes utter release."

With this new conviction, that man's inner world, long known, as we have seen, mainly as 'mind,' coupled more or less confusedly with other terms, was as much of the phenomenal or manifested cosmos as was the body, there came a fresh letting loose of that régime of the analytic phase which had been slowly replacing

[1] Aph. 65.

the syncretic phase in India's culture. The result is apparent in a new vocabulary for that inner world of the immaterial, and a new appreciation of its procedure, its uniformities, its order.

Conspicuous among the new technical terms used by Iśvarakṛṣna's school are:

1. *guṇa*'s, lit. it is supposed, either a group or the connecting link thereof.
2. *dvāra*'s, doors, gates, for ways of sense-access (*cf.* Bunyan's 'gates') and *dvārī*, gatekeeper.
3. *bhāva*'s (states of), being or becoming.
4. *vṛtti*'s, lit. turnings, goings-on, for functions.
5. *buddhi* (also *mahat*, great one), lit. awaked, for intellectual procedure.
6. *ahaṃkāra*, 'I-making, or -maker,' individualizing in sense-experience.
7. *abhimāna*, an equivalent of the preceding.
8. *anumāna*, inference, lit. serial connected thinking.
9. *kaivalya*, whole, complete, consummation.
10. *vyakta* and *avyakta*, manifested and reverse.
11. *prakṛti*, phenomenal world, both physical and mental.
12. *karaṇa*'s, organs.
13. *lakṣaṇa*'s, marks.

Not one of these thirteen words occurs in the early Upaniṣads. In the eight of the 'middle group,' 1 occurs in Śvetâsvatara and Maitri; 2 occurs once in Aitareya, once in Kauṣītaki, but not in a technical way, as, *e.g.*, in Aphorism 35: "those three organs (*i.e.*, 5, 6 and *manas*) are gatekeepers, the rest are gates." Neither is it yet technical in the Maitri (6, 30).

3 emerges, relatively untechnical, in Muṇḍaka and Śvet.; 4 has not yet emerged; 5 emerges in Kaṭha, Śvet. and Maitri; 6 as we saw, is used once untechnically in Chānd. (p. 130); as technical term it emerges in Śvet., Praśna and Maitri; 7 emerges in Praśna and Maitri; 8 as verb emerges first in Maitri (6, 1), but the noun, subsequently so staple a term in Indian logic, is not found; 9 is not found in this group, emerging only in the later Upaniṣad so entitled; 10 comes first into use in negative form in Kaṭha: " higher than the great is the *avyakta* "; already a technical term, Śvet. and Mait. have it also; but the positive form, used in the Aphorisms for phenomenal results, I do not find in any Upaniṣad. 11 emerges in Śvet. and Maitri; 12 as both *kāraṇa* and *karaṇa* emerges in Śvet. and Maitri, and 13 only in Maitri.

This is a tedious list for the reader, but only in this way do I deem he will clearly see, as in a mirror, the new influences that must have been infiltrating into the schools of the brahmans, influences which, as the technical usage in the Sānkhyakārikā Aphorisms suggests, are traceable to a common source. One term emerging in these middle Upaniṣads is absent from the Aphorisms, and that is the word *sānkhya*, occurring once, as we saw, in the Śvetāsvatara. This is a point of special interest, and suggests the following clues.

As a name for a definite system of teaching, the word *sānkhya* is one that was applied late, perhaps not in the first instance by teachers of the school itself. Perhaps a parallel case is the similar name, given at one time to the orthodox Sangha of Buddhism at Patna, of Analyzers: Vibhajjavādins, appropriated in the Commentaries for the one occasion only, but nowhere given them in their Canon. When Īśvarakṛṣna put down in writing the oral Aphorisms, the name had become accepted, but perhaps in the Ṣaṣṭitantram *this was not yet the case*. The Vibhajjavādins carried their case through in council and the name faded out with the effacement of opposition. 'Sānkhya' never came into front rank, but was *assimilated* by both brahman and Buddhist, and the name, *as a method*, survived. The mention of it with Yoga in the Śvetâsvatara may quite well be *a later insertion*, made after the acceptance of the name as that of a method. As the name of a recognized 'system' of philosophy, 'Sānkhya' belongs to a much later, if not clearly assignable date. As just method, infecting both brahman and early Buddhist teaching, the word 'sānkhya' is vaguely inclusive. Meaning literally 'well-' or 'connectedly-uttered,' it was applicable to naming, enumerating, distinguishing, valuing, in a word, to what we now call analysis. Thus in the definitions of the first book of Abhidhamma in the Pali Tipiṭaka, the word *adhivacana*, or equipollent term, is defined as "That which is *sankhā*, designation, expression, current term, name, denomination, name-assigning, interpretation, distinctive mark (of discourse) in this or that thing."[1] Hereon the Commentary has: "*sankhā* is uttering, the meaning being a predicating. What is it that is predicated? It is I, mine, another, another's, a person, a state, an individual . . . Tissa, Datta, a couch . . . these are ways of predicating."[2]

Here is no attempt at wording the distinguishing by name as, or as part of a process of analyzing Nor is the relatively pronounced taste for numbered categories

[1] Dhammasangaṇi, § 1306.
[2] *The Expositor* (P.T.S. ed.), p. 499.

(a taste we find already in un-Sānkhyanized Indian literature) shown up as part of such a process. And the same may be said of aphorisms in which there is worded awareness of making distinctions, *e.g.*, Aph. 15: *kāraṇa-kārya-vibhāgad*: 'because of discreteness between cause and effect.' We get particular phenomena called 'parts' or 'pieces' (*bheda*'s), but no word for the mental act of so viewing them, such as any form of the word *vibhaj*-. The word 'separate' is used mentally already in the Bṛhad. (4, 3, 23-30), and the self is pictured as divisible (*vibhakta*) in the Maitri, but the aphorisms, intensely analytic in procedure though they are, ignore the word. It is perhaps equally curious, certainly equally interesting, that although discriminating in ideas is to be found worded in the Second Collection (Majjhima-Nikāya) of the Tipiṭaka,[1] a technical term for the process is not met with, I believe, till the *Milinda Questions* of a later date. Here we find thoughts (*citta*) analyzed into seven classes, the term being "this second, third, etc., thought arrives at *vibhatti* (analysis)" as follows. The earlier, the Sutta, reference is where the Founder is said to have refused to say Yea or Nay to a large generalization, because he was "not a unitary speaker but an analytic speaker."[2] The Buddhists in the third century of their existence as a 'church,' building with minds largely influenced by Sānkhya *as method of thought*, could better realize and find words for systematized thinking as being definitely a process of analyzing. Thus it was one of the four orthodox ways of answering questions to give a *vibhajjavacanaṃ*, translated 'a

[1] *E.g.*, in Nos. 43, 44.

[2] *Ettha pi kho ahaṃ vibhajjavādo, nāhaṃ ekaṃsavādo* (No. 99: Subha-Sutta).

discriminating answer,' but literally 'an analyzing saying.'[1]

I come back to the 13 terms peculiarly characteristic of the Aphorisms. Taking first 5, 6 and 7, we find *manas* allied, not, as in the early Upaniṣads, with either *saṃkalpa*, or *dhyāna*, or *prajnā*, but with two new aspects of man's inner world: *buddhi* and *ahaṃkāra*, *manas* taking third place, a place more definitely circumscribed than is the case in the earlier thought. For the first 23 aphorisms, we have in these three, not *buddhi*, but *mahat*, or 'great one (or thing).' The wish is apparently to worth in the more the phase where the 'manifest' or phenomenal world reaches its highest limit, facing, so to speak, the unmanifest or Very Man. Suddenly, in Aphorism 23, the term *buddhi* does duty where had been *mahat*. Instead of the wording in 22: *prakṛter-mahaṃs, tato'hamkāras* . . . (out of matter the great one, thence I-making), we come upon *adhyavasāyo buddhi* . . ., and in 24, *abhimāno 'haṃkāras*. Here are, simply stated, equivalents for each of the two factors, which, with *manas* as third, constitute as it were the workshop of the phenomenal in man, wherein or whereby the bodily messages are transformed into a currency for the service of man: *puruṣ'arthe*. *Adhyavasāya* seems to have puzzled translators: 'Entscheidung' is Deussen's way; 'determination, judgement, ascertainment,' the way of others. Garbe prefers 'Entschliessung' (determination). It is of interest to read, that the Amarakośa, a late work, equates it with *utsahah*, exertion, a volitional term adopted in Buddhism, though its parallel was not. The literal meaning of the word *buddhi*: awakened state, is left unnoticed. And yet we

[1] *Anguttara*, ii. 46; *Dīgha*, Sangīti-Suttanta, p. 229.

saw how, in the Upaniṣads, merely physical awakening was gradually taken up into the psychical metaphor of spiritual awakening in the Kaṭha.

In that it had somehow got orphaned from the term *prajñā*, it was fitting that Sānkhya, in its honest psychological efforts, should have fixed on just this concept of the utmost reach of the mind as an awakening, as compensating for such a loss. Had the Tipiṭaka not cherished the word *paññā*, it is probable that the efforts in it to use *buddhi*, which are rare and sporadic, would have, as we say, caught on. *Buddhi* appears once[1] as a quasi-poetic equivalent of *paññā*. In the preference for the lengthened stem in *bodhi* and *sambodhi-parāyana*, etc., we have no longer a mental instrument, but an ideal. In the Aphorisms, *buddhi* is only the former. *Buddhi*, we read, is, as it were, the *raison d'être* of the senses, twice called *buddh'indriyāni*: these spread what they bring before it; it 'plunges down (*avagahate*)' into each sense-field (*viśaya*), as door-keeper of the 'doors,' or 'lights it up as a lamp,' working, in spite of general and special hindrances, for the benefit of the man or self.[2]

Of yet greater interest is the obscurer fate of the second *karaṇa* or, as this is rendered, 'organ,' namely, 'I-making' (*ahaṃkāra*). This is dealt with in two aphorisms only (24, 25), and very lean is the allotted treatment: "I-making is much-deeming; from it proceeds a twofold creation: one, the elevenfold group (of sense), the other the fivefold that-measure."[3] Further: 'I-making,' like *buddhi*, is modified (*vaikṛtah*), namely, by sense-impressions. This is all.

Now we find the word *abhimāno*: lit. much-minding,

[1] *Dīgha*, iii. 165.
[2] Nos. 26, 34, 35, 36, 49, 57.
[3] *Tan-mātra.*

appearing already as *abhimān-* in Bṛhad. and Muṇḍaka without imputation of vanity, simply as 'intending,' 'concerned with.' In this form it occurs also in the fine Tālapuṭa poem of the Theragāthā: *nibbānam ev'abhimāno carissaṃ*: 'I will fare my mind set on nirvana.' But the worsening that befel so many words through the earthquakes in Indian culture:—the seeking God within the man, the growth of monasticism, the impact of Hellenism, the rise of introspective analysis—befel also this word. Concentration on the man and his mind, taken with a growth of man's concern in the fellowman *as such*, brought about a seeing in that concentration what we have now come to call 'egoism,' on the one hand. On the other, a weakening of belief in the certain reality of the very man or self brought about for a time the notion, that to see the 'I' in apprehension or perception was an illusion, or 'Wahn' as Germans love to say. Everyman, in this, the most intimate fact in his knowledge,—the seeing the man himself in acts of intelligence,—was held to be deluded. And *abhimāno* came to mean, not the intensifying of *mano* in conscious perception, but an overweening sense that it is 'I' who perceive In truth, the recognition of the man or 'I' in the apprehending is the right analysis; the seeing illusion in *abhimāno* and *ahaṃkāra* is the error. This is anyway how I view the matter in historical perspective.

And now the remaining 'organ' (*karaṇa*) of the three:—what is left for *manas* in the process of coming to know? Here, in one aphorism and one only, we find, that the intermediacy of *manas* between the man and the senses, already affirmed in the Bṛhad.,[1] now serves as a delimitating the function of *manas*. Akin to the

[1] Above, p. 18.

other two organs, it is classed together with the organs and objects of sense themselves: 'Of the nature of both (is) mind; a purposive (or adjusting) sense, and of common nature with sense.'[1] And that is all. The only other reference to mind is to mention, in passing, its instability (*mano 'navaṣṭhānāt*), as one of the eight reasons for things being imperceptible (*ghātan*) in efficiency:—'remoteness, overnearness, mental instability (? inattention, so Deussen), sublimation, interposition, impairing of sense, overwhelming (*e.g.* stars by daylight) and merging in a mass.' (Aph. 7.)

I have been content to follow my betters and render *sadharmyāt* as 'of common nature.' But coming, as they do not, from Buddhist studies, I am tempted to see in this term the tidier logic of Buddhist analysis. This also reckoned *manas* as a sort of sixth sense-organ, but assigned to it as object, not the other five with their objects, but 'things,' that is, *dhamma*'s. True it does not bring in *saṃkalpa*, as the fitting sense-objects into a percept, say, a round convex outline, a colour, smell, etc., into an orange. But *mano*'s function is shown as the evolving, by and for the man, what we call things, concrete things, percepts, as well as things not present but imaged. And in view of the Buddhist categories, I incline to see in *sadhar.nyāt* a reference to (mind) "with its objects." I would add, anticipating later discussion, that in the Suttas we come across the different position, that the objects 'enjoyed' by *manas* are said to be, not *dhamma*'s, but those of the five senses. This does not exactly contradict the calling these objects collectively, when thus 'enjoyed,' *dhamma*'s instead of sights, sounds, etc.

[1] *Ubhaya-ātmakaṃ atra manah, saṃkalpakaṃ indriyaṃ ca sadharmyāt*, Aph. 27.

Nevertheless, it does suggest, for me, that we have here[1] a later editorial hand, changing *purisa* or *attā* into *mano*, so as to keep in harmony with the upgrowing doctrine, that the 'man' was so far a nonentity, that he was only to be found in body and mind.

We have next the new analysis inquiring into the mode of working the three 'organs' and the senses. This brings up a term to me of much importance, the term *vṛttih*: 'process,' lit. turning, rolling. In this form we do not find the word in previous teaching. With the prefix *pra-* it appears, in its 'first intention,' not only here, but already in Chāndogya (5, 13, 2): 'a mule-chariot rolling up,' but only so. As mental act it is emerging in the middle Upaniṣads: thus in Śvetâsvatara (2, 13) 'the first stage in Yoga-pravṛtti,' and in Maitri (6, 26): 'rightly is Yoga produced' (or carried on). In the Aphorisms, the simple *vṛttih* occurs in Nos. 28-31, showing us the essentially dynamic concept of mental phenomena. These were not 'states' but modes of action. And the process in organ and sense is thus described: "The procedure is a co-operating, simultaneous or consecutive, each having its own specific mark (*lakṣanyaṃ*); in perceiving (lit. seeing, *dṛṣte*), *buddhi*, *ahaṃkāra*, *manas* and a sense co-operate; in the imperceptible (*adṛṣte*, *i.e.*, the represented or imaged, as *we* say), only the first three. Each function (*vṛttih*) is an inciting cause to the next. (But) the benefit of the man is *the* cause (*puruṣa-artha' eva hetur*); (although) no organ is made-to-act by anyone (*na kenacit kāryate kāraṇaṃ*). Each of the three organs is thirteenfold (namely), as inducing, sustaining and illuminating *that*; and tenfold in what it can do, namely, inducing the inductible, sustaining the sustainable,

[1] *Majjhima-Nikāya*, Sutta 43.

lighting up the what may be lit. The inner organ(-ism) is threefold; the outer is tenfold, range-revealer to those three; the outer are of time present, the inner are of time's three modes." (Aph. 29-33.)

The Aphorisms are models of conciseness or, shall we say, caution in face of the little known. Very much has been read into them by Indian exegesis, too easily followed by European writers. Exegetists had their own problems in later values; it is positively refreshing to put these aside and rate these relatively modest sayings for what they actually say, rather than for what they do not say. They say nothing whatever about rejecting any Divine intervention or guidance in perception. They do maintain, that the mental and bodily organism is not functioning to please itself, but solely to serve him whom India had called mind-er, see-er, do-er. And that this agent was inherently divine is anyway not denied.

That Buddhist thought, perhaps at about the same time, was considering also process as *pavatti* (not as *vatti* only) and, in other terms, the specific mark *e.g.* in *lakkhaṇa* and time's three modes, cannot be considered here. Our present task is just to note how these terms were influencing the teachers of the middle Upaniṣads. But first a word about the three phenomena termed qualities, or *guṇa*'s, and those called *bhāva*'s.

In Aphorisms 12-15 we have an attempt to rationalize procedure, not in the man's organism only, but in the whole universe, by the *guṇa*'s. We read: "The Unmanifest, so also *pradhāna* is of three *guṇa*'s . . . *guṇa*'s are of the nature of joy, not-joy and indolence (or inertia: *visada*); their aim is illuminating, proceeding (*pravṛtti*), restraining (*niyama*); their function (*vṛtti*) is mutual crushing, supporting and engendering.

Goodness (*sattvaṃ*, the first) is held to be light (buoyant) and lighting-up; passion (the second, *rajas*) as inciting and mobile; darkness (the third, *tamas*) as heavy and cloaking; in function their aim is that of a lamp." Here we have man reading himself into the cosmos, nor is that lightly to be dismissed as anthropomorphic, since the later tendencies in modern science are doing so no less. To this extent is the Indian, for me, ahead of us in that his reading is not to project a Divine mathematician into the cosmic scheme, but rather a more typical man—a man in whom mind or thought subserves 'joy,' or the opposite, or in whom progress is clogged. In this subjectivism[1] I would see man as willer aiming at joy, swayed by passion, hindered by want of will and much else.

It is an important, yes, and a pathetic feature in the Aphorisms: (1) their steadfast sureness in the reality of the man (2) coupled with an eagerness to deprive him of the very essence of his manhood. (1) It is not only in an inferential way, that we see *the nature of the man* at work in the universe in the play of the three very human *guṇa*'s. It is in a way marking the advance of the spirit and words of scientific analysis, that we see his existence inferred—an asserting, it may be, against an upgrowing materialism on the one hand, or an apsychic psychology on the other, such as was infecting Buddhism:—"Because of the aim for another in aggregates, as the opposite (pole) to the (apparently unconscious play of) three *guṇa*'s and the rest (of the phenomenal world), because of a presiding over, because of there being an enjoyer, and because of procedure for the sake of final wholeness, the Man exists" (No. 17).

[1] Deussen, *op. cit.*, 427.

(I have translated the concise allusive clauses literally; I think *we* would render them more after this sort: The man really is, (*a*) because his instruments do not function for their own aims, (*b*) because the manifest working in nature of what are his qualities presuppose the owner of the qualities, (*c*) namely, of That in whom the qualities exist, (*d*) and who forwards his aims through and in those qualities and instruments, (*e*) he being the one who has an ultimate aim, the aim of coming to transcend that 'nature,' which is at present at once the qualities and instruments, as well as the field for their exercise.)

And then (2), when we have here, as it were, Plato shown us at back of Plato's Ideas, we find the man reduced to this:—And because of this oppositeness (as stated in the foregoing), "there is established (*siddhaṃ*) the witness-ship (or spectatorship) of the man, and of his detachment (*kaivalyaṃ*), of his indifference (lit. middleness), of his (mere) perceivingness, of his state of non-agent (*a-kartṛbhāvas*)." If he appears otherwise, it is the inferrer who mistakes the inactive lame man mounted on the shoulders of the blind man for the walker, thus: "because of connection with That (*prakṛti*, nature), the unconscious instrument (*liṅgaṃ*) is *as if conscious*, and in the activity of the *guṇa*'s, he the passive, becomes like a doer. For the sake of man's insight and consummation (*kaivalyaṃ-arthaṃ*), likewise of nature's (*pradhānasya*) aims (there is) even union of the two, the lame, the blind; hence is creation (or production) made (or effected)" (Nos. 20, 21).

In this futile effort to hamstring the man, so important was it then to keep him distinguished from and unidentified with his mind, that we are asked, on the one hand, to see passivity in man's *aiming at consummation*, and for it *using vision* (*darśana*), and in being partner with creative agency; on the other hand, to see the field and world of his instruments as having also (or 'even,' *api*) "an aim," namely, the setting him free, and hereby winning the right to have it said of these also, that they presuppose inherent manhood! We cannot have it both ways. Either 'nature' (*prakṛti*, *pradhāna*, *avyakta*) must be stripped of 'aims' and all that implies the man, or there is in nature also 'Man' working. And in seeing a nature which connived at man's aims, and thus involving manhood, proto-Sānkhya was really and only feeling after the true.

In the eight *bhāva*'s we have the idea of, not states so much as 'becomings' in consequence of acts or conduct. Here again in these brief sayings we have account taken of man as being in time no less than in space, albeit the outlook is left implicit. The eight becomings, then, are man's experience in consequence of his having pursued one way rather than another in eight chosen modes of conduct. Actually all that the Aphorisms word is that, of these: duty (*dharma*), undutifulness, knowledge, ignorance (refusing to know), waning of passion, its reverse, control, want of control, all are, in part, ready formed (namely, in man when born), in part, the causes of changes in him from birth, and even before. The results of the eight are respectively a 'becoming' in going upwards, a becoming in going downwards, departure from (the undesirable) and the opposite, a becoming of waning in the phenomenal, a becoming of more-wayfaring (*saṃsāra*), non-obstruction and the reverse.

In rendering the repeated '*bhavati*'s (becomes) I have kept closer to the text than such translations as I have seen. I cannot find it insignificant that this verb is here so repeated. I know too well how translators seem to make a point of evading this word, the literal uprush of which, in the early Upaniṣads, is so marked a feature. Yet it is precisely here, where the inner world of man is treated *as in time*, that the word is called for, and the call for it has been felt. It was one thing to affirm the man is, exists (*puruṣo 'sti*): it was another thing to see in this real man one in process of wayfaring, where, to him wayfaring hence, or coming hither, the great thing was that he should depart, or arrive armed in his progress with that growth, that becoming, of which Plato in the Phædrus wrote so earnestly.[1] When will our wise men come to see the very man as in process of becoming, and not in his body and mind only as such ?

We are now in a better position to appreciate the new world of thought in the eight middle Upaniṣads, of which I was speaking. The reader can verify the contexts in which technical Sānkhya terms are there seen emerging, contexts given above (p. 148 *f.*), and I need only give here a few instances.

Take first the Kaṭha—but no, not for a moment; look first at the way in which not the Kauṣītaki only —I have mentioned that—but the Kena too, seems to be uttering a warning note at the threshold of a new outlook. The former warns, that, in considering function, the agent, the man, must not be lost to view. The latter warns, in the solemn opening lines, that neither sense nor speech nor thinking nor learning suffices to reveal That Who is past comprehension. " Past these escaping the wise become immortal. . .

[1] Pictured as the soul, the self-mover, growing her wings, etc.

Other indeed is It than the known, and eke above the unknown . . . Known by awakening (*pratibodhita-viditaṃ*) it is (a somewhat) thought (*mataṃ*)." So known, "with the Self man finds immortality, finds energy (*vīryyaṃ*, 'will'), finds the true."

With the Kaṭha the new is beginning to infiltrate. "Know thou *buddhi*, driver of the chariot of the Man, and *manas* as the reins; *indriya's* his horses; the Man is enjoyer (*bhōktṛ*) of it all. . . . Suppress *buddhi* in the Man, the great self, the understanding self, the tranquil self." And evident is a selection, a rearrangement of the New: "Higher than sense is *manas*, above *manas* is *sattva*, above *sattva* is *buddhi*, above *buddhi* the unmanifest (*avyakta*)."

But in the Śvetâsvatara we are yet more deeply committed to the new. The new categories are cited as things known, especially in the (older) metaphor of man conceived as a wheel, *now* with triple felly, sixteen terminals, etc. Prose and verse are thickly sprinkled with terms not admittedly *called* those of 'sānkhya,' yet none the less new as compared with the terminology of the early Upaniṣads, and often assorting ill with the venerable tags which are ever recurring. *Buddhi* is accepted where once we found *vijñāna* and *prajñā*; *manas* is subordinated; *ahaṃkāra* peeps out once in conjunction with *saṃkalpa*. The three *guṇa*'s are confusedly used. We find *buddhi* and the very self spoken of as qualities (*guṇa*)! They are referred to as "threefold," and again as of indefinite number:—"he who is endowed with *guṇa*'s" (*guṇanvayo*);[1] "Who distributes all *guṇa*'s."[2] And the first *guṇa* '*sattva*' is used, as in the Kaṭha, in a way which seems to have called for exegesis to explain it, as either 'very

[1] Deussen: *bestimmtheithaft*. [2] Deussen: *Sonderheit*.

being ' or as ' intellect ' (*buddhi*), and not as the ' goodness ' of the Aphorisms. But emphatically, if not consistently, the Śvet. sees in *guṇa*'s, three or more, the qualities, not abroad and ownerless in a Prakṛti or nature, but inherent in a man, whether conceived as divine or as infradivine.

> " Saw the self-energy of the God (*deva*) hidden in his own *guṇa*'s (*sva-guṇair*)
>
> " Characterized by the three *guṇa*'s he roams according to his deeds " (1, 3; but *cf.* 6, 11: *nirguṇa*, p. 164).

Writers have variously estimated the degree to which the teacher in Śvetâsvatara is intent on opposing rather than adopting the new analysis of man. His exact position is at times made doubtful by discrepant recensions and obscurity of meaning. To me he seems on the one hand welcoming the new as a More in his outlook on man and the world, on the other, determined to harness the new in the service of what brahman teaching had earlier established as the true. Where the Aphorisms, concentrating on the mind as no less phenomenal, and hence worthable, than matter, are content to affirm the reality of ' the man,' without questioning the higher nature implicit in him, Śvetâsvatara never loses sight of that highest in man's nature, never wearies in making it explicit. In very humility it may be before that Highest, he falls back on a Vedic metaphor, and speaks of the Divine Mysteries as a conjuror's art, and of the Highest as the conjuror (*māyin*: 4, 9 *f.*, *cf.* 5, 3), a way of interpreting man's dulness (*moha*) in face of what he is yet unable to conceive, much less explain.

Whether or no it is a result of the view taken in the Aphorisms of man as an inert spectator, so that there might be no confusing him with his mental functions, there is certainly seen emerging in the Śvetâsvatara, especially in the sublime ode to the 'greatness of God' (part 6), the idea *devasya mahimā*, a new shade in the Immanence which insisted, in the lesson to Naciketas: That art *thou*! Always in the older word there was held up the ultimate "becoming Brahman," when the 'thou *as now thou art*' should be ready so to become, but the long, long way of attainment was not equally insisted on. For the man as at present merely potentially 'That' there was no cogent word, and none of the insistent teaching on growth that found utterance in Buddhism. Here we have the actual Deity, as immeasurably transcending the potentially divine in the man, made the theme. The verses (6; 11, 10, 12):

> The one God (*eko devah*) hidden in all things,
> Allpervading, inner self of all that has become,
> Overseer of deeds, in all things abiding,
> Witness, consummate (*kevalo*), without *guṇa*'s,
>
> * * * * *
>
> May he grant us entrance into Brahman!

might be the prayer of the Jew, the Muslim, the Christian, even when the Indian adds

> "The wise who contemplate him standing (persisting) in the self, they and they only have abiding happiness."

Man is here

> "resorting to him as a shelter" (3, 17; 6, 18);

he is not standing; he is gladly prostrate. A duality in self has been as it were forced upon the teacher, a duality in degree, such as is more clearly brought out in the following Maitri. Man's main concern *in time* is with what the Aphorisms call 'becomings' (*bhāva*'s): the results of his choice in conduct (*karma*), and of these the ode says: "God distributes all becomings, which were they absent, the deeds done would disappear . . . he continuing essentially other . . . he who is beyond the three times: the what-has-become, the becoming and the what-may-become (*bhavya*) or will become," as the Upaniṣads word past, present and future.[1] Did our translators not persistently ignore this idiom, my plea that life and religion were a 'becoming' strongly felt after in the Upaniṣads might be more patent. It may have been just this that prevents Śvetâsvatara from more than nominal approval of the doctrine of the very 'man' as inertly detached from his field and methods of creative energy (1, 9). As divine, but potentially divine only, his salvation lay, not in monastic quietistic detachment, but in using his new laboratory of yoga-practice. And it was in Śvetâsvatara's practice and tradition to see the man functioning "with the mind,"[2] not as the mind.

In the Upaniṣad usually looked upon as the successor in time of the Śvetâsvatara, the Maitri or Maitrāyana, and as having its last chapter and a half belonging to a yet later period than the rest, we see again an abundant yet also selective use of the terms of the Sānkhyan Aphorisms. It is of interest to find the word *sānkhya* used, as just in-calculable (*asānkhya*), but nowhere referred to any method, let alone 'system'; and this in the penultimate chapter (6, 20), so late, it may be, was the name Sānkhya applied to either. The '*guṇa*'s' are explicitly referred to as three, yet are elsewhere used of indefinite number. The three

[1] Usage here was not fixed. The Svetâsvatara (3, 15) has the present implicit, followed by *bhūtaṃ* and *bhavya*, not *bhaviṣyati*.

[2] Above, p. 18.

kāraṇa's (organs) are listed as in the Aphorisms, yet, when the simile of the chariot recurs, *buddhi* is ejected, and *manas* is seen, not as merely 'reins' but as driver, *prakṛti*, the world of phenomena, being brought in as whip. The first *guṇa*, *sattva*, is not mentioned as such, but *in a new series*: " *sattva* (goodness) is won (*prâpate*) from austerity, and from goodness *manas*; from *manas*, the Self," on winning Whom no one returns to birth (4, 3). In the later portion *sattva* is exalted from a quality of the phenomenal world to figure as the shrine of that intelligence (*caitanya*) who is the deity Viṣṇu, to whom, as for Śiva, the revived personal Theism of the day was attracting the brahman world (6, 38). The other two *guṇa*'s are analyzed each in a detailed list such as the proto-Sāṅkhyan sayings do not give us (3, 5).

Of special interest is the presenting the *guṇa*'s in an evolutionary series. " In the beginning was darkness (first *guṇa*) alone: that would (or might) be (*syāt*)[1] in the Highest (or Beyond: *pare*). Impelled by the highest, 'unevenness' supervened and 'passion' (*rajas*) appeared; this becoming uneven, goodness (*sattva*) appeared. *Sattva* being impelled flowed out as *rasa* (essence, juice): this is the part which, as knower-of-the-field (*kśetrajñā*), is in every individual (*pratipuruṣah*): only measure by self, reflected in each, possessing, as marks, purpose (*saṃkalpa*), judging (*adhyavasāya*) and much-worthing (*abhimāna*). Its forms are Prajāpati, Viśva and the like; the dark portion, students, is the same as Rudra; the passion-portion is the same as Brahman; the goodness-portion is the same as Viṣṇu . . . that one became threefold; he developed forth eightfold . . . infinitefold. . . . Because of

[1] Deussen's *muss sein* is not accurate.

having developed forth, he is become (*bhūta*); enters, pervades beings . . . he is within and without, within and without."[1]

We have here a notable effort to grasp a concept of the Highest which embraces both 'being' so-called and 'becoming.' This becomes clearer (1) if we heed the Sanskrit wording.

Further (2), if we note that it is the Maitri alone, which, in a list specifying the Ātman as permeating all deity-concepts: "Īśāna, Śambhu, Rudra, Prajāpati, Indra, Viṣṇu, Savitar (vivifier or sun)," etc., *includes Bhava*, 'becoming.':—"Him verily one should desire to know, He should be searched for." That all translations known to me either leave Bhava untranslated or render it by 'existence,' even if elsewhere they use 'becoming,' is a strange and a tragic fact. This blindness to the feeling after 'being as more really becoming,' this tendency to replace the static by the dynamic, the dynamic which is for me so patent in early and middle Upaniṣads, blinds us further to the new analysis which will have sprung from just this search:—the asking so often after the cause of this and that. We of a scientific era have been suckled on things-as-caused, on conditions and resultants, on that expansion of causation, the evolutionary outlook, and we do not sit up and take heed to this: that we still talk, many of us, in a popular way of 'happening by pure chance,' that we can measure our cultural acceptance of causality by Aristotle's date, that our 'evolution' is of yesterday, and a disputed theory still. We see, in the Upaniṣadic inquiries into origins—witness notably Śvetāsvatara's opening lines—and into the preoccupation with cause in early Buddhism,

[1] *Maitri*, 5, 2.

something as it were inherent in Indian as in human culture from all time.

My own hypothesis is, that the Upaniṣadic Immanence in its 'That art *thou,*' so irrational on the surface, started the reasonable necessity of seeing in the word 'art' of this rune its stronger adjunct 'art becoming,' and that herein and hereby was sown the closely bound up notion of 'becoming from what,' 'becoming into what,' in other words the necessity of studying cause and effect, together with that prominent feature in the middle Upaniṣads: the conceiving time in terms of becoming. "What is the cause (*hetu*)?"—a word unused in early Upaniṣads as a cultural term—"is it time, or our own becoming (*svabhāva*), or (external) become-things (*bhūtāni*), or the womb, or the man?"[1] Interest in cause as a co-product, or, a result of interest in seeing *being as becoming*:—this is what I see.

And very naturally it has led, in the Maitri, to a dethroning of the man from his glorious identity with the Highest. He has become a *pratipuruṣa*, an individual, opening the way to the 'plurality of selves' in Sānkhya; he should be *nirātman*, not the Highest Ātman: he is now called *bhūtâtmā*, self who has become, and who, in word-play, is said to be *abhibhūta*, overbecome, *i.e.* overwhelmed by the pressure of *guṇa*'s. And with this arose that way of seeing life itself as a worse and as a less, which is the smear of monasticism, a smear which makes the opening of the Maitri read as if a Buddhist monk had compiled it.

Of the remaining four middle Upaniṣads: Īśā, Praśna, Muṇḍaka, Māṇḍūkya, there is, in this brief treatment, not much to say that is distinctive. It is evident that

[1] What is the cause? Brahman? Whence are we born? Whereby do we live? etc. *Śvet.*, I, I.

the new analytic vogue is working, although there is scant tendency shown to adopt the new technicalities. Thus *prakṛti*, *avyakta*, *pradhāna*, and *guṇa*'s find no mention. The three organs emerge once (in Praśna), (but *citta* holds its own, 4, 8), and each is supplemented with inclusion of the potential, viz. *buddhi* and 'what may be conceived' (*bodhavya*), etc. Analytic progress is marked by the tendency to describe both parts and process, and not in the teacher only. A student pours forth questions till the teacher Pippalāda gasps: "Too much are you questioning; yet you are set on Brahman and I will answer" (3, 2). "Everything" this teacher resolves into what goes to make man's instruments, material and mental, actual and potential, but he does not rest satisfied with the distribution, with mere analysis. *He is not mastered by the fact of the 'more.'* He resolves everything into the resting-place (*sampratiṣṭha*) of the "supreme self, as birds resort to the tree." And hence every part of the man, actual and potential, is fundamentally act of "a see-er, toucher, hearer . . . conceiver (*boddhā*), maker (*karttā*: note! not I-maker), a self that is aware (*vijñānâtmā*), a man. He is resting in the supreme, imperishable self" . . . and he who thus knows everything becomes everything (*sarvajñaḥ sarvaṃ bhavati*) —note how we see the older rune 'Tat tvam *asi*' rationalized. When the man knows, he 'is' not, he 'becomes.'

I now turn to the opposite pole of man's mental activity, from the discursively analytical to the selectively developing; from that which came to be called *sānkhya* to that which came to be known as *yoga*.

In a preceding chapter I have called this direction

of mental activity esoteric, as distinct from the admittedly exoteric origin of the method known later as Sānkhya. And I have to show to what extent we can see that which was, in the early Upaniṣads, a tendency of thought, growing, in the middle Upaniṣads, into something that may fairly be called a consciously expressed discipline or method of culture.

That tendency of thought, a tendency inherent in man everywhere and at all times to turn observation on to, not the outer world alone, but also the inner world of consciousness, must have received a great stimulus from the mandate or gospel of Immanence, which, however and whenever first taught, we see being exploited in the earliest Upaniṣads. It is in this connection, rather than in any felt worth in introspection as such, that we see inward observation commended. It is an inner unity in things, more especially a unity in man's own composition, that we find sought after, as more 'real,' more 'true'—the two words, for India, are the same: *satya*—than the manifold, the diverse, the many. This unity is figured in several ways, chiefly by the heart, by a wheel, by a thread as connecting, later, by a tree as the birds' resort.[1]

Thus Yājñavalkya (or another in the Bṛhadārañyaka, 2, 15, 15): "This immortal man in this *ātman* . . . who is just this *ātman*, overlord, king of all: as all the spokes are held together in the hub and felly . . ." or in Kauṣītaki, "as the spokes are fixed on the hub" (3, 6) . . ." just so in this *ātman* all things, all *deva*'s, all worlds, all breathing things, all selves (or 'wholes' *ātmanaḥ*) are held together." (It is very rare to find self in the plural, but the word is elastic, like our spirit,

[1] *Bṛhad.*, 3, 9, 28; *Śvet.*, i., 4; 4, 7; *Kaṭha*, 6, 1; *Praśna*, 6, 6.

spirits, and more so, since it can mean, as has already been noticed (pp. 56, 83), the whole in anything of the nature of a compound—*e.g.*, Taitt. 2, 4.)

Again: Yājñavalkya: "do you know, Kapya, that thread (*sūtra*) by which this world and the other world and all beings (*bhūtāni*) become tied together?" . . . and, "do you know that Inner Controller who from within (*antarāyaṃ*) controls this world and the other worlds and all beings? . . . I know both. . . . Wind (*vāyus*) is that thread. By wind, as by a thread, these worlds and beings are tied together. Thus of a deceased one we say 'His limbs are unstrung'" (wind as breath has departed). . . . "And he who, dwelling in earth (and everywhere) in what is material (*adhibhūtaṃ*), and in what is spiritual (*adhyātman*), dwelling in breath, speech, sight, hearing, mind, skin, understanding (*vijñāne*) yet is other than these, whom they do not know, whose body (*śarīraṃ*) they are, who controls them from within, he is for you the self, immortal."[1]

Again: in Chāndogya (the teacher should say) "what is here, in this city of Brahman, is an abode, a small lotus-flower, within that is a small space. What is within that, this should be searched into; this verily one should want to know." "This for me the self within the heart smaller than a grain . . . greater than the earth . . . than these worlds . . . this is Brahman."[2]

And the manifold in experience was not of a plurality which could be materially or spiritually combined into a unity; it was the fundamental unity resolving itself, distributing itself, temporarily, into the manifold, in both thing and function. In the beginning the One

[1] *Bṛhad.*, 3, 7, 1.

[2] *Chānd.*, 8, 1, 2.

resolved Itself into *nāma* and *rūpa* (Bṛh., 1, 4, 7, etc.). "And in everything That enters in as razor in case, as fire in fireholder" . . . in breathing he is, as *nāma*, breath, in speech (he is, as *nāma*,) voice, in thinking, mind: these are just the names of his acts (*karmanāmāni*), and whoso heeds him *as one or the other* does not know him, for he is apart from (or in part in) these. He should be heeded as the self, for in the self all these are one. This self is the footprint of all, as one knows all by a footprint." Again (4, 4, 19): "As by mind is he to be perceived; on earth, the manifold is not (*na nānâsti*); he goes from dying to dying who here sees *just the manifold*." Again (Chānd. 6, 4): "the manifold must not be mistaken for the real; for the name given to any modification (*vikāro*) of *rūpa* is not a real thing."

From this unitary outlook we see emerging the practice desirable for maintaining and increasing it: "having this knowledge, having become calm, subdued (lit. tamed, *dānta*), resigned, patient, collected, one sees the self just in the self; one sees everything as the self; evil does not overcome or burn him; he overcomes, he burns evil."[1]

I can find in the earliest Upaniṣads nothing *less general* than these passages, nothing of which we can say: Here is not just a teaching of Immanence; here is shown a definite discipline, a religious practice, which is not adequately described by the general term Immanence. All that they show is the predisposition given by Immanence to the emergence of such a practice. There are, however, as I have said, in one Upaniṣad called early, two contexts where the word *yoga* appears for the first time, albeit with no such setting as to betray that such a practice had arisen.

[1] *Bṛhad.*, 4, 4, 23.

They occur in the Taittirīya. One is: " Verily other than, and within that one of mental form (*manomaya*) is self of *vijñā*-form; by it is that filled. This verily has the form of a man: faith is his head, order (*ṛta*) his right side, the true (or real) his left side; *yoga* the body (*i.e.*, the whole, *ātmā*); greatness (*mahas*) the foundation." There follows a next and final stage in the concept of the 'Man,' and that is bliss (*ānand*), but there is no development of that spiritual anatomy-chart. The other is in one of the many food-contexts, in which the older Upaniṣads are careful to study the man-in-a-body as belonging to the study of the whole man. In that, breathing and movements come in, of course; and it is as terms applied to breathing that we find the compound *yoga-kṣema*, meaning (technically or figuratively) " acquiring and maintaining breath," used for the first time:—" as *kṣema* in speech, as acquiring and maintaining in the inbreath and offbreath, as work in hands, . . . these are the recognizing of Brahman as food in man " (3, 10).

This same meaning given to *yoga*, but in a purely general sense, we find again in that early-middle Upaniṣad, the Kaṭha (2, 2): " The better and the pleasanter come to man . . . the wise man chooses the better . . . the fool, because of getting and keeping (*yogakṣemād*), chooses the pleasanter."

Now this general meaning for which *yoga* is here used died out in Upaniṣad terminology, and is echoed but once in the Gītā " to them I bring power to acquire and to maintain " (*yogakṣemaṃ vahāmi*; 9, 6). But it came to be taken over by the early Buddhists and invested with a high if poetic religious sanction, as we may come to see. As meaning an introspective practice, I do not find it used.

The unprecedented irruption of the word *yoga*, simple and compound, into the Taittirīya suggests three hypotheses: either this work is not rightly classed among the early Upaniṣads, but belongs to the middle group, *or* the compiler (or compilers) of it was original and not wholly in touch with his contemporaries, *or* the inclusion of *yoga* in the first context is the work of a later hand. I incline to the last guess, when, in Taittirīya I, 5, I, I note 'mahas' occupying the position given to 'yoga,' in a fourfold division of the concept of Deity.

I turn to the eight middle Upaniṣads:—do we in these find the idea of a definite religious practice of an introspectional, but not of an analytic nature, such as a teaching of Immanence might suggest, but such as we do not yet find in the earlier collection?

We certainly do. The Kena (which possibly ranks more truly with the earlier) does not do more than indicate the twofold tendency of: (*a*) diverging attention from sense, and (*b*) declaring, that knowledge of the Ātmā is not so much a matter of definitely worded knowledge which 'I know well,' or 'I know not,' as of "knowing in an awakening" (*pratibodhe viditaṃ*); we might say 'by intuition,' rather than by intellect. There is to be "an escaping past" sense and thought and speech; it is "other than the known, above the unknown."

The Kaṭha again dwells much on the attitude of mental control, notably in the discourse on the chariot (*cf.* p. 19, above); speech, it adds, and intellect (*buddhi*) are also to be suppressed (lit., cut). But it goes further; it introduces "yoga" as a means of penetrating to That Who "is hard to see, entered into the hidden, set in the secret place, dwelling in the depth, primeval," and "considering That as God (*deva*): so does the man-of-worth (*dhīro*) cast off pleasure and sorrow "[1]—a termination reminding us of the Buddhist 'fourth Jhāna.' And more: we here first come across *the awareness* of the introspective attitude put into words. It is led up to as contrasted with the more natural way in man of external vision:

> The Self-becomer (*svayambhū*) pierced openings outwards,
> therefore one looks outward, not within the self (*antarâtman*).
> The man of worth, seeking the immortal,
> beheld facing the Self, averting the eye (*avṛtta-cakśu*) (4, 1).

This new term we meet with again.

The four: Praśna, Muṇḍaka, Īśā, Māṇḍūkya, carry us little if at all along the new way. The Muṇḍaka gives attention to the centre of religious attention as the 'secret place'—but the Bṛhad. had anticipated this—and to the attitude as that of *dhyāyamānam*, or musing (3, 1, 8). Here again the Chāndogya has been there first, as we saw; but the present stage is a more conscious one. We are come aloof from the exercise of any externally applied wit: the student is to take as his bow the syllable OM; to it he is to adjust the self "sharpened by musing"; he is to pull the bow "with thought (*cetasā*) directed to the very being of That, and That as mark (*lakṣya*) he is to hit" (Muṇḍ. 2, 2, 3).

This figure of the arrow is repeated in the Maitri, but with a difference and with elaboration (6, 24). Musing or meditation, the usual rendering is in the latter work exalted to great power, since it is made the form of activity used in creation (*abhidhyātvā*). The Śvetâsvatara employs another graphic simile for it: that of the friction-stick, the lower one (*maraṇi*) is the body; 'OM' is the upper one; the work of rubbing

[1] *Kaṭha*, 2, 12.

to evoke the spark is musing (*dhyāna*), " and so may one see, hidden as it were, God (*deva*)." In the Praśna the attempt at union with the Divine is less physically represented in the phrase " becomes one in mind with the highest God (*manasi para-deve*)" (4, 2). The Īśā too dwells mainly on the joy in the vision of unity and the sense of confidence (6, 7). It is worth noting that the term, in the Praśna, " become one " (*ekī-bhavanti*), used already in the Bṛhad. (4, 4, 2) for the physical and mental contractions in dying, and so used still in the Māṇdukya—a verb which in the participle (*ekībhūta*) reappears in Buddhist *jhāna*—takes on here, in Praśna and in Muṇḍaka, a wider scope of spiritual union, but is not used by those fuller exponents of *yoga*, Śvetāsvatara and Maitri.

It is in the Śvetâsvatara and Maitri that *yoga* definitely emerges as a method, with both the noun *yoga* and the verb ' practise yoga ' (*prayojate*). The former (2, 8-15) gives details in method, stages and results. The latter gives a more technical category of ' sixfold yoga ' " for effecting this going to unity (*ekasya ekatvaṃ eti*)[1] of the One." Thus: " The practice (or usage) for setting-about (*prayoga-kalpa*) that (the becoming one) is this: breath-restraint (*prāṇayāma*); withdrawal (of the senses: so the exegesis, *pratyāhāra*), musing (*dhyāna*), sustained-attention (*dhāraṇa*), application (inception of thought: *tarka*), concentration (or absorption: *samādhi*). Such is said to be the sixfold yoga." This is as far as the middle Upaniṣads bring us in what has here developed into a conscious, analyzed, categorized practice, and we have certainly come very far, in comparison with what we found in the early Upaniṣads.

About it three words of comment. No serial proce-

[1] N.B.—' goes to,' not ' becomes.'

dure is suggested by it. This is fairly evident, not only from inspection of the six, but also from a comparison of two other lists of factors bearing on the same study: Buddhist jhāna and the Yoga-sūtras ascribed to one Patañjali. For instance, in the former, *tarka* (*i.e.*, *vitakka*) precedes *dhāraṇa* (*i.e.*, *vicāra*), and the whole procedure is called *dhyāna* (*jhāna*), and *jhāna* is elsewhere called a kind of *samādhi*. In the latter (II., 29) the six factors have become eight,[1] and are described with a detail unattempted by, and possibly unknown to, the author (or authors) of Maitri's part (6, 1-18). Here the serial procedure is evident. The later date is almost equally evident. Whether the Buddhist category, as formulated, is older than that of the Maitri is very doubtful. Recurring past count in the Pali Suttas, the fourfold (or, in Abhidhamma, fivefold) Jhāna *formula* is not for me of the early Sakyan teaching, and I do not place it earlier than the third century B.C. The Yoga-sutras Dr. James Woods places between A.D. 300 and 500, but the materials wrought up into Patañjali's compilation will have been much older. For instance, although the word *vṛtti* abounds in this, as well as in the Sānkhyakārikā, it is not found in Maitri or in earlier Upaniṣads. On the other hand, another stock term of the Yoga-sūtras: *nirodha*, meaning psychical restraint, namely of *vṛtti's* or the oscillations of mind, is already found applied to restraint of " voice, mind, breath " in the Maitri (6, 20). The early meaning of the word as used in Chānd. (8, 6, 5), and later in Praśna (1, 10) is that of transmundane exclusion only.

[1] Abstinences and observances and postures and regulating of breath and withdrawal of senses and fixed attention and contemplation and concentration.

I find no felt conflict anywhere expressed between the adopted exoteric analytic attitude, known as *sānkhya*, and the upgrowing esoteric intuitive attitude, known as *yoga*. The only joint occurrence of the two terms prescribes both as a means for "attaining" (*adhigamyam*) "the one God, hidden in all, one controller, the One among many, the cause (*kāraṇaṃ*)." But I do find, that virtually the preference comes, in Śvetâsvatara and Maitri, to intuitive, rather than to analytic study. The day of psychology-cum-logic, such as we see for instance in the relatively early Nyāyabindu sūtras, was not yet at hand. It is the control of mind, rather than its systematic development, which is the leading motive in the fine hymns of the Śvetâsvatara. These start with a bold inquiry into cause, but fall back at once on musing and *yoga* linked, as the method of those "who have seen the will of the self of God (*dev' ātmā-śaktim*) hidden in his own qualities." "May he endow us with clear intellect" is the prayer (4, 12), yet almost on its heels purpose (*saṃkalpa*) is called delusion, no less than touch and sight (5, 11). The Maitri too takes the same line. Senses and mind are revealers of the divine self within (6, 31), yet are the senses confusing guides and intellect is the cause of birth-wayfaring:—"where mind can be made to vanish—that is the highest state" (6, 34).

Very gradually an unhealthy period was supervening: the concept of a salvation lying in the turning away from the fuller life here for the fuller man, the man in the more as only to be evoked in the great laboratory of his normal life in the world—lying in the vain fancy of creating a premature yet inconceivable heaven by seeking it within. The recluse, the monk was re-fashioning the religious world of India.

CHAPTER IX

SENSE IN THE UPANIṢADS

I COME finally to that which in Western thought, when the subject is psychology, is not end but beginning. We have been considering the man (self or spirit or soul) expressing himself in and by mind; we have not inquired to what extent the early and middle Upaniṣadic teachers bequeathed to posterity any connected thought about the body as serving the man through sense. There has been much to say about *nāma*, but nothing about *rūpa*. Nor does inquiry when made reveal any such connected thought. There is no ignoring of sense, but neither is there any analytical exposition of it deserving the name. Eye and ear are more usually detached from the other three and, according, as we saw, to older precedent, treated of together with other three, to wit, breath, speech and mind. Touch occasionally gets a footing, but not bringing with it any insight into its essential significance as builder of man's knowledge of his world, such as we see dawning in Buddhist Abhidhamma and exegesis. Smell and taste flit in and out of the discourse, without any glimpse of critical interest shown, the latter acquiring importance metaphorically through the one word *rasa*, meaning both taste and essence. The teacher was in the first instance teacher of the things sempiternally most worth while, that is, of religion. And for religion, not in India only, the topic of sense belonged to the man-on-earth, and this was man in a lower way, a temporary way. *Rūpa* was man in the less, *nāma*, man in a more, using, *we* might say, he could not, a higher 'instrument.'

Nevertheless it were wrong to say those teachers left no characteristic sayings about sense. In the first place, they left no doubt that, in sense, man was up against a redoubtable force, against, as we say, edged tools. The inclusive term used from the early Upaniṣads for the senses, and persistent as usage, was *indriya* (*-āni*), a word meaning power or controlling power or lordship (*cf.* Chānd. 3, 3, 1, 3), and reserved for the organs of sense. The dying father is shown bequeathing to the son bending over him, not material possessions, but his *indriya*'s to the son's *indriya*'s, speech, breath, sight, hearing, taste, etc. (touch and smell omitted, Kauṣ. 2, 15).[1]

With the middle Upaniṣads a further term of power comes in, the senses being called 'gods' (*deva*). Kauṣītaki uses this term once, but the later Upaniṣads—Īśā, Muṇḍaka, Praśna, Śvetâsvatara—between them, frequently. It is a problematical term till we remember the disdeification undergone by personal Deism with the acceptance of Immanence, and the resolution of *deva* into meaning just anyone or anything exercising power *that was unseen*. With the latest of this group we witness the rehabilitation of personal Deity in such phrases as *para devo*: supreme god, for Brahman and Ātman, and other contexts, some of which are cited above.

The power of sense is further and more characteristically shown in speaking of the senses as 'graspers' and

[1] Dr. Ruben: "Zur altindischen Psychologie," a too short article in the Pathak Commemoration vol., Poona, makes the slip of saying "Yājñavālkya calls five expressions of life *buddhindriya*." The word *buddhi* is used only for physical awakening till we come to the Kaṭha and Sānkhya influence.

objects of sense as 'over-graspers' (*grahaḥ, atigrahaḥ*). in Bṛhad., 3, 2, 5. Yājñavalkya explains, that it is by in-breathing that we come to smell, by a *rūpa*, or thing-seen, that we see, and so on. No theory is put forward, here or elsewhere, resembling that of Greek *eidola* or Buddhist collision of sense and object, much less any question of any 'medium,' such as air. But the metaphor of grasping should not be taken too weightily. It is not followed up by any religious supplement on the dangers of sense, and is counterbalanced by Kauṣītaki's saying: "It is the breathing spirit (*prāṇa*), the intelligent self (*prajñātman*) that *seizes hold of* and animates (lit. raises up) this body" (3, 3).

Nowhere, I repeat, is there any serious attempt made to get what we should call a scientific, a reasoned statement about the matter. Such development as appears in the middle Upaniṣads is mainly in the way of the greater felt need, in the growing Yoga-vogue, of controlling the so-called controllers, the *indriyas*, the horses in the Kaṭha chariot, by man's servant, the driver *buddhi*, and his reins, the *manas*. Had there but been in that relatively toolless world a word for instrument, we might have found analytic thought sufficiently aided to beat out some sort of theory of defining and describing these wonderful and beautiful instruments; we might have seen *sānkhya* holding its own in rivalry with *yoga*.

But *yoga* had the teaching of Immanence mainly on its side. Man's vision was too much "averted" from the external to do justice to "the openings bored in him" (p. 175) outwards.

We have taken the senses first and in the end—so far—got no man. India took the man first, and in the end never did justice to his wonderful instruments or to what they might have revealed to him. We still wait for a culture which combines, to use Isaac Newton's phrase, an " intending of the mind " both ways.[1]

True as the essential teaching was in Immanence, it proved, for the loyal exploiters of it, in one other way hindersome. It wrought a tremendous work in the uplift of the concept of the man, but it barred the vision of human life to more than the visible world of sense. In its intense search for the self-that-was-More in a Self-That-is-Most, it contracted the long, long way of Becoming, and saw for the worthy (*dhīro*) nothing beyond this life's confines but That Most. Leaving this earth of sense-life he *might* " become Brahman." This was possibly his next step. The real next steps he virtually overlooked. He believed, I hold, believed reasonably, that he took a first step already in sleep, or other forms of unconsciousness. He admitted that he then found himself in another world of otherwise conditioned sense: a world, he testified, of sex and chariots, of varied experience and emotions, a world in short where he was still encased in a body wielded by mind.

Here was a sphere where analysis and where *yoga*, too, might have combined to help him to develop a new psychology—a psychology such as Bergson dreamed of in Europe, had we started otherwise. But the teachers faltered. To show the materials for such a psychology: here was one of the first and pressing tasks of original Buddhism, a gospel, as it proclaimed, sent out to " deva's and to men."

[1] A quotation I owe to Sir Walford Davies.

CHAPTER X

MAN AND HIS MIND IN ORIGINAL BUDDHISM (OR SAKYA)

No other book known to me has attempted to set out, with due regard for the history of values, what may presumably have been the *outlook on mind* held more or less in common by the men of the original Sakyan mission, the man or men who first went forth to teach that which in time became (in much altered form) the world-religion we know as 'early Buddhism.' There has been and is an acquiescence--an over-facile acquiescence—in that outlook as seeing the human being to consist in a fivefold agglomerate, known as *khandha*'s (Sanskrit: *skandha*'s), these occurring in the earliest utterances expressed as either monologue[1] or to a few disciples,[2] or also to bodies of laymen as "the divisions in which his teaching mainly runs."[3] To the critical writer, the fact (*a*) that the formula of the fivefold appears *as a gloss* in one account of the Tree-meditations, the fact (*b*) that the fivefold formula appears *as a gloss* in one Collection to the Third Utterance, called "Everything is on fire,"[4] the fact (*c*) of the Anguttara Pañcakanipāta omission should have given pause in this ill-founded conclusion. One day it will do so.

Meanwhile, to get a true outlook in the matter we have to put ourselves into the attitude of those first

[1] *Dīgha*, Mahāpadāna (No. XIV.).

[2] *Vinaya*, Mahāvagga, i., 6, 38 f.

[3] *Majjhima*, No. XXXV.

[4] *Vinaya*, Mahāvagga, i. 21, 2 f.; *Saṃyutta*, iii. 71.

teachers. They were trying "earnestly to accomplish"[1] the teaching of vision into what men should be and do. To attain this vision it was necessary to look into what men actually were, as body, as mind, as self. This I do not deny. But the primary quest of the Sakyan missioner always was: vision into what we ought to become.

If we turn to the world of Greek thought, we seem to find, at and from a certain period, a greater, a more detached interest in the quest of what man, in the midst of the "nature" to which he is bound, *is*. What he should become followed from what he was. He was to live and act "conformably to nature" (*homologoumenos tē phusei zēn*). As he emerged into a realization of himself as a world-knower and world-worder, the Greek was fascinated by the wonder of the senses and their world-pictures, and by mind as the mirror of these. And he was so much more of a mirror of them than a mover of them. His power over the external world was less than that which any child of our day may exert. Hence his poverty of wording concerning his own impact upon the world, as compared with his thinking and his wording and (in art) his working concerning the impact of the world upon him.

Where the early Buddhist exceeded his own primary aim, he did not get far, and when he strove to get further, he was prone to err and to stray from truth. He was alert as to the near way of the very gates of sense. And why? Because these were inlets less of knowledge than of obstruction and danger. They were to be guarded, not for the joy and more-life in the knowledge they brought, but lest the inpouring current they might become should overwhelm the little boat

[1] Recorded as the last words of the Founder.

trying to cross the perilous seas of what middle Upaniṣad and early Buddhist came to call the Faring-on (*saṃsāra*). This is, at any rate, the often emphasized teaching that we find, from that Third Utterance onward. And when (probably to make mission-touring a success) the first Sakyans decided to form themselves into an "order" of *sramaṇas* ('monks' is our nearest word), it is likely enough that admonitions in moral caution would be given. That the admonishing took on from the first ascetic aversion from all, even the wholesome joys of life is questionable, for the new gospel was for everyman, for the benefit of him as layman. And the Founder is shown, before his mission was launched, as aware that an ascetic ideal would be impracticable.[1]

That his ideal was saner than that is conveyed in the opening of a Sutta, the last in the Second Collection (No. 152). What he may have gone on to say has, as is elsewhere the case, been lost. A young brahman Uttara waits on him to learn, and is asked what his own teacher Pārasāriya teaches in the matter of the senses (*indriya*'s)? The reply is, that development (or culture, lit. 'making become') consists in "not seeing, not hearing." "In that case," is the rejoinder, "the blind and the deaf must be cultivating their senses." The student remaining silent, we get no further speech to him (as will surely have been the case), but a talk to the attendant Ānanda[2] on the difference between such a culture and "the supreme Ariyan culture of sense." This is, that sense-impressions are to be, not ignored, but recognized for what

[1] *Vinaya, op. cit.*, i. 5, 2 f.

[2] Such a falling back on Ānanda is a feature in other Suttas, and is suggestive of later apologetics. Ānanda's posthumous fame grew vastly.

they are, and perfect equanimity attained respecting them. In other words he who can see and hear first sees and hears, then "recloses eye and ear." But for "one who is in the way (*paṭipado*)," the arising of any sense-awareness as such causes him "loathing, abhorrence and disgust." Mental asceticism could no further go than that, and we have once more to mourn a wiser lost word, so unlikely is it that such a wise teacher would have had merely a monastic outlook wherewith to have helped forward, and that only indirectly, the young inquirer.

But when Buddhists tried to penetrate within the gates of sense, they were without orderly vision. There was an inner central gate, a sixth sense receiving, *i.e.*, it was said, "enjoying" what so came, and further, independent of sense, a hotch-potch of faculties or states, some simple, some complex; among these a few more or less inter-identical instruments of the spiritual life: *paññā, vipassanā, abhisamaya, paṭivedha.* Taken with body they made up a congeries, a "mere bundle" (*puñjamattaṃ*).[1] Such became gradually their man, their 'I,' their self. Thus they cut off the well-spring of that creative evolution which the early Upaniṣads discerned in the self. Their whole vision was but a transverse section just "going on," both microcosmic and macrocosmic. Even the goal of *parinibbāna*—the after-being of the perfected man at his last passing away—was but a mysterious vanishing from all possible worlds of rebirth into the void, worded only as a negation.

In a way they transcended the ignorance of their time and their world as to 'nature,' for they judged that nature to be teeming and moving and evolving

[1] A Buddhaghosa term.

from one cyclic cataclysm to new evolution and back again. They transcended the ignorance of their time and their world as to 'life,' for they raised the vague faith in survival to a natural law of life as a series of rebirths and redyings in a long, long upward way of purgation. But the blind spot of the spirit of their time and their world, as to a well-spring and well-goal of life and of all things, was reflected in a wavering agnosticism about the inner well-spring who is the real man, and then in a dogmatic nihilism concerning any such well-spring using the instruments of body and mind.

Hence it may be that, with far better opportunities in the way of materials to hand, we no more get a vision of *will* in Buddhist thought than we do in Greek thought. As the heirs of the latter and not of the former, we in the West have been taking a very long way round to come to a full realization of man's powers of reaction to, of impinging upon, the world which so constantly impinges upon him. We have not nearly come to it yet. But the outlook of the Buddhist on man as dynamic, as kinetic, was very favourable to remarkable inductions as to will, had he been capable of more worthily wording it.

Consider his materials: There was unquestionably a greater capacity for what is called *iddhi*, will-power, than there is now even in India, let alone the West. No one, save a materialist or a prejudiced sceptic, can study Buddhist literature and deny this. It is too cheap an evasion to write down all these thoughtful, sincere men as liars, as deluded all the time. Next, there was the faith in 'mind' (*chitta*) as infinitely ductile and plastic (*e.g.* Ang. i, 5), and in the sense-apparatus as so many *indriya*'s—that is, ruling or controlling things, faculties, not passive as mirrors, but engaged in clash and collision (*e.g.* Majjh. i, 111 *f.*). Next, there was the faith in the necessity of 'training the self' (*atta-dama*), however they conceived self (Dh. 80). Next, there was a keen sense of the importance of endeavour (*vāyāma*) and of energy (*viriya*), of effort (*padhāna*, *āyūhana*), together with a fourfold scheme of 'Best Efforts' in self-mastery (*B.P.E.*, § 1366). Next there was the belief in life-experience as work (*karma*) bringing forth results which were a sequel themselves of work. Next, there was life conceived as process, and as a cause-determined process. And, lastly, the belief in life as a very long period and opportunity of becoming of growth—a rising "on stepping stones of dead selves to higher things."

All of this is put forth here and there in a way that is quite explicit, in a way that, taken together, amounts to a world-dhamma, a view of things. But it is not in any way resumed and gripped as a view, realized as such. It is not held together by any clue or keyword about man's nature, such as today we might call a philosophical or a psychological principle. The Greeks and Buddhists laid hold, each of them, on a principle of natural causation. The Greeks applied it *to account for* serial order in the sense-pictures. The Buddhists applied it to teach how the series of sense-pictures and the resulting desires *might be shut off*. But neither Greek nor Buddhist was able to word a principle of will, nor of man as essentially a willer. The Greek's world-pictures developed into a concept of man as essentially and practically a static thinker. The Buddhist was too fluid altogether. For all his noble adumbrations of world-*werden*, of world-work, of training, of many lives rough-hewing man's will into holy living, he failed for lack of a vision of that will as the playing upon an instrument, and of man as the player.

Such is in barest outline the contents and extent of analysis of mind, to be found in the three Pali Piṭakas, the oldest complete canon of Buddhist teaching we have. To expand this sketch will be the burden of the following chapters. But first must come the inquiry, how far the sketch is true of the outlook on mind present to the missioners (mainly Brahmans) who *started* the movement destined to grow into "Buddhism"? No one save myself has yet attempted to do this. Writers have so far (I include myself prior to the last decade) been content to accept the outlook emphasized in the Piṭakas as representing justly that original outlook. Even they who refuse to see in the Piṭakas a work completed, in their present form, in the fifth or the fourth century B.C.—a refusal with which I am in agreement—have made no worthy effort to get at any earlier 'Buddhist' outlook on mind. To name only the two most eminent:—Rhys Davids, most guarded-in-word of men, recognized his own want of training in the 'mill' of psychology, and handed the matter over to me half a century ago, as to one emerging from it, to open up what Buddhism 'had to say about it.' Oldenberg, with a far longer and more distinguished academic career, showed, for all his capacity for exposition, a marked want of psychological insight. This is as evident in his most mature Buddhist treatise, *The Beginnings of Buddhism*, as it is in his better known *Buddha*. Nor does the *Buddhist Philosophy* of Berriedale Keith bring us any further. Always is there an absence of seeing that, *between* the birth of a new religious mandate, starting between B.C. 600 and 500, and its 'scriptures,' even the earliest known of such, dating apparently as 'holy writ' from some four to five hundred years later, it was humanly necessary that very considerable changes in religious values must have come to pass, and have influenced the form and tone and emphases visible in those scriptures.

To this criticism the rejoinder may be: Distinguish that outlook on mind of the founders of Buddhism from the outlook predominant in the Piṭakas if you can! It is an impracticable task. To this I would say: It is something gained that a distinction of the kind is worded as an ideal possibility. The next thing is to make an attempt to distinguish. For it is incredible that there is no distinction to make, so only it could be made. Let us see if a beginning in distinguishing can be made.

I take a doubtless very irregular procedure, but then I have a weakness for the irregular. I will sum up the conclusions I have come to on this original outlook in an imagined talk by one of Gotama's first disciples. I hear him saying: "We did not hold that 'mind' was in any way the very man. We never worded it as the man. We held that the man or self was that real being who valued things with mind, just as he is made to do in language, just as our teachers in what you call the early Upaniṣads were teaching. We held the self to be, as it were, the Man-in-man, the man as having, as it were within, a Most or Highest, as monitor, watching, warding, willing, wording him, just as you have That in 'conscience.' We called this Self the witness (*sakkhi*), the protector (*nātha*), the bourn (*gati*), the worth-seeking (*gavesitabba*), the light (*dīpa*), the refuge (*saraṇa*). We worded Him as *dharma* more than as self (*attā*), for He was all that we meant by *dharma*: the ought to be, the very word you have in 'will,' the word which stood for all we ought to become, just as a plant grows in the bud to the flower. All this we thought of in our use of 'self.' We never thought of 'self' as the ego in your idea of 'egoism,' or of 'selfish.' The self was for us rather your idea in 'spirit,' the man in the immaterial; yet not that only, but the man in the immaterial as having the Divine and as seeking the Divine.

"'Mind' for us was a way in which the man valued things. It is true that the man, as being *in a way* mind, was already being discussed in our day, but it had not yet won the weight it came to have. It was lurking in men's minds, that mind was in a way the man, and that man experienced *as* mind, but such opinions did not yet affect the sort of people we taught.

"We looked on mind as a 'more' (*bhūya, bhiyyo*) than the body, but as a somewhat working the body. But not as the fourfold complex with body as fifth which you find in the books. We never called mind and body *khandha*'s. The ways in which man valued things were for us either twofold: ways of body and mind, or threefold: thought, word and deed, as you say, or, as we said, 'action of body, of speech, of mind': *kāya-karma, vacī-karma, mano-karma*. Mind for us was a way in which man acted, and we called it *mano*, when we included desire or purpose or intent in the thinking. The thing thought we called *citta*. And the man conceived as awaking to new intelligent life on his surviving death we called *viññāṇa*. Sense too was for us a more in the way we considered the man. We did not worth it as a thing that made of necessity for his worsening, calling for revulsion. Sense opened up a more for him, and we were ever for the more.

And this was all."

Now this is for me just as much psychology as we can claim to see in the pre-Piṭakan teaching of the Sakyans. The expression "we were for the more" occurs in a Sutta as the refrain in the spiritual progress of a disciple, perhaps only an imaginary figure, called "Seeker" (Gavesin).[1] The meaning attaching at the birth of the Sakya mission to the word *viññāṇa* we have found existing in an early Upaniṣad.[2] In the Suttas we find it defined as not just a synonym of mind, but as (*a*) a continuum of flux, thus "*viññāṇa* runs on, fares on, not other" (*sandhavati saṃsarati naññaṃ*), and then is defined as "this speaker, worth-er who here or there experiences the result of good and bad deeds" (*vvāyaṃ vado vedeyyo tatra tatra kalyāṇa-pāpakānaṃ kammānaṃ vipākaṃ paṭisaṃvedeti*).[3] The definer asserts that this is how he understood the Founder to define *viññāṇa*. To the treatment he meets with I shall return. Here it is very clearly a name for the man as survivor, intelligent as such, and as intelligent incurring the consequences of his past. And this would seem to be implied in the use of the term in the suicidal episodes of two disciples, Godhika and Vakkali.[4] At the deathbeds of these two Gotama is said to see clairvoyantly a wraith, vapour-like, and to explain this as Māra, the Buddhist Satan, seeking the *viññāṇa*, who is one or other of the suicides, but seeking in vain. To render *viññāṇa* here by 'consciousness,' as we have done, is meaningless, as is

[1] *Anguttara*, iii. 215.
[2] Above, p. 76 *f*.
[3] *Majjhima*, i, 258.
[4] *S.* i. 120; iii. 124.

consciousness without the conscious entity. Warren at least put 'rebirth-consciousness,'[1] but that is really no better. But he knew how the term lingered on in its older meaning, long after it had been ruled as wrong to see in it the man persisting, in that we find it again in late Abhidhamma used for the man's dying thoughts.

It will have been noted that my Sakyan missioner repudiates the seeing any five groups or *khandha*'s in his mental outlook. And I believe that, with riper historical perspective, we shall come to agree with him. They are not for me in the first gospel. The marked preoccupation with the five *khandha*'s is for me too academic an emphasis for a gospel taken out to, not the monk, nor the School, but to man—" to devas and men." Let us take two contexts, where the five would surely have come up, had they been then formulated.

" Better were it, monks, that the uneducated manyfolk should conceive this four element-made body (*kāya*) rather than mind (*citta*) to be the self. And why? The body is seen to persist for a year, for two, three, four, five, ten or twenty years, for a generation . . . even for an hundred years, or even for longer, while that which is called *citta* or *mano* or *viññāṇa* arises as one thing, ceases as another, both by night and by day."[2]

Mind, as *citta* only, is then likened to the capering[3] of a monkey from bough to bough in forest trees, and then comes what is suspiciously like an appendix. Namely, the educated disciple heeds well the formula of how 'ill' arises in a mental causal series, and then

[1] *Buddhism in Translations*, p. 178, etc.

[2] *Saṃyutta* ii. 95.

[3] 'Catches hold . . . lets go.' I have a vivid recollection of the swinging thus along top boughs of Siamese apes, in the film 'Chang.'

he feels revulsion from—not body and mind, but from —each of the five *khandha*'s. The Sutta is repeated, as a variant of the same title, down to the above-given quotation, concluding with a different appendix, namely, the formula of the three *vedanā*'s, followed as before by the *khandha*-revulsion formula.

My conclusion is, that we have here, as we so often find, a fragment of an old saying, elaborated into a Sutta with later tags appended. We start with body and mind; we end with the five *khandha*'s.

I come to the second context. It is in the second compilation of the First Collection, and called Sāmaññaphala, or Fruit of Monkdom. With its predecessor it bears the oldest tradition in Suttas (connected discourses), for these two alone are named in the chronicle of the First Council as being then known by name. In it are described eight stages of prescribed mental studies, in which the disciple, having carefully prepared himself by much cathartic elimination in mood and thought, "much brings out and much bends down the *citta*"[1] to these. He first considers his body, its origin and composition, and how "for me the 'surviving-mind' (*viññāṇa*) is here nestled and bound (*sitaṃ ettha paṭibaddhaṃ*), just as a beautiful cat's-eye of pure water (looks when) strung upon a coloured thread." We have here the *viññāṇa* viewed as somehow 'in' or dependent on the bodily life, and as influenced by it, as the translucent gem would be, optically, by the colour of the thread.

Next, with mind thus attent, he exerts it similarly "in imagining from (or beside) this body another, a different (*aññaṃ*) body having shape and sense and features also, but viewed as mind." That is as *manomaya*, a term we have met with in early Upaniṣads,

[1] *Dīgha-Nikāya*, No. 2, p. 76 f.

and discussed. The term occurs now and then in the Fourth Collection, in the inserted gloss of Dhammapada, verse i., and elsewhere, and Commentaries are inclined to see magic in it, so long had its Upaniṣadic use passed from their ken. For me it is a witness of high interest in the newness of a study of mind *as such*, the mind coming to be distinguished from the man or self, and looked upon as a sort of subtle finer parallel to the body (*cf.* above, p. 57). Not a word on *khandhas*.

We meet with a slightly more elaborated treatment in another Sutta (or Suttanta) of the same Collection and subsection—probably later as being more sophisticated—the Poṭṭhapāda (No. IX.). Here the Founder is shown (as in his second Utterance) rejecting the suggestion made by the interlocutor, that the self (*attā*) is "gross and bodily," or that he is of mind-form, or of consciousness-form (*manomaya, saññāmaya*), having shape, or not having shape (*rūpī*). Here, whereas body, mind, 'consciousness' and the self are there at the start, we do not end with a single word whatever, in appendix or elsewise, about five *kandha*'s. Had the five been formulated when this patchwork of sayings was compiled, it is difficult to imagine that Poṭṭhapāda would not have preceded his reference to *saññā* by *vedanā*, the second *khandha*, and have proceeded to ask concerning the other two: *sankhāra*'s and *viññāṇa*. This comment will be appreciated only by readers who have noticed the untiring way in which the five are paraded in Sutta conversations, and further, who know the editorial habit of parading them when the conversation touches on the fact and functions of body and mind.

Once more: had the *khandha*'s been indeed an original feature of Gotama's teaching—and there is no evidence of such a teaching before his day—it is difficult to believe, that this feature, as held to be true and useful, would not have come into those sayings which are traditionally preserved as his parting injunctions, such as the seven lists known (later) as *bodhipakkhiya-dhamma*'s, and other sayings. But in none of these is there any mention of *khandha*'s. It is true alas! that in the Utterance recorded as his second, the five are paraded in usual Sutta fashion, and with the inevitable effect of weakening and dimming the force of the argument. For my part I am convinced, that we have here a case of the meddlesome hand of the editor.

We see this hand more clearly suggested in the 'First Utterance.' Here (*a*) the outline or charter for a New Word to man, to every man, has been narrowed down to a prescription for "one who has left the world" —a gospel for monks only[1]—(*b*) the word adopted for the goal of the religious quest, the thing sought and needed: *attha* (Sanskrit, *artha*) has been retained only in the negative form: *anattha-*, but the positive form, become with later literary growth too ambiguous, in that it meant also 'meaning' (as distinct from 'letter' or form: *vyañjana*) has been cut out, and four later ideals inserted; (*c*) a lengthy and pedantically worded appendix has been subjoined.

In the Second Utterance too we get the pedantically framed appendix. And we no longer have the inclusive pair of terms: *kāya, citta,* found in the Sutta discussed above. Instead of an inclusive term for mind, we find the four terms of the formula. We do not even get the three referred to as identical in the

[1] So reluctant do scholars seem in admitting editorial handling in the long life of the Suttas, that De la Vallée Poussin, accepting the narrowed outlook as original, sees in the 'Two Ends' a laxer and stricter observance *among monks*!

Sutta quoted from (above, p. 193), an identifying which is itself found only there, and which is also almost certainly late, so little do we see the Suttas using the three terms for mind as the one equating the others.

The Second Utterance in its essence is almost certainly a true tradition, and I give it here in two columns, the left containing what I see as truly or let us say, approximately original:

Body is not-self. On the one hand were this body 'self,' this body would not be liable to ill (*ābādhaṃ saṃvattevya*), and you would be able (to say): 'Thus let body be for me.' 'Thus let body not be for me.' Mind is not-self. On the one hand were this mind 'self,' this mind would not be liable to ill, and you would be able to say as to mind: 'Thus let mind be for me.' 'Thus let mind not be for me.' Since on the other hand neither body nor mind is 'self,' therefore are body and mind liable to ill, nor are you able (to say) as to either: 'Thus let it be for me.' 'Thus let it not be for me.'

Body is not-self. On the one hand were this body 'self,' this body would not be liable to ill, and you would be able (to say) as to body: 'Thus let body not be for me.' *Vedanā* is not-self. On the one hand were *vedanā* 'self,' this *vedanā* would not be liable to ill . . . (*continue as for* 'body'). *Saññā* is not-self. On the one hand were . . . (*continue as for* 'body'). *Sankhāra*'s are not-self. On the one hand were *sankhāra*'s 'self,' you would be able (to say) as to *sankhāra*'s: 'Thus let *sankhāra*'s be for me.' 'Thus let *sankhara*'s not be for me. But . . . (*continue as for* 'body'). *Viññāṇa* is not-self. On the one hand were this *viññāṇa* 'self,' this *viññāṇa* would not be liable to ill, and you would be able (to say) as to *viññāṇa*: 'Thus let *viññāṇa* be for me.' 'Thus let *viññāṇa* not be for me.' But since neither body nor *vedanā* nor . . . *viññāṇa* is 'self,' therefore is each of them liable to ill, and you are not able (to say) as to any . . . (*complete as for* 'body').

I do not quote the very monastic continuation, and have discussed it elsewhere. But the *khandha*'s are again brought in in a similar tedious refrain, a refrain which will have had a liturgical effect when droned out by an intoning in which India and South Asia have preceded us, but which retards and weakens the meaning it must originally have had, as a solemn warning from Founder to co-workers how to meet a growing tendency—a tendency which we saw Kauṣītaki warning against in his own choice of terms: seek not the speech but the speaker, not thought but the thinker. . . .

This warning must have had long reverberations in the early teaching, for it took shape, when perhaps the fivefold group-business was introduced, in a lengthened formula often cited in the Suttas, and called the "opinion (of permanence and of nihilism) based on the true group."[1] In it the uneducated man is said to be one who sees body or mind, namely, the four other *khandha*'s, as the self, or sees him as having body, or sees body in self, or the self in body, and so on for the mental four. The 'educated man' comes to the opposite conclusions, "not seeing" the body or mind as self, etc. The gradual growth of the so-called *anattā* theory may here be discerned. In the Second Utterance it is only called wrong to see body or mind as self. This does not preclude the self as 'having body and mind' wherewith to express itself. And had the idiom of the seventh and sixth centuries B.C. provided India with popular terms for instrument or tool, or 'use,' it is very probable that the discarding of man's reality in institutional Buddhism might have never come about!

That the current idiom as used by the founders,

[1] *E.g., Majjhima*, i. 300.

according to the Suttas, admitted that the self or man *did* 'have a mind,' let alone 'have a body,' is plain. Take the striking but quite overlooked saying in the Great Gosinga Sutta,[1] where Sāriputta is asked by his fellow-missioners to give the impression made on him by the glorious moonlit evening, and his view how it could yet be embellished. He replies: "In the case where a man[2] proceeds having the mind (*citta*) under control, and not under the control of the mind. Even as a gentleman might don just the suit he thinks fit for morning, noon or evening wear, so does the man dispose of the mind and not the mind dispose of him when he beautifies a night like this." If a Buddhist can, from this saying, see Sāriputta denying that the self "has" a mind, then indeed is 'the gentleman' his clothes and nothing more. Here is no possibility of evasion by saying: popular idiom was used by the founders when speaking to the general public, not to the "educated" few. Here we have the one disciple ranked foremost replying to the other disciple so ranked, and in the select company of their colleagues. Tacit repudiation of the formula just cited could no further go!

Moreover there is no question here of five *khandha*'s, either in the context, or as appendix. Where they appear as the latter is once more very strongly suggested in a little Sutta wherewith the long 'Section on Khandha's' in the Third Collection leads off. The opening episode has a very genuine ring about it. An aged sick man waits upon Gotama, and asks to be instructed "in what may long be for his good and

[1] *Majjhima*, No. 3ɬ, etc.

[2] The monk-editors have naturally limited the agent to 'a monk.'

happiness." "Surely, master," is the reply, "you are ill in body. Train yourself to say: 'the self will not become ill!'" The text, I hasten to add, has, for self, mind (*cittaṃ*). But since every one, Buddhists included, would admit that the "mind diseased" is a frequent fact and not disputed in ancient India, it is fairly clear, if the Founder is to be shown as the truth-sayer he was often called, that we must here read him as having spoken of the man as, *in one respect, namely, as very man, not liable to old age or illness.*

The 'householder' salaams and goes. He is then recorded as having come upon Sāriputta, who rallies him, why he did not further ask how he could keep "mind" well when body was ill. Instruction being welcomed, he then gives the old man the full benefit of the formula quoted above, as a panacea for bringing this to pass. That we have here an appendix added later I am not prepared to assert, were this the only evidence that we have. It must be laid beside other contributory evidence, and considered together with contexts, where the five groups or aggregates appear as the heart of the matter. For instance, No. 6, Sec. 2, of the Māra Saṃyutta, where the "recluse Gotama is instructing . . . the monks by a sermon on the five *khandha*'s."

That these make their *first appearance*, in the Third Collection, only in this, the fourth, and in the following Saṃyutta (that of the Nuns), there being nothing about them in the first two books: on Deva-intercourse, or in the third: the Kosala Book, is not without significance, and must come into our weighing. So must also the fact that there is no mention of *khandha*'s till the Tenth Sutta of the Majjhima, albeit the very first Sutta, in the paragraph on 'mind' (*mano*), yields an opportunity for resolving this into the four *khandha*'s. So must the absence of reference (to the best of my belief) in the whole of the First Collection till the lists of Fives in the Saṅgīti.[1] So must the absence of the five just where we should look for them: in the Fives of the Fourth Collection. The Sutta-Nipāta, usually reckoned as an early work, does not refer to them, not even in the poetic phrase "ebb and flux of the *khandha*'s" occurring in anthologies. These facts taken together seem to show, that in the Five-*khandha* doctrine we have an effort in mental analysis not belonging to the birth of the Sakyan mission.

That it took shape only when, with the growing cleavage between Brahmanism and 'Buddhism,' the teaching of Immanence, and even of the reality of the man or self was becoming discredited, is suggested by the explanatory attempt about it given by Buddhaghosa a thousand years later, an explanation possibly drawn from the Sinhalese Commentaries he recast into Pali: "Why did the Bhagavā speak of five *khandha*'s, neither more nor less? Because all similar states are grouped together; because the five are the measure of the hankering after the self and after what belongs to the self; and because in them are included remaining states."[2] It is true that this question touches only on the number, and not the fact of the grouping. This he handles in another work thus: whereas *khandha* signifies heap or mass, it also has a comprehensive and symbolic (or traditional, but lit. expanded: *rūḷhita*) meaning. As when, on cutting a portion of a tree, we speak of cutting the tree.[3]

Perhaps no other term could so conveniently have

[1] Last discourse save one.
[2] *Visuddhi-magga*, 478; trs. 564.
[3] *Aṭṭhasālinī*.

served to keep the then much emphasized plurality in the individual, his lack of essential unity to the fore as this clumsy term. And each of the five is defined in one Sutta in anything but a static light, such as the word 'mass' at first suggests.

But when it first emerged is wrapt in mystery. *Skandha* occurs but once in the early Upaniṣads, meaning 'body of doctrine' (*dharmaskandha*),[1] a meaning it often bore in the Suttas, and once in a middle (or later) Upaniṣad,[2] meaning merely a branch of a tree: "*tejas* or life-heat, proceeding from the heart through the lips ascends into space (*ākāśa*) like a column of smoke from branch to branch (*skandhāt skandham anusarati*)." Nor does the word occur among the psychological terms of the old Sānkhya aphorisms. There is therefore negatively made out a good case, that the term and number were a deliberate innovation made by institutional Buddhism.

In that institutional Buddhism it had an object to serve: the outlook on the man as merely an impermanent complex, with no essential reality. This object finally accomplished, it became gradually superseded, its clumsiness and overlapping terms being a hindrance to more exact thought. In the standard manual of the eleventh century, *Abhidhammattha-sangaha*, it is quite superseded, venerated only as a great tradition, and that to the present day, at least in Burma.[3]

The subject belongs more correctly to my next chapter. But (*a*) the emergence of the 'five' in the scriptures of the first activities of the 'Sakyans,' (*b*) the firmly accepted belief by writers on Buddhism that the 'five' belong to those first activities; these two con-

[1] *Chānd.*, 2, 23, 1. [2] *Maitri*, 7, 11.
[3] See below, Chap. XX.

siderations drove me to deal with it here. Not ranked with certain other formulas as the 'central teaching,' the 'five' still sit firmly as of the first teaching. And this I cannot accept.

I reject the *khandha*-classification, not only because contributory evidence points fairly strongly to its being an irruptive teaching, omitted here, figuring as appendix there. Such evidence supports my main position, but does not constitute it. This is, as I say elsewhere, that such religions as we call world-religions start with teaching to man, that is, every man, a new word about a More in his nature, life, destiny not before made plain, and *not* a new word about a Less in any of these. To tell man that the self that is he is not a central unity, with ways of coming to know and of expressing himself, but is merely the sum (or product) of those ways, is to teach a Less in his nature, life, destiny. Such a teaching I cannot pass, without its wrecking all that I see truly great and distinctive in the Helpers who found a religion *as Teachers*. Such an one might conceivably live a better religion than he taught—as healer of body and mind, as one of saintly living—but here I go with the votary—I see in that healer, that saintly liver, one who had it given him also to utter a new word about the man, and a new word that was and is *true*, not what appears to me, for a helper of any age to utter, to be a lie.

CHAPTER XI

PSYCHOLOGY IN THE NIKĀYAS

I. THE MAN OR SELF

HERE again I take the self first. I have said why I do so. That which we found about self, that is, the very man, in the Upaniṣads, was an unparalleled uplift in the conception of the human person. But it was not on that account that I took the self first. It was for a reason which now again makes me take the self first. We are now in a departure of Indian psychology which shows us, on the contrary, an unparalleled decline in that conception. But the method remains for me psychologically the right one; it is the evolution that went all awry, prompting us who get into this field to *overlook that changing aspect*, and to treat of the self or 'minder' under 'mind.' Such was my own erroneous treatment in the manual I am now rewriting. In that way we can get no light on the history of Buddhist thought.

Buddhist Commentators have helped to blind us. Their theory has been to despise the guidance of language, and say that, to get at very truth, the message of language as used by the manyfolk, that is, by friend Everyman, never gives the real truth, but is a mere matter of *sammuti*: common thinking, or convention, as we might say. Great teachers, 'Buddhas,' may use this to the manyfolk, but to the intelligent pupil they use terms in their 'highest meaning' (*parama'ttha-sacca-kathā*). This for me 'pernicious heresy' makes its earliest appearance in a notable Pali treatise begun probably in the first century B.C.,[1] and is fully set forth in an Abhidhamma Commentary which took its present form in the fifth century A.D.

If, as I have said elsewhere, we may judge by the Suttas, such a dual procedure was expressly repudiated by the Founder. So far as he had words—and what Messenger of a New Word does not now and then find that the right word is not there?—he meant what he said, "making no outer, no inner"—neither exoteric nor esoteric.

And language too, if it points to one thing more emphatically than to others, shows the man trying *to reveal himself* in relation to this and that, trying to get from the self 'within' to the other listening self not 'within.' Always it is the 'agent acting' that language ultimately means. Even when man has wrongheadedly substituted 'mind,' or other abstraction:—consciousness, desire, will and what not—for the self or man, language invests the dummy with the functions of an agent, when the dummy is but a collective name for the ways, the modes in which the agent acts. We have but to take up our doyen in psychology, John Locke:—"The mind very often sets itself on work in search of some hidden idea, and turns as it were the eye of the soul upon it . . . though sometimes too they start up of their own accord and offer themselves to the understanding."(!) And many parallels from his day to this might be cited. The self or man may be logically distinguishable from his ways, his acts, but he is always *there*. Our analysis is not sound

[1] *Milindapañha.*

if we banish him. How then does the mental outlook taught, or betrayed in the Suttas (including the Vinaya), speak of the 'self'?

Let us turn to the first utterance about him, the warning (given by teachers in previous chapters) against looking on body or mind as the self. If the reasoning here shown is to be valid, it is plain that, in the idea *attā*: 'self,' something more is implied than it is in our use of the word, or in the modern Buddhist use of it. The record says, that if self were identical with body, the body's power to choose would be omnipotent, that is, divine. The same is said of mind. Now this use of self is clearly other than our use of the word. The utmost we could mean, in such a context, is that were I just body, were all that I am included in body, I could *try*, better than my mere body now does, to be what I want to be. Mind, personality, soul would, as rolled up in body, make a stronger effort of will. But nothing more. And so, conversely, of mind, with bodily powers rolled up in it. But in the Indian meaning it is clear, that I should not be limited to trying. I should actually achieve. The meaning is that, in 'self,' we have a somewhat divinely, or if you prefer, superhumanly powerful, who is working through limited finite instruments, namely, body and mind, and hence cannot bring about a divine or perfect result. We have then, *to start with*, a concept of 'self' different from our own conceiving. And it is the concept of self which we found in the mental outlook of the Upaniṣads and of the Sāṅkhya aphorisms. This was the mental outlook accepted in Indian culture when the Sakyan mission began.

Take also the epithets applied to the self cited in the last chapter: witness, protector, bourn, light, refuge:—

in the first it is as witness of moral conduct that the 'self' is understood:—

> "There is no hiding-place on earth for him who evil works.
> The self for thee, O man, knows what is true or what is false.
> Yea, sir, the witness! you the lovely self despise,
> Who in the self conceal the self that's being wicked."[1]

Echo is this of a perhaps contemporary line in the Śvetâśvatara Upaniṣad (6, 11):—

> "the inner self of all,
> The overseer of actions, in all abiding,
> The witness . . ."

And in other contexts this moral Witness is referred to in terms we might use of 'conscience':—[2]

"Does the self reproach you not as to morals?"

"These are the penalties of wrong-doing: the self upbraids self. . . ."[3]

"Any moral layman established in the fourfold happy conditions is able to confess the self by the self, that unhappy rebirth is for him no more. . . ."[4]

> "By self incite the self, examine self
> By self, self-guarded thus, watchful of mind
> And happy shalt thou live. For self of self
> Is warder, unto self hath self recourse.
> Therefore train well the self. . . .[5]

And in the more literal sense of conscience too, as self-knower:—

"In so far as a monk knows the self to this effect: 'thus far am I in faith, morals, learning, self-surrender, insight, ready speech,' . . . he is called knower of self (*att'aññū*)."[6]

[1] *Anguttara*, i. 149.
[2] *Ibid.*, iii. 255, 267 f.; *Saṃyutta*, iii. 120.
[3] *Anguttara*, i. 57.
[4] *Ibid.*, iii. 211.
[5] *Dhammapada*, ver. 379 f.
[6] *Anguttara*, iv. 114.

"A monk who without deceit or guile manifests the self as he really is (*yathābhūtaṃ attānaṃ āvikattā*). . . ."[1]

In passing, note the way in which, in the more obviously *compiled* Suttas of the Second Collection, the dummy of mind is substituted for the self:—

"Ye should restrain, curb, subdue thought by mind (*cittaṃ cetasā*) (No. 20) . . . " possibly a stock phrase in current Yoga practice, but not one I have as yet met with in Yoga literature. It is, in the Suttas, more often used for 'thought-reading,' where the thought (*cetas, citta*) of some one is 'telepathically' discerned by the thought (*cetasā*) of the 'reader.'

Then the epithet 'bourn': the Pali is *gati*, as is also the Sanskrit; it means literally gait, going, and besides these, Macdonell gives 26 approximate meanings;[2] and then he omits 'passage.' In the Chāndogya Up. it is used for origin, descent, retrogression. In the Bṛhadāraṇyaka Up. it is used for way to the Highest:

"An ocean, a seer . . . becomes he whose world is Brahman . . . this is man's highest going (*parama gati*) . . . highest achievement . . . highest world . . . highest bliss" (4, 3, 32).

And the Kaṭha echoes:

> "Higher than the Man there is nothing whatever:
> That is the goal, that is the highest course.
> (*sā kaṣṭhā, sā parā gatiḥ*)." (3, 11.)

With these the Pali context is in sympathy:

> "Yea, 't is the self is warder (*nātho*) of the self;
> yea, and the self the bourn is of the self."
> (*Dhammapada*, 380).

[1] *Anguttara*, iii. 65.

[2] *Sanskrit Dictionary*.

Finally the epithets, 'light,' 'refuge.' The former figure, "in form of light" (*jyotirmayaḥ*), we saw is in the Upaniṣads applied to the self:

> "within the body in form of light" (*Muṇḍ*. 3, 1, 5),

and elsewhere (p. 41 f.). So also is the idea of a shelter or refuge or *Hort*:

> "ruler of all,
> great shelter of all (*sarvasya śaraṇam*), . .
> is the self." (*Śvet*. 3, 11.)

> "To that Deva, light of self-knowledge
> Do I seeking release resort as to a shelter." (*Ibid*., 6, 18.)

Here also the Pali context is in sympathy: "Live as they who have the self as light (or lamp), the self as shelter (or refuge) and no other," a context occurring some three times, and given as one of the final admonishings of the aged Teacher. Here *dīpa* has replaced *jyoti*, while the other (*saraṇa*, *śaraṇa*) is the same in both literatures. *Dīpa* is ambiguous; it may mean lamp, from *dīp*, to shine, or isle of refuge, from *dvi-āpa*, two waters, *i.e.*, land in a surrounding current. Dhammapada 25, and 236-8 gives both renderings, one in each context, or, some say, the latter meaning in both. But I believe I am right (against the Pali Dictionary) in seeing 'lamp' as meant in the admonition above, and not isle of refuge, for this reason: the word *dvīpa*: refuge, does not occur in the Upaniṣads, early or later. It is a Vedic word, but not used, so far as I can see, in the sense of a shelter or refuge, till the Mahābhārata, Part II. But *dīpa* as lamp, in the sense of guiding light, applied to the self, *is* used in Upaniṣads, and in those more or less contemporary with the birth of Sakya; thus in Śvetâsvatara, 2, 15:—

> "When with the nature of the self as-with-a-lamp (*dīpopamena*)
> A worker of Yoga beholds here the Brahman-nature . . ."

And in Maitri, 6, 30:—

> " Unending are the rays of him
> Who like a lamp dwells in the heart . . ."

and *ibid.*, 36:

> " As the persistence of a lamp is due to wick, support and oil,
> So these two, the self and the sun exist. . . ."

Commentators have been followed, as is usual, in deciding the choice; they prefer the more monastic meaning of refuge from drowning; but it does not follow that the primal tradition was known by them, who were ignorant of Upaniṣadic idiom.

Not that it matters much which rendering we find truer. That which does matter, matter very seriously, is the way in which we read the burden of the solemn injunction. Translators, lacking the imagination to place themselves in the place and time where and when it was uttered, have seen in the word 'self' purely the modern European, or for that matter, modern South Asian meaning: namely, in 'self' the average worthy man of today. They have seen in the word 'self' no more than what is meant in those cultures: a term for the positive purely human ego, somehow informing mind and body *plus* a somewhat known as 'character.' And they have actually seen, in the passage, a great inspired Helper of man bidding man thus conceived rely solely on his own wisdom and resources wherewith to attain salvation.

This shortsighted rendering has worked much harm for over two decades. Whereas the Buddhist formerly saw his hope of salvation to lie in faith in, and reliance on a Buddha, Dhamma, Sangha, he is now ever telling himself and us, that man must depend for safety here and hereafter on 'himself' alone. It is true, that the solemn injunction couples with 'self' the term 'dhamma,' to be taken as synonymous, since the phrase: "and no other" is appended to both terms. But however the second term is interpreted, we have it and 'self' made, it would appear, to supersede the more usual three terms: Buddha, Dhamma, Sangha. Both cannot well be true records. Here the Buddhist has, in so far as he knows his scriptures, been trying to thrive on a contradiction.

But *when that injunction was uttered*, the meaning attaching to the word *attā*, *ātmā*, was that which we have found adopted in the religious culture of India. *Attā* was implicitly, if not explicitly, Brahman = God, as somehow of and in the man:—'That art *thou*,' but this goes quite unnoticed in the renderings: 'be ye islands (or lamps) unto yourselves'; or the freer rendering: 'sucht hienieden Leuchte in euch selbst.'[1] We are here listening to a modern Agnostic; not to a truly religious missionary teaching the best religious wisdom *of his day*.

Most certainly, on the other hand, the speaker would not have pointed to the other, the threefold object of faith. The founder of 'Buddhism' lived when no man, himself included, was called Buddha; for him 'dhamma' meant the divine urge within to what ought to be, not a code of teaching; for him 'sangha' meant very largely a growing number of monks, inclined to be quarrelsome, and giving him much trouble and worry. The man who began by bidding men, in the admonitions of his day, "thoroughly seek

[1] Franke, R. O., *Dīga-Nikāya* (selected Suttas). I note that Oldenberg, in the posthumous *Reden des Buddha* (1922), remains blind:—"verharrt dass ihr eure eigne Leuchte . . . seid" (p. 103).

the self"; the man who, before he began his mission, is shown paying homage to 'dhamma' in "a great yearning for the great self":—this was not the man to bid men rely on the 'yourselves' they actually were, not potentially were, nor to seek refuge in a 'dhamma' not yet even uttered, much less compiled in category and code, nor in the 'sangha' as he knew it.

Such are some of the uses of the term 'self' in the Suttas, which can only be rightly understood when interpreted according to the Immanence of contemporary religious teaching. We have now to consider other uses, pointing to a different value which had come over the term, a value more akin to that which is down to today accepted as genuine Buddhism.

I take a little catechism which occurs very often in the Second, Third, and Fourth Collections. It is given at times to put a questioner, by a counter-questioning, at what was deemed a sounder point of view. Here it is, as used in this particular way:

A listener to a homily, in which a refusal to see body or mind as the self prescribed in the 'warning' discussed above,[1] has come to the conclusion: No-self in either body or mind must mean 'there is no one responsible'! And he asks himself: 'What self will deeds not done by a self affect?'[2]

The question goes straight to the heart of things. The arraigned thief or murderer pleads, he did not 'himself' steal or kill. 'Please, sir, 't wasn't I.' Or, 't wasn't the same 'I.'

The teacher is recorded as learning by thought-reading the doubt, and then follows the curious device

[1] P. 197 f.
[2] *Majjhima*, No. 109; *Saṃyutta*, iii. 103 f.

of talking 'at' the man by addressing another, here the whole class, which we met with above. The question is cited aloud, as "possibly asked himself by some fool,"[1] and the teacher proceeds, having referred to things arising only as they are caused, "What think you? Is body permanent, or impermanent?" "Impermanent, sir." "Is the permanent ill?" "It is." "Is it proper to say, of the impermanent, ill, and liable to change, 'This is mine; this am I; this is for me the self'?" "No, sir."

Here we see the questioner's reference to responsibility, which rests on the reality of a persisting self, swept aside. The one thing considered is this: 'Self,' we are taught, is a somewhat who persists, blissful and unchanging. But this 'self' you say, is transient and (liable to) ill. Hence, is the unsaid implication, the *attā*, the *ātmā*, who has hitherto been accepted, of Whom we have been taught, is not the man we are, whatever be his fate in a judgment.

It is the Self as divine that is here rejected, rather than the reality of any sort of a self. It is the Upaniṣadic, the Immanent Self Who is rejected from the nature of man. In the first vigour of the new teaching, it was not incompatible with it to see the very man as both divine and as 'becoming,' growing in his immense and infinite potency. But this outlook had undergone a palsy. Man was, as was his body, his mind, *a-nitya*, not lasting, brittle, crumbling, victim of change. 'Becoming' was being debased to mean mere change, and in mere change was nothing divine. There was a relatively new word come up to express this mere continuous occurring or repetition: *śāśvat*, Pali *sassata*: lit. hare-ish, from the bounds in the hare's

[1] Or 'futile man' (*mogha-purisa*).

going. Used but once in one of the older Upaniṣads: Bṛhad. (in the brief fifth Adhyāya, which is suggestive of a commentary on what precedes, and may hence be a later compilation), it occurs again only in the middle Upaniṣads, probable contemporaries of the first Sakyans—in Kaṭha, Īśā—and in the Gītā. Another such term, first occurring in middle Upaniṣads; Śvet. and Maitri, and in the Gītā, was *pariṇāma*, Pali *vipariṇāma*, meaning change or transformation (consequently also 'ripening'). Yet another term indicative of the altered, worsened outlook on 'the man' was the use of *puggala* for *purisa*. This word emerges only (in B.C. literature) in Pali works, sometimes in the compound *purisa-puggala*. In this the meaning (in the Piṭakas) is now depreciatory, now not so. But that *puggala* alone was depreciatory may be gathered from the exegetical definition, which is 'hell-swallower.'[1] It is difficult to render this difference in translation, and we translators have ignored that there is a difference. In this way we have misled. It is almost as if, with modern slang tendency, one wrote of men as 'blighters' or 'blokes,' or called them 'children of Satan,' 'miserable sinners.'

We see then that, both in the Academy and outside it, there had been arising a reaction against the wonderful teaching of the God-as-Man which we find the teachers in the early Upaniṣads exploiting. Here we need not judge the attitude in the Suttas to be derived from the successors of those teachers, nor the middle Upaniṣads to have been influenced by the later Sakyans. The reactionary movement may have been broad enough to affect both circles.

Let us revert to the little catechism. In it we see

[1] In late Sanskrit I understand it meant 'handsome person.'

between the Immanent idea of Self and the day in which the formula took shape, the emergence of a triad of terms closely connected, for some reason, in the current religious outlook: *anicca, dukkha, an-attā.* (The actual word *anattā* is not there, but it is as good as said in the context, and forms the third term in another formula: all things are these three, which finds strong emphasis in many Suttas, and is still held to be the very core of Hīnayāna Buddhism.) And then there is the fourth term: *vipariṇāma-dhamma:* a word not required logically, but strengthening the assertion, and probably, with this object, inserted in the compilation.

I have said 'emergence,' by which I mean a new outlook on 'everything,' and *a fortiori* on man, which had not arisen when the Sakya mission began with its original aim:—that, namely, of expanding the current teaching of Immanence into a practical mandate, of becoming by daily life ever a More in That Who man essentially is. Now it will be objected by the few who read the texts, that the little catechism is already found in the Second Utterance, cautioning disciples not to see the self in body or mind. How then can I speak of emergence?

I am impenitent, and abide by what I have said elsewhere four years ago. At the point where the citation in the chapter preceding this ceases, I wrote: "Here for me all that can be judged as genuine in the passage ends. It goes on in a way that is different, different in this: that the man or self is conceived in what is worse, is conceived as transient, as ill, as bent this way and that. And, as I said above, in my hypothesis of a gospel deserving to be called a world-religion, to go about bringing a new word of this sort to the Many cannot rightly, cannot possibly be the message in such a religion."[1] In what follows it is the monk who is valuing, the monk by whom the real message was carried down, becoming in his hands distorted as it went. And *it is the monk-values* that we see emerging in the little catechism.

We do not yet, in it, see the self or man as entity wiped out. It is only the Upaniṣadic Self, imperishable (*akṣara*), stable (*dhuva*), the unborn (*ajo*), permanent (*nitya*), hare-bounding (*śāśvato*), primeval (*purāṇo*), of Kaṭha and Gītā, the blissful (*ānand*) of the earlier Upaniṣads, who is here declared to be a conception impossible to hold *of man*. Man, as the monk saw him, was more fitly described in contrary terms.

This is equally patent in another now often cited passage in the Second Collection, No. 22, where it is claimed, that to affirm "the world, the self, in other words, this 'I' shall hereafter become permanent, stable, 'hare-like,' unchangeable, shall thus persist 'hare-bounding-like' is wholly, fully a fool-thing." Then follows the catechetical formula. That which is insisted upon, is not so much the non-existence of man as *attā*, as of the man as having the attribute of persisting or perduring identically.

That he does *so* persist is recorded as having been denied by the Founder. Gotama was of that older day when, with the still fresh teaching of Immanence, there was going on a feeling after the truth, that in being Deity, man is in truer language *becoming* Deity. Everywhere we meet with inflections of *bhū* (becoming), more than with those of *as* (being), save only in the formula "That art *thou*." And to the alternatives: 'all is,' 'nothing is,' he is shown as saying—the sentence

[1] *Buddhism* (1934), Chap. II.; *cf. Sakya*, p. 15 f.

has been replaced by a formula about the becoming of 'ill'—"Not so! All is becoming." But this great 'more-word' about man had wilted in the Academy, even while Gotama and his brahman mates were carrying it out to the Many, and terms for mere change, mere transience, as I have shown, were coming up to remind men, that identical persistence might be true of Deity, but not of man. If man 'became,' decay was bound to follow:—such was the newer materialistic tendency, against which the Founder fought at the outset in his 'second utterance.'

But the worsening in the concept of the man did not stop at repudiating identical persistence. That he had the joy of God in him had to go also, and 'ill' (*dukkha*) took its place alongside. And further: as if to ensure that all Divine attributes were ejected, a new word seems to have come into use: *attaniya*, in Buddhist Sanskrit *ātmaniya* and *ātmanīya*. There was another adjective for 'divine': *adhyātma*,[1] Pali: *ajjhatta*. But it was coming to mean merely the opposite of 'external' (*bahiddhā*), somewhat like our modern term 'subjective,' possibly coined by us because we had worsened the word 'self,' and so, the word 'selfish.' *Attaniya* signified 'attributes of the (divine) *attā*,' and it became correct to say:—in the five *khandha*'s is neither self nor 'selfic' attribute.

So far, since these five were just a more analytic body-cum-mind, the first teaching was being still maintained so far as the *reality* of 'the man' was accepted. But it did not stop there. The final depth of repudiation was to come. This was to reject, not only the reality of Divine attributes or nature in man, but the reality of any man whatever distinct from

[1] *E.g., Chānd.*, 1, 2, 14; *Kauṣ.*, 4, 2, etc.

body and mind. But this was a gradual growth during the two centuries after the passing of the first Sakyans. There was a half-way house in which Buddhist teaching halted for some time.

Three powerful influences were mainly instrumental in twisting that teaching from its original form: (1) the widening rupture with the established brahman teaching; (2) the growth, in north India, of monasticism; (3) the growing preoccupation of Indian culture with the analysis of mind, known as *sāṅkhya.*

The first (1), beginning with the Sakyan stand against the brahman attitude towards ritual, sacrifice and monopoly by birth alone, will in widening have drawn into the gap the central teaching of Immanence, a result analogous to that which has since been witnessed in Christian reform movements. The second (2) will have been mainly responsible for the pessimistic tone concerning the nature, life and destiny of man, and for the tendency among monks to suicide. (We read of a monk saying, that since, when monks got disgusted with "life and the body they stabbed themselves," martyrdom, on his intended mission, would be to him not unwelcome, since others would do the stabbing, meaning, probably, that *he* would not break a Vinaya rule against suicide [*Saṃyutta,* iv, No. 88.]) The third (3) afforded the 'halfway house.'

This was, that only in and through the body and mind—the five *khandha*'s—could the man be "got at." He could not be got at "as true, as persisting": *saccato ṭhetato*; or, in the later Abhidhamma phrase (with the instrumental, not the ablative): "with the sense of truly, ultimately": *saccikaṭṭhena paramaṭṭhatthena.* And it is implicit, that in this way he could not be got-at at all. He was not denied, as being but a myth, in so many words. But he remained what the Suttas are fond of calling *avyākata*: undetermined.

This is what I have elsewhere called the Humian position in Buddhism. One is inclined to judge, that the age was so interested in the growing *sānkhya* or psychological vogue, that it had become acceptable in culture to wave aside ultimates and rest content in analyses. The syncretic stage was passing; the synthetic stage had not yet come in. And so the Founder is often shown as silently refusing to make synthetic utterances, a silence which writers have accepted uncritically as both likely, and historically true. The reason may be, that they are more looking, in the great Reformer, for the Dissenter, and less for the 'Fulfiller.' If we bring in the editor of the Suttas, busy over oral, and then over written revisions, himself holding the values of a later day, we can see him hearing or reading, *not silences, but replies*, replies showing values he had, with his day, cast aside, replies which he soon found mutually discrepant, and *which he deleted*.

That term: "is not got at" (*na upalabbhati*) first appears in the Sutta cited as No. 22, and became a traditional way of stating the man as merged in mind. It is in the opening thesis of the Patna Debates of the third century B.C. It is also still used as a traditional form by Nāgasena in the Milinda conversations, even though the speaker went much further and categorically denied the reality of the self. (I have confessed myself tempted to see it, in this Sutta, as a later insertion, since exegesis, careful to define it in the comment on the Debate, passes it by in the Sutta, where the context is practically identical.) No term betrays more emphatically analytic preoccupation, taking so to speak a transverse section only in the whole of things, and losing sight of, and touch with, the behind and before, the A and the Z. The doer, as Kauṣītaki warned, is lost sight of in the doing; the doer's future is faded out in the deed. The fact that our own culture, from Hume's day to this, has followed a similar fate should help us to follow this stage of thought of India with more insight than we have yet shown.

There is yet another Sutta, this time in the Third Collection: 'Khema,'[1] where the Humianism is subtler than Hume's! Kosambi monks send greeting with a back and forth of messages to a sick mate in bed, that he gives proof of having won saintship. He denies with self-depreciation, and gets up staff in hand, to have the matter out. "Sirs, I say not I am body or I am mind. In both I've got the idea of 'I am,' but I don't discern that I am just *this* 'I am.' With the scent of a flower you say not, it's of the petals or colour or fibres of it; you say it's of the flower."

This isn't all, and he lands himself in another simile, in which the 'I am' conceit or fancy or desire is treated as a final disability which a proper saint must have got rid of. But as far as the flower, he would seem to be talking old stuff, pointing to the very man or self as the bearer of all that is 'flower.' The talk breaks away—has the editor been busy? Surely that flower had to be talked down!

In another figure, that of the wood and the faggots, the wood has had to be 'faded out,' as wireless idiom has it. The Founder, namely, is shown seeing men collecting kindling wood beneath the trees, and asking his followers whether they would say: It is we who are being collected? No, sir. And why? Because

[1] *Saṃyutta*, iii. 33; *Majjhima*, i. 141.

there's nothing there that is self or belonging to self (*attaniya*). Then, is the rejoinder, "put away (only) what is not of you, body and mind, these are not of you; these put away." The full analogy would be, that as the wood is to the fallen or cut fragments (grass, sticks, boughs and twigs), so is the self to his body and mind. I may be wrong, but it is with reference to the wood, the Jeta Grove, that I hear the matter being told. As are the faggots to the wood so are body and mind to the very 'you.' Compared with the very regular procedure in the use of the simile and parable—a very prominent feature in the Suttas—the way of this little parable is oddly discrepant. The relation of faggot to wood is left implicit, and the application of the simile is put forward and mixed up with the simile itself. Here is the parable restored to the form invariably used in Suttas:—

First the injunction (as in text) to 'put away' what is not of you. 'Body, mind: these put away from your notion of the true self.' Then the parable: 'Just as people in collecting in a wood faggots for burning and what not are not thereby collecting the wood itself.' Then the application: 'Even so put away,' etc., repeated. This body and mind is not you; put away these from your notion of 'you.'

The irregularity in the text may be apparent only to those who have made themselves familiar with the hundreds of similes in Pali literature, and with the adhesion to stereotyped form which is, here and elsewhere, the normal tendency in it. And I suggest, that although only the 'wood' and not the self has been faded out, the editorial object has been gained hereby: the wood would have made the picture positive; the self, corresponding to wood, is only mentioned negatively. Namely, body and mind are 'not the self.' And so we come to the illogical conclusion which, as we have seen, came to be deduced from that Second Utterance: because neither body nor mind is self, therefore there is no self! Coupled with the position of the halfway house:[1] the self may be neither of these, but he can only be 'got at' in, or as mind.

Witness to this preoccupation with mind is borne by the passages where there is room to guess that a term for mind has been substituted for 'self' or for 'man.' I have cited two such contexts. The one, that of the sick old man, bidden to practise keeping the mind (*citta*) well, in spite of the infirm body.[2] The other is to call, not the man or self, but the mind (*mano*) the enjoyer and referee of all the messages of sense.[3] The novelty, the iconoclasm in these words has not been perceived by us, partly because we also have dim muddled views about man and his instruments, partly because we seem, in the latter instance, to have found something corresponding to our own psychology of yesterday, namely, in a 'common sense,' co-ordinating special sensations.

It is true, that in the fivefold list of senses, with which Buddhist psychology is overmuch concerned, a sixth sense and its object are often appended: *mano* and *dhamma*'s, or things—a crude effort of analysis, inferior to that of Sānkhya where, as we saw, *mano* or *manas* is not ranked in the same category as bare sense, but is, with two other faculties, that which handles, conveys, interprets sense. But this context would, at first sight, seem to be a worthy effort in the same direction.

[1] Above, p. 218. [2] Above, p. 199 f.
[3] *Majjhima*, No. 43.

Well, let us glance at the Sutta: second Collection, No. 43: the 'Great Miscellany.' It purports to be a catechism, where Koṭṭhita puts questions on details of doctrine to Sāriputta. It is a most interesting patchwork, a miscellany indeed. And since the work of these two great brahman missioners was, not to set pattern catechism for students—that will have come after the first strenuous years—much less to ask and answer where both were reputed so wise, we may be tempted to see here the much later work of monks drawing up, from the mass of repeated Sayings (where only question and answer had been handed down), such a catechism for the Vihāra schools. But in the day when those two missioners were taking their mission out to the Many, the questions here patched together are more likely to have come from persons among that Many. And in that day, there is but one reply that Sāriputta would have given conceivably to the question: "Who"—notice, it is not What—"Who (*Ko*) enjoys (or experiences) the field of the five mutually independent senses? What is their 'resort-to' (*paṭisaraṇaṃ*: we have no good word)? He would have replied, it may be, to men who were *inclined to say:* It is the mind, "It is the breathing spirit, the intelligent self (*prajñâtmā*) who seizes hold of and animates this body. It is with mind that the man sees, hears, feels." Such are the replies his former masters had been giving, as we saw, to inquiring students. But here, the bitter irony of history shows him giving the very reply, it may be, that the inquirer was himself hoping to hear: "the mind."

It is easy to blame the editorial exegetist; it is dangerous to see as work of his whatever seems unexpected or incongruous. But where his opportunities have been great, and where his values can be shown as much moulded by powerful influences, we may be *driven* to the conclusion, that in our present sketchy knowledge of Buddhism we are being editorially spoonfed to a high degree. Too long have we been content to swallow scripture *en bloc*. We have after all only now begun to diet ourselves critically in Christian scripture. We can afford to be quicker in Buddhist scripture. How, for instance, as I have said elsewhere, can we afford to rule out as 'supernatural' all that the first Sakyans claim as experience from other worlds, and swallow whole all else that they are said to have said?

For instance, can anything be more plainly gloss inserted by an editor who sees man in and as mind, than the extra line imposed in Dhammapada 1 and 2?

> Things are forerun by mind (*mano-*), have mind as chief, are aspects of the mind.
> If with corrupted mind he speak or act,
> therefrom ill follows him as wheel the foot of drawing beast.

So in the reverse case of morals, in verse two.

Lines 2 and 3, 5 and 6 might have come straight from the Bṛhadārañyaka, where man is shown acting, experiencing, "with mind." Line 1, repeated in verse 2, *is alien.* The rest of the chapter: "the twins," is entirely in couplets, giving similar contrasts. Yet when I published my translation in 1931, I could not find that any of the many translators, or any one else, had ever drawn attention to the irregularity.

Before I can let my reader pass on from considering the decline of the Immanent Self in the Suttas, there are two contrasted passages I think he should have indicated to him. The one is in the Third, the other in the Fourth Collection. In both the phraseology is rarely distinctive compared with the monotonous Sutta refrains.

In the Nidāna Book (Vol. II) of the second Collection,[1] the Founder is made to ask Sāriputta whether he has announced the winning by him of *aññā*, *i.e.* 'the having-come-to-know.' With the growth of preoccupation with mind, and mind-ideas about the man,—further, with the growth of the 'arahan theory,' or belief in human consummation as possible already, and on earth—this word had taken the place of the older Sakyan term for the *summum bonum*: *attha*, the thing needed, the thing sought, the while it anticipated the use, in this sense, of 'nirvana' (Pali: *nibbāna*). It may be not too freely rendered by 'gnosis,' itself a newcomer into English. The winning or assurance of *aññā* the Suttas clothed in one of the formulas in which the state of arahan is announced, to wit, that rebirth is ended, the whole of the divine life having been lived and everything 'done that ought to be done' (*kataṃ karaṇīyaṃ*).

Sāriputta, as stated, demurs, that he had not said so in so many words. The dialogue is then spun out to accommodate the thematic formula of the Nidāna Book:—the causal origin of ill. We may cut this out, and come to what is more likely to have been the earlier 'version':— "How would you yourself say, how you have won *aññā*?" The reply is: "Through spiritual deliverance" (*ajjhattaṃ vimokkhā*). We can trace this word (*adhyātman*) emerging in all the early Upaniṣads as the adverb of reference to the self, the divine self, the God-in-man. I have said, it appears with a lowered worth in the Suttas, as just inward or

[1] *Saṃyutta*, ii., pp. 50-4.

personal, as nearly=to subjective, in contrast to the external. But here it would seem to be used in the older worth, tantamount to 'spiritual.' And it is surely Sāriputta the brahman *who would have used it in that older sense.*

(I am not so confident about *vimokkha*. The idea of release or deliverance runs through the Suttas, and who would say, that spiritual release is not, in man's forward growth, an important factor? But at best it is a negative worth, telling nothing of the positive 'becoming' which is the one thing which makes spiritual release valuable. For me the harping on the release-terms: *vimokkha, vimutti, mokṣa*, is part of the spore left in the records by the growing vogue of monasticism.)

I complete the reply imputed to Sāriputta:—"and through the waning out of all grasping (*upādāna*), in one living thus aware, the cankers (*āsavā*) do not flow and spread, and I do not deny the self (*attānaṃ ca n' âvajānāmi*)."[1] That he certainly did not deny the self is already assumed in his use of *ajjhattaṃ*, in the meaning it had in his day. But it must have been an awkward sentence for the exegetist Buddhaghosa, who did utterly deny the self; and it is not wonderful that he glides past it, saying only: "here is uttered the conclusion (*osānaṃ*) of what he said!"

But the reader may be puzzled at the reason *why* such a conclusion came to be made. I will tell him how I solve the problem for myself. First, we have, in the Sutta, the ancient half-forgotten tradition of something which Sāriputta *may* have said. It begins

[1] In my translation of the Nidāna-Saṃyutta, thirteen years ago (*Kindred Sayings*, ii.), I have here carelessly and unfortunately confused *avajānāmi* 'deny,' with *anujānāmi*, 'admit or allow,' thus altering completely the significance in Sāriputta's independent avowal.

with a noble, Kalāra, reporting that a monk known to them both, mentioned in Suttas, has left the Order and gone back to the world. Sāriputta's comment is that doubtless he didn't "find comfort" in it. That comfort, for the present and the future, he confesses he has certainly won. Kalāra then reports to the Founder, that Sāriputta has won assurance of *aññā*. Sāriputta is sent for, and is catechized, with the replies, in terms independent of formula, as stated.

Next, let us cut out the very usual bringing in of the Founder, as well as of the catechism, and see, *in the original fragment*, Sāriputta explaining to Kalāra, that "comfort" for him meant just that lovely sense of kinship with the Highest taught in the Immanence in which he as a brahman had been trained, and which led men to speak of the indwelling Divinity as "That from Whom I no more shrink away." He probably spoke in warmer terms, terms more like these, than the more reserved "I do not deny the self." Remember always that this then amounted to saying, "I do not deny the (Holy) Spirit."

Lastly, let us note that, with the emergence of *aññā*, coupled with the worsening idea of the 'self,' a saying or formula had arisen:—"Thus do worthy clansmen declare *aññā*: the Thing sought is mentioned, but they do not bring in the Self."[1] Now herein lies an Indian pun: *attha* is mentioned, but not *attā*. And puns *were taken seriously*, in a culture where was as yet no written word, for thus mistaken identities in words might be corrected, and contrasts drawn *out of the very likeness in form*. "The devas," say the Upaniṣads, "like puns." But the formula raised this difficulty:—how to reconcile Sāriputta's

[1] *Vin.*, Mhv. v. 28.

Self with "not bringing in the self" (*attā ca na upanīto*). The result has been an editorial compromise: "I do not deny (the verb may mean also 'despise') the self."

My solution may be held wrong, but I maintain, as generally true, that the survival of treasured fragments of Sayings conflicting with later values must have presented often such tasks to pious editors: men "committing deceptions who were incapable of telling a lie."[1] Venerable runes had to be preserved; new sayings had to be upheld.

The other passage survives apparently undoctored but in astonishing contrast to the usual tradition which fathers depreciation and even denial of the self on to the Founder. It is in the Sixes of the Fourth Collection, called 'Self-acting.'[2] In it a man, said to be a brahman (which is scarcely credible), comes to Gotama to aver, that in a man's actions the doing is not rightly to be called as 'by the self' or as 'by another.' The assertion may equally well be rendered 'there is no self-agent or self-agency' (*attakāro*, v. 1:-*kārī*). Gotama's reply is: "I have never even heard or seen such an opinion." (Curiously, the emphatic negative of a command *mā* is used for the categorical, not *na*, and we may have a corrupt recension of what was originally: 'Don't tell me such things! Never have I heard such!' But who may solve it today? The 'seen' is also baffling in a bookless age.) He goes on: Whenever you move a limb you are the self-agent(-cy). You admit there is initiative, and the man initiating."[3] The Founder's admission of ignorance can only have been left in as meaning: Such an opinion is

[1] Sir F. Pollock, *To my Grandson*.

[2] *Anguttara*, iii. 337 f.

[3] Below, p. 286.

your fancy. But there is evidence that, even in his day, reaction against the Immanence of the Upaniṣads was growing, begetting sceptical speculation. But we must leave it in its overlooked mysteriousness.

The reader of the opening chapters will have seen, that in and around the day when the Sakyan, or original Buddhist movement was born, Indian teaching, while it had introduced a striking and enthralling aspect of the Divine as the Immanent Self, neither lowered nor ignored that other aspect of Deity, which saw, behind His manifestations, a unitary, impersonal concept expressed in the neuter name 'Brahman.' If, in the newer teaching of God as the 'Self' or very man, Deity was brought from beyond the worlds into man, in 'Brahman,' Deity remained as the concept of the unattained Highest.

To this dual concept of the One, the first Sakyans brought their own new concept of a term it is hard for us to render exactly: their own concept of Deity as *dharma* (Pali *dhamma*). In this they sought to conceive Deity, as not only immanent, but as moving, urgent, ideal, as 'conscience,' as 'duty,' as 'the ought and ought not.'

We do not, in the Nikāyas, find any teaching bidding men seek or be guided by, or take refuge in, the supreme impersonal Brahman. And this may mean one of three things. Either (1) the first Buddhists were ignorant of the concept — which is impossible, if only from the preponderance of brahmans among the first disciples—or (2) they accepted it, teaching it in their own distinctive way, or (3) the concept in the Divine manifold they sought to teach insistently was a blend of the still relatively new Self-concept and their own new emphasis on *dharma*. As to this, I may remind readers of the cited context, where guidance is to be sought in self-cum-dharma, and "in no other."[1]

The second alternative was the recognition of Deity as Brahman in several striking compounds, herein resembling the way in which we have seen 'self' compounded: self-lamp-ed, or -islanded, self-refuged, *att'ādhipateyya-* 'having the self as dominant influence,' *atta-diṭṭhi* (opinions about), *atta-bhāva* (state of), and others. Thus we find as religious terms *Brahma-patti* (attainment of), *Brahma-vihāra* (abiding in), *Brahma-cariya* (living or conduct, *cf.* our 'godly life'), *Brahma-cakka* (wheel, *i.e.* Divine movement), *Brahma-bhūta* (God-become, God-realized). There are other compounds, such as *Brahma-cintita, -vāda, -ssara*:[2] where mere excellence is expressed, as we too say divinely fair, a divine melody, and the like, meaning only a very faint approximation to the real meaning of our words. And we may here possibly see a popularizing of the Brahman concept, current from this period and later, the exegesis of the term Brahma- being usually "in the sense of best" (*seṭṭha*). But to the five compounds first quoted, a very definite religious weight attaches. The first two (*-patti, -vihāra*) are given to a remarkable gospel of aiding the fellowman by will, taught by a brahman, and annexed by the Sakyans at a very early stage in their mission. (This theory put forward by myself eight years ago, I have as yet failed to see competently discussed.) I shall return to it later. *Brahmacarya* (Pali *-cariya*) and *Brahmacārī* were terms accepted under Brahmanism for the period and state of students of the brahman and noble classes. The life of such an one was strictly regulated, much

[1] Above, p. 209 ff.

[2] Divine thought, speech, voice.

as if he had been a novice in a monastery. It was a religious life, but the term means godly life, God-life, and should so be rendered. The Sakyans held that, not these years of pupillage only, but the whole life should be "godly," save that celibacy was required only for followers in the Order. The absence of it in the laity did not render life ungodly. The Charter of the first tours expressly enjoins the teaching of *brahmacariya* to "devas and men" generally.

The compound 'Brahma-wheel' occurs here and there in contexts similar to that of 'Dhamma-wheel' as a figure for the onward movement of conquest, transformed from that by violence to one of right and goodwill:

> For worlds of devas and of men
> Wayfarer made the Wheel Divine to roll,
> For all that breathes compassionate. (*Anguttara*, ii. 9.)
> Who rolls like thee the incomparable Dhamma-wheel?
> Sāriputta rolls it as I do, Wayfarer's son. (*Majjhima*, No. 92, *Sutta-Nipāta*, 557.)

The last compound, *Brahma-bhūta*, has a deeper-lying origin. The compound first emerges, in non-Buddhist literature, in the Bhagavadgītā, in three contexts.[1] The recluse is there said to attain the state so called, to "become Brahman," and "touched by Brahman (*brahma-saṃsparśam*)," the attendant experience being one of purity and infinite happiness, of light within and "supreme devotion toward Me." In a lengthy set passage in the Suttas describing the grown vogue of the genuine recluse (not the cenobitic monk) occurs a sentence resembling this yet unlike: "He tormenting neither the self, nor another self, lives, as to the seen, uncoveting, finished, become

[1] V. 24; VI. 27, 28; XVIII. 53.

cool, experiencing happiness, with the self become Brahman."[1] We cannot say with any precision when these things were first uttered. For me I repeat in brief, as I have more fully said elsewhere, they date from a time when, with a tremendous 'New Word' producing, among the more religious, profound reactions, there will have been felt the need to "come apart," in a way not so felt before, and ponder this thing about the 'man' apart from 'men.' It is worth noting too, that the epithet is found once or twice applied to the Founder. I believe that, in it, we have another link between 'Buddhism' and the period of its birth, a link which snapped and vanished in the adverse atmosphere of a more mental and spiritually worsened outlook on the self or very man.

That *dharma* meant duty or right or 'the ought' in conduct was no novelty attributable to the Sakyans. We find the injunction of teacher to pupil to "live according to *dharma*" in early Upaniṣads. But nowhere is the so living linked expressly with Immanence. The pupil is to look upon mother, father, teacher and guest as so many *deva*'s, but he is not told to love and reverence them because of the Most Holy Thing that they potentially are. Here was room for a new worthier teaching, and when we find the Founder of Sakya seeing in homage to *dhamma* the way to satisfy a yearning for the 'great *attā*,'[2] and identifying himself with this worship, before he began his mission, we surely see a very significant line which he intended his 'new

[1] *Majjhima*, No. 51, etc.

[2] *Mahattaṃ*. The word may mean the abstract of *mahā*, 'great.' The form *-attaṃ* is usually confined to poetry, *attānaṃ* being, as we have seen, the usual prose accusative. There is, however, an instance in prose where *mahattaṃ* is contrasted with a minor self (*Anguttara*, i. 149).

word ' to take. In seeing Deity in the ' ought to be,' ' ought to do,' ' ought to become ' implicit in the word *dharma*, he was bringing into religion the essential need of living one's faith, no less than was expressed in the word *Brahma-cariya*, the God-conduct. The *ātmā* idea was taking on new force as a concept of movement, of a dynamic cult, of a ' wayfaring ' ever further. In this way he started his world on a new line of psychological outlook:—the seeing in man and his mind not a ' being ' to be known and realized as such, but a ' becoming ' in a More, a Better. And, with all their decadence, the Suttas echo and re-echo this virtually from first to last.

CHAPTER XII

PSYCHOLOGY IN THE NIKĀYAS

2. MIND

THAT in the Nikāyas the outlook on the man or self is predominatingly one of mind in its manifold working should ever be kept in view. Sutta-episodes open with a man or men, in the natural, that is, the true presentation, as first and last persons, personages, individuals in an environment. But the tendency in the teaching is to resolve the man into so many parts of, or ideas about, the man. I need only refer to Suttas cited above as instances of practically all the rest: the sick old man on page 199; the inserted catechism on ideas causally treated in Sāriputta's assurance of salvation on page 225. I am not maintaining unreasonably, that conversations, and especially perhaps admonitions, can consist solely of personal episodes. I am only concerned to show, that in these, the interest is *usually diverted*, from the man as agent, to mental aspects of his life, whether these be discussed in terms of *khandha*'s or of sentiments or categories of tendencies and the like. All may be summed up approximately by saying, it is *dhamma*'s or mental phenomena for which our interest is claimed, rather than the man expressing himself by these. The man is 'being got at '[1] as *in*, if not as yet wholly *as*, mind. That this was, had been, a growth of the psycho-

[1] *Upalabbhati*, a term much used in this connection.

logical vogue later known as sānkhya, I have tried to show. That 'more' in the man considered under 'name' which we saw emerging in the Chāndogya, that idea of man acting "with the mind" which we saw emerging in the Bṛhadārañyaka, had brought about a seeing in 'mind,' a group of uniform processes similar to, analogous to those of the body, which we noticed in the Sāmaññaphala Suttanta.[1] This again, in course of time, become no longer a novelty, had developed into the *khandha*-analysis of the man, and the all but supersession of the man as agent and valuer by a speaking of him as 'mind.'

But let the reader not expect to find in the Suttas thorough-going consistency. This might be looked for, if the Suttas were, as some have judged them to be, the mediæval 'fake' of Ceylon monks. Actually they are as an old mansion, in which additions and alterations and repairs have been carried out, something of the original structure remaining.

Thus, we come across, in midst of all the preoccupation with parts and mental tendencies, a way of speaking which clearly, nay, almost with emphasis, refers to the mind *as the man's instrument*. Let us take examples of both this and of the prevailing method. Here is one of the *latter*:

"Two conditions are needed for release of mind (*ceto*): withdrawing work-of-mind (*manasi-kāro*) from what appeals to sense, and fixing it on the opposite."[2]

Here is another: "Answer them (inquirers of other sects) thus: 'All things are rooted in desire (*chanda*); have their origin in work-of-mind; (mental) contact gives rise to them; their confluence is feeling (*vedanā*); their chief state is concentration (*samādhi*); mindfulness

[1] Above, p. 194. [2] *Majjhima*, i. 296.

(*sati*) is their dominant influence; wisdom (*paññā*) is their beyond; and of all things release is the core (*sāra*).' "[1]

No isolated samples, however, suffice to show adequately the prepossession with mind and ideas about it (the man, the mind-er, being only implicit) which is scattered broadcast through this literature. Now take instances of a surviving interest in mind as used *by the man*:

Gotama is recorded as referring to thought-reading: "A certain man, brahman, declares by noted signs: 'thus is in you the mind, thus so and so is in you the thought (*citta*).' "[2]

Again: "For me the mind shall rise above every world; for me thought (*citta*) shall be inclined towards the waning out (*nibbāna*)."[3]

And we have seen where Sāriputta is shown speaking of the man who has the mind (*citta*) under control (*vasa*), and not *vice versa* (p. 199).

Measured by our own usage, we may say, that in the latter cases, the diction is that of the 'plain man,' the 'man of the street,' in the former cases, it is that of speakers given to mental analysis. It is true, as I have pointed out, that in the latter cases it is not just everyman who speaks, but a cultured disciple among his like. Nevertheless, the usual Buddhist explanation, where explanation is attempted, is to call the latter just 'conventional' modes of speech, not voicing what is 'genuinely' or 'supremely' true. For my part I repeat, that where we have the mind shown as man's instrument, we have survivals of a

[1] *Anguttara*, iv. 339. [2] *Ibid.*, i. 170.

[3] 'In you,' 'for me' =*te, me*, the 'oblique' form of 'thou' and of 'I,' and can be rendered by any oblique case: of, for, to, in, etc. We saw the like in the 'the ātmā' of or for me—*ma ātmā*, p. 28.

teaching which, *in its first exponents*, was familiar with the treatment of mind as just man's instrument, and not in any way superseding his presence and personal agency. Always in such phrases, where mind and body are on the stage, I see a door open in the centre at the back, and 'the man' appearing. In the former cases—cases of mental analysis—the door is closed. And in the Suttas we can see that door now open, now closed, more often closed than open. How very much closed it became, the reader who pursues these chapters to their end may realize.

What are the Pali terms used for 'mind'?

For our words 'mind,' 'thought,' 'consciousness' there were, as we have seen, several equivalents, the three principal ones being *mano* (also the variant *mānasa*), *citta* and *viññāṇa*. We have seen too in a unique passage that they are equated: *cittam iti pi mano iti pi viññāṇaṃ*, where *iti* [*a*]*pi* means "thus too," as if to say, choose which you will. For the purposes of that Sutta, that is to say, and more; in the definition of *cittaṃ* in the first book of the Abhidhamma-piṭaka, § 6, *mano* and *viññāṇa* are among the parallel terms. Moreover, the Buddhist scholar of today sees them as synonyms. But in actual Sutta-usage, each of the three has a distinctive shade of meaning. In *mano* we have the man valuing, measuring, appraising, and also purposing, intending: this we saw was Upaniṣad usage. In *citta* we more usually have the man as affective and affected, as experiencing. In *viññāṇa* we have the man as not of this world only, as 'soul.'

The volitional coefficient in the meaning of *mano* is of especial interest, in the absence of a fitter separate term like our 'will.' *Mano* was somehow informed with tendency to act; and if we see, in our own word, the will as not the servant of mind, dictated to by it, but the one active principle, engaged, *when called mind,* on a certain intensive form of activity, I hold we have the truth. The Indian was feeling perhaps after this when he worded '*nāma*'-activity in the word *mano* (*manas*), as a measuring with intent to act. The intention-coefficient was implicit only, and not always prominent, yet translators have occasionally felt the need of rendering *manas* by 'will' rather than by 'mind.' Namely in the Upaniṣads; I do not notice implicit volition so much in the Pali. When, in this, thought is voiced as purposeful, the more usual way is to use the causative forms, if I may so call them, of the stem *cit*: *celo, cetanā, cetayita.* This is not to say that these forms amount to a word as strong as our will or volition; I think my Burmese friends' insistence on *cetanā* as=to 'volition' is excessive, and regret I was by it induced to use 'volition' for *cetanā* in revising, in 1923, my *Buddhist Psychological Ethics. Cet-* was and remained a term of thought, but with the conational factor implicit, more so than in *manas* or *citta.* Thus Gotama, in ascetic struggles, is made to say: 'If I were to restrain, mortify *citta by cetas.*'[1]

In deciding anything about so delicate and elastic a matter as the range of any word for man's inner immaterial world, no hard and fast line can be drawn, but we may say with some confidence, that in *mano,* unaccompanied by prefixes of sentiment (*sumano* for cheerful, *dummano* for the opposite), we have the mind as active, literally, 'measuring,' judging, valuing. In *citta,* it is more usual to see the man as impressed, affected, with reaction thereto as implicit. More

[1] *Majjhima,* i., 242.

usual, I repeat, for here usage became less consistent, and we find here and there the manifold, the varied, *das Bunte* (to call in German aid, literally meant in the word), of man's affective experience, discarded for very outstanding efforts of will. Certainly it would be a mistake to assume, in *citta*, a passive receptiveness The Indian was too intelligent to look for this in anything wherein was life. For him the word 'action,' *kamma* (Sanskrit, *karman*), is the inclusive genus covering the threefold reaction of deed, word and thought (*kāyakamma, vacīkamma, manokamma*). And so it is a wide range in which *citta* is found: variety, inquisitiveness, instability, impulsiveness, as well as contrast with body (*kāya*, and, much later, with *rūpa*), and as both thinking and thought.

Some translators, *e.g.* Rhys Davids and Lord Chalmers, have preferred to render *citta* usually by 'heart.' And there is much, both in this variety and also in our own older literary diction, to make this plausible. We recall sayings ascribed to Jesus: "Out of the heart proceed evil thoughts," and "Why reason ye in your hearts?" Against this choice is the fact, that *hadaya*, heart, is also, as we saw in the Upaniṣads, given a psychological niche in Indian literature. Thus I found it, in translating Saṃyutta i., complementary to *citta*, "if we had approached any man-in-religion in this way his heart would have burst . . . his *citta* would have lost its balance."[1] And "I'll derange your *citta*, I'll crack your heart," rendering impossible one term only. *Hadaya* may also be said to have its distinctive meaning, as in our 'thoroughly,' or 'synergy.' Thus we read, in the Second Collection (No. 5), in a charming episode, bearing the stamp of

[1] Vol. i., 125, 207.

a true memory, of the interest felt by an ascetic, once a wheelwright, watching a brother in the craft intent on fashioning a tyre, and calling out how thoroughly he is working in the words: 'Methinks he planes from the heart heartily! (*hadayā hadayaṃ maññe tacchati*).' No, in our translating we want 'heart' for *hadaya*.

Now take an equally distinctive use of *citta*:

" Just as an ape in the forest, roaming through the woodland, clutches a bough, lets go and clutches another, so is what is called *citta* . . . ever changing as it arises and ceases."[1]

" Unsteady is the *citta* as any jigging ape."[2]

Note that in this, the Sutta-Nipāta's ape, it is the 'man' who is to the fore, not the mind of him, thus:—

" They grasp, they clutch, then loose their hold again,
As monkey gripping bough, then letting go."[3]

The monkey's inquisitive vagrancies proved of gripping interest in Buddhist tradition. Even when neither ape (nor for that matter, *citta* either) is named in Valliya's vivid poem, of the Monks' Anthology:

" Within the little five-doored hut an ape
Doth prowl, and round and round from door to door
He hies, rattling with blows again, again . . .
Halt, ape! run thou not forth! for thee
'Tis not herein as it was wont to be.
Reason doth hold thee captive. Never more
Shalt roam far hence [in freedom as of yore],"[4]

the Commentator, Dhammapāla, refers to the subject as *citta*, and cites the tree-traversing ape of the Suttas. And later still, Tibetan artists made the ape the symbol

[1] *Saṃyutta*, ii. 95.
[2] *Theragāthā*, ver. 1111.
[3] *Sutta-Nipāta*, ver. 791.
[4] *Theragāthā*, 125 f.

of the mind. Another artist, the poet Tālapuṭa, had the picture probably in mind when he composed his line:

> " O heart (*citta*) gone gadding after things that please,
> I call thee, heart, the breaker of my luck.
> I call thee, heart, despoiler of my lot."[1]

There is perhaps no more interesting achievement in æsthetic psychology than Tālapuṭa's beautiful poem,[2] a joy for the translator. Here I cite it for its recourse, almost throughout, to the device, not infrequent in poetry generally, but, I believe almost if not wholly unique in Pali, of the poet addressing his *citta*, as another might invoke his lyre. Never is *mano* or *viññāṇa* or *ceto* so addressed. And the singer's emotional fervour may serve as my excuse for having rendered *citta* throughout by heart.[3]

In the first sixteen stanzas Tālapuṭa, with, I hold, sounder insight tells of his spiritual yearnings as things he has himself experienced.

> When shall I come to dwell in mountain caves
> Unmated and alone,
> And with the vision gained
> Into impermanence of all that doth become . . .
> Yea, this for me, e'en this, when shall it come to be ?
>
> * * * * *
>
> O when shall I with thought (*sati*) composed intent,
> And clarity of wisdom (*paññā*) come to touch. . . .
>
> * * * * *
>
> O when shall I, hearing the call adown the woods
> Of crested twiceborn peacock (as I lie)
> Within the bosom of the hills,
> Arise and ponder how to win the Deathless—
> Yea, this when shall it come to be ?

---

[1] *Theragáthá*, 213 f. [2] *Ibid.*, 1106 ff.
[3] In my translation *Psalms of the Brethren*, P.T.S. ed.

and so on. The remaining thirty-nine stanzas are an adjuration of his *citta* to 'come to heel' and serve him loyally and strenuously in the Way of Becoming:

> 'Tis many years since I through thee was urged:
> 'Enough for thee the life within the home!'
> How now then, when I've left the world,
> Dost lack, O mind, devotion to the task?
>
> * * * * *
>
> Make welcome way of progress, of egress,
> Whereby to win the Deathless . . . so wast thou
> Wont, O mind, to urge on me.

Here, with a poet's licence, he inverts the relation, making the instrument agent, and the man the tool.

But so did I, as a child of my age, confuse this 'heart' or *citta* with 'this man' giving vent to these yearnings, that I failed to discern the muddle in which he also seems to have been embroiled. I went indeed a little further than did he, or than he could, in using, rarely and *metri causa*, the phrase 'my heart':

> Tell me, my heart, wherein am I at fault?
> (*kincāpi te, citta, virādhitam mayā?*)

which should read literally:

> Wherein again, for thee, O mind, has wrong-been-done by me?

'for thee' meaning, as I have earlier suggested, 'in thy opinion,' a meaning translators mainly ignore. It is our old English 'ethical dative.' The possessive grab of the 'my' has no equivalent in Pali.

I am not finding wholly wrong what I wrote in this work, in 1914, on our seeing "here, as in other literatures, the notion as of one's self and another self dramatizing, so to speak, amongst the flow of individual experience, and resolving the self into plurality" . . . "the poet apostrophizing his past subjective experience as a serial unity or continuum, *citta* being in this case the term evidently current for such a device, to the exclusion of *mano* and *viññāṇa*." It is very possible, that among the Hebrew terms rendered by soul, spirit: *nephesh*, *neshamah*, *ruach*, one only is used where there is apostrophizing. Indeed, Dr. Mattuck confirms me herein.[1] "Where the English version has the word 'soul,' the Hebrew word is, in all but one case, *nephesh* . . . a word which includes all of a man's being . . . is often used for the personal pronoun:—'May I = *nephesh*, die the death of the righteous.'"

I would now only word it all "in words a little different," as Margaretha would say. I do not see in the 'left-in' idiom: "the self upbraids the self," and similar passages, another self. It is one thing for the user of the tool to adjure, swear at, or take counsel, poetically shall we say, with the tool. It is another thing for the man, who feels the ideal self of him urging the actual fallible self of him, expressing this in sober prose. For the Indian, including the first Buddhists, there was here no duality; it was to word a *difference in aspects of the one unity*. I was too concerned to write a modern apologia for the Hīnayānist point of view.

It may next be asked, if, in *citta*, the mind-way or process include, in its meaning, the result or product? Does the word mean both thinking and 'a thought' or 'thoughtṣ'? I think I may say it is as vaguely inclusive as is our own term. The plural is found, but very rarely; with the exception of one phrase, only,

[1] In a letter which I am permitted to quote. Readers not more cognizant of Hebrew than I will read his further information with interest:—"in the phrase '[O] my soul,' the 'my' is indicated by the suffix only: *napshi*, which = 'my *nephesh*.'"

perhaps, in Abhidhamma and later Pali, *e.g.*, the seven thoughts (*satta cittāni*). The masculine plural, *cittā*, occurs in the *Milinda Questions*,[1] but I find the better rendering is that of the agent-noun: mind-ers, men having minds. The important formula I now go on to cite shows a use equally translatable by thinking and by thought (and quite properly by neither).

I refer to the fourfold formula known as the Brahma-vihāra's, literally, the God-abidings. (Here, the meaning of Brahman has been, in the last verse of a little poem about them, preserved in a practically unworsened worth:

brahman etaṃ vihāram idha-m-āhu.
God ! (or 'divine') (is) this state: here has one said.)[2]

I give the formula here to show the use of *citta*, but shall take it up again in the next chapter. "He with amity-consorted mind (*cittena*) abides suffusing each of the quarters . . . below, across everyway by everywhereness the entire world . . . with abounding expanded immeasurable unhate, unillwill suffusing, abides he." This is repeated for a *citta* 'consorting with pity, with goodwill, lit. gladness, and with poise.' Here is certainly no mixing himself up with or into mind. He *with mind* irradiates his fellowmen.

Why *mano*, why *ceto*, why some word for desire, for effort was not used, it is hard to say. *We* should certainly, I think, prescribe such exercises in terms of 'will,' or at least in terms of emotion, as more adequate, a coefficient of ideation being implicit. I can only imagine, that when the formula was fixed upon, the man had got so merged in mind, that it was deemed

[1] P. 110. [2] *Khuddakapāṭha* (last line). Sutta-Piṭaka.

he could 'put himself across,' as the saying goes, to his fellowman as 'thought.' And I could give a *Milinda* parallel to this use of *citta*. I am not sure we are much wiser in speaking, as we do, of 'telepathy,' of which this might be called a very remarkable experiment. Our fitter word were televolition.

I come finally to the third word of important tradition for 'mind':—one more usually rendered now as 'consciousness':—*viññāṇa*. Into that tradition I have already gone at some length,[1] and can here be therefore terser in treatment.

In the Suttas we may find *viññāṇa* as occurring mainly under a threefold heading: (1) the traditional treatment, (2) a generic term for mind-as-impressed and (3) a new and critical treatment, in which it is sought, sharply and intensely, to replace the traditional usage (1) by the aforesaid generic term (2). This is of great interest, for we see the change in values, not, as is usually the case, referred to only as a 'thing accomplished,' but as something coming to be.

And hitherto this has been passed over. To take two recent works: Dr. Har Dayal, in his *Bodhisattva Doctrine*, pleads rightly, that *viññāṇa* actually meant 'the man' as *consciously persisting*, in our sense of 'soul.' But whereas he quotes the two Māra Suttas,[2] of the Third Collection, where, with the body of a suicide lying dead, the clairvoyant goes on seeking the *viññāṇa*, who once made that body 'a body-having-*viññāṇa*' (*saviññāṇakaṃ kāyaṃ*), he ignores the trenchant discourse of the Second Collection, where we see the changed values emerging (Majjhima, No. 38),

[1] Above, p. 75 ff. [2] *Saṃyutta*, i. 120-22; iii. 124.

making it heresy to see in *viññāṇa* a persisting agent or 'soul.' Dr. N. Dutt, in his *Aspects of Mahāyāna Buddhism*, quotes the line from the First and Second Collections:

> *Viññāṇaṃ anidassanaṃ anantaṃ sabbato pabhaṃ* . . .
> *Viññāṇa* invisible infinite on all sides radiant,[1]

as a conditioned thing, disappearing when its conditions disappear, and virtually accepts the late exegesis, that we have here a 'dual' *viññāṇa*, viz., (1) a synonym for nirvana and (2) the fifth *khandha*. But the explanation surely is, that on the one hand the value in the meaning of *viññāṇa* had changed, and on the other the exegesis, cast centuries later into Pali from Singhalese, was written *entirely without historic sense*. It is no excuse, that our modern Indian writers should be without it also. But it is a strange and melancholy thing, that as yet the historic explanation is the one which writers on Buddhism incline to be most loth to adopt. That the very man (*ātmā, puruṣa*) should be described as "invisible, infinite, radiant" is good Upaniṣad teaching of the man as *vijñānamaya*,[2] he, as such, persisting as potentially Brahman Who is *vijñānamayaṃ*.[3]

The treatment of *viññāṇa* as generic, I mean, as coming into the growing analytical vogue, is seen in (*a*) its being classed as, not so much a part, as an aspect of 'mind' in the new *khandha* grouping, (*b*) its being compounded with 'datum' (*dhātu*) as *viññāṇadhātu* in the listing of senses, with *mano* as a sixth, thus: 'the datum of visual awareness (*cakkhuviññāṇadhātu*),' and so on.

[1] P. 148. [2] *Cf.* above, pp. 73-7.
[3] *Bṛhad. Up.*, 4, 4, 5.

There is another context, where *viññāṇa* occurs as *dhātu*, as one of six. First, the four elements, then space, then *viññāṇadhātu*. The grouping occurs, I believe, but twice in the Nikāyas,[1] and is probably old. It, so to speak, places man (*viññāṇa*) as a cosmic postulate among other five such, as not of one locus only in the cosmos, as having, like elements and space, a birthright in the worlds. But the later exegetic values had 'no use for' him as such; it turned him away from the 'worlds,' from 'becomings' (*bhavā*). Hence the Commentator *is not interested and passes by* with a mere word of paraphrase.

The third treatment of *viññāṇa* is, I repeat, of great historic interest, and should be studied. The Founder is made to arraign and sharply censure a monk (Sāti, a low-caste man, a fisherman) for having said, that he, the Bhagavan, taught, that *viññāṇa* "fared on, ran on as persistently identical."[2] The Sutta, which is compiled in a singularly vivid emphatic diction, makes the Founder, when this broadcast is repeated to him, summon Sāti, and elicit (as is the usual Sutta-procedure) a confession that it is true. The Founder then asks him: "What is that *viññāṇa*?" Sāti replies: "He, sir, is the speaker, the 'worther' (*vedeyyo*), who experiences here and there the result of deeds good and bad."

It is of interest to note, that the same definition is given, in the second Sutta of this Collection, of the self:—"That who for me is the self, the speaker, the 'worther,' who experiences here and there the result of deeds good and bad: now for me this self, permanent, stable, continuous, not liable to change, will as a con-

[1] *Digha*, iii. 247; *Majjhima*, iii. 31, 240.
[2] *Majjhima*, No. 38.

tinuity persist." And this is stigmatized as a jungle of (false) opinion. *Viññāṇa* then is here seen coming to bear the *later* meaning of consciousness, and no longer of self, soul, man.

Sāti is thereupon called foolish (or futile, *moghapurisa*) as forgetting, that the Teacher had told in many ways that *viññāṇa* was effect of a cause, and did not arise, without conditions. Sāti, silenced and in confusion, is then, in the usual way, talked-at through the listening disciples--a method which, if true, was possibly resorted to 'out of compassion.' These are put through a searching catechism as to how, because of sensations, sense-impressions (viz., visual and other *viññāṇa*), arise, mind-*viññāṇa*, too, arising, "conditioned by mind (*mano*)-cum-things (*dhammā*'s)." "See it, monks, as 'This is something that has become (*bhūtaṃ*).'" 'Become' even as a growing, not a static, thing comes to pass. So impossible was it for that age,[1] ay, and for more than that age, to conceive of the very self, *viññāṇa*, or man as also 'becoming' in his own inherently divine way, not the becoming-cum-decay of body and mind.

The early Upaniṣads had shown a supreme creator: Brahman, ātman, when creating, becoming thereby 'in his own inherently divine way' not less imperfect, but *other, more manifold in new ways*. And they had shown the man, in his potentially divine, less developed, as yet unconsummated ways, also becoming other, more manifold, and less imperfect. But dimness had come over this great vision: *Bhava*, 'becoming,' was still listed as an epithet of the Highest,[2] but the victorious

[1] The decadent age when this Sutta was compiled in its present form.

[2] *Cf.* above, p. 40.

term was and remained the inadequate *akṣara*, 'imperishable.' Maintenance, not growth, filled up the concept of the Divine, and maintenance meant persistence (*ṭhiti*), static being (*sat*), and not new coming-to-be.

The conversation goes on with an appending of passages from other Suttas, betraying its later composite origin:—the 'raft' simile is quoted, not introduced or explained; stock passages about four sustenances (*āhārā*), and the rising of human states from conditions (*paṭicca-samuppāda*). And we have one curious result, that the *viññāṇa*, which has to be accepted as an effect, is, as an *āhārā*, adduced as one of four general *conditions* of effect—a matter which doubtless could have been explained, but is not.

When in much later scholastic literature we see an association between *viññāṇa* and the dying person still lingering, it is not because *viññāṇa* is actually taught as being the person-in-survival. It is then taught as "rebirth-consciousness" (*paṭisandhi-viññāṇa*) or as "decease-consciousness" (*cuti-viññāṇa*), but there is no longer a teaching of anyone passing on. There is only an arising, in a new complex, somehow come together, of the result or effect of the latest *viññāṇa* on this side. Not the body alone was dying; the very Man in this decadent thought was dead. And in this Sutta he is being bled to death; the outcome of certainty about the mere conditioned nature of any *viññāṇa* is stated as resulting in the absence of any curiosity as to one's past, present or next state of life, as if no thought were to be taken as to personal responsibility. This is at odds with the teaching in most of the Suttas: in these men are ever being warned, that thought for future welfare should govern their behaviour here. Yet the incuriosity is not prescribed only in this context.[1]

The Sutta then gives a passage, unique, I believe, in the Piṭakas, about man's rebirth on earth as the result of parentage *plus* the intervention of a 'spirit' called *gandharva* (Pali: *gandhabba*). In this tradition, if such it was, I see the advent of the soul, self or man, encased in the invisible 'subtle body' of Indian belief, into the mother in the fifth month of fœtal life. It seems dragged in in this connection, but is not so. In the First Collection's Suttanta on Causation (No. xi), the advent of *viññāṇa* is said to be thus: "'Were *viññāṇa* not to descend into the mother, would name-and-form become constituted therein?' 'No, sir.' 'Were *viññāṇa*, after having descended into the mother, to become extinct, would name-and-form come to birth in this thusness (*itthattāya*)?' 'No, sir.'" And so we get the traditional meaning of *viññāṇa*, as man-surviving, *logically extended* to include man-pre-existing. I say 'logically,' only because I have not elsewhere found the term so used.

In this connection I have yet to comment on the survival in Buddhism of the Vedic term *nāma-rūpa*, name-and-form. The convenience, for Buddhism, of a term for 'the man,' in which the man himself is pushed out, is obvious. It remained archaic, scholastic or literary, a term of the formula; yet it survived for centuries, because of that convenience or because of its inclusion in a longlived formula, or because of both.

[1] *Cf.* . . . The reader can follow up this account in Chalmers's *Further Dialogues*, *Digha XV.*; *Saṃy.* ii., 26; S.B.B., V. But he will need to check certain translator's liberties with the text: 'organism,' *e.g.*, for 'become,' 'perception' for *viññāṇa*, etc.

Thus it was very useful to Buddhaghosa's nihilism.[1] The editors of the Third Collection also made an attempt, as we saw Sanatkumāra doing, to unfold a more in the 'name': "What is name and form? Experiencing,[2] perceiving, intending, contact, work of mind: this is called 'name.' The four great elements and the form derived from them: this is called 'form.' This is the name, this is the form, called name-and-form"—a context repeated by the editors of the Second Collection (No. 9).

We shall be keeping closer to historic truth if we do not, in these five terms, see more than quasi-synonyms of what could be meant by 'nāma': if we refrain from seeing in them anything meriting the name of careful analysis. All of them in later books have undergone more careful weighing, as we shall see. 'Perceiving,' for instance, (*saññā*) is used with much elasticity in the Suttas: it can be rendered here by 'awareness,' there by 'recognition,' and, in one set of formulas concerning what can scarcely be called other than figments of monastic imagination, we meet with, here a sphere of 'Not-*saññā*,' there a sphere of neither *saññā* nor not-*saññā*.[3] The nearest Sutta-approach to a definition runs thus: "Why do you say *saññā*? Because one perceives (*sañjānāti*). What does one perceive? One perceives blue-green (*nīla*), yellow, red, white."[4]

To return to the compound term *nāma-rūpa*: the formula to which the term owes its long upkeep in Buddhism is that famous as the 'Uprising-because of,' or Causal Chain. This was an application of the interest,

[1] *Visuddhi-magga*, ch. xviii., *e.g.* especially p. 593: "that he may the more easily put away this worldly concept of a being, a person."

[2] *Vedanā*. See below, p. 290 f.

[3] *E.g.*, *Dīgha*, iii. 224.

[4] *Saṃyutta*, iii. 86.

current in early Buddhist days, in causation as true for the mind, no less than for external things. The application sought to show that, causal uniformity being reliable, any psychic effect can be stopped by stopping the psychic cause. Hence it was important to get clear what, in mind, was the cause *x* of the effect *y*. Starting with 'ill' as the inevitably final effect in life, this, it was held, was conditioned by the three: death, old age, birth; birth was conditioned by the fact of becoming, this by the 'fuel' for becoming, namely grasping, experiencing, contact, sensation, and the fact of there coming to be a *nāma-rūpa*: each of these terms being affirmed to be the condition (*paccaya*) of the next. Nor is this all. *Viññāṇa*, pronounced, in the new way we have seen imposed, to be merely the result of sensation, is here made to precede sensation in this causal chain, and to be at once the cause and the effect of name-and-form. Sāriputta is made to say this to his colleague, also a learned brahman, Koṭṭhita.[1] Koṭṭhita calls out: 'How can such things be?' Well, listen, replies Sāriputta; 'even a wise man can learn from a parable. If you stand up two sheaves of reeds one leaning on the other, you will admit that neither will keep upright alone?' 'True.' Thus is name-and-form conditioned by *viññāṇa*, and *vice versa*.

That the *possibility* of adjusting the pull of gravitation in two lumps of matter *warranted the certainty* of this intercausal relation between immaterial *viññāṇa* and the immaterial *plus* material *nāmarūpa* did not apparently cause the Sutta editors a moment's doubt. I have a greater respect for the intelligence of those two eminent disciples, than to concede they ever were more than figureheads, borrowed to lend lustre, long

[1] *Saṃyutta*, ii. 80.

after their time, to such lame reasoning. Nay, I can hear them gently and benignantly laughing over themselves used as puppets, mixed with the woe they must have felt over the travesty of what they actually had taught.

I am not prepared to guess even, when the Cause-formula was first mooted, or whether, when it was drafted as such, *viññāṇa* could yet mean 'the man.' There is still, in modern Burma, the tradition, that the formula was meant to cover, not this life only, but also past lives and the next life.[1] In that case we have this life commencing with *viññāṇa* as if from the previous life "descending into the mother," in the old Sutta I cited, and there taking effect as name and form. But if *viññāṇa* no longer meant the man, but only mind (where alone man or self could be "got at"),[2] we may perhaps trace how, in a day of strong psychological preoccupation, man's life-development was worded in terms of mind. It was the advent on earth of a man-as-mind taking birth as just mind and body.

1 *Compendium of Philosophy*, p. 263.
2 *Cf.* above, p. 234.

CHAPTER XIII

PSYCHOLOGY IN THE NIKĀYAS (*Continued*)

3. MIND (*Continued*)

It may serve, I repeat, as a guide—in my opinion a true guide—to a better understanding of the evolution of Indian religious thought in Buddhism, if we never lose sight of the influence wrought over it by the growing vogue of mental analysis. Few things are so noteworthy, in the history of that thought, as the growing tendency, in both Brahmanic and Buddhist Sayings, to speak in terms of introspection, and to find new terms wherewith to do so. We have seen this in such terms as *buddhi*, *ahaṃkāra*, intuition (*pratibodha*), and inward vision (*avṛttacakṣu*).[1] In Buddhist Sayings these terms never took root. *Buddhi* is extremely rare:[2] *Ahaṃkāra* is not intelligently discussed as a sort of *māyā* (illusion) in work of mind; it is simply, with a twin term: *mamaṃkāra*:—making of a 'mine'—repulsed as a hindrance in Jhāna or 'musing' (whereof more later). 'Awakening' is, in the Pali *paṭibuddha*, simply physical, and I have not found in Pali the 'averted eye.' But the Suttas show a marked growth in a number of terms for both mind-ways and interest in this inner world—terms which are either, in the Upaniṣads, non-existent or uncultivated.

I refer to such terms as mean 'introspection' and 'constant awareness,' 'thinking' as an attending-to

[1] Chapters VII., VIII.

[2] In the absence of a needed Concordance, I have so far only found it in *Digha*, iii., 165, and in commentarial literature.

and a pondering-over: 'reflection' 'inferring' and 'scrutiny': 'knowledge' and 'wisdom' as marking different phases of cognition: 'radical' or 'systematic considering,' and a growing effort to describe spiritual effort in terms of *mental process.*

The first of these terms is of especial historical interest. It is *sati*, the Pali equivalent for the *smara*, 'memory,' which is included in that 'more' in 'name' which we found unfolded in the Chāndogya Upaniṣad. *Sati*, in the Suttas, is not wholly covered by 'memory.' To express the act of recollection, prefixes: *anu-* and *pati-* are used. Nor for that matter is *smara* adequately rendered by 'memory.' In this context, as in all Sutta contexts, it is evident that some such factor as 'attention' is meant. Thus, in the Upaniṣad, *smara* is called requisite for the 'hearing, thinking, understanding' of one who, in a meeting, is being addressed. And since, in the Pali books, 'attention' is required for other terms, the word 'mindfulness,' introduced, I believe, by Rhys Davids, is, on the whole, the best. It is even better than 'introspection'; it *includes this.* It denotes the requisite condition for efficient remembrance, or thought of any kind. It is lucidity and alertness of consciousness, whether externally or internally directed, but with special stress on the latter direction. It expresses that heedful thoughtful awareness which is the opposite of mental distractedness, and the essential preliminary to deliberation—a stress which finds picturesque wording in a well-known Sutta: that of the 'first aid to the wounded man' (*Majjhima*, No. 106), where *sati* is likened to the surgeon's probe. In Jhāna it was more especially a 'listening,' a 'listening-in' of a psychic kind.[1]

[1] *Cf.* below, Chap. XV.

The adjectives of the agent: *sato* and *satimā*, are often used in appreciation of the worthy man and are then very usually accompanied by the term *sampajāno*: 'he who knows,' *saṃ*: constantly (or well) and *pa*-: more or further. It is a difficult term to translate, but to exegetists perhaps so well known, that they pass it over—if that be the true reason for their silence. Definitions of terms are rare in the Suttas, being reserved for the Third Piṭaka, the Abhidhamma, but in the former there is at least a *referring* of both these terms taken together:—"What is the sustenance (or condition: *āhāra*) of control of the senses? '*Sati-sampajañña*[1] . . .' 'the sustenance of these?' 'Methodical thinking (*yoniso manasikāro*) . . .' 'the sustenance of this?' 'Faith.'" But more informative to psychological inquiry than such juxtapositions is the 'object-lesson' on the term in the Sutta where the Founder is shown admonishing his son and disciple Rāhula, who has obviously, to his father's knowledge, been 'deliberately lying.' The footbath is half upset, wholly so, inverted, with the comments: "Don't you see, Rāhula, how lessened, how empty, how chucked away, how topsy-turvy is the monkhood of one who sees no shame in deliberate lying (*n'atthi sampajāna-musāvāde lajjā*[2])?"

An admonition early immortalized in Asoka's Rock-Edicts.

The importance of *sati*, as showing the influence of current mental analysis on moral and spiritual training in early Buddhism, appears in the fourfold category, running throughout the Suttas, called the Four Presences of Mindfulness (*saty-upaṭṭhāna*, corrupted to

[1] The noun of *sampajāno*. *Anguttara*, v. 115.
[2] *Majjhima*, No. 61.

satippaṭṭhāna).[1] In this, the disciple is enjoined to reflect consecutively on body (*kāya*, not *rūpa*), experiencing (or feeling, *vedanā*), mind (*citta*, not *mano*, not *viññāṇa*), and things (*dhammā*). The simplest statement of the evoking this fourfold *sati* is, *e.g.*, in the Sangīti Suttanta, where it heads the list of 'fours': "Herein let a monk as to the body . . . as to experiences . . . as to mind . . . as to things continue so to look on these (taken separately), that he abides ardent, fully aware (*sampajāno*) and mindful, overcoming both the hankering and the dejection common in the world."

It is impossible to judge with any precision of the stage in the life of 'Sakya,' when the Four were first drafted. They are cited, in the touching poem, ascribed to Ānanda, in the Anthology, when mourning in loneliness the passing of his Chief:

> " And is the comrade passed away,
> And is the Master gone from hence ?
> No better friend is left methinks,
> Than to mount guard o'er deed and sense.
> They of the older time are gone.
> The new men suit me not at all.
> Alone today this child doth brood,
> Like nesting-bird when rain doth fall."

Lines 3 and 4 read:

> *n'atthi etādisaṃ mittaṃ yathā kāyagatā sati* (1035).

And it seems a pretty poor sort of comfort, such as I for one cannot hear Ānanda falling back upon, much less having been by " the Comrade " enjoined to do so. It seems, indeed, some guarantee of early drafting, that it has been put into Ānanda's mouth. Yet, if we turn to the Fours lists in the Fourth Collection—lists in which I see rather sources for materials elabo-

[1] Called in the *Divyāpadāna*, *smṛti-upasthāna*.

9

rated in the First and Second Collections, than bits detached from these—we see that these four *sati*-practices are *missing from the Fours*! They first occur in the Fives, of course, not as titular, but incidentally only, and subsequently. The only occurrence of the term *satipaṭṭhāna* in the Fours is almost an anticipation of a formula not yet drafted: "By himself he makes mindfulness present, and causes another to practise in making it present."[1] Is not this, taken together, suggesting to us that, when the Fours were (orally) collected in the gradual compiling of the Fourth Collection, the formula known as the Four Presences of Mindfulness was not yet drafted? I know that, according to the Long Suttanta of the Founder's Passing in the First Collection, this formula is recorded as one of the 'things' (*dhammā*) the Order was enjoined, "having learnt them by heart, to practise, make-become, teach often for the persistence of the godly life and the welfare of many."[2] And there too, in a preceding section, is Ānanda recommended to practise the formulated *sati*.[3]

But I am not hoping to carry with me readers who, because they find certain formulas inserted in the great patchwork, such as this Suttanta admittedly is, are content to accept such insertions as actually spoken in such a form at such a date. Only they who lack the rudiments of historical sense would be thus content. I cannot hear a dying veteran, who had, if we go by the records, just bidden his disciples seek guidance and refuge in the Man or self or soul, and in His inner monition (*dharma*), "and in nothing else," go on to point to a resolving that Man into four bundles of bodily and mental states, the Man himself lost to view. It

[1] Vol. ii. 218. [2] *Dīgha*, ii. 119. [3] *Ibid.*, 100.

is true, that if we see, in that source of guidance and refuge, merely the 'self' *as we use the word*,[1] the case is altered, but it is altered historically for the worse, as I have tried to show.

With the four items in the formula I have dealt already in part: the fourth: *dhammā*, that is, *dhamma* in the plural, we may consider a moment. Psychologically the term is of interest, and the various renderings of the plural form: as 'truths,' 'states,' phenomena (*Erscheinungen*), etc., betray that its complexity has been felt. We may at once dismiss the notion, put forward in Stcherbatzky's *Central Conception of Buddhism*, that in 'dhamma' we have a metaphysical monadic unit. *This is valid for no period in Buddhist thought save its mediæval stage.* There is nothing of the kind that can be critically shown as entering into the Piṭakan idea of *dhamma*. And it is with this idea alone that we are here concerned.

It is fairly clear that *dhamma*, singular and *dhammā*, plural had a different value in the Piṭakas. We are ourselves not unfamiliar with such a difference, *e.g.* in such words as will, wills (legal), interest and interests, and the like. But the difference need not be pressed too far. If *dharma* implied an 'oughtness': something to be borne (in honour, in memory) and *dhammā* meant 'things,' whether material or of the mind, there was not therefore nothing of implicit 'oughtness' in the plural use. There is, in our 'thing,' an analogous 'oughtness.' We have but to consider the use of the word (*ting*, *þing*) in our Northern tongues for meetings, political and other, to consider what it is 'fit to arrange.' And as to elasticity in use, we need but compare the Johnsonian definition of thing as "not a person".

[1] *Cf.* above, p. 206.

with his Shakespearean quotations of 'thing' *used for a person*, both in honour and in dishonour.

In the formula, *dhammā* are explained as beings 'things taught, to be learnt,' herein agreeing with the occasional use of "things" in the Bible:—"if a soul sin through ignorance concerning things which ought not to be done" (*Lev.* 4, 2), and "I have uttered things too wonderful for me" (*Job* 42, 3); and "Thou hast shewed thy people hard things" (*Pss.* 60, 3). And those 'things taught' are specified as five hindrances, five *khandha*'s, the world of sense, factors of enlightenment, four truths:—the carefully prescribed path of category and formula.

As meaning material things, it is not easy to find *dhammā* used. As affix, *-dhamma* is frequent, meaning 'having the quality of': *e.g. maraṇa-dhammo* (man is), a dying-thing, or 'liable to die.' With the growing interest in mind-analysis, it was inevitable, especially in spiritual topics, that *dhammā* should come to mean preponderantly 'things-of-mind,' mental experiences. But this does not, need not, for us, in view of our own scriptures, render less advisable the translating of *dhammā* by 'things,' wherever possible.

Mind-ways, not necessarily introspective, find frequent expression in the complementary terms *vitakka* and *vicāra*.[1] The former is the usual word in the Suttas for active work of mind as turned on to an object, for restless discursive intellection. Without the prefix, it meant argument, dialectic, logic. And *takka* we find depreciated when compared with the *dassana*, or vision—we might call it intuition—not won through intellect. More of this later.[2] *Vicāra* meant persistence in the thinking, the onset of which

[1] Pron. *vichāra*. [2] Chap. XVIII.

was indicated by *vitakka*. But the two are not so explained till the Abhidhamma definitions were compiled.

In the terms I have called reflection, inference and scrutiny, we have the prefix of repetition and collection, *pati-*: *paccavekkhati*, *paṭisañcikkhati*. Both words belong to the vocabulary of vision, as do several other Piṭaka terms, Buddhism in this respect multiplying such as had been or were being used by the Upaniṣads:—*anupassati*, *samanupassati*, *samanupekkhati* and others. The first-named: 'reflection,' had the same double usage that we have, as this context shows:—The Founder is recorded as admonishing his son Rāhula: " 'What is the use of a mirror (*ādāsa*)?' 'To reflect, sir.' 'Even so must we reflect and reflect in all our work of body, speech or thought, namely, this that I want to do would be harmful to myself or to others.' "

The second term, inference, which came, in Indian psychology, to stand for all mind-work exclusive of perception, *anumāna* (*anuminitabba*) is all but absent in the Nikāyas, albeit the act of inference is clearly indicated.[1]

The other term—I have called it 'scrutinizing,' but without insisting that this is the only fit rendering—is, in a list of complementary terms we may safely call relatively early,[2] opposed to a term of great interest, which I shall consider presently: the causative of 'to become.' In this list there are three versions of contrasted definitions of two terms of very great significance in the history of Buddhism: *paṭisankhāna*, *bhāvanā*. The former is a Pali variant of our old

[1] See *Saṃyutta*, i. 56; *Majjhima*, i. 96; *cf. ibid.*, ii. 135, 158.

[2] *Anguttara*, i., p. 52 f.

friend *sānkhya*, meaning literally a re-computing. Together with *vibhajana*, or dividing-up, it would seem to be a word coming into use for the growing interest in, and awareness of, analysis of, man's inner world. And this 'computing' is described as a process of *paṭisañcikkhati*. In all three versions, this is a constant factor; the other, '*bhāvanā*,' is each time a variant: riddance, making-become, *jhāna*. The constant element is (*a*) the discernment that unworthy behaviour in deed, word and mind sows evil result here and hereafter, (*b*) the decision to renounce all such and 'make-become' worthy behaviour.

The phrase cited above (p. 256) 'radical thought' calls for comment. Literally translated, *yoniso manasikāro* is 'from the matrix-mindworking.' It is often used in the Suttas as indicating the only way of thought which could bring about desirable moral results. The Commentarial definition of *yoniso* is *upāyena*, 'by method, systematically.' I am not satisfied that we have here the original point of meaning. The Upaniṣads do not help us; it is very possibly a Sakyan invention. But I incline to think the sounder interpretation for original Sakya would be to seek the warrant of true thinking, not in the rationalistic way of induction 'from the root of the matter,' but in the way of Immanent religion, namely, in thinking which was guided by the inner control (*antaryāmin*) of Dharma, thus 'from the root of the *Man*.'

The word 'work of mind,' in later ages, underwent interesting specialization, whereof more later. In the Suttas it is not specialized, that is, when without the *yoniso*. As we have seen, it is given as part of the content of *nāma* (p. 251), in *nāmarūpa*, but that only meant it was an equivalent term, not a specific quality.

These are not all the new wealth of mind-terms emerging in the Suttas. There are also *vicaya* and *vīmaṃsā*, the *vi-* indicating discursive intellection, the stems, respectively, a heaping up, and a derivative of 'to think,' the Vedic form *mīmaṃsa* never occurring in the Suttas. *Cintā*, again, though rare, makes an interesting entry in the context: "There are four unthinkables (*a-cinteyyāni*), which may not be thought about (*na cintetabbāni*), thinking about which would be for him madness and disaster: the wisdom-range of the wise (*buddha*), the musing range of the muser (*jhāyin*), the result of the deed, thinking about the worlds."[1]

As to the reference to different values in terms for 'knowledge' and the 'wit' that is 'wisdom,' by these I mean the words *ñāṇa*, with *ñāṇa-dassana*, *aññā* (literally the stem *ñā*, to know, with the prefix *ā*, this being equal to the German prefix *er-*), and *paññā* (*ñā* with prefix *pa-*). *Dassana* is another vision-term for knowledge, meaning literally 'seeing.' The use of the compound 'knowledge-and-vision' was ever growing in Pali literature. So was another word for insight: *vipassanā*, possibly unknown in the early decades.

Ñāṇa meant just knowledge in either a next to hand, or a lofty sense. Thus the thirsty man comes to a well and sees water. He knows, he sees, as the old religious refrain ran; he had *ñāṇa*. But he cannot get at the water.[2] On the other hand the term describing the breaking in on the muser of new insight is also *ñāṇa*. Thus the refrain in one version of the new message inspiring the Founder is described as: "Coming-to-be! Coming-to-be!—at that thought there arose in him a vision into things not called before to mind, and

[1] *Anguttara*, ii. 80. [2] *Saṃyutta*, ii. 83.

knowledge (*ñāṇa*) arose, wisdom (*paññā*), lore (*vijjā*), light (*āloko*) arose."[1]

Aññā, meaning rather coming-to-know or learning, used as such in agent-form: *aññātar*, learner, emerges, in Vinaya and Sutta Piṭakas, as what might be rendered as gnosis, or 'saving knowledge.' I drew attention to this earlier.[2] The compounds, just emerging in the Suttas (in their prose, not in verse), are in the Abhidhamma drawn up in a category. Thus: "There are these three faculties: the not learnt I shall learn (*aññāt' aññāssāmīt'indriya*); knowing (*aññ-indriya*); the faculty of 'one who has come to know' (*aññātāv'-indriya*). In the three Sutta references, the only one where there is more than a mere list, the Itivuttaka (53),[3] it is of interest to note, that the verses following the list do not recognize the three as fixed terms:

> To the pupil training, in the straight way walking,
> By ending (of his sins) first cometh knowledge (*ñāṇaṃ*).
> Straight follows gnosis (*aññā*); then, by that gnosis freed,
> To such doth knowledge (*ñāṇaṃ*) come to be. . . .

This justifies the rendering of *aññā* by 'learning,' 'coming to know.'

Of interest also is it to witness, how the 'idea-about,' in abstract noun and list, is submerging the 'man'; the man who in Immanence was so much in a More, is dwindling to a man in the Less. The first of the three in the category—constituting as it does a noble legend to inscribe over any school portal—and the last 'stay put' in the triad, for any practical use they may ever have had; the middle term, the manless abstract, occurs not rarely, in such contexts as were quoted above. But in all these variants let the reader

[1] *Dīgha*, ii. 33.
[2] Above, p. 225.
[3] *Dīgha*, iii. 219; *Saṃyutta*, v. 204.

not overlook the emphasis in them conferred by the prefix *añ-*, *i.e.* *ā*, the German *er-*. *We* have to express this by either learning, or by coming-to-know. How much this idea of knowledge as a progressive advance meant, or was coming-to-mean, in the early Upaniṣads, I have tried to show. How much it meant in *original* Sakya it is my constant effort to try to show. I shall return to it.

In the word *paññā* we have interesting confirmation of this. Here, to the stem *ñā* is added the dynamic particle *pa*, from *pra-*, to which Whitney assigned the meanings 'forward, onward, forth, fore.'[1] The high worth in the term shown in the early Upaniṣads is strenuously maintained in the Suttas, and persists in the treatise Visuddhi-magga of the fifth century A.D., this being possibly due to the traditional respect in which the triad *sīla*, *samādhi*, *paññā*, as comprising the whole teaching of Buddhism, was yet held. In the Abhidhamma no term has attracted so many accessory terms or quasi-equivalents as has *paññā*. In the Suttas no term is more prominently defined. The 'eye of *paññā*' or *paññā*-vision is thus described:

> The eye of flesh, the *deva*-eye,
> And eye of wisdom best of all (*anuttaraṃ*).[2]

"He who has *paññā* is said 'to know' (*pajānāti*); what does he know? That 'this' is ill; this, the cause of ill," etc. "We speak of *viññāṇa*:—in how many ways is there *viññāṇa*? One is aware; of what? It is pleasant, it is painful, it is neither. Are the two mutually involved or separate? And is it possible, considering them apart, to declare that they are different? That is not possible; they are mutually

[1] *Sanskrit Grammar*, § 1077. [2] *Itivuttaka*, § 61.

involved. What one discerns, of that one is aware; of what one is aware, that one discerns. What then distinguishes them? *Paññā* is to be made to become; *viññāṇa* is to be understood."[1]

Vedanā (experiencing) and *saññā* (perceiving) are also stated here to be bound up with and not different from *viññāṇa*. And then: "In the sense of something distinguishable from the five senses by pure *mano*-awareness, what is knowable (*ñeyya*)? That space is infinite; that awareness is infinite; and that 'there is nothing whatever.' By what does one know (*pajānāti*) the knowable? One knows by the eye of *paññā*? What is the aim of *paññā*? *Paññā* has the aim of higher knowledge (*abhi-ññā*), thorough knowledge (*pari-ññā*), and of eliminating (*pahāna*)."

From the tendency to think in negative terms, and from the shrinkage in the outlook on life characterizing Indian thought in the latter pre-Christian centuries, the term *pahāna* ('riddance' often renders it well) played a great part in early Buddhism. It is more religious than logical. *Abhiññā* came to have a more specialized meaning, that of 'psychic' knowledge—one in which it is, by no means exclusively, used within the Suttas.

"All," comments Buddhaghosa, "are modes of knowing; only the prefix is different." He then by a simile which, whether original or not, he uses in at least three of his works, compares *saññā*, *viññāṇa*, *paññā* to the different reaction provoked, at sight of the precious metals, in a child, a citizen, and a metallurgical expert. The first sees in them coloured objects; the second sees *also* in them tokens representing utilities to be got; the third is *also* able to judge as

[1] *Majjhima*, No. 43.

to their origin and their fashioner. Thus *viññāṇa* includes the work of perception and also general notions. But *paññā* includes both these, and also " by an uplift of energy attains to a revelation of the Way."

A Commentator was bound to be exegetical. But the concluding clause is a deeply interesting comment on the statement above: '*paññā* is to be developed.' The verb—*bhāvetabbā*—is literally 'must be made to become.' It is constantly used in connection with the meditative self-training of the Buddhist student. With it may be compared similar terms—*anubrūheti*, *vaḍḍheti*, develop, make to grow—used in connection with mental culture.

In their arising is involved creative, constructive effort. And this is intuition or insight, that effort of " intellectual sympathy by which the mind can place itself within the mobile reality " of things.[1] *Paññā* was not simply exercise of thought on matters of general knowledge and practice, nor was it dialectic, nor desultory reverie. It was intelligence diverted by—or rather *as*—concentrated volition, from lower practical issues till, as a fusion of sympathy, synthesis, synergy, it 'made to become' that spiritual vision which had not been before.

So I wrote over twenty years ago, and here I am content to repeat myself. Not because I am content to stop where I did, but because I may, by repeating these lines, better show where they, in showing promise, fall short.

Let me first say, that by the foregoing I see in 'wisdom,' Rhys Davids's rendering, a word nearer to *paññā* than 'insight' or than 'reason.' *Paññā*, as

[1] Bergson, *Introduction to Metaphysics*.

I rightly point out, is no mere intellectual 'convolution' of thought; India, and especially the early Sakyans, sought in it to show the very man-as-growing; not only as 'coming-to-know,' but, also as *coming-to-be*. But wisdom too—as my master, Croom Robertson said—"is a term of practical import; is not mere insight, but conduct guided by insight . . . good conduct is wise; wise conduct is good."[1] And in the practical import is nothing static, but the advance such as, in Jesus, we read, kept pace with the growth (*proekopsis*) in stature of body.[2]

But the growth I saw in *paññā* was too much the dawning of vision *in the mind of the contemplator*, too little the actual becoming in the contemplator himself. If there is, in the new word of Gotama, any advance on the teaching of contemporary brahmans, it is that, in the figure of the Way or Wayfaring, he taught man as essentially not 'being' but becoming, a 'becoming-er.' And in *paññā* or *prajñā* he had, and his mates had, a term that was not just coming-to-know, but mainly a coming-to-live that was wiser. *Paññā* expressed not only the spiritual 'vision' that was new, but the life which was the object of that vision, the living man who was growing.

There is a term to which I have repeatedly drawn attention, often used in the Suttas to intensify the verb 'he knows' (*pajānāti*): the word *yathābhūtaṃ*. This is not a Vedic term; the vocabulary of the Upaniṣads knows it not; it peeps out in the Mahābhārata; it may be called, more than most, a Buddhist creation.

Our equivalent would be, when it occurs with 'to know,' 'knowing things as they really are.' And we are reminded of Matthew Arnold's earnest insist-

[1] *Elements of Psychology*, 1896. [2] *Luke* ii. 52.

ence on disinterestedness of vision; when he tried to raise the ideal and mission of criticism in literature as an "endeavour to see things as in themselves they really are"; of his warning that "whoever sets himself to see things as they are will find himself in a very small circle"; his one thing needful for this being "simple lucidity of mind" (in other words, *sati*).[1]

But the Pali phrase is "to know things (to 'see things' also occurs) *as they have become.*" Is there no significance in this being the term we find, and not such a word as *yathā-santo*: as they *are*? "See you, Sāriputta, that it has become? See you, Sāriputta, that it has become?" is the surely not accidental, or invented repetition! "Yea, master, it has become," is the response, "by right wisdom one sees it as it has become."[2] I do not wish to force the awareness, in this idiom, into life and the worlds as a 'becoming.' The past participle *bhūta* is, by itself, common enough in Vedic literature. But when we find time's three periods worded in the Upaniṣads as "what has become, is becoming and will become" (*yad bhūtac-ca bhavac-ca bhaviśyac-ca*), we feel we are in a world with a more dynamic perspective of reality than one in which this is worded as 'what has been, is and will be.' Or, for that matter, than the later Buddhist world, where that dynamic perspective has been dropped, and time is worded only as 'the gone by, the not come, the re-uprisen' (*atītam-anāgata-paccuppanna*). However, I do not expect to carry readers along with me yet. We have adopted an evolutionary view in the world of matter; we confess in education a conviction, that

1 Discussed in my 'Seeing Things as they really are,' *Buddhism*, Rangoon, 1903.

2 *Saṃyutta*, ii. 47.

mind as well as body is a becoming. But we, with India, have yet to discern, as the very essence of the self or soul or man-in-man, that he, in a slower but perennial growth, is one who is becoming, growing, evolving.

For the present, the point here submitted is that, in the foregoing, it has been shown, that the vogue, in the early centuries of Buddhism, of preoccupation with analysis of mind, resulted in an interesting, unmistakable increment in terms for 'mind-ways,' or 'mindings.' These two last terms are fitter than 'mind'—a dangerous word as tending to be conceived as substance more than as process; as an 'is,' rather than a 'becoming'; and to be used as a dummy-man. Every one of the mind-terms cited is process or way rather than state. As to a new awareness of inner-world *processes*, that too is a Buddhist development, but discussion of it will more fitly come when we have done with terms for distinguishable *factors* in processes.

CHAPTER XIV

PSYCHOLOGY IN THE NIKĀYAS (*Continued*)

4. TERMS AND CONCEPTS OF WILL

In the Pali and Jain scriptures we find, as we do not find in other Indian scriptures, at least of early date, the triplet: action of body, action of speech, action of mind (*kāyakamma, vacīkamma, manokamma*); or, as we more concisely but less adequately say, word, thought and deed. We know that the triplet is a feature in the early Persian thought which we associate with the work of Zarathustra, but that we do not find it in the early Upaniṣads, nor in the Bible, which does not get beyond the linking of word and deed, nor in the plays called of Shakespeare, albeit in the Book of Common Prayer it emerges. When this threefold expression of man's activity as such (*-kamma*) came into use in the Sakyan usage we do not know. Its occurrence in the Piṭakas may be called fitful; thus it is frequent early in the Fourth Collection, and early in the Third; it is rare in the First and Second Collections, and, in the last named, we also get word and deed given alone. But wherever the triad does occur, it occurs as an unquestioned and accepted way of wording. I incline to see in it, as Indian, an idiom of original Sakyan teaching.

There is one important branch of Piṭaka teaching where it is not brought to the front—a branch where we should have looked for it. This is in the field of the analysis of man as expressing himself in body and mind. As such he is scheduled otherwise, viz. as having 'a beminded body,' as *nāma* and *rūpa*, as five *khandha*'s, as having body, mind and 'mentals' (*cetasikā*). But when conduct and the consequences of conduct, past, here below, or hereafter, come to be considered, then it is that the triple category finds place, *e.g.* notably in the after-death tribunal, where it occurs eight times: "My man! you have not been doing well with deed, word, thought," etc.[1] Again:

> "Let him commit no evil whatsoever,
> Throughout the world, in speech and mind and deed."[2]

Again:

"They whose conduct in deed and word and thought is virtuous, for them is the self a dear friend."[3]

Whenever and wherever it originated, it was a notable vantage-ground taken by man in summing himself up. For here he associated himself in plain terms with his deeds; he was not surveying himself as a static beholder, nor a passive creature of destiny, but as actor, as doer, and as such as willer,—as a chooser, that is, and as a 'becomer.' He looked behind, he looked forward. He saw how he, as agent, is no creature only of the hour that now is. He saw himself in the perspective of the worlds. As were his actions, so was he now, so would he be. He was not just played upon. He was actor, maker, *Werdender*.

And it is because we of the Western world have come to realize this in our own way and our own wording, that we have found a place, in our summing up of the man, for will and willer—albeit some among

[1] *Anguttara*, i. 138 ff.; *Majjhima*, No. 130. 'Deed' is more literally 'body' (*kāya*).

[2] *Saṃyutta*, i. 12; 31, etc.

[3] *Ibid.*, i. 71.

our nations have not won to the latter word. So much the worse for these. It has taken us a long time to get even only so far as we have got. And India never got even so far. But she felt early and much after what she had somehow come to know. We in our 'coming to know' have largely ascribed this to something that we call 'will.' India did not word 'will' as Latins and Teutons, her Aryan brethren worded it. The root of the word was in her Aryan heritage as it was in ours. That which we developed in *Wal(h)* she held, but developed only slightly as *War*:—choice. It is not likely that the very different fate of these two forms of a common root, if common indeed it was, has been a matter of mere accident. The history of this pregnant stem has still to be written. When it is, much of the history of the Indo-Aryan and European Aryan will be involved.

India, to repeat myself,[1] used her word *var-* in narrow ineffectual ways. It was used for one or two models of choice: for a boon, for marriage-custom; and again as meaning "of chosen, choice or elect quality," a usage frequent in later Pali. It appears much, with Buddhists and Jains, in compounds with *ni-*, *saṃ-*, to express hindrance or self-restraint. But I do not find any words (due may be to oversight) in which *var-* has attained to a force and worth approaching that of *val-* in *e.g.* *uelle*, *uolo*, *uoluntas*, or *will* and *wollen*, and *Wahl*.[2]

We cannot imagine a literature where occasion for wording what we will to be or do does not arise. When with such an occasion we find no direct and distinctive

[1] Above, p. 108.

[2] Even in *svayaṃvara*, we find the maiden saying, not 'I choose this man!' but 'I take (*gaṇhāmi*) him.' *Jātaka*, No. 31.

word for will, we look at least for a makeshift term, a term which is not the word that would be named as the usual, and main meaning, *e.g.* *manas* (mind) and *saṃkalpa* (fitting together). When we are called upon to render in Vedic or Pali such a direct distinctive sentence as that of the healing Jesus: 'I will! Be thou clean!', whether he meant just 'I am willing,' or the expression of a supreme effort of healing will, we are dumb. We could only say: 'Mayest thou be clean!' or 'Of thee I am one healing-desiring' (*te ahaṃ tekiccha-kāmo*). It is true that *manas* and *saṃkalpa* (Pali: *saṃkappa*) *imply* will. Many years ago Regnaud, in his pioneer Upaniṣadic *Matériaux* (p. 93), saw in the *saṃkalpa*, *manas*-in-action, and hence took it to mean "desire (*kāma*) or volition." And if we found it meeting us wherever, in the context, we should look for some reference to man as willing, my point would be weakened. But it is precisely the very rare and irregular use which is made of the term, in both *Upaniṣads* and *Piṭakas*, that sharpens my point. Into this I have gone already (Chap. IV.). I showed how it could hardly be maintained, that *saṃkalpa* was used to express any very fundamental aspect of man, much less the most fundamental aspect. Thrust for a moment into relief, in the 'More' that was in 'name,' in the Chāndogya Upaniṣad, as being 'more than mind,' it is dropped forthwith, *citta* being declared to be yet a More than it. It was not an indispensable, a constant in India's concept of the man, as much for instance as was *prajñā*, *manas*, *kāma*.

How then did early Buddhism treat it? In formulas we see it lifted to an important place. When the figure of the Way came to be drafted as a formula of eight modes of deed, word and thought, *saṃkappa* comes second. 'View' must be right or fit; 'intent' must be so no less. And more. I have it on good authority[1] that in an ancient Chinese version of the First Utterance, the Way is called not eightfold, but simply and solely by a term which virtually equates *saṃkappa*: the Way of Intent or Purpose. Again, when we come to the more advanced stage in mental analysis revealed in the first book of Abhidhamma, we find *saṃkappa* given a definition peculiar to itself and to one other term: *vitakka*. Each is called "lifting the mind on to its object, disposing, adapting, applying it." Here is something that is certainly volitional, albeit the equating it with *vitakka*, a strongly cognitive term, weakens the result. We should see in the definition a state of mode of 'attention.' And modern attention to 'attention' has done something to place our psychology on a more dynamic footing. Nevertheless the word 'intent' remains *the least emphasized* of all the terms making up that inadequate octad known as the much praised 'eightfold path,' and, speaking with the drawback of no Piṭaka Concordance, I would say, its occurrence in the Suttas is relatively rare. And however much we press it into the service of a will-term, it remains mainly a term of intellection. Thought in it is tending to overt action, but thought, not will, dominates the meaning.

How then did Sakya go about to find fit words for her Message, which was so clearly, so emphatically a call to the will of man? The modern Buddhist, if conversant with Abhidhamma, will emphatically say: *cetanā* was used for will. Readers of the still standard

[1] See my *Buddhism* (1934), p. 115. It was A. J. Edmunds who quoted to me the version.

Manual, the *Abhidhammattha-sangaha*, translated by the late S. Z. Aung and myself as *Compendium of Philosophy*, may have seen what is there said about it. I had said, in 1897, in an article published in England and in Burma, that early Buddhism presented for me the curious paradox of a gospel of the will of man, without a fit word for will. And I recalled Matthew Arnold's quip, that in spite of the term 'solecism' becoming current, the men of Soli had no use for such a word, just as the Irish, maybe, do not term a certain word-coil 'an Irish bull.' Groping by etymology I had found *cetanā* too intellectual for equating with will. There *was* 'conation' in the fact that its mediæval definition included, as its 'taste' (*rasa*), *āyūhana*, 'effort towards.' But this definition included *saṃvidahana* (placing-in-detail-together) and *saṃsandati* (linking-together) as its 'occasion' and 'meaning.' Hence, even in the fifth century it was *mainly cognitive*.

It is interesting, that in the Suttas the word is brought into line with action, thus: "I say that *cetanā* is *kamma*." But then follows: "When we have *cetayita* (lit. made-thinking), then we make action of deed, word and thought."[1] Thus here too the thinking, the *citta*, is shown as the precedent of the act. I was very willing twenty-five years ago to be corrected by the lore of Burma. And the meagre inadequate treatment of will in my *Buddhist Psychology* of four years later is due to this most friendly rebuff. I am not nearly so willing today; I think I was in the main right; I regret the rendering of *cetanā* by 'volition' in the later edition of my *Buddhist Psychological Ethics* (1923). I am trying here to make good.

[1] *Anguttara*, iii. 415.

It is a known feature in the expositions of the votary, that he finds, with entire absence of historical perspective, everything that is true and wise in his creed from its very beginning. *His picture is all foreground.* He does not see, that even if a truly inspired man began to paint it, he may not have found a fit pigment ready to hand. And that his effort to paint what he had to show, with such pigment as he had then and there, *may be one of the finest features in his work.* Let us imagine Gotama inspired to teach the brotherhood of man. What a difficult task it would have been, where and when no man ever spoke of even his dearest friend as his 'brother,' or even *to* his bloodbrother by that word. He would call him just *tāta*, a word used for filial relationship as well. He had not even a word for 'my neighbour' such as the Hebrew knew well. What then were the makeshifts used for will by the Sakyans as the best 'pigments' to hand?

There would have been a worthy word in *kāma*, a word as strong in generations before Sakya as was our 'conation,' and much less academic than this word. We have seen above the man worthily summed up in action as proceeding by *kāma*, *kratu*, *karma*, and resulting experience. But whereas *kratu*, a strong active term, had somehow become obsolete, *kāma* had become debased to mean sensuous and sensual experience. Its earlier breadth lingers in the Suttas: 'one who desires the self (*atta-kāmo*)' or 'the good' (*attha-kāmo*), 'goes whither he will' (*yathākāmaṃ eti*) and the like. But monasticism grew and deepened this debasement. That breadth lingers also, to my thinking, in the word for the next world: *kāma-loka*. This is usually taken to mean 'where man hereafter still has, in a body,' sense-experience. It is more likely, it meant the land of desire, the 'better land' the land *where we fain would be.'* It virtually meant just this in the Edicts of Asoka: the term for it in his day was *svaga* (Pali *sagga*, Sanskrit *svarga*), and of it he wrote: "To attain heaven (*svaga*):—what than this is more desirable (lit. more to be done)?" (Girnar, ix. 9.)

However much *kāma* may have worthily stood for will, and by Bloomfield called an equivalent, it is ever rendered by 'desire.' This word is for us one of the most composite in our psychology; it is a blend of will with idea and feeling. My teacher, most fastidious in defining, worded it thus: "Desire is to emotion as appetite is to primitive wants of the system. Any sense-feeling or emotion may, as determining action, where uneasiness is persistent, be called desire. Desire is wishing as opposed to willing."[1] Used unanalytically, and by constructive genius, we see, in the French equivalent, the very well-spring in the man:—"Prométhée, Prométhée, est-ce toi, toi qui voulais affranchir l'homme des liens de la fatalité? . . . Les hommes t'ont donné mille noms symboliques: audace, désespoir, délire, rébellion, malédiction. Ceux-ci t'ont appelé Satan, ceux-là crime; moi, je t'appelle DÉSIR! Vérité! vérité! tu ne t'es pas révélée; depuis dix mille ans que je te cherche. . . . Depuis dix mille ans l'infini me répond: désir, désir!"[2]

Turgid! the Englishman, the modern Frenchman may possibly say, but nevertheless a great, a moving, a true saying. Prometheus, as the incarnate will, seeking a More, a Becoming, a very synergy of man's essential nature. It was the tragedy in Buddhism, that it branded man's seeking, here called desire, "as Satan, as crime," rather than as that without which

[1] *Elements of Psychology*, p. 235. [2] Georges Sand, *Leila*.

there could be for him no salvation. I am not saying that the many translated contexts where this is done always use literal equivalents of the Pali terms; indeed I called attention in 1897 to the way in which the word 'desire,' *désir*, *Verlangen*, had been ridden to death by translators, glad, perhaps, to escape literal renderings by so fine-sounding a word. I rescue my list from its present oblivion.

Pali terms rendered as 'désir,' 'desire':—

upādānaṃ	By Burnouf.
tṛṣṇā	By Foucaux (*Lalita-Vistara*).

Pali terms rendered by 'desires':

kāma .	By Oldenberg	
nekkhammaṃ	,, ,,	(abandonment of desire)
sitā	,, Fausböll	(lit. clinging bond)
sineho .	. . . .	(lit. viscosity, sticking)
chātatā	. . . .	(lit. hunger)
chanda		
ussāda	. . . .	(lit. upsitting, arrogance)
taṇhā .	. . . .	(lit. thirst)
paṇidhi	. . . .	(lit. aiming, aspiration)
ākāsaṃ	. . . .	(lit. space, puffed-up)
visattikaṃ	. . . .	(lit. dart of)
ejo .	. . . .	(lit. moving)
jappitāni	. . . .	(lit. mumblings, prayers for)
nirāsāso	. . . .	(lit. yearning)
anāsāso	. . . .	(ditto)
chandarāgaviratto .	. .	(not dyed with passion and desire)
āsavā .	. By Max Müller	(lit. having creeping canker)
kāmā		
taṇhā		
vana .	. . . .	(lit. forest or wood)

Henry Warren went so far as to explain that desire and seeking were 'to be taken as equivalent' to passion, lust, covetousness and thirst.[1]

[1] *Buddhism in Translations.*

It is clear that the word 'desire(s)' has been ridden to death. Nevertheless translators will have judged, by the contexts, that the mental state they tried thus to word, a state of unrest, mobility, seeking, wanting—analyze it as we may—was very prominent in the Piṭakas. Further, that there were many Pali words to express it, even if *they* lit usually on only one English word. Lastly, the contexts leave us in no doubt that the attitude of the *compilers* towards this fluid state was one of deprecation, of depreciation. I choose at hazard three of the contexts: "In whom desire (*taṇhā*) has departed before death . . . he is indeed a sage."[1] "From wish (*chanda*) originate dear objects and the greed that prevails in the worlds and desire (*āsā*) . . ."[2] "Stop the stream valiantly, drive away desires (*kāme*)."[3]

I am not so incorrect as to say that other words, such as 'pleasures,' 'lusts,' are not made to take their turn with 'desire.' For these we should not in any scriptures expect anything but deprecation, qualified or unqualified. But desire, especially in the singular, is for us, to speak truthfully, an a-moral, or un-moral, not an immoral term. Either then we must feel critical towards our translators for lowering the value of 'desire,' or we must see we are dealing in the Piṭakas with a literature, in which the terms judged fit to be rendered by 'desire(s)' share the fate of the dog, which, being called a bad name, is hanged. There are for us desires and desires. And one bad name is to call desire 'craving,' 'hankering'! My husband chose the former word for *taṇhā*: 'thirst,' and I chose the latter for *paṇihita* (*panidhi*, rendered above 'aiming'). Now in extreme thirst, 'craving' is not exactly a

[1] *Sutta-Nipāta*, 865. [2] *Ibid.*, 355, 856, etc.
[3] *Dhammapada*, 383.

despicable state. And in religion it has, to express aspiration after the Highest, been raised to sublime verse: "As panteth the hart . . . so panteth my soul. . . ." But monastic Buddhism came to see in the word *taṇhā*, the very source of ill. "What is the origin of ill? It is this thirst making-again-to-become,[1] which delights in this and that," is the (probably much edited) formula of the "four truths" in the First Utterance. And the stopping of ill is the stopping[2] of this thirst.

Is there then any qualification by which other terms for desire, cited above, assume a favourable meaning? Yes, the term *chanda* stands, not condemned unheard, at least not always. Here it is in good company:—

> ". . . learning (*vijjā*)
> Linked by desire (*chanda*) and energy
> with faith, insight and concentration."[3]

and aiming at things of worth:—

> "Ay, mine was once desire (*chando*) to learn those doctrines. . . ."[4]

Further, there is no blame for the word in a possibly late-added Sutta, where Ānanda reveals an orthodox but limited appreciation of it. Asked by a brahman as to the object of the God-life lived in his Order, he replies, it is said, "'For the putting away of *chanda*.' 'That would surely be an unendingly impossible thing.' 'Well, had you not *chanda* when you sought me out today, and when you found me, was not that wish abated?' 'It was.' 'Even so, in the monk who, become arahan, has lived the life, done what was to

[1] *I.e.*, 'belonging to rebirth.'
[2] Often wrongly rendered by 'cessation of.'
[3] *Sutta-Nipāta*, 1026. [4] *Saṃyutta*, i. 202.

do, . . . is released . . . that *chanda* which he had, to win all this, is it not abated? If so, is there not an end?' "[1]

If now we are to see in *chanda* a worthy equivalent of will, we must see in the Buddhist saint a will-less automaton. More than any instance does this episode show us that *chanda* was but another word for wish, or want, *i.e.* just a mode of the will which is essential in manhood, whether stunted or relatively consummated. I am not, in so saying, finding the definition of the arahan, as a perfected man, other than lamentably imperfect. No man on earth has realized and carried out all that man can become. The higher a man attains on earth, the more will he become charged with fuller, stronger will. It is but the passing wish that arises and passes, and this is apparently all that was, in the Piṭakas, at least as represented by the words imputed to Ānanda, understood by *chanda*.

This term is, it is true, used in a more intensive way in a certain formula, but it is there used with a different meaning, as I shall show (p. 294).

The Piṭakan editors would seem to have been at pains not to cast out *chanda*, or even some form of *kāma*, from qualities held desirable. We not only find *chanda* listed with such esteemed words as energy, effort, endeavour, exertion, but also its face saved by the prefix *dhamma-*: 'righteous desire.' We find also, in Abhidhamma and Commentary, the compound *kattu-kamyatā*, 'state of desire to act,' as synonym for *chanda*. I have sought, I repeat, for many years to do justice to these reservations and distinctions not without some special pleading. It was impossible, without a sense of injustice done, to read the many

[1] *Saṃyutta*, v. 272.

fine calls in the Nikāyas on what *we* should call the will, the earnest exordiums to energy, to "noble quest," to progress in the Way, the lovely "faith in what we may become,"[1] and then to note how translators and narrators glossed it all over and emphasized only "extinction of desire"!

Yet after all Buddhism has been its own worst enemy. Ānanda, whose reputation grew with the aftermen in proportion to the way in which his contemporaries seem to have snubbed him,[2] makes out that the saint has no *chanda* any more. Hence, so far as that meant 'will,' will was not of man's essential nature. The saint could no longer 'become,' hence he had ceased to will. The brahman groped after will in his conception of the Divine Desire in creation. The Buddhist, harping on *anicca*, *anattā*, repudiated in the highest sense all becoming, all will. When we read such vigorous will-words as these: "When a man is not thoroughly aware of some blemish, he will not bring *chanda* to birth, he will not strive, he will not set energy afoot to get rid of it," we ask, how can we say there is no will worded in Buddhism? When we read those words of Ānanda's, we realize that, for Buddhism, such activity was not of the very life of the complete man, but was only an episode, was only the "writhing" of the learner.

But it was not only in salving terms of desire, when need dictated, that Sakya vindicates its call to man's will, to choose, to be faring onward, to be growing. There is in the Suttas no more distinctive feature than the increment in words for effort, and, in effort, initiative. There is in the Suttas nothing more striking

[1] Wordsworth's *Prelude*.
[2] In Mahāyāna Sūtras he has become very distinguished.

than the constant use of the dynamic term 'to make become,' the causative of the verb 'become.' The latter, as I have shown, was a new feature peeping out in the Upaniṣads, but it became discredited, for the same reasons as 'becoming' (not 'making become') lost honour in Buddhism. 'Making become' is a rare feature of the Upaniṣads. So too is little if any stress laid in the Upaniṣads on the necessity of *constant personal effort* in bringing to pass the holy life.

To illustrate in succession: (*a*) *Viriya*, which I find *but once* in the Upaniṣads, takes a prominent place in character-training. It is included in the categories of the Way, of the Faculties and Strengths, of the Limbs of Enlightenment. In the definitions of early Abhidhamma, it is, in fulness, second to the long list of *paññā*-equivalents, defined thus: "*Viriya* is mental inception of energy, striving, onward effort, exertion, endeavour, zeal, ardour, vigour, fortitude, unfaltering verve, sustained desire, unflinching endurance, and firm grasp of the burden, right *padhāna*."[1] The last, meaning strenuous effort, I shall mention later (p. 295). It is also used, and not *viriya*, in the title of the formula enjoining 'Right Effort,' in which the man is bidden, in order to make good things arise and maintain them, and to get rid of bad things and hinder their arising, "engender desire (*chanda*), endeavour, start energy, grip the thought (*citta*)."[2] But there is here no sign, that the very essence of mind is involved; there is only a suggestion of mind as attacked by mind—we are reminded of Satan "divided against himself." Moreover, energy, effort, is not will; they are only modes of exerting will.

But we can at least say that the Sakyan had only

[1] *Dhammasangaṇi*, § 13. [2] *Dīgha*, iii. 221, etc.

just missed stumbling upon a notable doctrine of will. Certainly he was no Quietist. His inner world was seething with energy.

> O see my forward strides in energy!
> (*passa viriya-parakkamaṃ*)

is a recurring note in the Monks' Anthology (167). The Community was

> Of strenuous energy and resolute,
> Ever advancing strongly . . .
> *āraddhaviriye pahitatte niccaṃ daḷha-parakkamaṃ* (224).[1]

So responds a nun. The conception of the believer's remainder of incarnate life had been transformed. It was not the endless round of *saṃsāra*, growing up in Indian monasticism, which we have renamed 'transmigration.' It had for the first Sakyans become a progress in the Godlife. It was a way of growth in many worlds. Here is a notable 'growth-word':

"Growing by the five growths the Ariyan woman-disciple grows with the Ariyan growth: she becomes one who lays hold of the real (*sāra*) and of the excellent (*vara*) things in her person, to wit, faith, morals, learning, giving up and wisdom."[2]

The books hover about this vital notion of growth, about the Way of Growth (*vaḍḍhi-paṭipadā*), but just miss gripping the truth, that their central tenet of the Way is just that:—growth of the 'man,' not only of his instruments, along the agelong way of the worlds.

'The books,' I repeat; I am certain that, long before the day of the books, the Founder and his man gripped that truth; it was of the very centre of the teaching reckoned best in their day. It was the widening rift between that teaching and the aftermen, the over-

[1] Mahā-Pajāpatī. [2] *Saṃyutta*, iv. 250; cf., *Anguttara*, v. 137.

shadowing interest in 'mind,' the growing monasticism, with its Man as a Less, that brought about the missed grip.

I have said that, in using words for effort as makeshifts for will, the contexts link with these 'initiative.' This word is some form of the stem *rabh*, or *rambh*, to take hold, with the prefix *ā*, 'on to.' And I referred (p. 228) to one outstanding Sutta, where the idea of inception-in-the-act was made to testify to the real presence, in the act, of personal agency. By the teaching that grew up in Buddhism, an act was but the result of another preceding act, whether physical or mental. As the jingle says: 'fire burnt stick, stick beat dog,' etc. But in linking 'the datum of initiative' (*ārabbha-dhātu*) with self-agency, and the fact that *viriya* is time and again alluded to as *ārabbha-*, *āraddha-*, the Sakyans brought the terms for effort very near to an implicit doctrine of will, such as, in its broader more inclusive sense, *we* understand it.

> Wherefore from such let him keep well apart—
> The sluggard and the poor in energy (*hīna-viriyaṃ*).
> Let him consort with those who live aloof,
> With noble eager contemplative souls,
> With men of constant quickened energies (*niccaṃ āraddha-viriyaṃ*).[1]

Mr. Woodward's 'quickened' is good work, and more literary English than the more literal rendering of energy laid hold of, or set on foot, begun, started, initiated.

I come to (*b*): the novel and repeated use of 'making become.'

As I have often said elsewhere, this word has lost

[1] *Iti-vuttaka* (S.B. Buddhists, VIII), iii. 3, 9.

for us the power it once had in its Anglo-Saxon form, *e.g.*[1] in such lines as

> Falleð in ðat welle-grund,
> ðer he wurde heil and sund,
> and cumeð ut al newe:—

" there he became whole and sound," our more fortunate German neighbours having preserved their *werden.* This is not to say, that the equally archaic ' become ' has no strength: " . . . is become the head-stone of the corner ":—' become ' so used is as strong as its discarded rival. But as a fact we *tend to avoid using it*; its later ambiguity in ' to befit ' weakens it. Hence translators, in evading, give us no idea of the very frequent occurrence of both ' become ' and ' making become ' in the Piṭakas. In a recent translation of the Sutta-Nipāta anthology, in the Harvard Oriental Series,[2] of sixty occurrences of the twin forms, *only one* is rendered as ' become '.

> He strips the veil from things and so becomes (*bhavati*)
> the peerless all-enlightened. . . .

As a very opposite case, let the reader consult the most recent translations of the Pali Text Society, by Messrs. Woodward and Hare, *The Book of the Gradual Sayings* (the Fourth Collection), and see what a different atmosphere of growth and coming to be is created by literal truth in the English. Listen to this, in the third volume, p. 61:

" And while he contemplates these the Way comes into being . . . that Way he follows, makes become, makes more. . . .

> Now am I bound-to-become one turning no more back;
> I shall become a further-farer in the life divine."[3]

---

[1] *Cf. Manual of Buddhism* (S.P.C.K., 1932), p. 90.
[2] By Lord Chalmers.
[3] *Anguttara*, iii. 75.

I seem to hear my first Sakyan missioner saying of these lines: ' they give rightly what we taught, the man as in a becoming more and more, faring to the Most.' It is the more strange to find, that in the only German translation by the German Buddhist monk Nyanatiloka these lines and the dozen or so preceding them have been entirely omitted ! a most unlucky editorial accident. And consider the following opening to a Sutta of the Second Collection (the sequel to the opening, here, and in general, is too often a monastic elaboration). I have cited this elsewhere and more than once, but it needs repeating. It betrays that an order of *śramaṇa*'s (Pali: *samaṇas*), so living as to " let their light shine before men " as " an ensample of godly life " was, when this Saying was first uttered, a New Thing.

" People know you as being *śramaṇa*'s. If you are asked ' What is that ?' admit that you are, but say to yourselves: 'We will take up and practise those things which make the *śramaṇa*: thus will our profession become real, our pledge a thing that has become (*i.e.* is true, *bhūtaṃ*). And our use of what we need to live by, will become fruitful and profitable, and our leaving the world will become not sterile, but fertile and full of result.' You should train yourselves thus: to be conscientious and discreet. You may then think: ' We have done that. So far is enough; enough has been done. We have won what we sought as monks. There's nothing further to be done.' I declare unto you, I protest unto you ! See there be no decay, no falling off in your quest while yet anything further remains to be done ! What further remains to be done ? Train yourselves saying: ' Very pure will we become in conduct of deed, word and thought. We will neither exalt the self, nor despise the other man.'

Then you may say: 'We've done this as well. So far is enough' . . ."

The Sutta proceeds as before, in a series betraying monkish preoccupations, for us here a detail, if a lamentable detail. That which is not a detail is the view of life as a process in becoming. The reader can hardly fail to note the persistent use of 'become' (*bhavati*). Yet let me tell him, that in the only English translation[1] yet published, the word 'become' *is not used once*! And this too:—In the only German translation yet published,[2] the word *werden* is not once used either, not even for the 'we will become'! The four occurrences of *bhava-* forms are thus paralleled:

become real . . . *soll wahr sein* (!)
become true . . . *wirklich*
become fruitful . . . *sollen* . . . *erlangen*
become not sterile . . . *soll nicht* . . . *bleiben*
will we become . . . *wollen wir sein* (!)

Comment is needless. Neither translator has been gripped by the ever-recurring notion of a coming-to-be. He has not seen in it what I see in it. Do you, reader, decide for yourself. But, in deciding, become for the nonce an Indian of the sixth century B.C., not a modern Englishman or German.

Time alone, together with much riper study of the Pali sources than I as yet find among Buddhists or writers on Buddhism, will judge as to the significance of the perpetual insistence in the Piṭakas on the religious life as a coming-to-be. Let us now glance in conclusion at two important phases in the teaching, where we find the concepts of will and becoming combined in

[1] *Sacred Books of the Buddhists*, V.: 'Further Dialogues of the Buddha,' 1915. By Robert (Lord) Chalmers, No. 39.
[2] K. Neumann's.

very interesting and abnormal forms of initiatory and sustained effort. I refer (1) to the exercises called 'God-abidings' (*brahma-vihārā*) to which reference has already been made, and (2) to 'effectuating' or *iddhi*.

(1) I do not here repeat the evidence I have put forward,[1] that the cult was not originally Sakyan but was annexed from another body of teachers, but I remain convinced that this was so. The exercise, to be practised on an individual by an individual, was one that we should rightly call, not telepathic, but televolitional. A man abounding in, filled with, either amity, or pity, or glad goodwill, or poise, balance, was enjoined to will another out of his own abundance, making-become in him the corresponding wealth of one or more of these sentiments.

Now in the formula, where the recipient *in spe* is no longer an individual, but a whole quarter of the firmament (!), there is no attempt made to use any makeshift for that 'will' which we, were *we* treasurers of the tradition, would undoubtedly use, nor for the 'Becoming,' which the man is shown as (*a*) experiencing in himself, in psychic generosity, (*b*) willing to bring about in the other man (or quarter). He is said to act "with a mind (*citta*) accompanied by amity," or the rest. But an outstanding term is brought in, to give requisite force to the strenuous will-effect that is called upon. He is said to 'suffuse' (*pharati*) the object with such a 'mind.' We might, with one translator, shift the direct and indirect object and say 'he is to radiate such a mind on to such an object.' Or, reverting, 'irradiate such an object with such a mind.' The term *pharati* may very well have been adopted with

[1] *Sakya*, Chap. XI.

the practice. But when the Sakyan poets got on to the idea, they joined their 'make become' to the 'suffuse,' thus:

> Passion for him gone by, hatred he should repress,
> He should *make-become* mind that is friendly, the boundless,
> Ever with zest by night and by day let him *spread* (*pharate*) over all quarters the thing that is infinite. (*Sutta-Nipāta*, 507.)

In the only other reference, in this work, we have just *āsevamāno* (practising, following). As Lord Chalmers renders the verse (71):

> Alone! In season due
> practise goodwill and poise,
> pity and kindliness, (thereby to win) release,
> unthwarted by the world.

It is possibly the lack, in this very notable and for us yet alien exercise, of a strong word for the essential attitude in the man-imparting, that has resulted in the practice being as yet so misunderstood. Writers treat it as mere benevolent contemplation. Even Buddhaghosa, who gives us a quite vivid picture of the volitional efforts entailed, treats the last, (poise= *upekkhā*) as if the willer, after an orgy of philanthropy, needed to suffuse *himself* with fresh balance! That the object might be a friend distraught, needing steadying influence, is not in his thoughts. And when we take up the other Anthology, that of the Monks and Nuns called Elders (*thera-therī*), we are struck by a double defaulting. Namely, the 'Sisters' never make allusion to the fourfold practice, and the monks, when they do allude to their being void of enmity, or, as with Revata, more positively, to amity, as a dominant sentiment, never allude to the practice of 'suffusing' the fellowman therewith. There is a moral loveliness in his verses:

> Nay, *mettā* I avow, made infinite,
> well trained, by orderly progression grown,
> even as by the Buddha it was taught.
> with all am I a friend, comrade to all,
> and to all creatures kind and merciful;
> a heart (*citta*) of amity I cultivate,
> and ever in goodwill is my delight.
> a mind that cannot drift or fluctuate
> I make my joy; the sentiments sublime
> that evil men do shun I make-become (ver. 647-9).

But at best it was, as he says, just sentiment. It is true that, in the Commentary, we not infrequently meet with sayers of poems who were said to be experts in 'amity-musing' (*mettā-jhāna*), absorbed in it even when waiting at doorsteps for alms. Subhūti, for example, was famed as best of 'unlimited' abiders-without-enmity (*anodissaka-araṇa-vihārīnaṃ*).[1] The only woman so distinguished was Sāmāvatī, wife of king Udena, a laywoman, not a nun. But even in such cases the monks at least were only exercising sentiment.

The silence of the nuns is a point which I ought, in my translation of their verses,[2] to have noticed. Their leaving the world was in no small measure the result of a 'woman's movement' for greater freedom, domestic and social; their verses betray this. Others left because of bitter bereavement. Both of these classes of nuns would not be normally fit to discern, that in no way could they better vindicate their breaking of narrower ties than by the broader sisterhood and motherhood to be practised in the 'God-abidings.'

[1] *Anguttara*, i., p. 23 f.
[2] *Psalms of the Sisters*, Pali Text Society, 1909.

Buddhism has even been rapped over the knuckles for a benevolence limited to sentiment in meditation. But originally the act described as "amity-accompanied thought" was as truly an effort to transmit love or pity or comfort by will, as if the willer had either spoken words thus fraught, or had written them —*i.e.* in those days, sent a verbal message.

Maybe we are so myopic because we have never tried the practice. The only person I know who tried the practice with apparent striking result is not a Buddhist. Maybe we are myopic, because we do not yet, even with the very word on our tongue, realize all that we mean, actually, potentially, by 'will.' And being myopic, we do not here see how sorely, in those old days of a great new word, the word that *we* have was needed. Not having it, the Sakyan pressed into service a quite special word for a special effort of will: *pharati*, and withal his own great word 'to make become.' Yet even now, Buddhists persistently render the noun *bhāvanā*: 'the making become,' by 'meditation.' Meditation! as if the first Sakyans were a dreamy quiescent lot of Quietists, brooding over men and things, and not the ever active John Wesleys of their day!

(2) Into the subject of *iddhi* I shall go at more length in a later chapter. I only mention it here as a notable term, without adequate English equivalent, to indicate in the man, a more, a *plus*, a super this or that, in the use of which the Sakyan teachers brought in words for desire, effort and the making-become—brought them in, in the unconscious need for such a word as we have in will. *Iddhi* might refer to an external 'more,' such as wealth and other means of enjoyment; Rhys Davids was at pains to show this.[1] Its

[1] *Dialogues*, i. 88, *n*. 4.

more special, because more religious use was in meaning an inner more in the very man, such as he, at a stage in his becoming different from that of the 'average' man, could express by mind and body. So doing he became in one or more specified ways what we now call a psychic phenomenon. So doing he may be said to have been exerting power or potency, and the word is often so rendered; but Pali words for power[1] are not adduced to define *iddhi*. I have not indeed found any definition of it in the Piṭakas; there is only description in detail, and that in an oft-quoted formula.

But the dynamic procedure to train so as to develop it, where possible, shows work in mental analysis that is of interest. The procedure was in a formula called Steps of (or to) *Iddhi* (*iddhipādā*):

"These four steps to *iddhi* made-to-become, practised, advance the going further and further: what four? (1) Here a monk brings about a step-to-*iddhi* accompanied by combining concentrated effort with a 'mantra' (*chanda*).[2] (2) . . . by combining concentrated effort with energy. (3) . . . by combining concentrated effort with thought. (4) . . . by combining concentrated effort with examination (*vīmaṃsā*)."[3]

There is no guarantee given that any one or all of these would prove effective training. The More aimed at was, as we know, too elusive to be won by routine alone, or at all. But the formula is an interesting example of the plan, pursued in a bookless world, of a man diverting (superbending *abhininnamēti*) his inner energies to an idea or group of ideas, which then became

[1] *Bala, daḷha, anubhāva.*

[2] Why I see this the *other* meaning of *chanda*, *cf.* my *Gotama the Man*, p. 222.

[3] *E.g. Dīgha*, iii, 221.

the while his "dominating influence" (*adhipateyya*), just as *we* might confine attention to a given chapter in a book.

And with this method the will-makeshifts of making-become and effort in close conjunction should be noticed. The one term 'making become' (*bhāveti*) is constantly linked with certain important teachings, such as the Way:—you did not 'know' or 'realize' the Way; you made it become (*maggaṃ bhāveti*). Jhāna too, or preparatory 'musing' (whereof more presently):—you 'made become a way thereto.' So for the seven Limbs of Enlightenment. Sometimes the term used in these strenuous exercises was to engender or give birth to (*janeti*), in which case it is always wish or desire that is to be produced, as in these Steps to Iddhi, and in the four Right Efforts, where the practiser is said to engender desire, to endeavour, to start energy, to grip the mind (or thought), to wrestle.

The last term: *padahati*, is shown in the four Steps, in the noun-form *padhāna*, translated above, with *samādhi*, as "concentrated effort." Exegesis saw in it supreme energy (*uttama-viriya*), but the teaching rarely got hold fruitfully of the noun. (It may be remembered what a different meaning *padhāna* came to have in early Sānkhya).[1] With the verb-forms it was different; no compound in spiritual growing is oftener used than the past participle *pahita* with *attā*, for the man who has the self 'wrought' or 'bestriven.' I have used 'the self established' here, but judge I was wrong. Buddhaghosa, zealous perhaps to see everywhere the man as unreal, sees in the compound *pahina*: "sent away," and interprets as *pesitatto*. When I compare his exegesis with that of Dhammapāla (Udāna-

[1] Above, pp. 147, 160.

Commentary), I incline to think, I may have done Buddhaghosa an injustice, and that his *pesita* meant also a 'sent forward' (*nibbāne pesitacitto*). The unknown Sutta-Nipāta commentator is not in disaccord with this, when he explains by *mutt'ajjhāsaya*, or *v.l. uttam'ajjhāsaya*:—inclination (or will) set free, or, at the highest power.

No writer, Buddhist or other, has so far joined hands with me over this seeing in Buddhism a gospel of Will put forth in the teeth of there being no fit word for will, and in the significance thereby to be seen in the insistence on initial effort and the making-become. It is true there is just now a bad slump in research into early Buddhism. It has had its day of dawn, late last century. It has not yet, save in these efforts of mine, entered on a day of sunrise *with respect to the point* I have here discussed. Yet it is one that professing Buddhists could join in forwarding, so greatly does it enhance the value of their creed as having at one time been a New Word in the world, a new message not yet fitly discerned, and so, not fitly worded, by man.

Yet very true it is, that neither then nor now has this religion been looked upon as a gospel of will. We have only to look at the few formulas claimed as both central and original to see, that in not one of them is any worth attached consciously to man's nature, life and destiny as that of ever willing to become a More, a More which implicitly or explicitly is making for a Most. The fivefold *khandha* doctrine has nothing about this, nor has the eightfold way as so taught; the four truths get rid of all allusion to will under the 'bad name' of 'thirst,' and the three Marks: 'transient, ill, not-self' are merely negative. Why is the First Utterance whittled down, from the call it was to choice, to a mere statement how well one Man got to know quite well about two ends and a Way, and how to get rid of thirst, *i.e.* will?

It is an interesting history if a tragic one. To a great extent Buddhists were their own hinderers. They did feel after the truth, that man, as he becomes better, is not as it were dressing or painting himself with something external, but is undergoing an inner change. Yet they ever feared the idea of change, as if change were of necessity change for the worse. Never are the words transient or change or otherwise-ness (*aññathatta*) used save as ushers-in or guarantees of ill. Buddhists pictured spiritual progress as a making become, yet they strained every nerve to suppress the tendency to 'becoming': *bhava*, *i.e.* rebirth. They spoke of saintly advance, yet they aspired to cut short vital progress by a stopping or ending (*nirodha*) of that way of life in the forward wayfaring in the worlds, and by hustling on a final change: a *parinirvāna*—for which not a single man on earth was ready. In resisting the brahmanic conception of the real man as unchanging (for so brahmans *came to hold*), and as even now, did he but really "know" it, actually Very God, not potentially only, they ejected this static man from the mere flux of man's activities, and said of these activities: Behold the only man. "A man," I read in the words of a Buddhist monk in a current magazine, "is only the co-ordinate combination of human activities and matter." (!)

Now we cannot get very far in an adequate notion of will without a willer. We may cheat ourselves with 'thought,' by figuring this as an objective inner world of impressions and ideas. We may cheat ourselves with 'feeling,' by figuring this as waves of somatic resonance and what-not. But we cannot get on thus with 'will.' Because will is a self-directing. We saw that, according to one Sutta, will, expressed as 'element of initiative,' *of necessity implied the agent.*[1] Will without willer is meaningless. But the Buddhists, in diverging from Brahmanism, on the ground (judging by the Suttas) of protest against ritual and birth-monopolies, *first* stripped the man of the brahmanic Divine Immanence, *then* finally stripped the "activities and matter" of the man, *i.e.* self. Thus they barred the way to all that a clear view of initiative, effort and making-become implied. In such considerations as these there may lie material to account for Buddhism, with no word for will in its world-heritage, failing to find or annex any adequate term for that self-directed activity which in those makeshift terms it fostered well.

Could we but tell how it came about, that we Western Aryans, in our longer trek, if longer indeed it was, lit on our fine will-terms, we might better tell why the South-eastern Aryans did not. Did not at least when Sakya was born. *Before* that day there had been *kāma* and *kratu*. *After* that day India laid hold of *śakti*, or 'ability to become and to do.' But *vara* never developed as the true twin of 'will' (*val*).

[1] Above, p. 228.

CHAPTER XV

PSYCHOLOGY IN THE NIKĀYAS (*Continued*)

5. FEELING, SENSE AND THE KHANDHAS

If it is difficult in a modern work to treat separately of feeling and sense, it is harder still when we are inquiring into what the man of old had to say about them. Feeling in general terms is our being affected, or acted upon. And affection would be, in form, the better word. Yet how could our psychologists speak unambiguously about sense as affection, or about our "being affected"? Or, if we followed a now outdated psychologist, Bain, and said "Feeling is excitement"? Feeling, in our psychology, has come to mean sense of touch, emotion, and consciousness in general, *e.g.* 'this table does not feel when I strike it.'[1] Much the same ambiguity exists in other European languages. We cannot therefore wonder if we find no greater precision in Indian literatures.

The word *vedanā* I have till now consistently rendered by 'feeling,' for this reason, that in my own field *vedanā* is, when analyzed, consistently resolved into what is pleasant, painful, and what is neither, or is neutral (*a-dukkham-a-sukha*).[2] Yet the word, and very possibly the older meaning conveyed by it, was a 'knowing,' (from *vid-*) anything that we are impressed by, anything that we, unlike the table, 'experience.' In

[1] Croom Robertson, *Elements of Psychology*.

[2] *E.g.*, *Majjhima*, No. 44.

this more general sense it appears in the formula of the Causal Chain:—"because of sense, contact, because of contact, *vedanā*." If I touch anything, or if it touch me, I do not necessarily experience it as pleasure or pain, nor am I, mainly, aware of it as neither. Mostly it is as something that I am just aware of, that I possibly 'perceive,' certainly, that I am impressed by. Hence it is necessary, if the reader would rightly understand *vedanā*, that he should read it in as general a sense as our 'feeling' implies, and not as 'hedonic' sensation, or as emotion only. But just because of the latitude required, I do not hold with those who render it by 'sensation.' Here again, it is true, our tongue lends a wide range. But the unusual or wonderful is ruled out by the Pali contexts. It is the narrowness of 'sensation,' as sense-message *only*, that is not faithful to the originals. *Vedanā*, we are told, may be mental (*cetasika*) as often as bodily (*kāyika*). And while its 'content' may be called pleasant or painful, it must be remembered, that whereas the pleasant (*sukha*) may refer to a wide field of impressing objects, from a taste up to nirvana itself, the painful (*dukkha*) covers for the pious Buddhist the whole of life, as summed up under decay, disease and dying. There is, moreover, one Sutta (*Majjhima*, No. 59) where, with a suggestion of impatience about the 'just three,' the Founder is shown as saying, it was in a way equally correct to speak of two modes of *vedanā*, or for that matter of three, five, six, eighteen or one hundred and eight, all and each of which he had taught, the conclusion being (as not a matter of pedantic categorizing), that "the 'wayfarer' ranks under the pleasant all that is pleasant wherever he descries it."[1]

[1] *E.g.*, *Majjhima*, No. 59.

Other terms meaning consciousness more precisely affective or emotional I do not find in Pali; I find only words for this or that mode of feeling or emotion: several for unpleasant feeling, several for the opposite. Words for forms of dislike are numerous; less so, words for liking; a word to equate with our love does not exist; I had to treat of it (in the *Encyclopædia for Religion and Ethics*, art. 'Love,' Buddhist) under six headings. It was necessary to butter this great word over different words used in the Suttas, such as the overmuch used *mettā*, amity, with the contradictories to its opposites, *adosa* (no-hate), *avera, araṇu, avyāpajjha, appaṭigha,* the often more sexually inclined *rati*, and the notable term *anukampā*—which is a genuinely Sakyan 'discovery'—not omitting pity (*karuṇā*), gladness (*pamojja*), and *muditā*, a joy-term, but used as in the German *Mitfreude*, for sympathetic joy. The 'six headings' were parental: mother love and filial love; fraternal and kin love; friendship; sex love; love for an inferior by a superior and *vice versa*; æsthetic and ideal love. Love for humanity I do not find worded as we word it, but it is included in a sentiment of 'friendship' (*mettā*; or amity) for "all creatures, all breathers" (*sabbe sattā, sabbe pāṇā* or *pāṇāni* or *pāṇabhūtāni*).

The word *anukampā* (vibrating because of, or after, along, toward[1]) is also used with this universal breadth, either as specified above, or as being felt for "devas and men" as in the first mission-charter (*sabbapāṇabhūtânukampī, lokânukampāya, atthāya . . . devamanussānaṃ*).[2] I have perhaps too exclusively rendered

[1] *Cf.* Whitney, *Sanskrit Grammar*, § 1077: *anu* : 'after, along, toward.'

[2] Vinaya, Mahāvagga, I. 11.

this great word by 'compassion.' Etymologically it is right and so is 'sympathy,' both meaning a 'feeling-with,' or as we say, 'feeling for.' But in its 'second intention' compassion has, for us, taken on a meaning of 'stooping to help,' of one, in some way better, better off, helping another who is 'under-dog.' And this acquired meaning is not really in the word *anukampā*. A closer acquaintance with contexts shows this. It is showing kindness or goodwill where no such inequality may exist. And I wish here to correct if and where I have so far blundered. In my *Sakya* I have guarded myself in rendering very elastic the using of 'compassion' (pp. 294 ff.), but I might have gone further and not seen our 'compassion' in the sentiment prescribed, in the Singāla Suttanta, for wives towards husbands, and servants towards masters. Our 'goodwill' is probably nearer the mark.

Anukampā is noticeably absent from the Sutta better known than most, the Metta-Sutta,[1] the most altruistically eloquent perhaps of all Piṭaka sayings. Here it is *mettā* which is raised above its meaning of 'friendship' to its fitter aspect, of universal goodwill as a *motherly* caring-for, the climax being thus:

> As mother her own child lifelong,
> her only child would warding be,
> so let him also make-become in creatures all
> the mind immeasurable.
> Ay, amity for all the world, even
> the mind immeasurable let him make-become,
> upwards and downwards and across,
> unbarriered, without anger, without foes,
> whether he stand, walk, sit, or lie;
> till drowsiness be gone from him,
> let him this inner wareness keep:
> God! have they here this biding called.

---

[1] *Khuddakapāṭha*, and *Sutta-Nipāta*.

That amity should, in the Piṭakas, be much exploited, and that parental and conjugal love should be on the whole at a discount, is only to be expected from a literature compiled and selected by a society of monks,—where, too, Immanence, presiding at the birth of that society, had diverted any tendency to see in external Deity the relation of father or mother to child. Prajāpati, Father of devas, men and *asuras* (disdeified *devas*), was no longer heard exhorting his children to be good and kind (*Bṛhad.*, 5, 2), nor did the learned believer any more address him as such (*ibid.*, 1, 5). Friendship and the friend are words far more frequent in the Piṭakas than in the Upaniṣads. And whereas the *guru*, as confessor and virtual dictator to his pupil in later Hindu literature, is unknown in both Vedic and Pali sayings, the *kalyāṇa-mitto*: the 'lovely' friend, is highly appreciated, albeit his position as such is nowhere made institutional. We find Ānanda saying: "The half of the God-life is friendship, companionship, intimacy with what is lovely (or with one who is lovely): *kalyāṇa*: a word which may be equated with *kalakâgathos*, or with the *prosphilē*:—'Whatsoever things are lovely,' of Ep. Philippians." "Nay, not so, Ānanda, nay, not so. It is not the half, it is the whole of the God-life. Of one with such friendship it is to be expected that he will make-become, make much of, the Way . . ."[1] "It is because I am a *kalyāṇa-mitto* that beings are set free from birth, old age, disease, dying and sorrow . . . It behoves you too, sire, to train yourself in becoming such a friend. To become this, you must be diligent in what is good. Your court ladies and gentlemen will follow your example."[2] "A

[1] *Saṃyutta*, v. 2.
[2] *Ibid.*, i. 87. 'Sire' is the king of Kosala.

monk who is a good friend, companion, intimate, serving, attending, honouring good friends, emulating their ways of thought shall fulfil the training, the moral life . . ."[1]

As I have said elsewhere, it will be new to most readers to hear that, as against thirty-three references to the 'friend' in the Old Testament, there is in all the early Upaniṣads but *one* instance of a word for friend in the phrase 'favouritism to friends.'[2] Even that is in the Maitri, probably later than the birth of Sakya. Mitra, the 'friendly' *deva,* is invoked in passing, as in the earlier Taittirīya, but this shadowy double of Varuṇa is not a live note in the teaching. It is only in the monastic Piṭakas that the figure of the man as friend to man, the woman to woman, first enters into Indian religion:—

> Then she to this poor almswoman drew near
> who was my fostermother in the faith.
> She taught to me *dhamma* . . . hearing her words
> before her I sat down to meditate.[3]
>
> Then came I where a woman mendicant
> shared with me food and drink and welcomed me,
> and said: Come forth into our homeless life.
> In gracious pity did she let me come—
> Patāchārā— and heard me take the vows.
> And henceforth words of wisdom and of power
> she spake and set before my face
> the way of going to the crown of life.[4]

The woman, too, whom we meet seeking the mustard seed, Kisāgotamī:—

> Friendship with noble souls throughout the world
> The Sage hath praised. A fool in sooth grows wise
> If he but entertain a noble friend.[5]

---

[1] *Anguttara*, iii. 118. [2] *Mait.*, 3, 5.
[3] *Therigāthā*, ver. 69 f. [4] *Ibid.*, 124. [5] *Ibid.*, 213.

And Sundarī:

> To thee I owe it, O thou noble friend,
> thou loveliest of the Therī sisterhood,
> that I the threefold lore have gotten now . . .[1]

The clearing of other relations out of the life of the Indian woman must have 'made-become' with a novel stimulus this amity, compassionate and ideal, with members of her own sex, in spiritual sisterhood and motherhood. It is perhaps the more strange, that I have yet to find any episode, such as the Commentators, and not the Suttas only, loved to relate, revealing a friendship, or at least the expression of it, rivalling that between David and Jonathan.

But when we need, to express the relation, the word 'love,' it is less surprising, that a gospel grown monastic has no consolation to offer save 'Hands off,' or to the bereaved sufferer: 'Well! but you were asking for it!' The death of the only son calls up but this:

> In bondage to the dear and sweet how many a *deva*, many a man
> woeworn submit themselves to lord of death's command.
> But they who, earnest night and day, cast out the lovely form,
> dig up the root of woe, death-bait so hard to pass.[2]

"Yes, householder, our dear ones bring sorrow and lamentation, pain, suffering and tribulation."[3]

This is all. Yet so near had the Founders brought the next world that it is wonderful to find the passing son, as able and ready to being ***a message from,*** and set up ***a tie between, that world and this***, made so utterly absent from the outlook of the aftermen.

[1] *Therīgāthā*, 331.

[2] *Udāna*, ii. 8, trans. by F. L. Woodward, *S. Bks. Buddhists*, viii. 1935.

[3] *Majjhima*, No. 87.

From love, it is, for us of Christendom, natural to pass to faith and hope. Here there is need, in current opinion of Buddhism, for a word of criticism and suggestion. 'Hope' is as absent from the wording of the teaching as it is from that of the Gospels. It is true that, for these, as for the Suttas, the "hope of all nations" was held to have been on earth, turning longing into a blessed 'moment' (*khaṇa*: moment, is Pali for 'opportunity') for satisfaction. But there was, in both the next step (and many after that), need for hope in the life of the satisfied one. The Epistles make this good:—"the hope that is in you," etc. The Suttas, so to speak, 'went one better' here. They cultivate *expectation*. *Āsiṃsā*, 'hope,' the desiderative of *āsa*-, to long for, is hard to find. But *pāṭikankhā*: "is to be expected," is often declared to be the result if a certain way of life is followed.

"So long as the Vajjians meet, rise up and do what is to be done in concord (*samaggā*), so long is growth to be expected of them and not decay.[1]

"The man, Moggallāna, who is not aware of his own faults 'as they really are,' of him it is not to be expected, that he will engender desire, will strive, will start energy for riddance of them. He is like a brass bowl from market or stithy, never used and cleaned . . ." Sāriputta is then made to state the opposite case.[2]

As to faith, a curious belief obtains among some Buddhists, especially among 'verts,' that in Buddhism is no faith, only knowledge. This is of course not the case where the writer is a student of Pali literature. Such may possibly be so far uncritical as to see, in what the 'Buddhas' say, so many *ipse dixits* of the

[1] *Dīgha*, ii. 14. [2] *Majjhima*, No. 5.

'Buddha,' as does *e.g.* Dr. Barua, in his essay 'Faith in Buddhism.'[1] But they will not be so inaccurate as to rule faith out of Buddhism early or late. They who do so would appear to see in 'faith' the acceptance of an article of belief, which is to be accepted on authority, and is indispensable to salvation. But here too, any careful reading of the Suttas, such as is now possible to the English reader, if only the translations are to him accessible, will show, not only that there is as much formulated matter of creed or dogma in them which is to be 'believed in' (*pasanna*) as in any other creed, but that there is the certainty of being cast into *niraya* (purgatory) if wrong views are held.[2]

This is, however, not a controversial work; my business is to indicate the attitude in the Nikāyas toward the sentiment of *saddhā*, which translators agree in rendering by faith (or belief or assurance). Now it is true that I do not find any episode so eloquent of belief in belief as the Gospel saying of the epileptic's cure:—" the father of the child cried out with tears: Lord, I believe! Help thou mine unbelief!" Or the Johannine saying: "Dost thou believe on the son of God? . . . Lord, I believe! and worshipped him." But the Suttas make it clear, that *saddhā*—and whether we translate by faith or belief or trust, or confidence or assurance, the meaning comes to the same, namely, that we act with the idea, combined with the desire, that we are making for what is both true and a better—that *saddhā* is the initial step or expression in taking such a course. Thus, in the Second Collection, No. 70,

[1] *Buddhistic Studies*, ed. Dr. B. C. Law.

[2] "If a man hold wrong views, Lohicca, I declare that one of two future births will be his lot, either purgatory, or rebirth as an animal." (*Dīgha*, No. 12, i, p. 227.)

"Take the case of a man in whom *saddhā* is born (*saddha-jāto*), he draws near, then attends (in person), then listens, then learns, then remembers, then scrutinizes the aim, then approves; hereupon desire is born, with this he ventures (*ussahati*), then he weighs (*tuleti*), then strives (*padahati*), as one who has a bestriven self (*pahit'atto*), he wholly realizes what is supremely real, and penetrating it by wisdom sees. Now if it had not been for faith he would not have drawn near "[1] . . . and so on.

In accordance with this series, faith is put first in a category of five, the five *indriya*'s, or senses, which (*a*) are suggestive, in a day of interest in mind-analysis, of a religious attempt to equate five spiritual faculties with the five of psychophysical sense; (*b*) were ranked as of importance in doctrines; (*c*) were an early effort, relatively speaking, at categorizing. Namely, they were in existence as a Five when the compilers of the Fourth Collection drew up their Fives, for they head the list and at some length, viz. as five 'strengths,' when *e.g.* such fives as the *khandha*'s are absent. Here again, effort (*viriya*) follows faith, deliberation is worded by *sati*, guidance not of earth only by *samādhi*, whereof more presently, and progress is called *paññā*, which in the same Collection is identified with a 'making-become.'[2]

Another instructive context is in the talk to the rich lady-supporter Visākhā, in the Fourth Collection, where the consistent votary is shown as thinking on those who have gone to a well-deserved happy world, and saying: "Such faith exists in me as they had when on earth, whence has come their present happiness."[3]

[1] *Majjhima*, No. 70. [2] See above, p. 266.
[3] *Anguttara*, i. 210.

We even find the Founder made to say, in the Bhakti-vein: "Of them who do but believe in me, do but love me (*mayi saddhamattaṃ pemamattaṃ*) all these are wayfarers to the happy world."[1]

And that disciples have left the world "from faith (*saddhā*)" is ever given as the one sound motive for such a step. If any valid distinction can be drawn between faith in early Buddhism and faith in institutional religions (including later Buddhism), it is that, in the former case, the faith is a hopeful assurance in the fact and possibility of man's nature, life and destiny as a Becoming, becoming ever a More towards a Most, rather than a sentiment culminating in the worship of a person seen as external.

Faith, hope and amity are nowhere, as in Christian Epistles, grouped, in the Piṭakas, in a category. They are detached 'sentiments,' *i.e.* complex expressions of the man through mind, where 'feeling,' largely detached from sense-impression, plays a strong part. No lack of regard is paid to the importance of the last, amity, in Buddhism; it is things about the other two that needed saying. Nor is there, to my knowledge, any list of sentiments or emotions to be found in Piṭakan books, even in those given to definitions. The only well-recognized and well-repeated cataloguing I find is in the field of feeling as sense. And I now turn to what the Suttas give us about that.

Sense.

This is perhaps less remarkable than what they, with such evident interest in the fact and nature of sense, *do not give us*. There is perhaps no greater contrast between ancient Indian psychology and our

[1] *Majjhima*, No. 22.

own early efforts, than the relative pains we are at to discuss the mind-work on impressions of sense, when these are succeeded by their products, sensation being suspended,—as when we remember a scene—and the Indian absence of attempts so to discuss. Mediæval Buddhism made some attempt to make good, as when the eleventh-century manual gives an analysis of the process (*vīthi*, way) of cognition through sense and after. Even there—but we can keep that till the end.

The five senses are, in the Nikāyas, now called *indriya*'s (*i.e.* controllings; 'faculties' is practically a literal rendering, viz. a power or ability to do), now they are called *āyatana*'s (*i.e.* place, sphere of meeting, or origin, or happening—I quote the Commentator). As such the term includes both organ (for which there was no word) and object of sense. They are also called, without explanation, *dhātu*'s, data or elements. Also, but rarely, 'doors' (*dvārā*, or gates), a term much more used in exegesis, and one which superseded the Upaniṣadic *suśayah* or 'openings.' Now it is possible that any or all of these collective names were in use at the birth of Buddhism; more we cannot say. We know that *indriya* is first used for senses in the middle Upaniṣads, viz. the Kaṭha; in the earlier, the term, in the singular, is used for vital power or vigour only. And in the Suttas, we meet with the five senses in detail usually without any collective name. There is a triad of such names occurring in the Anthologies of monks and nuns: *khandh'âyatana-dhātuyo*: groups, spheres, data:

> . . . That *dhamma* hearing: all about
> The body, mind, sensations, what they bring,
> And all the data of our knowledge . . .[1]

[1] *Theragāthā*, 1255; *Saṃyutta*, i. 196.

So I tried to make readable the compound '*khandha*'s and the rest.' So again in poems of the nuns:

> *sā me dhammaṃ adesesi khandhāyatanadhātuyo.*
> she to me *dhamma* taught about all that,

a line thrice repeated with one variant:

> *adesesi dhātuāyatanāni* ca.[1]

We have here one of the stock ślokas (two padas of eight syllables each), of which there are many, especially in the Nuns' anthology, and for my part I see in it a decorative flourish that will have taken a century and longer in which to emerge. It is in an increasing literature which is purely oral, that we not unnaturally look for a growth in category-cum-formula mania. The five senses, sometimes with *mano* added as a sixth, with their respective objects:—the seen, the heard, smells, tastes, the tangible, *mano*'s object being *dhamma*'s: things, or objects of mind,—are often enumerated with pedantically unnecessary iteration, without being called by any of the collective names mentioned. The Sutta teachings would gain greatly in directness and impressiveness if those names had been used from the first by the monk-compilers in the Kaṭha style, which is more like that of modern literature, and said, *e.g.*—

> The senses (*indriyāni*), they say, are the horses;
> Sense-objects (*viṣayaṃ*) what they range over;
> The self combined with senses and with mind
> wise men by name the enjoyer (*bhōktṛ*) call.

The Sutta-way is rather thus: "Because of sight (lit. eye) and visible shape (*rūpa*) arises visual consciousness (*cakkhuviññāṇa*); the collision of the three is contact. Conditioned by contact rises feeling; what one feels

[1] *Therīg.*, 43, 69, 170.

one perceives; what one perceives (*sañjānāti*), one thinks about (*vitakketi*); what one thinks about, one is obsessed withal (*papañceti*): hence obsessions concerning past, future and present objects beset and infest a man. Because of hearing . . ." here the mill turns afresh, when apparently the teacher's purpose had been equally well carried out, had he said here: So it is with the other four senses and mind.[1]

What can have been the reason for the difference in Buddhist method? Scarcely help in committing to memory. It is true that 'refrains' in Sutta prose are a very frequent feature, but they are not a constant feature. And if repetition and refrain were held necessary for learning by heart, why then the Suttas would be nothing but either these or metric pieces. But it is not so. Not seldom we come upon prose passages with as little repetition as anything in Upaniṣads or with ourselves. I venture to think, that the repetitions were indeed intended to make a major impression. But not so much to be of verbal assistance, as to rub in more thoroughly *the depreciation of the man*, as being in body and mind. The repetitions are specially frequent where the topic is either sense (and what it leads to) or *khandha*'s. Here is another emphasizing the transience and hence ultimately the 'ill' in all sense:

"Viññāṇa comes to pass, monks, because of a dual thing. What is that dual (thing)? Because of sight and because of visible object arises visual consciousness. Sight is transient, changing; its state is 'becoming-other-ness.' Visible objects are just the same. So this dual thing is both mobile and passing away. . . . Visual consciousness, sprung from a condition, from a

[1] *Majjhima*, Nos. 18, 148.

relation which is transient, changing, having 'becoming-other-ness,' is itself no less so. Now this kind of consciousness, happening because of a transient condition, whence shall it become perduring? Visual contact—as the collision, coincidence, encounter of these three phenomena is called—is transient, changing, having 'becoming-other-ness.' Arisen because of a transient condition, whence shall it become perduring? Come into contact one feels, is aware, perceives; hence these states also are mobile and passing away, transient, changing, having 'becoming-otherness.'"[1]

This longer formula is repeated for each of the other senses. It was a teaching by monks to and for monks:—to this had the mission to 'man' of the Sakyas come.

As to the psychophysical nature of the 'collision' (*sangati*)[2] or contact (*phassa*), no attempt is made throughout the Piṭakas to analyse it. Nor is there any felt need, in all five senses save touch, for mention of a *medium* between sense-object and the organ. But we can imagine that, for a country and a time, in which archaic analyses could locate colours 'in the heart' as seat of mind, it was no far step, so to transcend the bare touch-notion in contact, as to feel no need for either a material medium, or for the outleaping *eidola*-emanations of Greek thought.[3]

Whatever was actually held to take place in all contact, we find no underlying hypothesis of an illusory world or of a creating intelligence within. The association of *māyā*, the cosmic illusion of other and of later Indian thought, is absent from the whole of Piṭaka Buddhism. The only allusion in it to *māyā* is just the

[1] *Saṃyutta-N.*, iv. 67 f. [2] Also called *sangaha*.

[3] Even Aristotle only makes some sort of medium for sight a necessary condition (*De Anima* II, vii.).

craft of the conjuror, or analogously of any clever dialectician, in making you believe what he willed. The idea of *māyā* as a feature, a cause, in the 'ill' of life is never intruded, each or late, in Pali literature, so far as I am acquainted with it. On the contrary, the five forms of sense-impressions were eventually held up as ultimate realities among the elements making up the human complex. It is they that were real where the man, the recipient of the impressions, was not a reality. They were catalogued as 'things existing' perceived by that which is non-existent.'[1] I have pointed this out repeatedly, but still the idea is abroad—where the literature is little known—that the Founder explained the ills of life as due to *māyā*. The only approach to this, in the Suttas, is that *happiness*, in so far as it is based on the life of sense, is like mirage or the conjuror's trick-craft.

Sensation in experience became effective on external elements being brought into suitable focus, with organs made of similar elements within us. To effect contact of sense between without and within a threefold conjuncture, as we have seen, was needed:

"If (1) the action of the eye is not cut off, but (2) external visible objects do not come into focus,[2] and (3) a correlation according is not set up, there is not to that extent the manifestation of a corresponding degree of *viññāṇa*. (The same results when conditions 1 and 2 only are given.) But if the action of the eye is not cut off, if external visible objects come into focus, and if a correlation according is set up, then the corresponding degree of consciousness is manifested."

[1] *Compendium of Philosophy*.

[2] Literally: avenue; *āpāthaṃ āgacchanti*, *Majjhima-N.*, No. 28.

This is repeated, as is usual, for the other senses in turn. The widespread theory of 'like being known only by like' was considered to be implicit in these, the earlier doctrines. The elements were either (*a*) belonging to the self or internal, or (*b*) external.[1] Later it is referred to as an ancient doctrine.[2] But speculation concerning nature or mind is not a Buddhist characteristic. We find the more positive statements that variety in contact is due to difference in organ or an object. And from difference in contact, difference arises in feeling, perception, volition, etc.[3]

The picturesque metaphor of the Upaniṣads: 'grasper' and over-grasper' for sense-organ and object, I do not find in the Nikāyas.[4] There are other metaphors, most of which are for ethical, or for what we might call evangelical exhortation. But in two or three there are points of philosophical interest. In the Sutta called 'the Snake,' of the Sense-sphere Saṃyutta,[5] a man ('Everyman') is represented as fleeing for his life from four great snakes (the four elements), five assassins (the five *khandha*'s), with love-of-pleasure (*nandi*) in their midst with drawn sword. He hastens into a village, which he finds empty and about to be destroyed by bandits. Rushing away he comes to the perils of the sea, to cross which he has to make a raft and scull himself over with hands and feet. The Sutta gives its own exegesis. The empty village is the six organs of sense (*āyatanāni*), which any wise man declares are empty things and void. Note the

[1] *Ajjhattikaṃ*, *bahiddhā* or *bāhira*.

[2] *Atthasālinī*, 313; *cf.* my *Buddh. Psy. Ethics* (second ed.), lxviii.

[3] *Saṃyutta* ii. 140 f., P.T.S. ed.

[4] Above, p. 180 f.

[5] Vol. iv., p. 172 f.

more advanced nihilism in the Commentary:—" because they are common to many and *without a headman.*" In this connection it is well to remember that the traditional notion, quoted in the Upaniṣads, of the 'man seen in the eye' became a true symbol of the indwelling agent, whether conceived as divine or human, rather as both. The village-sacking bandits are the six objects of sense, each organ being conceived as 'hit' (*haññati*, meaning also smitten, hurt, slain) by objects seen or otherwise sensed as attractive or the reverse.

The notion, in sense-experience, of 'empty, emptiness' (*suñña, suññatā*), became as characteristic of Buddhist teaching and of its late metaphysic as *māyā* was not. It cannot possibly have been a feature in the original folk-gospel. Worthy in so far as it meant, that the 'worth while' in what makes for salvation is not to be found in the sense-messages as such, it would have ruined the attractive force in a folk-gospel. The needed emphasis in this is positive, of the More; not negative, not of the Less. The clearest statement of emptiness as an ideal may be read in the Second Collection (the only Collection giving any weighed attention to the notion), in Sutta 121. Here the residence of disciples in a disused lay-mansion is termed a relative solitude or emptiness; forest residence is relatively more of an emptiness; in it the ideal of complete aloneness becomes conceivable, an ideal described as "thoroughly purified supreme and uttermost," wherein "the mind (*citta*) leaps forward, is satisfied, stands firm, is released," an excellent ideal for the monastic recluse. Different is the description in Sutta 43, etc., where the world's emptiness is said to be being void of the self and what is 'self-ic'—a value of the 'man' in the Less. The not-Divine is substituted for the preceding value of the worth-whileness of getting rid of things relatively hindersome to growth in spirit.

To what extent the two values became fused in mediæval Buddhism lies outside my scope.

It was natural that persistence in mental analysis would lead to interesting developments in—*e.g.*, the nature of touch and things tangible (*phoṭṭhabba*), and the relation of these to sight and the seen. Of this more when we come to later developments.

One word more in relation to sense: what did mind as sixth sense imply? Does the catechism in the Second Collection, called the Great(-er) Miscellany (No. 43), throw light upon this? The question occurs:

"These five senses (*indriyāni*) have each a different field, different range, not mutually enjoyed. Now what is their common resort (*paṭisaraṇa*)? And who enjoys their field and range?"

"Mind (*mano*) is their common resort, mind enjoys their field and range."[1] And this is all. The following questions go on to deal with the physical bases of sense. Now the early Indian way, as we saw, had been seeing in *mano* an intermediary instrument between sense and the man or self. "By (or with) the (*manasā*) one sees," etc.[2] "And the word I have rendered resort, 'a going back or repeated going back,' appears in that early Indian way as just *śaraṇa*, in the sense of refuge, protection, *e.g.* by Prajāpati, by Death, etc.[3] In the Sutta we get the word for refuge modified, by *paṭi*-, to mean a constant or usual process, and we get the source and *raison d'être* of protection *left out*.

In the Commentary we get a curious double result.

[1] *Majjhima*, No. 43. [2] Above, Ch. II.
[3] *E.g.*, *Chānd.*, 2, 22, 5; *Śvet.*, 3, 17; 6, 18, etc.

First a touch of developed mental analysis; *then*, the older way consigned to an illustrating parable. *Mano*, it says, as *paṭisaraṇa*, is the *javano-mano*, *i.e.* the apperceiving, or fully aware mind (a term of much later analysis). As enjoyer, it is five-gate-ish, partaking by way of being charmed or repelled or muddled. This, the hedonic, the monkish, outlook does not get us far. But then, with gusto, a parable shows us a king receiving revenues from five villages. In these is no charm and the rest, but there *is* such in the proceeds of the money-values of what is paid in kind. But this belongs more properly to later discussion. The thing to note in the Nikāyas, as quoted, is the substitution, unexplained, undefended, of mind for the 'man.' We must be, in the text of the Sutta, where and *as finally it was compiled and written down*, at a good distance in time from the date and teaching of the Upaniṣads.

Again, the expression: doors or gates (*dvārā*), which became a technical term in the scholastic psychology of cognition, is in the older books but a picturesque simile. The only *formula* in which it there occurs is in that of sense-control called 'guardedness as to the doors of sense.'[1] But that the figure was ready, even in the earlier days, to fall into rank as a scientific term, and may even then have been often so used, appears from a parable in the Nikāyas of a 'six-gated fortified city' through the gates whereof come messengers, bringing a true message. The moral is that there are more ways than one of apprehending the gospel. And the six gates are explained to be the six organs of sense, 'mindfulness' being the doorkeeper.[2] But here

[1] *E.g.*, *Majjhima*, No. 107, etc. The abstract term is only in Abhidhamma.

[2] *Saṃyutta*, iv. 194.

the older teaching is not superseded. The messengers address themselves to no instrument, but to the man himself, "seated in the midst of the city." It is true he is called *viññāṇa*, not *purisa*. But then the messages, called the *yathābhūtaṃ vacanaṃ*, 'the word of the very true,' will not have belonged to that city only. *Viññāṇa* was the man awaiting messages from "a city which is to come." Is it not significant that here is no mention of *mano*?[1]

Khandha's.

In conclusion one more word on the five *khandha*'s, or rather on the four, excluding the body, which in Abhidhamma are called *arūpino*, or bodiless, lit. formless. These were *vedanā* (with which I have dealt above), *saññā*, a vague term for any kind of awareness, but somewhat more specially defined in exegesis; *sankhārā* and *viññāṇa*. Of these it only remains to add a few words.

For their order no reason is given in the Nikāyas; they are just sprung upon us. But in it I seem to see their being so 'sprung' in a period of changing values lying between the earlier days, when the self was far from being ejected, and a time when this was taking place. If the drafting of the fivefold category had happened in the latter, I fancy that the more complex number, '*sankhārā*,' might have come last. *Vedanā* naturally came first; the activities it covers lie next to physical sensations. Is not this how European psychology reasons? And had not Buddhism, when this fivefold scheme was drafted, ousted, or gone far in ousting the psychological datum of man-as-valuing

[1] *Cf.* above, p. 76.

from place of priority? Centuries later we see a quasi-readjustment had taken place. Buddhaghosa treats of *viññāṇa* (No. 5) *before* treating of Nos. 2, 3 and 4. And the *Compendium* also places it first after *rūpa*, but calls it *citta*.

Saññā may have got associated with naming at an early date; we find it so associated in exegesis. But when defined in the Suttas, it is said to be just perceiving this or that colour. But then *viññāṇa* is, when defined in the Suttas, really nothing more than just *saññā*:

"Why do you say *viññāṇa*? He is aware (*vijānāti*), therefore one says *viññāṇa*. Of what is one aware? Of tastes: sour, bitter, acrid, sweet, alkaline, non-alkaline, saline, non-saline."[1] Elsewhere the reply to this question is: "one is aware of what is pleasant, unpleasant or neither."[2] To a similar question *saññā* is described as "one perceives (*sañjānāti*) something is blue-green, red, yellow, white."[3] But in treating of sensations, no stress is anywhere laid on visual and sapid sensations being different, in respect of requiring a different aspect or functioning of mind to make them experienced as such. Exegesis too is here incurious, albeit given to note difference in prefixes, such as we have here. I should go beyond our book, if I suggested, a more discriminative force lay in the *vi-*; no notice is taken of it. Thus by Sutta-definitions of *saññā* and *viññāṇa*, the place for the latter would seem to be, in the four, that of second or third.

But it may have been, that when the new Buddhist academical life was taking shape, the worlds were not yet banished from earnest attention, as came to pass (and has come to pass with us); it may have been only

[1] *Saṃyutta* iii. 86 f. [2] *Majjhima*, No. 43. [3] Saṃy. *loc. cit.*

logical to include, in a summary of experience, the still inexpugnable man; and man under the name associated, as we have seen, with that earnest attention. Or again, whereas the man was still in the field, he was included under, shall we say, a lay name, but under the name most fitting a mental summary: *viññāṇa*, rather than *satta* (being) or *purisa*, or the new and deprecatory *puggala*.

Left in for this reason or that, and so termed, the 'man' was put, not first, but last. Why? Man, on the one hand, was furthest from the body. *Rūpa*, it must be remembered, was not so much 'body' as 'seen-thing,' or 'shape.' We are most obviously aware of man as the seen thing. We are least obviously, least overtly aware of him as the 'man,' the knower (*viññātar*), the self. On the other hand, has it not been urged, that India began her psychology, not with sense, but with the self? This is true, and we have seen that it was so. But in the *khandha*-category we have come a long way from that beginning; we are in a downward path of decadence in the study of man's inner world, a path making for materialism and atheism. In that downward path, the faith in 'becoming' sickened and died; the reality of the man did so too; he was being reduced to (*a*) what we see (*rūpa*), (*b*) what we infer from the ways of *rūpa*—an inference of the value which our thought would have if, on seeing the new wireless-directed aeroplane 'Queen Bee' at work, we should conclude no man was directing it.

In the third phase *sankhārā* we are confronted with another term which seems to have much of historic evolution to tell us, could we but hear. It is a word we do not find in pre-Buddhistic literature. The translation of it has ever been a poser. *Now* it is used in a wide loose sense to mean 'all things,' 'the world,' 'life':

> *Aniccā vata sankhārā* . . .[1]
> Transient, alas! are all component things;
> their nature 'tis to rise and fall,

is a famous catchword, associated with the passing of the Sakyamuni, and today forming perhaps the only Pali phrase a Buddhist knows. *Now* it is used to cover a very dumping-ground of 'states,' upwards of 50 in number, some, complexes, some, simple, to which the various renderings of 'confections, conformations, predispositions, *Gestaltungen*, *Hervorbringungen*, activities, syntheses, etc., have been given.

In the Suttas is one passage clearly limiting them to three:

> "How many *sankhāra*'s are there? Three, the *sankhāra* of body (*i.e.* deed), the *sankhāra* of speech, the *sankhāra* of thought (*citta*).

These are then defined respectively as inspiration and respiration; attending and pondering (*vitakka*, *vicāra*); *saññā* and *vedanā*. Why, or how (*kasmā*) is this so? is then asked. The not very enlightening reply is, because each pair is "bound up with deed, thought and word respectively, thus having first attended and pondered, one then breaks into speech." Not even thus much of explaining is given to the two others. Teacher and questioner are said to have been Dhammadinnā, the nun, and her former husband, the layman Visākha.[2] And at the close of the talk, the Founder has it all repeated to him by Visākha and says, 'as she spoke so had I spoken.' (Thus did a few women in the Order win its suffrages!) Here we see *sankhārā*

[1] *Dīgha*, ii. 157; *Therag.*, 676; *Dhammapada*, 277.
[2] *Majjhima*, No. 44.

understood as certain preceding *conjunctures* to activities of deed, word and thought.

So also in the Sutta, cited above, on each of the *khandha*'s, we read:

" Why do you say *sankhāra*'s? Because these compose what is compound. And what is the compound they compose? They compound *rūpa* in order to *rūpa-ness*, (*rūpattāya*), (*vedanā*) in order to *vedanā-ness* (*vedanattāya*), . . . and so on . . .[1]

" Just as one cooks rice-gruel to make rice-gruel," continues the Commentator, " or a cake to make a cake, so is this being brought together by antecedent conditions and wrought up into a (mental) compound termed *rūpa*. . . . By 'composing' is meant 'striving along, kneading together, effecting.' Together with the mental production of *rūpa* are compounded the feeling (*vedanā*) and other states associated with it. The essential mark of a *sankhāra* is 'being work of mind,' " or of purpose (*cetayita*).

This is a very rare instance of a Sutta bringing in the abstract form to aid in explaining, especially as these five forms are unique in the Piṭakas, and only one so far has been met with in Commentaries: *viññāṇatta*, or awareness, viz. in the Petavatthu *exegesis*: " just as in a burning corpse, from the departure of 'consciousness' no pain is felt . . ." And the conclusion seems forced upon us that, in this Sīha-Sutta in the Khandha-Samyutta, we have a something on the *khandha*'s later in time than the three *sankhāra*'s as named by Dhammadinnā.[2] She has not a word to say about abstracts. She does mention the five *khandha*'s—

[1] *Saṃyutta*, iii, 86 f.

[2] Complicating the assumption that the first two Collections (Nikāyas) were compiled from the third and fourth.

starts off with them. But it is passing strange that she establishes no connection whatever between them and her 'three *sankhāra*'s,' a context which is not found elsewhere.

But as to that, her talk and that preceding hers, the two Vedalla Suttas, are a very patchwork of partly disconnected themes. Teachers were not *writing* their discourses, much less entire books, when the Nikāyas took shape. And it is possible, that many Suttas were compiled from a number of briefer Sayings, handed down for generation after generation, recognizable by some tag or 'text,' *e.g.* 'The Three *Sankhāra*'s,' '*Viññāṇa* and *Paññā*.' And so we get the nun's traditional talk with Visākha made to begin with 'five *khandha*'s,' in a Saying on the term *sakkāya* ('the true,' or 'the very group'), showing the growing worth in man as being not a unity but a manifold; then made to continue on other tags; then coming to the text: 'three *sankhāra*'s,' where the *sankhārā* as a *khandha* play no part.

Actually in orthodox teaching, the *sankhāra*'s became not three, but some 52, of which more later. About these:—the wherefore of the placing of many of the items under this head appears to be, not so much to show a composite activity of mind in each, as to find some pigeonhole wherein to store *the increasing number of terms for mental life, taking shape with the growth of mental analysis*. For instance we find wisdom (*paññā*) listed as faculty, and as strength (or force); we find zest (*pīti*, or rapture) included as an emotional expression not fitly coming under *vedanā*; and so with the term, a Vedic term, of 'one-pointedness of mind' (*citt'ekaggatā*) an equivalent for *samādhi*, and others.

This then is the historical interest which I see in the origin and evolution of *sankhārā* in the human manifold. First an effort of insight to include, in that manifold, the consciousness of *constructive activity* as an essential factor in the *mano-kamma*, or activities of mind. Then, the referring to this group, or the dumping in it, the *further results* of mental analysis. Here, it was felt, was this and that in man's inner world: now where shall we, become aware of an ever greater distinguishable variety of experiences, list them? In the unique 'three *sankhāra*'s' we see this constructive, or rather reconstructive activity, linking *x* and *y* as conditions requisite for a given effect.

That the constructive activity as such was of tremendous significance, in that, from man's infancy, it was building for him the way in which he interpreted the world without him—this I do not think we find in the Nikāyas. Some suggestions of it we may meet with in Abhidhamma, but we should go too far were we to see it felt after, in the context *Saṃy*, i, 61 f.; *Anguttara*, ii, 47 f.: that "in this body-*cum-viññāṇa* was the genesis of the world, the stopping of it and the way thereto."

Nor do I hold, that the fourth *khandha*, for all the constructive activity suggested in its name, was meant to be set over against a relative *passivity* in the others. If this had been the case, we should, I think, have come upon a word for passivity. We do not; on the contrary, we find the word 'work of mind' (*manasikāro*) and action of mind (*mano-kammaṃ*) used in the most inclusive sense. It is true that the Indian, with the rest of the ancient world, looked upon knowledge as mainly a receiving, a being 'hit' or impressed. It is true that, with the rest of the ancient world, he could make very little efferent impression upon his world. But he was not one to whom the quiescent, the to-be-acquiescent made the stronger appeal. (Remember that the sitting brooding Buddha-*rūpa* is a late ideal.)

Much more and much earlier it was the *awareness of causation* which made on him the profound impression we note, in both middle Upaniṣads, and in all the Piṭakas. And causation is essentially a way of mobility, of change, of process. We see it shaping the meaning in 'the three *sankhāra*'s,' as we see it in the definition of forming something about-to-be in the *sankhārakkhandha*. The modern Buddhist scholar sees in this group the reply to my "no word for will in Buddhism," for does not its list open with *cetanā*, and has that not been accepted as meaning 'our volition'? I do not quite see eye to eye with them here, and I have said why above. Were their view sound, the *sankhārakkhandha* would have been defined as just *cetanā*, and not as much else of a different nature. But I think, that if we see productive and progressive activity in the original idea, and *then* the dumping-need supervening, we shall get as near to the history of this 'aggregate' as the jealously burying past permits.

In fact, had the monk-world of the Order confined their mental analysis to the fourth: the man (*viññāṇa*) as worth-er and 'of the worlds,' and to the third: man's activity, as constructive, in all the phases of reaction to what was without *and within*, that analysis would have been both sounder, and not superseded in our present era. The *khandha* notion of 'heaps' of an analyzed manifold is neither psychologically true, nor was it of the original teaching, nor was it useful. For all purposes of religion and ethics we get a far truer and more useful picture of (*a*) the man or self, (*b*) the instruments he wields in body and mind, than when he is treated by way of the transverse section and arrested in his life-process, as five groups. If we read the Suttas attentively, we see that the plan actually followed is much more that of (*a*) and (*b*), and that the *khandha*-plan is intrusive and hindersome. The plan followed is virtually the setting forth of process. Thus:

"Thinking results in desire; through desire objects are divided into what we like and what we dislike; hence envy and selfishness, hence quarrelling and fighting."[1]

"Conditioned by contact arises feeling: what one feels, one perceives, what one perceives one thinks about, what one thinks about one is obsessed withal."[2]

"Because of some datum there arises perception, opinion, thinking, volition, wish, aspiration. And according as the datum is low, mediocre or lofty, so will all these be."[3]

And a longer process was cited above under 'faith': one of trusting, drawing near, attending, listening and so on.[4]

These instances might be multiplied indefinitely and show a persistent effort to set forth mind-ways as orderly causal process, as emphatically, if of course not solely, a Buddhist concept. Perhaps the most notable example is (*a*) the generalized statement of cause and effect, (*b*) the monastic application of this to show the life process as leading up (or down) to 'ill.' Sometimes we get (*a*) introducing (*b*): (*d*) "this being, that comes to be; from the coming to be of this, that

[1] *Dīgha*, ii. 277.
[2] *Ibid*. (condensed): 'Obsessed' = *papañcasaññā*.
[3] *Saṃyutta*, ii. 153.
[4] *Majjhima*, Nos. 70; 95.

comes to be. This not being, that comes not to be; from the stopping of this that is stopped."[1] And then (*b*): " That is to say: Conditioned by ignorance, *sankhārā*, conditioned by *sankhāra*'s, *viññāṇa*; conditioned by *viññāṇa* name and shape," and so on with senses (the six), contact, experiencing, thirst, fuel (or grasping), becoming, birth, old age and dying, then 'ill' (grief, lamenting, suffering, sorrow, despair)."

Sometimes we don't; we get one or the other in isolation. The former (*a*) is a great generalization true for all time, the vision, at the time, of a great man. The latter (*b*) is a vision of the Less. It sees value and profit only in the latter half of the generalization:—stop the effect by stopping the cause, that is, if you would stop 'ill.' That to produce 'well,' *le bien*, you should *set this or that cause in motion*, is passed over.

But in all these process-words we need no *khandha* division. For good or for worse the division was brought in. I am waiting for the historian's judgment, that of the original teaching it certainly was not.[2]

[1] *Saṃyutta*, ii. 28, etc.

[2] I have no explanation to offer for the curious choice of 'five' in it. But I have somewhere read of 'five' as the Indian village unit: four men and a headman. And we have seen (p. 315) how the simile of the 'village' was used. Some day a better known Pali exegesis may link that unit and the *khandha*'s.

CHAPTER XVI

THE OTHER-WORLD MIND

UNDER this title: the other-world mind, I am dealing with the three subjects familiar to readers of Buddhist works, as *jhāna*, *iddhi* and *abhiññā*, terms which we may render as musing, will-potency (or psychic potency) and super-knowledge. I have treated of each of these in some detail in Chapters IX, XII and XIII of the book entitled *Sakya*; hence I can write of them here more briefly. In calling them collectively other-world mind, I am going a little beyond any present theory put forward in either Buddhist or European books. I am judging, namely, at least for purposes of this exposition, that in the so-called psychic experiences coming under these three heads, we have the man or self experiencing largely through the 'other' body which is ever somehow encasing him, called in many books of East and West the 'subtle body,' a body which becomes in deep sleep, swoon and after death his main and active instrument, just as during waking earth-life his visible body is functioning.

I have already said (p. 125), that teaching in the Upaniṣads is vague and vacillating about this dual body. Strange to say, in Pali literature, whereas there is any amount of acceptance in things abnormal and supernormal, the 'other body' finds, so far as I know, no mention. And I say this so that the reader may distinguish my theory from anything that the Nikāyas have to say on other worlds. I am not saying, it is easy to guess why we read nothing in them about another body. There is at least no foolish talk in them (in, *e.g.* the anthologies: Petavatthu and Vimānavatthu, which deal wholly with human beings who have passed on and are being 'psychically' interviewed from earth) of a 'disembodied' or 'discarnate' personal existence. The persons so interviewed are too clearly embodied for that, embodied in a way to which no idea of the ghostly or subjective is applied. No explanation whatever is either given, or felt to be needed. The early syncretic mind of India, as of other lands, was childlike enough to take much more as real than it could 'prove' or cared to prove, that is, explain by certain very limited premises.

And nowhere, in the Piṭakas, have I found such experiences as are given in those two anthologies, or others in the Suttas, judged, by the original compilers, to be of "such stuff as dreams are made of," much less explained as experienced by a morbid mind. Indeed it would have been impious in many cases to have given that reason. It survived in the Sayings, that the Founder himself both had such experiences, and in relating them made no effort to explain them away. For instance, he is made to say, after recounting a 'visit' paid him by a deceased lay-patron: "Good! Ānanda, what can be known by inference, you have here known. That *deva* was verily Anāthapiṇḍika."[1] The Founder is also made to say, that to be conversing with *deva*'s who are present is to be experiencing a purely happy world (or environment), namely, when in the enjoyment of *jhāna*. He is also repeatedly recorded as saying that he had learnt certain things from devas. And certain of his chief

[1] *Saṃyutta*, i. 56.

disciples are said to have been adepts in all three of the above-named practices. Psychic experiences, then, especially that of levitation, were accepted as unquestioned happenings from the compiling of the Nikāyas to the day of Buddhaghosa. But no care was taken to inquire into the human instrument called in them into play.

Jhāna.

Jhāna means just 'thinking,' from the stem *dhī, dhyā*, and must not be held by the young Pali student as a derivative of *jhāyati*: to burn, from the stem *kṣā*. It has been shown that, whereas in the earlier Chāndogya Upaniṣad, *dhyāna* appears as just one 'more' in man's inner furniture among many others, in the later Maitri it reappears classed as one phase in a sixfold 'yoga,' or inward-directed discipline.[1] In the Buddhist Suttas, it retains its unclassified vagueness; it is ever recurring; nothing is more pervasive; but it remains as an attitude which is nowhere defined, not even in Abhidhamma. Other terms associated with it are in the latter defined, such as *samādhi* (called also *adhicitta*, or higher thought)[2], and *citt'ekaggatā*; it is not. Nirvana (*nibbāna*) we find queried and defined, *bhava* (becoming) also, and other terms, but not *jhāna*. It was an old and accepted term. *Samādhi* (lit. to put continuously on to, compose, concentrate) and *citt'-ekaggatā* (one-pointedness of mind) are both defined. In Abhidhamma, they mean "stability, solidity, absorbed steadfastness of mind . . . absence of distraction, balance, unperturbed mental procedure, calm." In the Second Collection, too, we find *samādhi* analyzed, but in different terms:

[1] Above, p. 73.

[2] *Anguttara*, i. 229 ff.

[3] Dhammasangaṇi, §§ 11, 15.

"What, lady (*Dhammadinnā*), is *samādhi*? What are its outward signs (*nimitta*)? What is its equipment? What is the making-*samādhi*-become?

"One-pointedness of mind is *samādhi*; the four presences of *sati* are its outward signs; the four right efforts are its equipment, and the practice, make-become, increase, in those things are the making-*samādhi*-become."[1]

Now there emerges time and again in the Suttas a fourfold formula called 'first, second, third and fourth *jhāna*,' and into the second of these stages those two terms enter, thus: the four stages describe the man as eliminating successively the intellectual activity present in the first, when he may be said to win the second, and the hedonic factors of consciousness when he may be said to win the third. The fourth is the winning of perfect *sati* (lucid, alert mentality) and of indifference (*upekkhā*) or poise. And number two is called "born of *samādhi*" (*samādhi-ja*) and "a state of one-fixedness" (*ekodibhāva*). Thus those two terms are used as factors in a wider genus of *jhāna*.

It should be noted that the word *yoga* does not occur in the formula. There is, in fact, nothing in the formula that points distinctively, as did *yoga*, to *intensive introspective* 'meditation.' Intellection as such is to be banished, as is emotional distraction; but the practiser is not to be in any sort of quasi-drugged or muzzy state, in trance, coma or ecstasy, nor absorbed in thought. He is to be mentally composed, lucidly alert, equable. I suggest that what we have is rather the attitude of the watcher who has made his mind a *tabula rasa* and is waiting to learn.

That which may, in his next experiences, come to

[1] No. 44. Sometimes rendered, not judiciously, by 'rapture.'

be experienced is one thing in the Suttas, another in the Abhidhamma treatment of Jhāna.[1] In many contexts in the Nikāyas the fourfold *jhāna*-formula is made to precede the experiencing of one or all of the psychic states called *iddhi* and *abhiññā*, *e.g.* in the Second Collection, Nos. 36 and 51. The musing was apparently considered to be a *preparatory practice, favourable to the inception of psychic experience.* Nothing is said as to this inception being possible, probable, or neither. The psychic states are just enumerated serially as being one and all experienced in turn, and making the impression on us, on me at least, that the compilers *had not themselves any experience at first hand of what they were recording.* They would have told it so differently if it had been so.

But if, in what they have handed down, there was ever any living truth, then this systematic musing was a training, not, as writers now say (myself excepted), for either a monastic pushing away from the attention, of 'the world,' natural or social, nor a sort of scale-playing in mastery over the thoughts, but a training in readiness to receive supernormal experience.

I will here repeat evidence bearing me out. In the Fourth Collection, it is said, access is gained to devas (good men of the next world and of the world 'beyond') in '*jhāna*.'[2] In the Second Collection Gotama is said to reply, that a purely happy world is made present, when a man in fourth *jhāna* has devas present and conversing with him.[3] In the Abhidhamma, Book I, the *jhāna*-section begins with the words: "at what time one makes-become a way for access to the world of the seen (*rūpa*, *i.e.* the Brahma-world, or world

[1] See below, Chap. XVIII.
[2] *Anguttara*, ii. 184.
[3] No. 79.

'beyond'), he enters into *jhāna*-stages. In the Vimānavatthu Commentary one of the first missioners, Moggallāna, is said to enter *jhāna*, that he may get into touch with the next world and report what he finds has been the happy fate of individuals who were worthy on earth.

So far I have found writers on *jhāna* entirely ignoring this and other Piṭakan evidence, and in consequence leaving out other worlds, which in original Sakya were so real and so much present. Or else, they see in *jhāna* that which we call mystic experience.[1] For me (as I have said), early Buddhism may be rated as 'mystical' or not; or it may be rated as akin to Yoga (of which it shows no awareness) or not. But its early 'musing' or *jhāna* cannot rightly be identified with the outlook in either. *Jhāna* was less obscure than the one, and was not the inward attitude of the other. In its broadest, its most real, because its, for us, most practical meaning mysticism is *converse, usually solitary, with the unseen.* Converse is access, is comm-union, not union. Attention is really turned outward. When, if ever, the earth comes to accept this humbler, more practicable aspect of mysticism, instead of using terms of an as yet inconceivable union with an as yet inconceivable Highest, we may then come to hold in wider worth a mysticism, that is not only attainable by a saintly aspirant now in this continent, now in that century, but one that is a way for the help of the many, *ye keci sikkhakāmā*:—whosoever are willing to learn (*Dīgha*, ii, 101).

[1] *E.g.*, Professor F. Heiler, *Die Buddhistische Versenkung*, and Professor E. Hauer, *Der Yoga als Heilsweg*.

Iddhi.

We have seen that in the early meaning of the early, the Vedic term *dhyāna*, original Buddhism or Sakya attained a very distinctive position: the admission that there were mindways, showing themselves at least in some men (and women), capable of reacting to impressions given by beings not living in this world. That in such persons—persons we are now agreeing to call 'psychic'—these impressions were made by way of a sensitive organism or body, which was not that engaged in the activities of earth-life, is nowhere admitted—this I have said. That an organism needed to be one 'in touch with' other-world conditions does not seem to have occurred to such mental analysis as entered into Sakyan consciousness. In this respect we are in our own psychology no further than were the first Buddhists. And greatly will a generation to come wonder over this.

In *jhāna* they were as a man who at night puts out the light in his room, that he may the better from his window look out for what stars it may then become the more possible for him to see. That they had to get rid as far as possible of what earthlife was bringing them—this the formula makes clear. Why, for what purpose this was to be done:—this, when the formula was drafted, had been lost, lost in the newer values, in which the nearness, the watching sympathy of the worlds, the striking example set them by the founders had been worsened in minds bent mainly, if not solely, on earth. John Bunyan would have handed those aftermen a muckrake.

It was not held absolutely necessary, that the *jhāna* posture and attitude should preface that experience of abnormal will known as *iddhi*, but the fact that some contexts give the latter as preceded by the former strengthens the theory, that both were such experiences as we call abnormal, and not the latter only. *Iddhi* is a break-down from *ṛddhi*, a word derived by Whitney from either (or both) *vṛdh*, to grow, *rādh*, to succeed. Had there been a word like our 'will,' it would probably have here been used. *Iddhi* covers a number of achievements, bodily and mental, which we of average powers may will to do, but when we try we fall short. Thus the first is that rising and temporary remaining in the air unsupported, which we bring to pass, in a lesser degree, whenever we jump, in the 'high' or 'long' jump. The long jump is used in the later *Questions of Milinda* as an example of the domination of thought, *i.e.* will, over weight of body. Were our athletic jumpers' wills stronger, they might rival the achievements, well witnessed in the last century, of Daniel Home. Indeed, it is the want of an adequate word for will, or the 'synergy' which includes bodily action, that causes the Buddhist compilers to talk queerly about converting *citta* into body or the reverse.

The formula of *iddhi*-varieties runs in the Nikāyas as follows:

"Being one he becomes many; having become many, he becomes one; here visible, there invisible, he goes without let or hindrance through wall, through rampart, through air; he makes immersion-emersion in earth as if in water; he walks on water unbreaking it as if on earth; he travels seated crosslegged through air as if he were bird on the wing; he can handle and stroke with the hand the moon and sun, mighty and powerful though they be; he has control over the body as far as Brahmā-world."[1]

[1] *E.g. Dīgha*, i. 77 f.

Writers on early Buddhism, with one exception, Dr. H. Beckh,[1] push this matter of *iddhi* aside after the method of repellent rationalism. I believe that in time psychical research, coupled with historical criticism, will find in it, not merely a ruined pillar to be glanced at and passed by, but a subject that merits sympathetic consideration. The concluding clauses look extravagant enough, but less so to historical criticism. The inmates of the near world included a presiding *deva* of the sun and one of the moon, who might be clairvoyantly seen, and even, as if in modern séance, 'stroked.'[2] And Brahmā-world in the person of one or other of its inmates could be within reach of any psychic desiring intercourse. Such an one was believed to have interceded with the Founder on behalf of men needing him. It must be remembered that our not yet discarded notions of 'up above' for other worlds did not exist for the first Buddhists; we can see them coming in. Translators have here misled us.[3]

Mindful of this, we may come to see the list as showing restraint rather than extravagance. The clauses show where achievement may be possible, given a stronger will than is possessed by the average man. It is noticeable that undergoing ordeal by fire without injury finds no mention. The carrying on life under earth or water is not pushed to the pitch we might have expected, in view of tested experiments made under modern medical scrutiny of the former. But my aim here is not to inquire into abnormal bodily achievement. It is the recognition of the reality of abnormal will

[1] *Buddhismus*, ii. 72 f.

[2] *Parimaseyyaṃ parimajjeyyaṃ*.

[3] *E.g. Dialogues of the Buddha*, i. 280 f. (There is no "went up" in the Pali.)

'at a higher power,' and the assigning to it a special and interesting word that is the business of this book, a word which so far from being taken over from an earlier literary tradition, occurs but once in the early (or in later) Upaniṣads,[1] and only once in the *Bhagavad-gītā*,[2] both times in the sense of experiencing luck. To what extent, if any, the abnormal power of will testified to in *ṛddhi* or *iddhi* has ever been attributed to an abnormal conjunction of activity in the *body as dual* I cannot say. So indifferent are most of us to the possible existence of the other body, let alone the psychology of our mind-ways in working it, that it may yet be some time before inquiry into it comes to assist 'abnormal psychology.' But evidence in the matter of other-world communication points to a general heightening in power, and swift effectiveness of will in other worlds, as compared with our earth-average.

Abhiññā

This term (lit. much-, or super-knowing) is scarcely ever used in the specific meaning it came later to have to denote five, and then six modes of a higher power of cognition. More often it is used as a gerund: "having thoroughly known (of themselves)," so used in a stock saying. And also as noun in another stock saying, where this or that is said either to conduce, or not to conduce to seven things, of which *abhiññā* is one. (In the edited First Utterance, the seven, *abhiññā* the second, amount as yet to only four.[3]) In these contexts only is the word used in the First and Second

[1] *Bṛhad. Up.*, 5, 14, 7. [2] II. 8.
[3] *Vinaya*, Mahāvagga, I. 6.

Collections. In the Fourth, the term 'six *abhiññā*'s' has crept in as a patent insertion (*chaḷ-abhiññā*),[1] but the term does not occur as a list in the Book of the Sixes. But in the third Collection, we meet with the interesting inconsistency, that now the *abhiññā*'s are five, now they are six.[2] And this, as I have said in Sakya, is probably due to the later addition of a sixth, which in no way tallies with the first five.

I take this sixth first, the rather to show the contrast and clear it out of the way. The wording is not always identical; the usual way is: "having of himself thoroughly known (*abhiññā*) and realized, through the waning of the cankers (*āsavā*), even in this life, release of mind, release in wisdom, he abides therein." There is here indicated a power of insight, but the object is religious and ethical, not that of psychic development. The term *āsavā* too, meaning lusts, becoming (*i.e.* life- and world-opportunities of becoming) and ignorance (a fourth, 'opinion,' gets added later), is intrusive and alien to psychic interest. It is an interesting fact that, in the Visuddhi-magga, written in the fifth century A.D., this sixth item is dropped from the chapter called that on *Abhiññā*'s. The Commentaries, however, show no discrimination in the matter. That on the Second Collection calls all the six a training in insight into the advantages in morality! (*sīlānisaṃsa-dussan'-atthaṃ*).[4]

Of the other five the first is but a restatement of the *iddhi*-formula.

[1] *Anguttara*, i. 258.

[2] *Saṃyutta*, ii. 216. There appear to be five only in the Aśokâvadāna. J. Przyluski, *La Légende de l'empéreur Aśoka*, p. 395.

[3] *Ibid.*, ii. 217; *M.* No. 6.

[4] *Papañca-sūdanī*, i. 1-54 (P.T.S. ed.).

The rest are:

(2) " With the *deva*-hearing, pure and surpassing human hearing, he hears both (sorts of) sounds, whether distant or near;

(3) he knows (or understands, *pajānāti*) fully comprehending (*paricca*) with the mind (*ceto*) the mind of other men, other beings;

(4) he remembers the variously circumstanced past residings.

(5) he by *deva*-sight, purified surpassing human sight, sees beings."

Here we are concerned with psychophysical supernormal attainment. The reader will admit as much, but so crude is as yet our comment on the foregoing category, usually called sixfold, that I have yet to meet with any one who has queried the contrast between 1—5 and 6. But I have further comments to make.

(*a*) The arrangement at first sight looks haphazard. That *iddhi*-modes were placed first is, conceivably, because the list of these may have been an earlier, a very old attempt to distinguish and catalogue. Or it may have been so placed as referring to external effects, things done by supernormal will, Nos. 2-5 being rather of the nature of afferent experience. But that psychic hearing should come first in 2-5 and psychic sight last *may suggest first-hand knowledge* in the cataloguers. Even we—some of us—know that (i.) things seen are the result of a blend of touch and visual experiences, but that in hearing we are relatively independent of touch; that touch is a sense depending more on contact, *under identical conditions*, than is hearing, and is therefore harder to get than aural psychic results; (ii.) in hearing we come nearer, in speech, to the impact of another will upon us, than we do in sight. Hence what we now call clairaudience is an experience nearer to the normal than any other. In No. 3 again we are grading off in every degree from the normal. The power of inference from what is normally seen and heard differs greatly in individuals, and has provoked much debate when experts in what we call thought-reading have given apparently supernormal exhibitions. Such power of normal inference is taken into account in the Suttas, but the three modes of it are all called 'wonders' (*pāṭihāriyā*). The first kind is either by *iddhi*, or what we might call intuitive insight, or it is by *ādesanā* 'indicating,' either by signs (*nimitta*) observed in another, or light is thrown on the other's thought by words heard "from men, or not-men, or devas."

In No. 4 we are certainly up against a rare gift, but one which is, to judge by evidence, very intermittent and of all shades of difference from the normal. Children have been known to show such memory in a startling degree, and I went into one such case myself in Rome recently. Pali literature does not once adduce children as the usual cases of it; it is the Founder himself who is usually shown exercising it. But it may be, that No. 5 "*deva*-eye" or 'clairvoyance' seemed to the compilers of the list to be yet more rarely come by, if indeed the list goes by degree of supernormality. The word 'residings' (*nivāsa-*) will seem strange. But it should be noted that there was no word in Indian tongues for 'lives' in the plural. And 'becomings' (*bhavā*) had, perhaps, in this old formula come to be so used. In the enlargement which follows, the work of other compilers, the word 'births' (*jātiyo*) is first introduced.

(*b*) I have not, in three of the four cases, given the full formula. I have a strong belief that in these a deal of padding has been added. This is in Nos. 3, 4 and 5. In 4, there follows a wordy account of lives recalled, from one only, to a 100,000, even to æons, then details of having been of such a family, rank, etc.—foolish stuff and most unnecessary, since no heed is taken of any 'becoming' in a more or a less of the survivor, and no care is taken, in asking followers to believe such a fairy-tale in time, to support it by any authority worthy of credit. In 5, on the other hand, the growth or becoming, in what the man of *deva*-vision is held to see, is of first importance. But we hear not a word of what is so frequent in the Suttas, the seeing of worthy advisers and helpers in the unseen watching the men of earth and giving, or for that matter taking, information and advice. The man so gifted is not represented, as was the Founder so often, and some too of his men, seeing and conversing with a *deva*, but is, as it were, on a sort of judgment-throne, watching men surviving death both here and in the next (*i.e.* 'other') world. I incline, I repeat, to the inference, that we have here implicit the absence of any first-hand acquaintance, in at least the latest compilers, with supernormal, *i.e.* psychic vision. Had there been such acquaintance, it would have been told much more simply and differently. It may be we have here the traditional telling of what some Moggallāna actually saw in a vision.

(*c*) If it be questioned whether our terms clair-audience and clairvoyance fit the gifts under Nos. 2 and 5, I only use them because they are more intelligible for us than the literal "*deva*-eye," "*deva*-ear," and because they are, I think, juster than the very misleading renderings mostly used of celestial or heavenly ear and eye. In some contexts they are used for cases of telepathy.

(*d*) If it be asked whether, in the Piṭakas, one or more of these psychic gifts was during life a permanent or a transient attainment, there is one context bearing on this that is worth quoting. In the First Collection, No. 6, is a conversation recorded as between a disciple Mahāli of Vesālī, and Gotama. Mahāli asks whether a disciple, Sunakhatta, who had been clairvoyant but not clairaudient, had been himself the cause of the lack in the latter gift, or whether there were no *deva*-sounds that anyone could hear. "Nay," is the reply, "they are real, those deva-sounds; they are not things of naught. . . . But Sunakhatta has only in a one-sided way made concentration become; were he to make-become the double concentration he might enjoy both gifts."

(*e*) Attainment, as well as practice towards this, in these gifts is represented[1] as being a matter, not of desire only, but of desire as worded by the strong term "longing for" (*ākankhati*), where the prefix *ā* stresses the weaker meaning in the verb. "If he were to long to . . ." (*ākankheyya ce*, and *sace ākankheyya*).

To this extent then do we find early and even original Buddhism revealing a notable and distinctive advance in the recognition and analysis of the man of abnormal mind. And by 'abnormal' I am not doing it the injustice of saying the morbid or the pathological mind. The sanity that shines out in the Co-founders —some may except our friend Moggallāna—has drawn the appreciation of the outside and modern world.

[1] In Second Collection, No. 6; *cf.* No. 120, etc.

They held, no less than did the apostles of the Jesus-mission, that "these were not things of naught"—mere subjective illusions—nor experiences of only unbalanced minds. Either the records show a telling of wide-awake sane experience at first hand, or reveal at second hand a reverent valuing of the More in the many ways, by which it was given to a man or woman of special ability, or more-will, of earnest aspirations, to develop, to 'make-become' his or her nature.

CHAPTER XVII

THE WORTHY, OR ARAHAN(T)[1]

Our psychology, divorced in infancy from religion and philosophy, is so much concerned with the normal or average man—I should better say, mind—and, more lately, in 'abnormal' psychology, with the divergence, mainly in falling off, from that normal mind, that it has taken little if any count of the man as abnormally excellent, or 'gifted,' or in the process of growth or 'becoming' leading thereto. Nor do I find in earliest Indian literature, that in it the birth of psychology included any analytic interest in the man as supernormally 'worthy,' let alone 'holy.' Men were shown as better or worse, and a few as markedly so. But I have found no distinct psychological criteria by which the better man was held to pass muster. That the Piṭakas show us such a term for the supernormally 'worthy' man, and such criteria definitely worded, is a distinctive development in Indian psychology under early Buddhism.

In this distinctive development are two special features: the name for such a man, and the estimate of him as having actually, as man, attained consummation even on earth, or of him as sure to attain it in his next rebirth.[2]

[1] I am glad to be able here to be brief, referring readers to Miss I. B. Horner's forthcoming essay on this subject.

[2] This is an alternative usually found in the Fourth Collection, *e.g.* i, 232, 245; 9 references in all.

The name is *arahan*[1] (other forms are *arahant*, *arahat*, *arhat*: all are grammatically justifiable) from the stem *arh*, to deserve, or be fit, and we do not find this word applied to outstanding worth of any kind in man before the appearance of a Buddhist literature. In early and middle Upaniṣads the verb is now and then used to mean 'fit' or 'able-to,' in the contexts: 'fit to explain,' 'unable to refuse,' etc. The adjective occurs also now and then, meaning fit or proper. The noun I do not find. In the Gītā the verb, as enjoining an 'ought' to be or do, is much more frequent, but neither here is there the noun. It is apparently only in the Brāhmaṇas, that we read of "a worthy person" (*arahant*) as upholding the dignity of a Soma ceremony, but nothing further is said about him.[2] He is, as we already have found him in the Rig-Veda, just the worthy, fit and pious fellow: layman or priest; kindling the fire to Agni:

arhantas cid yam indhate,

or liberal-handed praising the sacrifice to the Maruts:

Arhanto ye sudānavah.

When, on the other hand, we take up the First Piṭaka, and read of the traditional episodes in the birth of 'Sakya,' we are in an *arahan* picture almost at the outset. It is true that, in these, the verses first inserted call the, shall I say saint? a "brahman." But after the bodhi-tree enlightenment episode, the Founder arrogates to himself the term in verses where he is made to say:

ahaṃ hi arahā loke !

I verily am worthy-one in the world !

---

[1] *Cf.* the Far Eastern corruption to *lohan*.

[2] *Cf.* Śatapaṭha Bṛ. 3, 4, 1, 3 and 6.

The Jain term *jina*, 'conqueror,' he is also made to claim, but this fades out, and the founder is seen claiming the threefold title of *tathāgata, arahan, sammāsambuddha.* Thereupon all the first converts appear as so many *arahans*, five, then six, then eleven, then sixty-one, then a thousand, plus the sixty-one.[1] Not that the Sakyans alone claim the title. Discounting for my purposes its use by the new company who came to be called Jainas, or Jina-men, we find a *religieux*, a fire-worshipper (possibly a missioner from Persia), entering into a sort of competition in psychic power with Gotama, repeatedly claiming: "None the less he is not *arahan* as am I," thus linking up this term with the older one of *rishi* (Pali: *isi*), a world-forsaker believed to have the power to bless, but more especially to blast. Elsewhere in the Vinaya the word *arahan* hardly occurs. In the Sutta-Piṭaka the word is frequent, but no longer as meaning one given to affect others with supernormal power. Either we hear of others who become "yet one more arahan in the world," or the word occurs in discourse on saintly standards of worth, these including the psychic powers I have discussed in the last chapter.

Notable in such discourse are certain formulas, giving expression to the attainments constituting a man *arahan.*[2] These are four; and since they amount to analytical judgments on the mental equipment of such a man, I give them in full:

(*A and B*) "He alone, withdrawn, zealous, ardent, with the self bedriven (*pahitatto*), not long after abides in the attainment of that supreme goal of the God-life, for the sake of which sons of (good) families rightly

[1] *Vinaya*, Mahāvagga I.
[2] See my Index vol. to *Saṃyutta*, Introduction, P.T.S. ed.

leave the world, having of himself known it thoroughly and realized it even in this life: namely, birth has waned out (*khīṇa*), the Godlife has been lived, done is what should be done, no beyond for these conditions."

(*C*) "This monk is called *arahan*, in whom *āsava*'s are waned out, who has been a liver, done what ought to be done, has laid down the burden, has attained the very Aim (*attha*), has the fetter or rebirth utterly waned out, is, having rightly come to know, set free."

(*D*) "Then the knowledge rose up for me: Unshakeable for me is release of mind; this is the last birth; there is now no further becoming."

It is clear from these, that in the *arahan* peculiar to Buddhist culture, we have a picture of man as having done, finished, attained to all that was in the mind of the compilers as to things held most worthy, man as perfect, as consummated. To us it may seem very much too much to expect of any man 'here below.' It was an outcome of a culture preceding, accompanying, that of Sakya, in which the notion of man had undergone the tremendous uplift given it in Upaniṣadic Immanence. In that, man was capable of 'becoming Brahman' (albeit not in this world), because in essence, in potentiality he *was* Brahman. The early Buddhists had eliminated the divine indwelling self, and as if by way of compensation they had substituted the ideal, attainable on earth, of a perfect purely human self, with certain abnormal potencies of will included.

That a man should so attain, it was not necessary that he should have *first* 'left the world.'[1] Nor was he conceived as absorbed in his own salvation, regardless of fellowmen. His other-regarding virtues are

[1] On this debatable point see *Kvu* (*Points of Controversy*), Bk. IV. 1; also *The Milinda Questions*.

detailed in what is perhaps a very early saying, the talk between Gotama and Visākhā.[1] In it, *arahan*'s are taken as examples of positive (not merely negative) morality; of modesty, also kindness and sympathy for all beings. They are further commendable for certain monkish abstinences; for monks were the great majority of those who, or for whom, the title was claimed:

> The yellow robe, that goodly dye,
> That freed souls wear without disgust,
> The banner of the arahan . . .[2]

And I cannot recollect coming across a woman who, or for whom, the title was claimed, who was not wearing that banner; thus Sundarī presents herself to the Founder, in her poem, in terms of the *arahan* diploma:

> Thou art buddha! thou art master! and thine,
> Thy very daughter am I, issue of thy mouth,[3]
> Thou very brahman! even of thy word.
> Accomplished now is my appointed task,
> And all that drugged my heart is purged away.[4]

Pajāpatī, his fostermother, a leading nun:

> And now I know my living frame's the last.
> No more Pajāpatī shall come to be![5]

Another, Bhaddā Kapilānī:

> We both have seen, both he and I, the woe
> And pity of the world, and have gone forth.
> We both are *arahan*'s with selves well tamed;
> Cool are we both, ours is *nibbāna* now.[6]

The epithet "become cool" (*sītibhūta*) was as much a keyword as was "with *āsavas* waned out" (*khīṇâsava*).

[1] *Anguttara* i, 211. [2] *Therag.*, 961.
[3] Milton has of this a curious echo:
Thou art my mother! Thou my author, thou!
[4] Verse 336. [5] Verse 160. [6] Verse 66.

The Commentator is not behindhand in attesting to their attainment; the *envoi* to the dual anthology classes nuns with monks:

> Excelling in all virtue, *arahan*'s,
> Who wrought all that 'twas possible to do,—
> These Psalms, their utterances when *aññā*
> They did proclaim, or whensoe'er it was . . .

and, in the episodical exegesis, is equally emphatic.

Among these *arahan*'s, of both sexes, were some who were gifted teachers. And for that matter many of the first Sakyans were. They doubtless betook themselves to retreat when need of it was felt. But genuine anchorites, fleers from men, ascetics, wrapt up in their own spiritual welfare, it would not be true to call them. As cenobites they claimed to live together in joyous harmony[1] and

> where arhans live, delectable the site.[2]

I repeat, that the idea, the psychological concept of the *arahan* appears to have emerged in the early, not the first years of Buddhism, as a maintaining the older ideal of the very man or self, as being capable of sublime becoming or growth, but with the crowning idea of indwelling Deity cut out. I never find, when the arahan is holding the floor, that we are looking at man as a bunch of five *khandha*'s. In him we have yet the very man, the man-in-man, as I have called the *attā*, the man who is *bhāvitatto*, he who has the self made-to-become, the man who is *pahitatto*, he who has the self that has striven. When the later nihilism refused to see in the human being *any self at all*, the concept of the arahan suffered a logical worsen-

[1] Verse 161. [2] *Saṃyutta*, i. 233; *Therag.*, 991.

ing. It was less impressive to see perfection in a body-mind complex, than it had been to believe one saw it in a man *whose* was the complex. And accordingly I find the *arahan* but slightly and coldly treated in mediæval Pali. Of mediæval Buddhist Sanskrit I know too little to make the same conclusion.

Now it was a brave effort to worship the ideal man, when immanent Deity had been eviscerated. It was a worthy clinging to a Best, a Highest, a Most, when the last vestige of That Who had been looked to as such had faded out of the Buddhist consciousness. In his last rôle the *arahan* stands before us as the little earth-god, elect in virtuous qualities, powerful in abnormal psychic gifts—the 'gifts' of his own labours in 'making-himself-become' in an immeasurable vista of past lives—a little god of a brief day, till the final death of the body should launch him into a *pari-nibbāna*, an utter waning out, when and where his track would be to men and devas untraceable,

> In whom the *āsava*'s are driėd up,
> Whose happiness dependeth not on food;
> Whose range is in the 'void' and the 'unmark'd'
> And liberty:—as flight of birds in air
> So hard is it to track the trail of him![1]

become a No-thing to men for help or guidance or salvation, save only as an inspiring memory, one to whom prayer could amount to nothing further than meditation on an example set, with pious will to follow after.

It may seem unfitly grudging to call such a man unfitly named as 'saint,' a name which, in '*Heiliger*,' Oldenberg, for instance, ungrudgingly bestows. Whether we call him 'saint' or 'holy' depends on

[1] *Therag.*, 92.

what we thereby mean. In the *arahan* we see perfection as at one time conceived accorded to this and that human being. But what of perfection not yet conceivable, but as yet to be conceived? In the world of 'science' what should we think of men who said 'our scientific knowledge and proficiency is now perfected; henceforth we can estimate the perfect scientist in terms of these'? It is not in the *arahan* that we should seek the holy, the saint. Much more is it in the words ascribed to Gotama: seek ye what further remains to be done (*uttariṃ karaṇīya*).[1] Much nearer do I find the man to holiness, bound for a goal he could not yet perhaps even conceive, who sang:

> Would that I could create what ne'er decays
> For the decaying, for the fevered fret
> The waning out: the peace that's uttermost,
> Incomparable safety from the toils,[2]

than the man who worded with serene complacency:—

> Now have they prospered, all my highest aims,
> To compass which I sought this still retreat.
> The holy lore and liberty, my quest,
> All lurking vain conceits I've cast away.[3]

The former, Suppiya, is said to have been "yet striving for arahanship"; the last, Sivali, to have won it. But in the former I seem to see the aspirant for the inconceivable, for That for which we have no words, the schoolboy mindful of the home no school can ever supersede; in the latter I seem to see a walled garden, windows with the blinds drawn down.

Now for me the saint is a 'holy' man just in proportion as he is working to 'become' with casement looking on the misty horizons, with garden unwalled,

[1] Above, p. 288. [2] *Therag.*, verse 32.
[3] *Ibid.*, verse 60.

with a measure not of this world, with "the best yet to come."

The *arahan* idea, the man conceived as finished, done, perfect, was bound to wither and die. Buddhism of today has, so far as I can see, no use whatever for him. It aims at ideas about the man, not at the Man. And this was surely because in the past he was measured by the standard of the known, the realized, the taught, the measure yet conceivable on earth. That man, in his earth-body (over which even the *arahan* was judged not to have perfect control),[1] may attain quasi-divine perfection can only be held at the fearful cost of a shrinkage in the idea of perfection, even of such as we can yet conceive. The Most has been brought within what is at best here but the More; the Best has been bent over to the limits of a Better; the Highest stands as only a Higher.

It is generally admitted that the best human body here is very limited. We realize this, not only in our watching over 'records' of strength, etc., longevity, standards of art and the like, but also the moment we look into the psychically abnormal. A body far outstripping the best we can normally, by and in it, achieve is easily conceived. The same is true of mind, especially when we study what in telepathy and televolition is conceivably possible. We have never honestly taken into education any methods for 'making-become,' as such, the fallows of our will; we train will haphazard as an adjunct, not as the very radium of our being.

With present facts before them, it is curious how lightly acquiescent Buddhist and other writers have been in the theory which claims consummation for

[1] *Milindapañha*, p. 253.

any man of earth at any time. The composer, the executing artist cannot give us the supreme music of the spheres; he has to communicate through instruments better or worse, all of them limited. And hearing his better, we dream of music that is a Best. Man too has to 'become' in a More towards a Most by worthing, valuing ever a better against a worse. By all this he grows. When instruments for comparing are ultimately discarded, then maybe will come to pass the word uttered long ago: "Yea yonder! the Man yonder! I am HE."[1]

[1] *Bṛhad. Up.*, 5, 15.

CHAPTER XVIII

PSYCHOLOGY IN THE ABHIDHAMMA-PIṬAKA

MY book is mainly concerned with beginnings, else may it be thought I have left too scanty space for Abhidhamma psychology. It should anyway be remembered, that the work of the Third Piṭaka is largely to analyze, and in so doing detach from their contexts, doctrines already put forth in the Sutta-Piṭaka. Hence I have been forestalling much of what had else awaited us. Here I wish only to bring out a few points revealing work done on these doctrines, as it was carried on in the School, and not by way of addressing the congregation, or conversing with the individual inquirer. Work so done is the subject-matter and method of the Suttas.

In the two to three centuries preceding the redaction of at least four of the seven books of the Third Piṭaka, the day of the master-minds of the founders was too recent, perhaps, for their utterances to be considered objectively, much less critically, whence might have sprung development of theory, psychological or other. And there had come about such a breaking away from earlier tradition,—a tradition which had started with the immanent Divine Self—that we cannot wonder, if constructive imagination was held tightly down to working out the legacy, whereof the Ābhidhammika compilers were the heirs.

The one exception to this sterility in development of theory is the system of twenty-four relations, the listing and analysis, that is to say, of all the types of relations observable between mental phenomena, under the aspect of causality. This work in development I have shown, holding good reasons for thinking so, was produced later than the preceding books.[1] I refer to the last book (including probably the penultimate book) called the Paṭṭhāna, or analysis of mental events as having a causal basis. But even that exposition lacks concise theoretic discussion.

Perhaps the most convenient way for the European to summarize this Piṭaka is to see in it an attempt to be exhaustive on the subject of

(*a*) terms and their meaning,
(*b*) propositions and their interrelations,
(*c*) debates in syllogism.

Under (*a*) come the first two books and the fourth: Dhamma-sangaṇi, or Compendium of things of body and mind; Vibhanga: terms under doctrinal 'sections' and Puggala-Paññatti, or Designation of human types.

Under (*b*) come (i.) an older set of sentences called Mātikā ('openings' [for discourse]). These form an unexplained preface to the first Book, and may be all we have left of what, in the First Piṭaka, is always put where we might put Abhidhamma, namely, after Vinaya and Sutta (or Dhamma, doctrine).[2] (ii.) The Dhātukathā, or talk on elements (*i.e.* mental elements). (iii.) The Yamaka, or book of couples and the Paṭṭhāna.

Under (*c*) comes the fifth (but once the last) book: debates couched in syllogistic dialectic, called Kathāvatthu, or subjects for talk. It is exegetically claimed

[1] *JRAS* 1925, 111 and below, p. 383.
[2] Thus, "learned in Vinaya, Dhamma and Mātikā," *Vin.*, Mahâvagga, x. 1, etc.

for these, that they were uttered at the Conference and Revision of Oral Sayings at Patna in Asoka's day. This is probably true. But it is fairly evident that, after the first section or two, the rest constitute an accretion which may have taken some time to get enrolled. It is also likely, that the more or less spontaneous utterances of the first debates, on matters of utmost importance in the history of Buddhism, were subsequently redacted in more pedantic dialectical form as exercises in the new logic. The book is the oldest known instance of Indian logic.

(*a*) In the first book, after the superseded but venerable Mātikā, we come immediately upon a developed and more orderly statement of the contents of a limited number of types of thought, which we find anticipated—if this be historically correct—in the latter Suttas of the Second Collection (No. III: the Anupada, or 'successively-arising' Sutta). In this is an appreciation ascribed to the Founder of the gifts and character of his beloved friend and leading disciple Sāriputta (who predeceased him). The occasion is referred to the outcome, for Sāriputta, of a couple of weeks spent in introspective vision (*vipassanā*) of the serial uprising of *dhamma*'s. He has spent his wisdom "vast and extensive, joyous and swift, acute and penetrating, in this way, thus:

"For instance, bhikkhus, Sāriputta, aloof from sensuous desires, aloof from bad ideas, enters into and abides in First Jhāna, wherein attention is applied and sustained, which is born of solitude and filled with zest and pleasurable feeling. And the presentations in that First Jhāna, to wit, thinking applied and sustained (*vitakka, vichāra*), and zest and pleasurable feeling (*pīti, sukha*) and singleness of object (*citt'ekaggatā*), and contact, feeling, perception, volition, consciousness (*citta*), desire (*chanda*), choice, effort, mindfulness, indifference, adaptation of attention (*manasikāra*)—these are for him serially determined; these, as they arise, are for him things understood, and as they are present and as they depart, are for him things understood. He discerns: 'Verily these presentations that were not, have become; having become, they again depart.' And he with regard to them abides neither drawn to, nor averse from them, independent, not captivated, but free, detached, his mind placing no barriers." He understands: "There is a way out beyond, namely, by expanding that."

With pedantic meticulousness the compilers make Sāriputta go through the exercises approved in their way of Four Jhānas, and carried on to a musing on a curious set of five other forms of Jhāna called formless (*āruppa*), often made to succeed the first four, and to come to the conclusion: "He understands: 'There is no way out beyond; it is not to be found by expanding that.'"

I would ask the reader to look into this much more critically than I did (α) when I was writing the first edition of this work, and even (β) when I was commenting on it nine years later in the Preface to the second edition of my *Buddhist Psychological Ethics*. The 'more' in criticism under (α) is given in (β). Thus:

"The Sutta (Anupada) is . . . an obvious patchwork of editorial compiling, and dates without a reasonable doubt long after Sāriputta had preceded his great friend and leader in leaving this world. We have first a stock formula of praise, spoken in not one context only of Sāriputta. Then *ex abrupto* a tradition about a fortnight of systematic introspection. Then *ex abrupto* three more formulas of praise. And that is all. The Sutta . . . is a little 'wreath,' a Kranz, or album of Sāriputtiana, handed down probably in the Sāvatthi memorized records, or only put together, and that badly, when the records were, long after, committed to writing."[1]

I then try to make out a case for Sāriputta having been introspectively inclined, but without fit evidence. If he indeed composed the verses ascribed to him in the Anthology—and why not ?—it is not very likely that by the phrase *ajjhatta-rato*, he meant "who loveth introspective work." I have here been, as we all are alas ! too often, prompted by a Commentator putting into Pali a tradition of a long past date, when *adhyātma* had meant "things pertaining to the Spirit or Self," but which had, after centuries of crucifying the reality of the Spirit, come to mean just 'internal,' almost our 'subjective.' Even so, I do not see Sāriputta (or any one else) reasonably taking delight (*rato* is a strong word: joy, love) in disembowelling himself psychologically. Much more do I see him, a very brahman, seeing in *ajjhatta* a somewhat nearer to the Hebrew Psalmist's

> He that dwelleth in the secret place of the Most High
> Shall abide under the shadow of the Almighty . . .
> Thou hast made the Most High thy habitation;
> There shall no evil befall thee. . . .

But the intrusion of two words: *anupada*, and *vavatthita*, 'assigned,' which are not of the older idiom, suggest a later editing, and show us that, when this editing took place, the period of the compiling of the naïve

[1] Preface to Second Edition, 1923.

crude analyses of the Abhidhamma-Piṭaka was not far removed in time.

And more: the Anupada cataloguing is short as compared with the overweighted complexes within a complex-specimen in the Dhamma-sangaṇi: 16 items compared with about 50. Nevertheless in that briefer catalogue two distinct lists are lumped together: five terms connected by 'and' (*ca*), and eleven terms without 'and.' Had but one list been got in, 'contact' (No. 6) would, by Buddhist tradition, take its proper place at the head of the 16. And another curious item: in the Dhamma-sangaṇi, when the given "good thought" has been at length 'disembowelled,' we get the following coda: "Now these, or whatever other incorporeal things there are on that occasion, these are *dhamma*'s that are good." And "or whatever other" as a made word, "*ye-vā-pana-ka*," recurs as a technical term. They are *e.g.* "desire, resolve, attention, equanimity, pity, sympathetic joy, abstinence from bad conduct in act, speech and livelihood." But in the Sutta we find, among these seven, the first three: desire, resolve, attention, incorporated into the sixteen, not merely appended. It is an odd little irregularity, wherein the Commentary does not help us. Had Buddhaghosa written it, he with his greater erudition might have noticed both this, and have referred to the parallel attempt at introspection in the Anupada Sutta. But he, it appears, had asked a colleague to compile the Pali Commentary, a man we only know under the name Chulla-Buddhaghosa,[1] and he reveals no knowledge of the Sutta.

Under (β) I would say: In the striking refrain: on the way out beyond and the need of getting there by ex-

[1] *Gandhavaṃsa*, JPTS., 1886, p. 68.

panding this or that, namely, by growth or becoming, I see Sāriputta teaching,

"turning even as I the wheel,"

as the Master is recorded more than once to have said of him. But in the last clause I see a very libel on both. It is the sort of teaching we saw had come up about the *arahan*, the man finished, done, lived. In a teaching of Becoming there could not possibly be for the man of earth any finality. Ever was there an *uttariṃ*, a *pāraṃ*, a further, a beyond. Nor do I see either finding a true getting-beyond in introspection. In musing (*jhāna*), yes: a hearing *how* to get further. In life, yes, even more, for in the test of living lay the means of getting further. But I cannot hear Sāriputta, after his fine refrain has been put to a number of items he probably never even heard of, ending with the conclusion, that there was nothing beyond, and no further expansion to be made. It is unlike that which we find him made to say in the Suttas: "I praise not standing still; I praise growth" (Anguttara, v, 96).

After the Dhamma-sangaṇi has presented us with its much longer list of all the items judged to be intuitable in the first of the 'eight good kinds of *citta*,' it sets to work defining each term. Here we get lists of approximately equivalent terms, together with now and then an informative defining clause. Of the clauses, we are told that *vitakka* is a "much imposing of mind (upon)," and that *vichāra* is a serial adjusting and focussing of thought.

Of the lists, I will only stay a moment on two such sets of equivalents. All are very short, at times tautological or mere repetitions, but as to length with two striking exceptions. These give an account of (i.) wisdom (*paññā*), and (ii.) effort, or energy (*viriya*), and I have mentioned them above.

" Wisdom on that occasion is understanding, search research, searching *dhamma*, discernment, distinguishing, differencing, erudition, proficiency, subtlety, criticism, reflection, scrutiny, breadth, sagacity, a 'guide', insight, intelligence, a 'goad'; wisdom as faculty, as a 'strength,' as 'a sword,' as 'a height,' as 'light,' as 'glory,' as 'splendour,' as a 'jewel,' as absence of illusion (or bewilderment), as searching *dhamma*, right view: this on that occasion is wisdom " (§ 16).

" Effort on that occasion is the mental inception of effort, the moving out, the moving forward, exertion, endeavour, energy, upheaval, vigour, fortitude, state of unfaltering effort, state of sustained desire, state of unflinching endurance, solid grip of the burden, effort, effort as faculty, as strength, right endeavour: this on that occasion is effort " (§ 13).[1]

'Wisdom' in number of items far surpasses 'effort,' and greatly excels also the lists of Chāndogya and Aitareya Upaniṣads.[2] But as to 'effort,' it is in Indian culture a *very new thing to find a list about it at all*, and we shall not understand the old Buddhist tradition rightly, if we heed not this fact. In the wisdom-parade of terms a yet older tradition is being worthily supported; in the *viriya-for-will*-parade we more definitely see *how* Buddhism, although it fails as yet to see this, was most truly in Indian culture a creative force. And let us not fail to note how, in the first term of the definition, 'inception of effort' there is a

[1] Where my translation here differs from that in my translation (1900 and 1923), it is in keeping more closely to a literal rendering.

[2] Above, chap. IV.

surviving echo of that Sutta in which the very man or self is seen *in the act of initiative.*[1]

It is important to note, that in this and the second book, Vibhanga, we have come quite away from the 'man,' who is both appealed to and discussed in the Suttas. We are entirely in a field of notions about his *citta* and his *rūpa*. The first book starts with analyses of a delimited number of forms of *citta* which are acclaimed as 'good' (*kusala*), and another such number of such as are 'not good,' and yet again of a number which are indeterminate, or not called either (*avyākata*). The books themselves betray no awareness of novelty in treatment, but, for exegesis, such treatment is distinguished by the technical term *nippariyāyena*: *i.e.*, by non-applied, non-episodical method, any rounded-off saying in a Sutta being called a *pariyāya*. Indeed, this is the only partition recognized in the Rock-inscriptions of Asoka, when referring to portions of the Buddha-community-sayings, which he commends to the special attention of the Order. But the negative form *nippariyāya* does not, I believe, occur in the Sutta-Piṭaka. So much is the 'man' kept out of sight, that, in commenting on the Jhāna-definitions, the exegetist[2] asks who is, or where in the formulas is, the *subject*, since they are admittedly a 'way' (*magga*) or 'course' (*paṭipadā*), and "where there is this there must be a wayfarer or proceeder (*paṭipaṇṇaka*)." It was a very striking concession, for the chief exegetist Buddhaghosa is often at pains, both in his Commentaries and much more in his Visuddhi Magga, to banish the man or self as unreal, unreal in any way. I feel sure he would never have written or endorsed Buddhaghosa Minor's

[1] Above, chs. XI., XIV.
[2] *Aṭṭhasālinī*, on Jhāna.

'concession.'[1] For him "there was Way, but no goer"!

Another less important point in these analyses of consciousness is, that whereas the *citta*-forms analyzed are, as I have said, entirely de-individualized, and intended to apply to what we should call the normal man as type-thoughts, we do not find any terms for either 'type' or 'normal.' The translator never raises the question. Similarly, no attempt is made to categorize in any special way the mind in genius or in the otherwise abnormal, *e.g.* the psychic mind active in the *iddhi* forms or *abhiññā*, which we have been considering, nor the mind in the mentally defective, the incurably (*a-tekiccha*) wicked as Devadatta was supposed to be, nor the mind in the animal.

I am not herein wishing to express surprise or depreciation. Our own psychology is still pretty new, and it is only today, so to speak, that we are ourselves beginning to investigate abnormal psychology in any form. But there is a belief, that animal rebirth and human rebirth were equally true for original Sakya, and this I do not accept. We see a very few allusions to rebirth as beast creeping—suspiciously like glosses—into the Upaniṣads. We see it grown to full maturity in Pali Commentaries (and here and there in the Piṭakas), in the former in the shape mainly of stories wherewith to entertain and edify congregations. With growing numbers, rival sects and no fixed pay of any kind, it was ever peculiarly necessary for the Order to draw their *parisā*, or congregations, by stooping often to be the jongleurs and balladmongers of the

[1] Let me here confess that, in *Sakya* (p. 174), I had overlooked the *two* Buddhaghosas. My apologies to Buddhaghosa Minor (Chulla).

unlearned folk, to which the Suttas so often refer as *assutavā* (unlearned) and *puthujjana* (many-folk). And in Ceylon, on feast-days, this may still be seen and heard.

At the same time, it would not have been strange to find other than the utter silence there is about the animal mind in Abhidhamma. Beings (*sattā*) of which we are ever hearing are coextensive apparently with *pāṇā*: 'creatures,' lit. breathers. There came into Buddhism less of a logical dividing line between such, sub- or super-human and just human, than our own tradition and prejudice reveal. Yet they, with a creed of pity, and anticarnivorism for all beings, have not extended their intellectual curiosity to the different modes and limits of those which were, as they held, undergoing an unhappy phase in life's unending pulsations. The wealth of sympathetic insight into animal life, shown in the huge collection of so-called Jātaka tales, wherein beast and birds speak and act much as do men, the belief that rebirth as animal was a fate more likely than not awaiting the everyman you were addressing if not yourself:—" Those who leave this world and are reborn as human beings are few, but those who . . . are reborn in purgatory, among beasts, among the shades (*peta*'s) are many . . ."[1] make this total omission somewhat strange. No Commentary on Abhidhamma tells us, if I mistake not, that those *citta*-analyses are to hold good for animals, or if not, why not. And the Suttas give us but a sad head-shaking over these: "I might talk on in many ways, so hard is it adequately to state the ills of the animal world."[2]

As to treatment of mind without man, there would almost seem, in the third book on terms named above,

[1] *Anguttara*, i. 37. [2] *Majjhima*, No. 129.

to be an attempted compensation made by some one who was clearly familiar with that Nikāya in which less injustice is done to the reality of the man than in the other three—I mean the Fourth Collection or Anguttara. In this book (*a*, 3)[1] we get in the title *Designation of Man*, and, in the contents, where the designation is like that in the Anguttara, by way of one item, two, and more items, we find a large number of actual quotations from Anguttara contexts, albeit unacknowledged to be such. I do not think we are thereby justified in theorizing about this work being deliberately modelled on either the Anguttara, or the Suttanta in the Dīgha Nikāya called Sangīti, also numerically arranged. Somehow this arrangement had found its way into the new Buddhist 'Vedas,' possibly as mnemonically helpful; and now one group of compilers, now another followed the vogue.

Much more important in this question of the Fourth Book and the Fourth Collection, especially the former, is the making the 'man' himself their subject, and not only 'ideas-about' his instruments, body and mind, more than is done, relatively more than is done, in Books I. to III. and Collections I. to III. It is true that we have the man called by the term which indicates a lowered, worsened view of him than had been the Indian view of a day gone by. I mean the use of *puggala* (according to the Commentaries a derogatory term) for the term *purisa*=*ātman*=potentially Brahma. I have dealt with this in a previous chapter.[2] That the man was, under this name, no more the child of splendid nature and destiny, *quâ* man, as brahman teaching had shown him to be, had apparently come to be accepted, much as Puritan England accepted the

[1] In the Piṭaka, No. 4.

[2] Above, p. 214.

man as a 'child of sin,' a 'sinner,' without realizing the loss that religious teaching had thereby suffered.

The emphasis on the actual existence of man of this or that type, which is so curious a feature in many Fourth Collection Suttas: "There are, there exist in the world two, three, four men (*i.e.* classes of '*puggala*'s') . . . is not followed in this Abhidhamma book.[1] Possibly because the catechetical form precludes it. Where you start with the question "What are the men called so and so?" or, "Who have this or that quality?", the fact that they exist is admitted. It is more likely, however, that the reality and worth of man never really came *here* into question. He was a complex of *dhamma*'s, no more: such was the position taken up by the regnant majority, called at the Patna Council Analyzers: Vibhajjavādins, the majority in whose hands the actual composition of the Abhidhamma-Piṭaka may have lain. The matter of chief importance, in these later books, was to settle, once for all, what all the terms and definitions about man in the Suttas amounted to. It was *in the analysis* of all that could be said about him that they were interested, else had they never gotten so strikingly emphatic a *nom d'occasion*.

And it is a very striking development in analytic statement, both psychical and physical, that meets us in the first book, the Dhamma-sangaṇi. Human consciousness has been schematized as experiencing now one, now another of a certain number of types of contents. We have the average good, the average bad mind unrolled, not too atomistically, but with a clear sense of process; we have then the mind as engaged

[1] Discussed in the Winternitz Festgabe (and in *Indian Culture*, July, 1935) as 'A Vanished Sakyan Window.'

in a beyond or unseen, so far ethically undetermined, that 'it' might be taking a worldly (*lokiya*) interest only in its experience; we have finally the mind as engaged on the same subject, but out of supramundane (*lokuttara*) interest only, in the aim, that is, of winning singlemindedly the goal *then* deemed highest, and called nirvana.

A word here of comment. The words 'good' and 'bad' are used only in the sense of 'felicific,' or causing welfare, and the reverse. Indeed, my late Burmese colleague, S. Z. Aung, preferred the rendering 'meritorious' and 'demeritorious.' If, in other words, your thoughts, your *mano-kamma* was *kusala*, you won so much to the good (*puñña*) in your account with that *automatic* result in the after-life, curiously accepted by Buddhists in the teeth of the Pali scriptures. I have rejected this rendering, because had *kusala* meant this, we should find *puññavant* used, together with, or in preference to, *kusala*. We do not. *Kusala*, *akusala* belong to the Upaniṣadic, the Vedic tradition, and in them, as meaning just our own good and bad in a moral sense, I believe we have also the original Sakyan tradition.

After analyzing thought of these two kinds, we come to indeterminate (*avyākata*) *dhamma*'s, and things are less simple. "What are they? When, as the result of good acts having been wrought, having been stored up in connection with (life in the) sensuous sphere, sense-experience has arisen, accompanied by indifference (*upekkhā*) having a sense-object, then there is (included in this experience) contact, feeling, perception, purpose, thought (*citta*), indifference, one-pointedness; mind, indifference, life as faculty (*indriya*): —these, or whatever other incorporeal *dhamma*'s there are on that occasion—these are indeterminate." And thereupon the definition of each of these proceeds much as before.

I must confess I am more at a loss to understand what here is meant than I seem to have been nearly four decades ago, when I was translating this 'Compendium.' If I get it at all, it is that, under the aspect of being a result of some good thought one has had in the past, this impression *is un-moral*. But in so far as it is itself a thought (*citta*) it must come under either what is good or what is bad. With the former of these two sentences the Commentary agrees. And fortunately, for all that it matters, in rightly comprehending the things that are, in Buddhism, worth while, we can leave it at that. But as analysis it is not anticipated in the Suttas.

Abhidhamma definitions, while they are certainly a notable psychological advance over anything achieved in earlier or contemporary Indian literature, may not be satisfying to our own logical tradition. They consist very largely of enumerating synonymous, or partly synonymous, terms, such as we might call overlapping circles.[1] But they reveal to us much useful information concerning the term described, the terms describing this term, and the terms which we may have expected to find, but find not. And they show the Sokratic earnestness with which these early Schoolmen strove to clarify their concepts, so as to guard their doctrines from the heretical innovations, to which ambiguity in terms would yield cheap foothold.

As instances of the light thrown for us by this mass

[1] I refer, of course, to the well-known Euler circles in Formal Logic.

of conscientious cataloguing, we may note a few purely psychological definitions:

"Which are the phenomena that are (*a*) of the self, (*b*) external?

"*Ans.* (*a*) The spheres (fields) of the five senses and of *mano*; (*b*) the spheres of the five kinds of sense-objects and of mental objects (*dhammā*)."[1]

* * * * *

"In what respect is this or that *khandha* (*a*) of the self, (*b*) external?

"*Ans.* (*a*) That *khandha* which, for these or those beings, is of the self, is self-referable, one's own, referable to the person. . . . (*b*) That *khandha* which for these or those other beings, other persons, is of the self, is self-referable, their own, referable to the person."

We have here the field of object including not only all that is directly presented to my experience considered as the subject, but also all that is subjective for others.

"What on that occasion is the faculty of *sati*?"

"*Ans.* The mindfulness which on that occasion is recollecting, calling back to mind; the mindfulness which is remembering, bearing in mind, the opposite of superficiality and of obliviousness . . . this is the power of mindfulness that there then is."[2]

This term has been discussed above. I have added the Abhidhamma definition to make clear the comprehensiveness of its meaning. That, etymologically, is memory, or remembering; practically, it is clear thinking on past or present.

[1] § 1207 f.
[2] § 14. *Sati* derives from *s*[*m*]*arati*, 'to remember.'

"Opposite of superficiality" is literally "state-of-not-floating,"—"like pumpkins and empty pots on the surface of the water" is the comment—"but sinking on to the object of thought," and again "non-floating and apprehension (*upagaṇhānā*) are its essential marks." In it, the man in consciousness reminds himself of what he has (his past being wrought up with his present), like a treasurer detailing his revenue to a king. Past, present, future, the threefold time-distinction, is constantly cited, but the problem of forgetfulness and reinstatement, and the conditions of reinstatement, usually alluded to among ourselves as association of ideas, are still not raised as matters calling for definition.

Coming now to Abhidhamma elaborations of the simpler Nikāyan analysis of sensations, it is here that we find distinctions in time brought forward. This analysis reveals an increase in precision of statement rather than in theory, or added matter of observation. But it remains the fullest experiential statement of sense-consciousness which ancient literature has given us. It occurs in the first book, and is included under the inquiry into material qualities in general or *rūpa*. The four elemental material qualities are 'underived,' *no upādā*, or irreducible; the sense-organs, and all sense-objects, *except those of touch*, are derived, that is, from the underived elementals. Hence the ancient Hellenic theory that 'like is known by like' may be considered as latent in this arrangement,[1] although it is only in Buddhaghosa that I have found it made explicit: "Where there is difference of kind there is no

[1] Empedokles, Plato, Plotinus, who accepted it, were all influenced, through Pythagorism or elsewise, by Eastern thought.

stimulus. The Ancients say that sensory stimulus is of similar kinds, not of different kinds."[1]

Each of the five special senses, and then the *mano*, the sixth sense, is set out in a fourfold formula, carefully worded and voluble as compared with the jejune statement of organ, object *plus* contact, of the Nikāyas. Summarized, the formula takes account of (*a*) the sense, invisible (the fleshy organ is not included) and reacting, (*b*) the object invisible also (as presentation) and impinging, and (*c*) the contact. Further,

(1) the fact of possible sensation;
(2) the actual impact of object;
(3) the actual impact of sense;
(4) the resultant actual impression and possible results in the four incorporeal aggregates.

The severance of (2) and (3) is explained by the Commentary as indicating (2) involuntary sensation, *e.g.* an unexpected seeing of lightning, and (3) voluntary seeing, 'looking,' for example, or 'listening'—adjusted movement of attention of "one who by his own wish, seeking to look at some object, concentrates his vision."

And in all four statements, there is the detailed time-reference—'has seen, sees, will or may see,' 'has impinged, impinges, will or may impinge.' Sense is emphatically stated as an experience in time no less than in space.

"What is that *rūpa* sphere which is not derived? (*a*) The sphere of the tangible; (*b*) the water element. What is (*a*)? The earth, heat and wind elements; the hard, the soft, the smooth, the rough, pleasant contact, painful contact, the heavy, the light. . . . What

[1] *Atthasālinī*, 313.

is (*b*)? That which is water, watery, the viscid, viscous, the binding quality in *rūpa*."

I reserve till a final chapter the interesting psychological developments found in the Commentary on these simpler attempts, attempts which none the less are themselves striking developments on anything we find in contemporary Indian literature.

One more word on the development, first found in this first book, of that dumping-ground of mental analysis, the fourth or *sankhāra-khandha*. In the first place we find the different thought-arisings (*cittuppādā*), good and bad, distinguished as being with a conscious condition precedent, or without one. In the former alternative the thought is called *sa-sankhārena*: 'with a, shall I say? predisposing cause.' Thus, when an act of mind takes place, it may be that the doer was impelled to do it (*a*) through advice, (*b*) through a command, (*c*) through an inner monition: —this from the Commentary, where it is called a new term, and where (*c*) is not referred to Dhamma, so completely had the earlier conscience-force in the term faded.

So far Dhammadinnā herself might have been the exponent. We are not far from her dual *sankhārā* of an act of mind.[1] But we are then plunged into the following, anticipated only in the list or 'mixed grill' given in that other Sutta, the Anupada:[2]

" What on that occasion " (*i.e.* at the genesis of the first type of good thoughts) " are the four *khandha*'s? . . . What is the *khandha* of *vedanā* (feeling or experiencing)? The mentally pleasant, mentally happy, pleasant happy experience born of thought-contact which is thought-contact-born pleasure, happiness,

[1] Above, p. 323. [2] Above, p. 357.

feeling: this on that occasion is the *khandha* of *vedanā*. What . . . is the *khandha* of *saññā* (perceiving)? That which on that occasion is perception, perceiving, state of perceiving: this on that occasion is the *khandha* of perception. What . . . is the *khandha* of *sankhāra*'s? Contact, purpose (*cetanā*), initial and sustained application, zest, concentrating; the five moral powers—faith, energy, mindfulness, concentration, insight; vital power, rightness of views, intention, endeavour, mindfulness, concentration; the forces of faith . . . insight (*as above*); the forces of modesty and discretion, disinterestedness, amity, understanding; no-covetousness, no-malice; composure, buoyancy, pliancy, fitness, proficiency, rectitude of consciousness and its properties, mindfulness and intelligence, calm and insight, grasp and balance—these, or whatever other incorporeal causally induced phenomena there are on that occasion, exclusive of the aggregates of feeling, perception, and of consciousness—these are the aggregate of *sankhāra*'s."[1]

The contents of this fourth aggregate are re-stated with the explication of each of the other types of good and of bad consciousness, the items varying according to the typical nature of the psychosis analyzed. The second type, for example, lacking the intelligent or intellectual character of the first type, all the constituents implying understanding, insight, etc., are omitted, and so on.

This is a notable elaboration in what my teacher, Croom Robertson, used to call 'bodying out a thought,' as compared with the simple description of this particular 'group' in the Nikāyas. And it is probably

[1] § 62.

intended to express, not what is present in consciousness at every flicker of the type evoked, but the field of choice, the range and potentiality, in the conscious activity ranked under the given type. These typical good and bad types of consciousness that are being analyzed are each and all said to be caused on occasion of a mental object, either a sense-impression or a *mano*-impression. And the contents of the mental complexes of an Ariya-sāvaka—a saintly student—would differ greatly from that of the average layman whom he taught, when some external object evoked in each the same type of consciousness.

Viewed in this way, the analyses are not so overdone as at first sight they seem to be. They are all in keeping with one of the chief tasks of the Abhidhamma compilers: the jealous guarding of the doctrines of the Suttas, in their oral preservation and transmission, from errors arising through vagueness and ambiguity of language. And thus it is that they have left us a mass of exponential detail with no exposition of theory. The doctrine (*Dhamma*) had been declared, learnt and handed on in set verbal forms. In *Abhi*-dhamma the teacher, conversant with Dhamma, and teaching it in his turn, possessed, in the definitions of these seven supplementary books, a thesaurus of knowledge helping to clarify his knowledge and his expositions. He set himself, as I have said, to eliminate from the doctrines, thus adapted to individuals and small groups, all that was contingent in narrative, viz. the episode eliciting the pronouncement, the comparative method of conveying its meaning, the parable and the simile, appealing to this or that hearer. The bare judgment, or predication, was thus registered, and its terms defined. The result is not attractive reading, but the purpose was doubtless served. Taken altogether we have, in Abhidhamma, not a well-constructed philosophical system, but all the materials for one. "Dhamma," wrote the late learned Ledi Sayadaw in his essay on Abhidhamma, "is taught in two ways: in formulas suitable for memorizing . . . and in instruction imparted directly and specifically to individuals. By the former method the matter is analyzed either in outline or in detail, without regard as to whether perplexities may arise or not. . . . Now the great field of Abhidhamma instruction is one of formulas, . . . wherein one must keep in view, not only those who are listening on any one occasion, but the general course of the doctrine according to the meaning and the letter. Thus will the teaching make for increase of analytical knowledge in those Ariyan students who have learned the doctrines, and for the acquisition, some future day, of analytical knowledge by ordinary folk."[1]

But this elimination of what was contingent matter does not exhaust Abhidhamma generalizing. Had this negative work been all, we might have had the not-to-be-regretted result of a Piṭaka shorn of some of its length. By the logic of consistency or symmetry, the Ābhidhammikas judged it right to apply their doctrinal formulas, psychological and otherwise, not only to normal humanity, but also to supernormal humans like the arahans, and to those companies of devas on different planes of life, to which normal humans were, as religious beings, habitually aspiring.

With the conclusion of the analysis of thought (*citta*) and material instrument (my term, not Buddhist),

[1] *Yamaka*, ii. (P.T.S.), pp. 222, 229; translated by me in *JPTS*, 1914, pp. 116, 124.

i.e. rūpa, the book continues its catechizing in sections which I could, did space permit, show to be later accretions, and which may be no more than subsequent rehandling, or 'work done on' the foregoing. The first called, at some undetermined point of time, the deposition section, or summary (*nikkhepa*), treats of *dhamma*'s in triplets: things as they are *x* or *y* or neither. It is here that we first come across the distinction of *dhamma*'s as *citta* and *cetasikā*, *i.e.* as thought and as thought-properties or constituents—a division which came in time to supersede the more cumbrous overlapping four mental *khandha*'s. The former are defined as the five sense-awarenesses and *mano*, the latter as the other three *khandha*'s. Later on these came to be reshuffled. A further anticipation of this is that, in the fifth book, Kathāvatthu, we find a list of *sankhāra*'s with *vedanā* and *saññā* all called *cetasikā*.

There then follow two accretions I have called Appendixes. The first defines pairs of terms and phrases found in the Suttas; the second is looked upon as a commentarial analysis (*vibhatti*) of Section III., and brings in later terms. It will be a little strange to readers to learn that the word nirvana (*nibbāna*) never occurs in the book till Appendix I., and then only once. One or two other terms are apparently used for denoting its range in thought, namely, 'the un-included' (*apariyāpanna*), and, later only, 'unconditioned element' (*asankhatā dhātu*). This is the more remarkable in that, in the mind-analysis of Part I., supramundane musing is solely concerned with compassing this other-world aim.

(*b*) Of the three books analyzing propositions I here say nothing, since their aim is not psychological analysis. But with this exception: in the last book, the Paṭṭhāna, a new term is suddenly sprung upon us, not as new, but as an accepted technicality. This is the word *bhavanga*, a corruption, I incline to think, of *bhavangya*, an abstract of the verbal noun *bhavan-*, 'becoming.'[1] It is the only occurrence of it in the Piṭakas, but in later works it is fairly frequent. In our work it is listed as one of several immediate conditions in a resulting awareness: namely, in the awareness of attention (*āvajjanā*, a word which is etymologically our own 'ad-vert-ing'). Both terms are later idiom than that of the Suttas, and form part of the analysis of a full cognitive act, from the latent continuum or flux (*bhavanga*) of the awake but unimpressed mind to the apperception and retention of the finish. It is a sort of anticipation of our (overworked) term subconsciousness. That it should take the form of a dynamic, not a static, term is for me significant, as the reader of this book will understand.

In its opposition to the renascent Indian static ideal, Buddhism needed such a term. Once lit upon, it proved to answer a need. In the fifth book, Kathāvatthu, we find a word for full consciousness: *sammukhībhāva*, but the complementary term has *apparently not been found.* This is supplied by the Commentary *only about that term.* And I judge that, in the time interval between that text and its commentary, this term emerged. It was wanted for vital continuance when the act of waking advertence, which we now call attention, is absent. The vital continuum with its potentiality of attention-in-perception was ever

[1] *Bhavanga*, in Anguttara, ii. 79, is a misediting for *bhavagga*. In my Tikapaṭṭhāna edition, *Tikapaṭṭhāna*, i. 159 (P.T.S., 1923), I show myself misled by it.

proceeding (becoming). They needed this word 'potential.' They had no Aristotle and did not find it. But they found *bhavanga*. More hereon later (407 f.).

The recognition of a flux of, to word it negatively, inattention as a feature in the analysis of man's inner world is all that I find approaching the subject of the subconscious or the unconscious as such. Of dreams I find in Abhidhamma no treatment. It is only in the Milinda Questions that we find them discussed. In the earlier centuries with which I have dealt, there was no felt need to seek terms for subliminal consciousness. There was the accepted belief in the dual body. You were using either the one or the other. And the irrationality of the dream may well have seemed a blending of awareness belonging to the two, just when sleep was supervening or departing. Our psychology may eventually find here many needed explanations. But when, under the influence of monastic teaching, India was turning away from a belief in the nearness, the co-presence of the other world, the consciousness of the earthbody was becoming for her the great preoccupation, and it was then that this awareness 'here below' began to be figured as either attending or inattending.

(*c*) I have but sampled the assiduous analysis and defining in the Abhidhamma, partly because of it there is no end, partly not to overweary the reader. But the outstanding book, the Debates, translated as *Points of Controversy*, will repay psychologically a brief comment.

For instance, in the VIth Book, one of the debates is concerning the thesis: That space is visible. The orthodox rejoinder, contesting it, is:

" If this is so, you commit yourself to saying that

space is visible material object and element; hence as such it is either blue-green, yellow, etc., is cognizable by the eye, impinges on the eye, enters the avenue of sight as do such objects. But you deny this. You must either affirm or deny, that because of eye and space visual consciousness arises. If *not*, your proposition falls through. If you agree, well, you cannot cite any Sutta to establish this. All that the Suttanta says is: 'Because of eye and visible object visual consciousness arises'—with this you agree. Hence you must either call space visible object (*rūpa-*), or fail to maintain your position.

"Proposer: If I am wrong, you must nevertheless admit, that you 'see' the interval between two trees or two posts, the space in a keyhole or in a window. Surely then space is visible."

The Commentary explains, that in space it is a '*mano*-door-consciousness' which arises, not an 'eye-door.' In *our* diction we infer space rather than 'see' it.

The comment is of interest, but might easily have been improved upon. Why is the work of *mano* here not called *takka*: logical inference? It occurs in the sacrosanct Suttanta: "So far as anything can be ascertained by *takka*, thou hast ascertained it."[1] And Buddhaghosa's comment is that the mode of *takka* here would be *anumāna*: inference (a later term). But it is over the function of *mano*, as my book has perhaps made clear, that Buddhist psychology leaves much to be desired. (Nor was Aristotle, for that matter, any better).)[2] Thus: the objects of their sixth sense—*sensus communis* I used to call it—of *mano* were

[1] *Saṃyutta*, i. 55; *Kindred Sayings*, i. 80.
[2] See the writer's *Will to Peace* (Ernest Benn), p. 63 f.

dhammā, or as we might say presentations, or, with Hume, impressions and ideas. Further, this sixth sense, figured as gate or door, received and co-ordinated all the more elementary, the simpler objects of the five senses. Hence the objects of *mano* are by the Buddhist books (and from the first) shown to be complex. But *ākāsadhātu*, the element of space, is a simple object. Yet we read nowhere any intelligent discussion on this dual capacity of *mano* both to apprehend the simple and to co-ordinate simple impressions into complexes or percepts.

With the term *bhavanga* I have already dealt (p. 378). Had it been in use when the Kathāvatthu was compiled, it would certainly not have been left to the Commentary to use it in explaining the section where it was needed (*Points*, p. 243). It was certain that such a term would come to be needed. The Sāsana paid early and assiduous attention to attention. And for this reason: consciousness, awareness, only arose when a stimulus arose (see above, p. 312). What then was mind, where, how was it, when, as in sleep, or latent awareness, no cause was arousing it, calling it into actuality? Was it a sort of potential being, one with the life-flux? There were no words for the subconscious, the subliminal, the potential. In the Kathāvatthu we see in this and that discussion the need of all three terms, albeit the need is not felt as such.

Here are a few other points of psychological interest in the same work:

(*a*) Consciousness conceived as (α) acts of minding or awareness, and (β) co-efficients or adjuncts, some constant, some contingent, called 'mentals' (*cetasikā*) came, I repeat, to occupy a leading place in South Asian Buddhism. Nevertheless we can note, that the validity of such a classification was once a controverted point. Thus: "if there were 'mentals' of *citta*, why not make out 'contactals' (*phassika*) as adjuncts of contact (*phassa*)?" (VII. 3).

Another curious point, ethical as well as psychological, is the contention, that mind (*mano*) and its specific objects (*dhamma*'s) are unmoral; so also are knowledge (*ñāṇa*) and mindfulness (*sati*), when no sense-impressions are present to render them liable to moral stain. Here, as is the case in much prescientific dialectic, the weak analogies of language are oftener referred to than the facts of living experience.

(*b*) In connection with the process of cognition, the Kathāvatthu makes repeated use of a sequence which we do not find previously: "adverting, ideating, co-ordinating application, attending, purposing, anticipating, aiming." The sequence may possibly not imply consecutiveness.

(*c*) The duration of a *citta*-unit was clearly a controverted point. And the logic of analogy again appears in the attempt to harmonize mind with life and the cosmic process. The Suttanta (we should say 'scriptures') spoke of a threefold unit of duration: the nascent, the static, the evanescent. Was not the 'morning-noon-evening' such a unit? Could not mind-process be made to fit with that? And was the process really a momentary unit? Did *deva*'s, in the immaterial sphere of mind (*arūpa*), only live there for a mind-instant? Did not they lack bodies with the duration of youth, maturity and old age as vehicles for the succession of innumerable mental flashpoints?

The later *khaṇika-vāda*, or 'momentary theory' of thought-life is here seen emerging. It is but adumbrated in the Nikāyas (above, p. 193).

(*d*) The perdurance of past consciousness too was a problem: how could the remembered past persist in present consciousness?[1]

Arguments in the later Kathāvatthu chapters show a familiarity with some of the 24 causal relations (*paccayā*), detailed with terrible reiteration in the Paṭṭhāna's citing them technically, *e.g.* "by the causal relation of immediate succession." This may seem to argue, that the Paṭṭhāna is after all not a later work. But if we, in arguing, take a Pali book as a unitary composition, we shall get nowhere. The *paccaya* terms do not occur till Section XV, and it does not require much examination to see, that the Kathāvatthu is, as I have said, an accretion in time. The Paṭṭhāna may well have been compiled even entirely, between compilation of Sections I. and XV. of the other work.

Another term apparently needed, felt after, in the Kathāvatthu is our newer term 'fore-conscious.' Namely, in a controversy on the forms of 'bias,' or latent tendencies (*anusaya*: lit. 'continued lyings'), in man (*Points*, p. 253 f., *cf*. p. 234), were these, as *latent*, unmoral, and only moral when *patent*? Where the word 'potential' seemed needed, I have used it guardedly (p. 242), and only, I think, in translating the Commentary. The Commentary is trying, like a good chairman, to help out matters in the discussion. Do we actually possess past consciousness, or is it perished? A man, it explains, may be endowed with (*samannāgata*), or again, he may have actual acquisition (*paṭilābha*) (of consciousness). There is a pathos in this felt need of the right word, and not finding it.

There is more matter of psychological interest in

[1] *Points*, p. 90.

the Kathāvatthu, but I have limited myself to that in which it may be said, that the subject is not merely touched, but just a little scratched. If readers will consult the analytical table in our translation, pp. xviii-xxvii, they will see, that such questions appear to have been raised now by one now by another of all the eighteen schools which the Commentary claims took part in such debates, earlier or later. The Andhakas of S.E. India were, it would seem, psychologically the most keen. The orthodox or *Sthavira-vādin* attitude in these matters is by no means always the more intelligently alert or convincing. Perhaps it could hardly fail to be otherwise. To be orthodox usually implies being *that which has done with growing.*

That the amount of inquisitive alertness, revealed in the past by heterodox schools, led to no more fruitful results than we have on record is also not surprising. These early psychologizers had inherited a certain positive body of data due to observation of mental procedure. But in their controversies we seldom if ever find that their intelligence has learnt this lesson: what was got was due to the mental alertness exercised by the man, or the men 'who saw' (*cakkhumanto*) about *the things we find.* If we are to get further, we must not only argue from these data; we must get more data, and in the same way. We too must observe and see. We must compare; we must measure; we must record the results. They were not yet an old Church, but already theirs was the backward view: "Is it not said in the Suttanta? Was it not said by the Exalted One?"

In one way, an all-important way, theirs was not the backward, by which I mean, the original view. They no longer held that the very man or soul was real; he was but a bundle of *dhamma*'s. And it was to protest against this, the newer view of the majority at Patna, of the 'Analyzers,' that a minority, from Vesālī chiefly, called Vajjians and Mahāsanghikas (of 'the great company'), met the former in debates such as were, in the scholastic edition of them we have in the Kathāvatthu, held in wordy war over this subject. No longer, for the Analyzers, was the man not to be confounded with his instruments, body and mind; he had come to be, for all that definition could do, just those instruments; "not to be got at" in any true, ultimate sense. The Analyzers, called in the Commentary Our-own-speakers (or the word Sakavādin may mean Sakya-speaker), ask, what is the ground of the soul's persisting? They are told by the man of the 'old brigade,' called here the Man-worder, it is by 'becoming' (*bhava*). The shallow rejoinder refers to 'becoming' as the growth of animal and plant life only, where it is of necessity followed by decay. That the Man-worder, if worthy of his great tradition, would have maintained, against this, that the soul is neither animal nor plant, and hence not limited, as are they, in his becoming, we cannot know. The editors would look to it, that any such argument was not permitted to be recorded. Were they not committed to a gospel, a philosophy of Man-in-the-Less?

That we have, in these soul-debates of Book I. of the Kathāvatthu, a very dressed account of what actually took place is much overlooked. My Burmese colleague and I did so when we were translating them, and I had not his excuse of being a Buddhist. It is true that now and then the last word is left with the Man of Vesālī. And once it is in the Commentary that his argument has been permitted to survive, a curious and precious jetsam. The debate has turned on the presence of a real man, not mind, in the achievement of a psychic feat (*iddhi* or *abhiññā*): Is the man an indispensable factor in such? The Analyzer *contra*: "Do you maintain his reality solely on that ground? If so, is he also real when *not* exercising *iddhi*? How do you support that?" The defender is merely made to say to the first of the three questions, "No, he is not only real then." And the matter, after the usual rejoinder claiming refutation, is then dismissed. But the Commentary gives us what the Man-worder may very well have said: "He judges that supernormal power is wrought, not by external agency, unconnected with the man's faculties, but is of the very self (*ajjhattaṃ*), hence there must be a user of those powers. Else are *they* the fiction; yet you admit they are genuine occurrences."

Is Saul also among the prophets? Or how was this 'left in'?

CHAPTER XIX

DEVELOPMENTS IN THE BOOK "QUESTIONS OF KING MILINDA"

FOR a fuller treatment of this all-important work in the history of Buddhism I refer my readers to my essay, *The Milinda Questions.*[1] Here I can but glance at the interesting glimpses of development in theory of mind, such as appear to have been mooted in Indian, then perhaps largely Buddhist, culture, midway between the Abhidhamma and the fifth century, when we know, with some certainty, that the exegesis on the Piṭakas took its final written shape in Pali.

I have discussed how the outstanding work of the *Milinda-pañha* apparently came into being:—a work in three distinct sections of different dates, and very greatly man-handled by orthodox editors in Ceylon, before it was circulated as a unitary composition. The 'questioning' in the first part is probably a genuine piece of early reporting, at a day when the practice of committing things to writing was quickly growing, the 'teacher of writing' being adduced more than once. There is a desultory taking up, dropping and resuming of topics, between the Greco-Bactrian king Menandros and the Buddhist monk Nāgasena, which

[1] *Trübner's Oriental Series*, 1930. The text of the *Milinda-pañho* (Trenckner) has been reissued by the R. Asiatic Soc., London. The translation referred to is in *S. Bks. of the East Series*.

precludes the idea of an original composition in dialogue. In the second part, on a number of 'dilemmas,' such an original composition, without this desultory procedure, is just what we find, and it was probably a later essay, not compiled from scribes' records.

The dialogue branches into a great variety of subjects, religious, ethical, monastic, philosophical, but it is occupied for some fifty pages (in the translation) with purely psychological matter, and for some fifty more with psycho-philosophical matter as to 'soul.'

One statement, not without interest here, is the measuring what we should call growth in holiness, graduation in saintship, in terms of increasing ability in intellection, or play of intellect.[1] The problem is how to reconcile the orthodox belief in the omniscience of the Buddha with the necessity of his having to consider (or reflect, *ā-vajjana*, lit. ad-vert) before cognizing anything he wished. In reply, seven types of *citta*'s are described, forming a scale in mental culture (*bhāvitattaṃ cittassa*) from the least trained up to the supremely trained or Buddha mind, *i.e.* of the supreme type of Buddhas, known from this time onward as *sabb'aññu*, omni-scient,[2] who gave themselves to enlighten and help mankind. In each grade, the mind is described as being brought quickly and easily into play about a greater range of subjects, remaining stiff and sluggish in action about a diminishing range of subjects.

[1] *Questions of King Milinda* (*Sac. Bks. East*), i. 154 f.

[2] In the Suttas (*Majjhima*, No. 71) he is shown emphatically repudiating omniscience. Buddhists have overlooked this. *Cf.* what is said above on seven '*cittāni*' and *citta* (p. 243).

'Culture,' here, is our old friend 'make-to-be,' 'cause-to-become,' associated above with developed intelligence (*paññā*).[1] Perhaps 'development' or 'evolution' is at least as fit a rendering. The supreme type of mind is (*in our terms*) to be so 'evolved,' that its thorough knowledge concerning everything knowable is, at any given moment, and with respect to a given subject, either actual, or potential with a potentiality swiftly transformable into actuality. The scheme is interesting as showing both the importance of intelligence or intellect in the Buddhist scheme of religious values, and also the oneness in kind between all human intellect, even up to the intellect of those who were ranked as and above the *deva*'s.

Concepts of mental functioning are discussed much after the earlier fashion of the Nikāyas, and usually during the repudiation, by the sage, of the position, that the 'man' can be 'got at' in any ultimate sense. Nāgasena, answering to his name as his first reply to the king, declares 'himself' to be but a mere convenient label for a number of parts and aggregates. "For here the man is not got at."[2]

It is of historical interest that he here uses the opening phrase of the Kathāvatthu debate (I. 1) and its term for entity or soul: not *attā*, but *puggala*. In fact, throughout his dissertations, terms other than *attā* are used: *puggala*, *jīva* (life, vital spirit),[3] *vedagu*, sentient agent.[4] *Jīva*, in the Sānkhya school, is the

[1] "Wisdom should be made to become" (p. 93, 266).

[2] "*Na hi ettha puggalo upalabbhati.*" Rhys Davids's rendering 'For there is no permanent individuality' is too free and goes too far, or not far enough. 'Permanent' finds no mention in such *anattā* talk.

[3] *Questions* (*S.B.E.*), 48, 86, 132.

[4] *Ibid.*, 86.

empirical soul, the intermediary, so to speak, between the organism and the absolute or noumenal soul. And it would almost appear as if *attā* had, at least for a time, come to signify merely the personal appearance or visible self.[1]

The mental processes discussed are chiefly those to which attention was given in connection with the Nikāyas. But there are points of added interest.

The sage has replied that "if he die with natural desires still at work in him, he will be reborn, but if not, no." Milinda asks if through reasoned thinking one "is not reborn." Nāgasena: "Both by reasoned thinking, sire, by wisdom and by other good qualities." "But are not reasoned thinking and wisdom just the same?" "No, sire, they are different. Sheep and goats, oxen, buffaloes, camels, asses are capable of reasoned thinking, but not of wisdom."[2] Reasoned thinking and wisdom are then described by the respective essential features of mental grasp and elimination or severance, just as a reaper grasps with one hand and prescinds with the sickle.

'Reasoned thinking' and 'wisdom' are *yoniso-manasikāra* and *paññā*, discussed above. We should have possibly named dogs, elephants, monkeys, for the beasts named here. But clearly, not the most intelligent animals are meant; merely 'animals' in general. Now, in the Nikāyas, the ability and habit of *yoniso-manasikāra* is the basis of all higher spiritual training. The term may possibly have depreciated a little during the centuries. If not, the crediting of animals with it lends point to the anomaly, pointed

[1] Or in popular diction? In the translation *attā* is translated by 'image,' *i.e.*, in a mirror.

[2] *Questions*, i. 50.

out above, with regard to inquiry into the mind of animals.[1] The association of *paññā* with 'elimination' dates from the Nikāyas, as we saw. It is, at the same time, exegetical, and not exhaustive of the import of the word. "Illumination," says the sage, a little later, "is also its mark. . . . It causes the splendour of wisdom to shine; it reveals the ariyan truths . . . as a lamp brought into a dark house (a Nikāyan figure)." Again, like the wind, it has no abiding-place.

More interesting yet is the distinction, seen in 'wisdom,' that whereas *paññā* analyzes, it is itself unanalyzable. It can value; it may not be valued. Thus, as I have said in the *Questions*, do we see monastic Buddhism giving back, with the left hand of a surviving tradition, what it explicitly took away with the dexter finger of the right hand. *Paññā* was made to take the place of the man, self, soul, and figure as his dummy. In the Aitareya Upaniṣad it appears as the crowning aspect of an ineffable but most real Man=Brahman. In the Milinda, *paññā* remains; the Man is ejected.

There is an echo of Majjhima discourse in the little tag hereon: "The king said: 'These three: *viññāṇa*, *paññā* and in creatures the *jīva*, are these *dhamma*'s different in word and meaning, or one in meaning, different in word? *Viññāṇa* has the "mark" of being aware (*vijānāti*), *paññā* has the mark of being-wise-about (*pajānāti*); the *jīva* in creatures (=beings) is not got at."[2]

To pursue this psycho-philosophical question a little

[1] Above, p. 365.

[2] *Milinda* (text), p. 86. The translation of the last clause is, again, too free.

farther, the soul, as *jīva*, or *vedagu* (knower), was still conceived as a will-entity or agent, who, were he immanent, would, in order to *know*, not need to act through the intermediacy of the different channels of coming-to-know, to wit, the five senses and *mano*.

" What is this, sire, the ' soul ' (*vedagu*) ?"

" The life [-principle] (*jīva*) within, which sees through the eye, hears through the ear . . . and cognizes phenomena through mind, just as we, sitting here in the palace, can look out of any window we wish, east, west, north or south." . . . " If this *jīva* acts as you say, choosing its window as it likes, can it not then see through any one of the five senses, or so hear, so taste, etc. ?"[1]

And later:

" But if, sir, there be no such thing as a soul, what is it then which sees objects with the eye, hears sounds with the ear, . . . or perceives objects with the mind ?"

The Elder said: " If the soul does all this, then [it would not need the specialized apparatus of each sense] it would see, hear, etc., more clearly if the sense-organ were removed; but it is not the case that we see, hear, etc., better if the eye-aperture, etc., has the organ removed; hence there is no agent in sensation independent of the specific functioning of each sense."[2]

The form of animistic philosophy, against which this argument is a protest, may well have been the *jīva* theory of the Sānkhya-Sūtras. This was but a convenient fiction or schema, by which the else inconceivable action of the noumenal soul, called *pūrūṣa*, *ātman, or kevălă* (absolute), upon body, sense and *mano* might be expressed in words. Thus the *pŭrŭṣa* was

[1] *Questions*, i. 86. [2] *Questions*, i. 133.

indifferent, impassive, separate; the senses acted mechanically. But sensation became conscious life when *jīva* glowed in it, like fire in hot iron, or as a red blossom in a crystal, the *pŭrŭṣa* losing nothing thereby.[1]

The really important point that arises out of this, at first sight, somewhat futile argument of Nāgasena, is his immediately following enunciation of natural law in mental procedure, wherein lay what some would hold to be the main support of his case. He first emphasizes the fact (briefly stated in the Nikāyas) of the orderliness in sense:—we cannot taste with the stomach, or the external skin; each channel of sense has its own procedure.

The king is then made to ask whether a sense-impression always has *mano*-consciousness as its concomitant. "Yes." "Which happens first?" "First the sensation, then *mano* functions." The king asks whether sensation induces this perceiving by an injunction, whether, i.e., perception bids sense to supervene. The reply is, there is no such intercourse; the sequence happens through (1) 'inclination' or natural tendency, (2) existing structure, (3) habitual process, (4) practice. These conditions are severally illustrated by similes: (1) by rain-water running away according to natural *slope*; (2) by the one means of egress and ingress used in a walled city; (3) by the usual order observed by the waggons of a caravanserai—first waggon, second waggon, etc.; (4) by the arts of writing, arithmetic and valuation, skill succeeding clumsiness through association set up by practice.

[1] *Cf.* R. Garbe, *Sānkhya-philosophie*, pp. 305 f.; *Sānkhya-Sūtras*, Nos. 99, 356. In Jain doctrine, it is the soul (*jīva*) that is 'coloured' (H. Jacobi, *Trans. Hist. Religions Cong.*, Oxford, ii. 63).

It was this idea of a uniformity or habit, without and within, evident if not to be accounted for, that Buddhism accepted, as substitute for the 'man' of its earlier teaching.

Further discussions on mental process yield some more definitions. The other concomitants of the happening of a *mano*-consciousness, beside the 'contact' on occasion of sense (between sense and its object), are stated to be feeling, perception, purpose (onset of) and sustained attention. These amount practically to the four immaterial *khandha*'s, and are to be understood as the contents of a state or process of consciousness on occasion of sense. 'Contact' is illustrated by two rams butting, two cymbals clashing.[1] But, as we shall see, the *wherewithal* in the collision does not seem to have been conceived as matter in the case of sight and hearing. 'Feeling' is well described as 'the being experienced and the being enjoyed.' The character of 'perception' is cognizing—becoming aware, *e.g.* of visible objects, that is, of colours (Buddhist psychology still assigning only colour to bare visual impression). Thus a king's steward, visiting his treasure-house, perceives the variously coloured treasures. 'Recognizing' is a possible rendering, but in the term (*saññā*) the corresponding prefix *paṭi-* is lacking.

'Purpose' (*cetanā*) receives a definition of some interest. In the Abhidhamma-Piṭaka it is described by mere derivatives, throwing for us no light on its connotation. This is not far amiss if the term meant bare volition, or conation, since we have here an, or shall I not say *the*, irreducible element of mind. Now the function, or mark of purpose, in these *Questions*,[2] is declared to be twofold: (1) deponent, and (2) causa-

[1] *Questions*, i. 92 f. [2] *Questions*, p. 94.

tive; to wit, (1) thinking (or being caused to think), and (2) concocting or devising (to give effect to the thought). "As a man might prepare, concoct a poison and drinking it, give it also to others to drink." This dual idea was maintained up to Buddhaghosa's time. By him it is likened to the working and making to work of a peasant-farmer, and of a master-craftsman. And he applies the orthodox fourfold definition of his time to the term (*cetanā*), showing it to imply 'being made to think,' 'effort,' 'fixing,' 'arranging.'[1] It would therefore seem to be the motor element in consciousness with the further implication of direction or purpose, and may thus be better rendered by purpose than by conation. The latter, as bare reaching out, or activity put forth, is aimed at in an *indriya*—*i.e.* a power or faculty—analogous to the sense-powers, and called *viriya*. As described in the Abhidhamma-Piṭaka (see above, p. 362), its equivalents are so many applications and modes of the unworded 'will.'

All this, on the other hand, suggests rather an aspect of the whole consciousness and character (habitual potential consciousness) at any given moment. In such terms as *cetanā*, the effort is being made to dissever, in a psychosis, all the nuances that go to make up the complex of consciousness.

The twin terms: initial and sustained mental application recur.[3] In the *Questions* they are likened to (*a*) a carpenter fixing a shaped plank into a joint, and (*b*) the reverberations of the (*a*) blows dealt in shaping a metal pot: (*a*) is the applied attention, (*b*) repeated pulsations of attention thus directed.

This analysis of consciousness ends with a reflection

[1] *Visuddhi-Magga*, ch. x. [2] *Bud. Psy. Ethics*, § 13.

[3] Above, p. 260.

on the difficulty of "fixing all those mental phenomena involved in a single impression, on occasion of sense, telling that such is contact, such feeling, etc.," as if a man in the Bay of Bengal were to taste the water and say in which river the drops had originally come down[1] —a metaphor quoted by Buddhaghosa. The factors were distinguishable, but not experienced as isolated, no more than the many flavours enjoyed in the sauce blended by Milinda's chef.[2]

The term *sati*, or mindfulness, is twice discussed; the second occasion suggests a later development, almost identifying the word with mindfulness of the past, or memory, and offering the earliest approach to a theory of association of ideas existing in Indian literature. The sage has stated that *sati* arises both through inward perception and external signs. He is then asked: "In how many ways does *sati* spring up?"[3] Seventeen ways are enumerated, but they fall properly into the two above-named groups, with the exception of two. These two amount to a statement of our own 'association by way of similarity and of contrast,' and apply of course to subjective experience in general, whether presentative or representative. "*Sati* arises," we read, ". . . from similarity . . . or difference of appearance . . . as on seeing one *like* her we call to mind the mother . . . ," or remember that such a colour, sound, etc., is *different* from that of a certain thing. The other 'modes by which mindfulness arises' are carelessly strung together, and only deserve

[1] *Questions* (text), 87.

[2] *Ibid.*, 63. It became nevertheless orthodox doctrine to hold, that no two *citta*'s of sense-reaction could arise at the same moment. There was swift succession and apparent simultaneity. Ledi Sayadaw, *JPTS.*, 1914, 149.

[3] *Questions*, i. 78 f.

mention because, so far as I know, there is no other inquiry of the same date to place beside the list. Briefly, then, recollection by purely representative effort is said to be effected by direct intellection (*abhijānana*), by discursive *cetanā*, by the 'making-to-become' of trained intuition in 'super-knowledge,' *i.e.* in remembering one's own former lives and, lastly, by ordinary revival of past experience as compared with present thoughts. This is more especially effected when that experience was of a striking nature, causing deep emotion. Milinda would recollect easily his coronation, Nāgasena his conversion; both would easily recall a pleasant or a painful episode. External suggestions of a visible or audible nature are also enumerated. The subject is then dropped.

Not less psychologically interesting is the exposition of a theory of dreams.[1] The physical conditions of dreaming are stated to be: firstly, the constant condition of 'monkey sleep,' that is, of a state between waking and deep sleep; secondly, the variable antecedents of morbid health, biliousness for instance. The other kind of antecedent, through which alone the dream has any relation to impending occurrences, is deva-influence or deva-induction. The meaning or object of this *deva* (*dibba*) intervention is accepted as current lore without criticism. As telepathic procedure, where the agency was of a physically more ethereal, or mentally less *canalized* composition than the recipient's mind, the occurrence would not seem supernatural to an Indian. It is added that the dreamer would not read the sign; he would relate, and an expert would interpret —a 'wrong means of livelihood and low art,' according to the ancient teaching ascribed to the Founder.[2]

[1] *Questions* (text), 297 ff.

[2] *Dialogues*, i. 17.

In deep sleep the consciousness (*citta*) is stated to have 'gone into,' that is, become one with the *bhavanga*, or flow of organic life, and 'does not go on,' does not recognize or discern what is pleasant or unpleasant. For consciousness, in this merely potential state, not being a continuum, or persisting being, is practically non-existent. To what, if any, extent the life-flow moments include moments of what we now term subconscious mental life, I have yet to learn.

Finally, concerning the achievements in that 'more-will' which India termed *ṛddhi* or *iddhi*: the talk here, though as ever desultory, is of interest. The later term *iddhi*-by-resolve (*adhiṭṭhāna*) is used)[1], as if a word for will had been further groped after. But in description, it is 'thought' (*citta*) which has to be the makeshift-term:—"Can anyone go in this bodily frame to the far North (*Uttără-kuru*), or to other worlds?"

"Yes, sire, there are persons who can go with this four-element-made body to Uttara-kuru or to Brahma-world; or to any other part of this world." "But how can they?" "Do you admit, sire, having ever jumped three or six feet of ground?" "Yes, sir, I do; I can jump twelve feet." "But how?" "I cause this idea (*citta*) to arise: 'there will I alight!' With the genesis of the idea my body becomes buoyant to me." "Just so, sire, does a monk, who has *iddhi* and mastery over *citta*, lifting up the body in consciousness, travel through the air by way of *citta*."

To this I have alluded already.[2]

Again, when Milinda is puzzled how a man, who has will and mastery over mind, can vanish, and reappear

[1] Appears in modes of *iddhi* in *Paṭisambhidā-magga*, ii. 207; but elsewhere (i. 107, etc.; *Dīgha*, iii. 229) not so associated.

[2] Above, p. 336. *Questions*, 84 f.

in the Brahma-world, which is supposed to be distant a four months' journey of a falling body from the earth,[1] "as soon as a strong man could stretch forth and bend in again his arm," he is asked to think of anything he ever did at his birthplace (Alasanda=Alexandria, in Baktria), two hundred leagues away. He does so. "So easily, sire, have you travelled so far?"[2] comments the sage, likening will-locomotion to thought.

[1] Note how the idea of an ultra-mundane 'up above' has now emerged. *Cf.* above, p. 337 *n*.

[2] *Ibid.*, 82.

CHAPTER XX

SOME MEDIÆVAL DEVELOPMENTS

SCANTY space in a volume already bulky remains to discuss, even in outline, the addition and modifications to be found in the great thesaurus of Buddhist exegetical literature. Nor is the time for such discussion fully arrived. Since the first edition of this work appeared (1914), the Pali Text Society, founded by my husband in 1881, has published 36 volumes of Commentaries. And there remain yet some ten or a dozen volumes in preparation. But no one has as yet made these works in their entirety the subject of critical study,[1] and my own acquaintance with their contents is very limited. I know a good deal more about the most famous of the early mediæval exegetists, Buddhaghosa, than I did twenty years ago; since then I have edited his 700 odd pages of original treatise: the Visuddhi Magga, or Way of Purity,[2] and have as general editor seen many of those 33 volumes through the press. But adequate study of them and the rest must remain with younger hands. For these ('hands,' my Asiatic friend, means 'men'; ask any sailor !) the work will be to this extent rewarding, that it is a yet unbeaten track; what they say will be a new word. Thus I have not seen as yet any distinction made between (*a*) the older materials on which each exegetist worked, and (*b*) his own

[1] Dr. E. W. Adhikaram, a former pupil, has forthcoming an essay on the Commentaries in Ceylon.

[2] Translated P.T.S. ed. by Professor P. Maung Tin.

contribution, often representing later changed values. And that this has not yet been recognized has done much mischief to the true, *i.e.* historical outlook on Buddhism. Thus the out and out nihilism of both Buddhaghosa and his contemporary Buddhadatta, which saw no real 'man,' spirit, soul, not as permanent entity only, but as any entity whatever—saw 'him' as 'merely a bunch of dhamma's' (*puñjamattaṃ dhammānaṃ*)—is a going further than the more cautious view of the Analyzers 6 to 7 centuries earlier, that the man "cannot be got at in a genuine ultimate sense." The Founder had said, it is recorded: "See that you take not the limited handicapped body and mind as the man or self." These nihilists did take them as just 'he.' No one as yet has discerned this altered position.

The history of the Commentaries has to be studied in close conjunction with (*a*) the tardy beginning of writing thoughts at length, *i.e.* books, in India and south Asia, (*b*) the resulting complicated descent of the oral and then written records. Thus we have first, the probable commitment to writing (on a thin metal scroll, long before palm leaves were used) of heads or texts, or it may be of what we used to call 'the argument.' Exposition was left to free, if trained, speech, like the modern sermon. Long after, the free exposition began also to be put into fixed oral discourse. Metrical discourse will have preceded the prose in these early fixings. Much will have yet been left to free exposition; we may compare here our fixed 'Lessons' from 'Holy Writ,' with sermons. Then writing came in, as a needed safeguard—so the sentiment runs in the earliest known testimony: the Dīpavaṃsa of Ceylon of 300 to 400 A.D.—came in in the last century B.C., possibly slightly earlier in India. The fixed expositions, poetry and prose, were set down as *pāṭha* or 'text'; the frills of exposition became written *aṭṭhakathā* or commentary.

Then early in the fifth century we hear of Buddhadatta and Buddhaghosa going in succession from India to Ceylon, and of the latter both writing his famed treatise in Ceylon and also of his recasting the *aṭṭhakathā*, which had there been written in Sinhalese, into Pali, this literary diction from the Prakrit dialects having become the churches' orthodox tongue. Hence it is that in the *aṭṭhakathā* of each work we get attached a 'word-comment,' the result of saying *x* (a Sinhalese word) is in Pali *y*.

Now it is in historical sifting on these lines that work is mainly to be done. And then only will it be fit to discuss contributions to Buddhist psychology to be found (*a*) in the older expositions *handled by* those mediæval exegetists, from Dhammapāla and those above-named, including forgotten writers, credit for whose work has been laid on Buddhaghosa, making him a very Omar Khayyam of exegesis, and (*b*) in their own fifth-century and later contribution.

So far as I have tried to anticipate these future maturer labours, I here reproduce with some revision what I published twenty years ago.

Buddhadatta, Buddhaghosa and Anuruddha (*Ceylon*, ? 1,000 A.D.)

I will call these Bd., Bgh. and A.

Whereas Bgh. expounds his psychology in terms of the five-aggregate division, Bd. opens his scheme with the fourfold division of A.'s *Compendium*—viz. mind, mental properties, material quality, Nibbāna.[1] He writes in metrical Pali, stopping at times to supply his own prose commentary: "*Citta*, that is, being aware of what is within one's range . . . minding everything inclusively; one's own life-continuum." And later: "*Cetasika*'s, that is, conjoined with *citta*, or becomings-in-*citta* (*citte bhavā*). These also, like *citta*, form the subject to object, as such forming a single class. As resultants or non-resultants in consciousness, they are divisible into two classes. As productive of good or bad result or neither (literally: as good, bad or indeterminate) they form three classes. As belonging to consciousness concerned with mundane experience, with rebirth in worlds of sublimated matter, with rebirth in immaterial worlds, and with subjects whence all rebirth-concerns are rejected, they form four classes."[2]

He then enumerates all the 'mental properties' to be distinguished in analysing that first type of a good and happy thought or *citta* on occasion of sense, detailed in the Abhidhamma-Piṭaka, and discussed in an earlier chapter (pp. 361 ff.). He also introduces the important distinction, not brought out in the old original analysis, of some mental properties being constants (*nīyatā*)[3] and some contingent or occasional. "These five: pity, sympathy-with-joy, aversion from evil in act, speech and life, are inconstant; they arise sometimes [in such a type of consciousness]."

This distinction is clearly worked out in A.'s *Compendium*. We cannot yet compare Bd. and Bgh. But

[1] I do not say that we do not meet with this division in, and its acceptance by, Bgh. My point refers only to emphasis.

[2] *Abhidhammâvatāra* (P.T.S. ed.), p. 16; *cf.* p. 1.

[3] The *Compendium* term is here *sadhāraṇa* and its negative.

the later *Compendium* shows clearly that, at all events, for psychological analysis, the 'five-groups' system has fallen into the background, and consciousness is resolved into *citta* and its coefficients of *cetasika*'s, some of which are constant coefficients, that is, which are, in any given moment of consciousness, present, some not.

This, in the *Compendium of Philosophy*, is much better worked out than in the older writer. We there see that, in such a given moment, mental analysis declares, as being distinguishable factors, or nuances, seven constant coefficients, the Pali for 'constant' being 'all-consciousness-common-to.' These are contact, feeling, perceiving, purposive intellection, individualization,[1] [the accompanying awareness of] psychic life, attention. Without these there can be no supraliminal consciousness. Besides these there may or may not be distinguishable six occasional coefficients, the Pali for 'occasional' being, in Bd., not-fixed, not certain (*a-niyāta*), in the *Compendium*, 'scattered' (*pakiṇṇaka*), distributed. These are initial and sustained application, deciding, effort, zest, desire-to-do, or intention.

These thirteen, the later work adds, are all neutral, morally speaking; they combine with other factors of consciousness which are distinguishably good or bad 'implicates' of *citta*.

Such then is the evolution of this dual category. First, *citta* only; with the stray mention of *cetasika*, singular in number, in one Nikāya. Then a group-word only—*citta-cetasika dhamma*'s, in the books of the (later) third Piṭaka. Then the second term, now plural, appears as a list in the fifth book of that Piṭaka. Then

[1] P. 94 f.

the two terms described as separate philosophical categories in the fifth century; finally, the latter category, with fuller treatment, in the eleventh-century manual. And in that manual the five aggregates are enumerated but once, in a philosophical, not a psychological section, just to paraphrase the ancient term *nāmarūpa* (mind-and-body),[1] before they are again and finally let go.

That a positive, if a very slow, evolution in psychological specialization is here to be seen, seems fairly clear. It may not be admitted in centres of Abhidhamma learning. I am not sure that the habit of regarding matters historically, so new as yet in our own world of science, is cultivated there at all. The theory of *citta* and its properties or coefficient *cetasika*'s, in this or that group of conscious syntheses, is pursued in the *Compendium* with a good deal of very arid and to us also sterile numerical summarizing—an aftermath, I am tempted to think, of the so long preponderant booklessness in Indian culture. More instructive, and revealing a more notable development in analysis, is the doctrine of function (*kicca*) and of process (*vīthi*, *pavatti*). And here, whereas the *Compendium* reveals advance in summarization, it is in Bgh. and Bd. that, at present, we detect the original sources of its evolution.

In discussing the fifth aggregate—*viññāṇa*, or consciousness in its typical sense of coming-to-know, cognition,—Bgh. enumerates fourteen modes (*ākārā*) in which there is *viññāṇa*-process,[2]—viz. at reconception, in subconsciousness (sleep, etc., *bhavanga*), in *ad-verted* attention (*ā-vajjanā*), the five modes of special sense-impressions, recipience [of the same], investigation,

[1] *Compendium*, p. 198; *cf.* 23.
[2] *Visuddhi-Magga*, Ch. xiv.

determination, complete apprehension, and registration, and finally, at death. "At the end of registration, procedure is once more *bhavanga* (unconscious or subconscious). Then when *bhavanga* is again cut across, the course of consciousness having again acquired [the necessary] antecedents, adverting recurs, and so on, there being repetition of this procedure by way of the natural law (*niyàmâ*) of consciousness, until the *bhavanga* perishes. In each new life (*bhava*, literally 'becoming'), the lapsing of the last subconscious *citta* is called decease (*cŭti*, falling). . . . But from decease [comes] again conception, and from conception again *bhavanga*—such is the procedure in the unarrested consciousness-continuum of beings faring on through eternity. But whoso attains arahanship, to him when consciousness has ended, renewed birth and death have also ceased."[1]

The eleven modes of the cognitive process are briefly described previous to this passage. But they have not the appearance of being stated for the first time. No explanation of them *as process* is judged necessary. And since Bd., in the fourth chapter of the work referred to, also names these fourteen modes of *citta*, it is probably right to conclude that they both were but handing on an analytical formula, which had evolved between their own time and that of the final closing of the Abhidhamma-Piṭaka.

But the exposition of the cognitive process is more clearly and concisely stated in the later *Compendium*. However swiftly an act of sense-perception may be performed, it was held that, in every such act, seventeen moments or flashes (the metaphor is mine) of consciousness took place, each moment being con-

[1] *Visuddhi-Magga*, Ch. xiv.

sidered to involve the three time-phases of all 'becoming,' namely a nascent, static and dissolving phase. "Hence," we read, "the process [of sense-cognition] is thus: When, say, a visible object, after one *citta*-moment (1) has passed, enters the avenue [or focus] of sight, the life-continuum (*bhavanga*) vibrating twice (2) (3), its stream is interrupted, then the adverting moment rises and ceases (4). Immediately after, there arise and cease, in order, the visual impression (*viññāṇa*) aware of just that visible object (5), recipient consciousness (6), investigating consciousness (7), determining or assigning consciousness (8), then seven flashes of full perception," or apperception (*jăvăna*) (9-15); finally, *if* the percept is sufficiently vivid, two moments of retention or registering consciousness (16, 17). This phase etymologically is very differently named: *tad-ārammaṇa*, or *that*-object—that and not another= identifying. "After that comes subsidence into the life-continuum."[1]

The later commentaries illustrate this multiple, if momentary, psychosis by the following simile: A man lies asleep with covered head beneath a mango tree (stream of unconscious life or *bhavanga*). A wind stirs the branches (preceding *citta* 1 and vibrating *bhavanga*, 2, 3). This causes a mango to fall by him (arrest or disruption of unconscious life). The man is waked by the falling fruit (adverting, 4). He uncovers his head (sense-impression of fruit, 5), picks up the fruit (receiving, 6), inspects it (investigating, 7), determines what it is (determining, 8), eats it (full perception, 9-15), swallows the last morsels (registering, 16, 17), re-covers his head and sleeps again (subsidence into *bhavanga*). ('After-taste' had perhaps been more apt for 16, 17.)

[1] *Compendium*, 126.

Such is the type of procedure where the impression is vivid. With fainter impressions, inception may take longer, or there may be no process of registering, whence comes retention and reproduction. There may even be no moments of full cognition, or, in the faintest stimuli conceivable, no sense-impression, but mere momentary *bhavanga-calána*, *i.e.* organic 'vibration.'

This is certainly, in its meticulous analysis, its so to speak microscopical introspection, a considerable elaboration of the simple Sutta statement, quoted in a former chapter, of *mano* as the resort of, and the indulger in, all the impressions of the special senses.[1] Nevertheless, the validity of that statement is piously upheld by Bgh., when he is discoursing on *mano*. This is in the Commentary on the first Abhidhamma-Piṭaka book, a work containing better psychological matter than the more normative treatment of the *Visuddhi-Magga*. The work of *mano* is there explained in reference to that passage.

Quoting it, he goes on: "Those objects which are the field and range of the five senses are also enjoyed by *mano*. . . . Each object (colour, sound, etc.) enters the focus [of consciousness] by two doors or gates. The object of sight, for instance, when it becomes the condition of *bhavanga*-vibration, by striking on the visual organ, at that instant comes into the focus of the *mano*-door. Just as a bird coming through the air and alighting on a tree, at the same moment shakes a bough and casts its shadow on the earth, even so is the simultaneity of sense-stimulus and *mano*-access." Then follow adverting of *mano* and the rest of the process. But in work of *mano*-door only, there is no sense-impact. This is when, on a later occasion and

[1] P. 223.

being no matter where, we recall some previous sense-experience—"the sight of the beautifully decorated shrine, the pleasant voice of the preacher, the odour of votive wreaths, the meal enjoyed with colleagues. Or we may, when lying on a hard bed, recall a soft, easy couch enjoyed at such a time. Thus to the adverting *mano* the tangible object seems to enter the door of touch, and to make the pleasant contact present. But there is no such impact at the time."[1]

It is worth while to pause here and once more on the word *paṭisaraṇa*, 'resort' or 'referee.' We have seen it, without prefix, used in the Upaniṣads for the Self. We have seen it, in the Suttas, lowered to mean *manas*, mind. In the Commentary on the word we see the older tradition revived and shifted to a particular 'self': the Founder. "Disciples sometimes invite the Master's teaching by saying: 'Things have the Bhagavan as their root, their guide, their resort. Well for us if he reveal the meaning of this that he has just declared . . .' then a parable: Things of all four planes coming into the focus of his omniscience, are said to resort to the Bhagavan; they make him their resort, they go down together . . . thus 'contact' comes to his discernment asking: 'What is my name?' 'Thou art contact in the sense of seeking. . . .'" The four mind-*skandha*'s ask in turn . . . "each receiving a name according to its nature."

Visual consciousness, it goes on, is mere seeing visible object. . . . There is here no scope for the three radicals: appetite, ill-will, bewilderment. These affect the *mano* (or *javana*). How differently, had Buddhism been "founded on Sānkhya,"[2] would this have been worded!

[1] *Atthasālinī*, p. 73. [2] A notion held by Garbe and Jacobi.

Later on, the *mano*-element ('element' as being 'empty of substance' or 'entity') is described as "*following* the sense-impression, as having the essential mark of cognizing sights, sounds, etc., the property of receiving the same, the resulting phenomenon of truth (literally: thusness), and as its proximate antecedent, the vanishing of the sense-impression. . . ."[1] Its physical basis is the heart, and although the door-objects, which are not similarly bound, pass on, this is the *locus*, this has the function of receiving them. The investigating moment and the rest come under that developed activity of *mano* termed 'element of *mano*-consciousness,' and correspond more or less to what our text-books call representative cognition, much of which is always implicit, if perhaps latent, in an act of sense-perception. And where the work of mind is not largely automatic, and swiftly determined and apperceived, as on most occasions of sense, but is dealing with unfamiliar and problematical assimilation, we may presume that Bgh. would admit that *citta*-moments, predominantly of investigating, determining, etc., might be indefinitely multiplied. Unfortunately he has left us no work devoted entirely and systematically to mental analysis. And if there be any such later work by another hand, it is not yet accessible.

The location of mental functioning in the heart as its basis or 'site' (*vatthu*) was an old tradition, which is not worded in the Piṭakas,[2] but emerges in the Commentaries. I have it from Burma that the canonical silence was intentional. The wise Founder

[1] *Atthasālinī*, 263. Note the orthodox scholastic mode of definition.

[2] Let the reader not be misled by translations of *citta* (mind) by 'heart.' See above, p. 239. *Cf. Compendium*, p. 277 f. Note by S. Z. Aung.

judged that to assign a cerebral basis for mind would not be accepted by his age (!). Be that as it may, the evasion is, in the Abhidhamma book Paṭṭhāna quite marked. Thus:—The bases of the five senses are enumerated; then: "That *rūpa* on the basis of which apprehension and comprehension take place. . . ."

A complete exposition of this Commentary, however, would reveal much more incidental psychological matter of interest. For instance, it does not pause to point to anything problematical in the phenomenon of contact on occasion of sense, either in the physical necessity, except in touch, of a medium, or in the apparent anomaly of *rūpa* in contact with that which is *a-rūpa* (matter with mind). And it makes no dogmatic statement concerning this. Nevertheless remarks are let drop guarding the psychological position. Thus: "'Eye impinges on visible object (*rūpa*)' only means eye receiving the mental object (*ā-rammaṇa*)."[1] Again, when he alludes to the *Milinda* similes for contact—the rams butting and cymbals clashing—Buddhaghosa justifies the use of 'impact' as between consciousness and mental object only in the sense of attaining, achieving (*sampatti*).[2] And, generally speaking, the cause of feeling lies in the nature of consciousness itself, "just as the heat of melting lac is in its own tissue though ascribed to burning coal without."

There is a great deal more sagacious psychological comment scattered thickly up and down this Commentary, and to some extent the following Commentary[3] on the *Vibhanga*, or second book of the Abhidhamma-Piṭaka.

[1] *Atthasālini*, 309. [2] *Ibid.*, 108 f.
[3] Edited by Rev. A. P. Buddhadatta, P.T.S. ed.

Some day the psychology of Bgh. will take its lawful place in the history of psychology. It is as yet premature to attempt a digest of the contribution made by him. I will only quote two more remarks given in *Buddhist Psychological Ethics*, to show, by these alone, how unworthy of a truly catholic perspective it will be, to take account of Aristotle's psychology and not of Bgh.'s when made accessible.

The work just mentioned, a translation of *Dhamma-sangăṇi*, has replied to its query: "What is included under visible object?" by stating, first, colours, then forms of magnitude. On these the Commentary remarks: "Here, inasmuch as we are able to tell 'long,' 'short,' etc., by touch, while we cannot so discern 'blue,' etc., therefore long, short, and so on are not to be taken as visual objects without explanation. It is only by customary usage that we can speak of anything as *visible* object which appears as long or short, great or small, etc., etc., when so placed as to compare with something else."[1] This may not bring us up to modern psychology, but it is a farther step towards Berkeley's (rather one-sided) view, that whenever we are seeing, we are really, in mind, touching, than is Aristotle's mere hint: "There is a movement which is perceptible both by touch and sight."[2] The reader may find it interesting to link this argument with that in Chap. XVIII., p. 380, above, on the question of the visibility of space.

Once more, in commenting on the question: "What is included under the organ of touch?" he writes:

"The organ of touch (literally, the material organic compound, or body, *kāya*) is diffused over the whole bodily form just as moisture pervades an entire cotton

[1] *Atthasālinī*, 317. [2] *De Anima*, II. vi.

rag. With the exception of this quality of unspecialized organ, the sense ranks with the others. To the objection that, if the sensitive surface be so general, it would convey confused impressions, the reply is that, without this extensity, we should not get all the touch-differentiations that we do get. In an ultimate sense the organ of touch is both everywhere and not everywhere. Not everywhere to the extent of being in things as seen or as tasted, etc. We cannot segregate sensations as we can grains of sand: hence qualities appear to, but do not really, coalesce in the object."[1]

One more contribution by Bgh. to a theory of the work of touch must find mention. It will have been noticed that a binding quality was reckoned the essential feature in the element of water. The other three elements were also assigned such a feature: extension (not solidity) in earth, the calorific in fire, mobility in wind or air (*vāyo*). About water: he exempts this from the tangible, inasmuch as that which is felt, in a concrete liquid, is the other three elements, not the bindingness or cohesiveness of them. We feel its resistance, viz. its extended quality, we feel also its heat or cold, we feel its movement. It is these three which we apprehend through touch. For him, as for us, touch was the most fundamental of the senses. The other sense-organs and objects, he goes on, are relatively speaking as cotton balls striking other cotton balls on elemental anvils. But touch is as the hammer itself, smiting through its cotton sense on to the anvils.

Leaving the field of sense-cognition, another noteworthy contribution by Bgh. is his recording what was probably the current development of the meaning

[1] *Atthasālinī*, 311.

of the term I have rendered as 'zest' (*pīti*). This word in the canonical books is usually associated with either *sūkha*, pleasant, happy feeling, or *pamōjja*, joy, gladness, and it was very generally rendered by 'joy.' S. Z. Aung has strongly maintained that *pīti* is not so much an emotional as an intellectual quality, and, at least in its lower power, stands for 'interest.' Thus the 'interest' of pursuit as compared with the *sukha* of realization is, by Bgh., likened to the thirsty heated traveller's quest compared with his reaching water, shade and rest.

But if *pīti* be not emotional, it is unmistakably emotion. 'Emotional' is, has to be, used as the adjective of feeling. And *pīti* is classed, not with feeling (*vedanā-kkhandha*), but among the complexes called *sankhāra*'s or *cetasika*'s. It is not simply pleasurable feeling (*sukha*). But neither is emotion to be so defined. Emotion is feeling accompanying an idea, the being 'moved' with a coefficient of representative consciousness. The canonical description of *pīti* allies it with terms of gladness, mirth and enthusiasm.[1] Bgh. gives, as its essential features, the being pleased, expansion, and elation.[2] He also gives us the five grades of *pīti*: the thrill of eagerness, the momentary flash, the flood of enthusiasm, as waves breaking over us, ecstasy or transport, and rapture. And all the instances given refer to an idea or group of ideas as the proximate cause. Hence, whereas no one word need suffice, 'joy' as the more exultant, uplifted form of interest or zest is by no means always a mistranslation. And as the Commentary on the Anthology of the monks and nuns renders by *pīti-sukha* their emotion on reviewing their own struggles to the goal, so do I

[1] *Dhammasangaṇi*, § 9. [2] *Atthasālinī*, 115.

judge that Bgh., and even my excellent collaborator, would use *pīti* in translating Professor Bergson's fine passage on the intellectual joy of creative effort and attainment. Once we get at the psychologically composite backbone of *pīti*: "intellectual excitement over an object felt as desirable,"[1] we may render the word by whichever of the above-named terms—none of which, not even 'joy,' is bare feeling—the particular context seems to demand.

This mood of intellectual commotion, ranging from interest, eagerness, or zest up to rapture, is too important in all religious psychology for us to dismiss the Buddhist discussion of it for yet a few moments longer. The emotion, writes the Commentator, reaches maturity and climax in composure and serenity of mind. But the prior working of it is a sort of mental intoxication. We may pass over his metaphors of the first three and the last: the 'goose-flesh' thrill, the lightning flash, the boiling surge on the shore, the expansion of a blown bladder.[2] It is on *pīti* as elation, or transport or ecstasy, that he enlarges. And here, far from our Western and Greek-trained sobriety, he takes the elation[3] and transport physically as well as mentally, representing those possessed of this rapture "caught up to the third heaven," as St. Paul might say, "whether in the body or out of the body I cannot tell—God knoweth,"[4] or as he himself says, "making the body elated, so as to accomplish a measure of leaping into the air." He then tells two anecdotes from his abundant store: how an Elder M. dwelling at N.

[1] Discussed in my *Buddhism* (first ed. *only*), p. 231.
[2] *Visuddhi-Magga*, Ch. iv.
[3] *Udagya* = *ud-ag-ya* (up-top-ness).
[4] II. Cor. xii. 2.

contemplating the full moon at a shrine, and thinking how at the Great Shrine all the faithful must just then be reverencing the Buddha, dwelt on the idea of Him and in a throbbing (*ubbega*) ecstasy like the chords of a lyre, rose in the air and stood again in the courtyard of the Great Shrine. Thus too the daughter of well-to-do folk at Y., near the minster Z., left at home while they went to church, stands at her door looking in the bright moonlight up towards the hill-shrine 'shining like a heap of pearls,' and longing to hear 'the sweet Dhamma-discourse.' Thereupon throbbing ecstasy arises and she too leaps into the air, arriving in the congregation before her parents. They question her and are amazed that she should have come as only arahans were wont to travel.

Pīti therefore at this degree of intensity was held to have produced, in the past at least, a similar super-normal result to the power of supernormal will,[1] without apparently any express preparation or exertion of will.

Bgh. gives his cases in much the same tone of habitual, unsurprised faith that an orthodox Christian would use in alluding to miracles. But I have not yet found him attesting his own experience of such results, nor that of his contemporaries. And his chapter on *iddhi* in the *Visuddhi-Magga*, to which he here and there refers his readers, is to me clearly not that of one who spoke from first-hand experience. In this chapter, now in its long-delayed English dress,[2] the reader will be able to judge to what extent the Jhāna exercises, pre-scribed for making the mind (*citta*) 'concentrated, purified, pliant and fit,' seem calculated to induce

[1] *Adhiṭṭhānā-iddhi*, see above, p. 336.

[2] *The Expositor*, i. 153 f. Trs. by P. Maung Tin (P.T.S. ed.), 1920.

the extraordinary power of will which, in the *iddhi*-adept, were reckoned able to convert mind into body, or body into mind, as if the repudiated Ātman Himself were immanent in either.

The work of Bgh. cannot be finally appraised in these fragmentary remarks, typical of the very unfinished state of our 'excavations,' but so far we can say, that his intellect, clogged as it is by all that usually handicaps the scholastic mind, dominates the development of his own tradition: unsound philology, unsoundness as to historical evidence, the losing, in detailed work, all conspectus of the whole, whether that whole be the movement, from its inception, of the tradition he represented. His diction, moreover, becomes at times involved and ambiguous. He was no longer writing for a culture with no literature. But there is a world of difference between his commentatorial phraseology and the limpid periods of the author of the *Milinda Questions*.

We know, moreover, enough to be doubtful as to the probability of coming upon any attempt to theorize on the problem of representative cognition, or of the association of ideas. Apparently he resembled in this respect European philosophers prior to Hume and Hartley— for Spinoza's statements[1] carry us no further than Bgh.'s as psychological theory, though they are better summaries. Until, in fact, the *neurological inquiries* of Cartesianism were set on foot, no strong impetus arose to make the apparent parallelism between the physically associated and the mentally associated a matter for philosophy to theorize about. But the problem of the functions of the pineal gland and the deductions therefrom set the savants thinking anew.

[1] *Ethics*, II. xvii., xviii.

"I wonder," wrote Spinoza, "that one who had so often taken to task the Scholastics for wishing to explain obscurities through occult qualities, could maintain a hypothesis, beside which occult qualities are commonplace! What does he understand, I ask, by the union of the mind and the body?"[1]

Now Buddhist psychology postulated a seat, literally, site (*vatthu*), for each of the ways in which the organism was, as Professor Bergson might say, canalized for access to external impressions, or rather for the access of those external conditions, in consequence of which *citta* or consciousness was called up. These were the five special sense-peripheries, and, in the older books, "that material thing on the basis of which apprehension and comprehension take place,"[2] a thing which, in all the (much later) commentaries, is explained to be the heart (*hădăyā-vatthu*). The brain is scarcely mentioned until the *Milinda*,[3] and though the etymological parallel of nerves (*nahăru*) is always included, in the enumeration of the thirty-two main constituents of the body, it is apparently in the sense of 'sinews.' There was therefore no physiological induction concerning the 'canalization' of sensory disturbance. Hence any corresponding theory of 'latent mental modifications,' based on a theory of neural tracks and so forth, is no more to be expected in Buddhist than in European mediæval psychology. And so far as I have seen, Bgh. is content to push no further the adumbrations of theory we met with in the *Milinda*, but simply to give the facts, the results of representative cognition, without

[1] *Ethics*, v., Preface. He is referring to Descartes.
[2] *Compendium*, 278.
[3] *Questions*, 26: *matthalunga*. *Khuddakapāṭha*, III., mentions it; *Majjhima*, in its list in No. 10, omits it.

feeling called upon to frame any new theory to suit the 'non-entity-non-soul' axiom of his tradition which he loses no opportunity of upholding.

To judge, however, by S. Z. Aung's able presentment in his introductory essay to the *Compendium of Philosophy*, the later mediæval and modern psychological literature of Burma and Ceylon has not only evolved a detailed theory of reproductive mental procedure, but claims to have evolved it from the so-called Method of Relations, formulated with interminable detail in the last book of the Abhidhamma-Piṭaka called *Paṭṭhāna*. We have as yet no access to the original documents containing these later developments to which Aung owed his philosophical training. But I imagine that it will have been the contact with Western thought and criticism, and not his authorities, which prompted him to propound and to reply to the query: "How is memory possible, if the subject be not the same for any two consecutive moments in life?"[1]

I have put in a plea that special attention may be given to the philosophy of relations (*paccāyā*), and its application to mental processes.[2] Here is not the place to discuss it, and the question itself given above is philosophical, and not psychological. We are not, however, out for psychology pure and simple, and shall do well to pause a moment over the subject on which we may get more light in the near future.

Paccaya is not exactly our relation. It is nearer to that kind of relation which we call *causal*. Thus, in the Commentary on the Book of Relations we read: "*Paccaya* here means *because-of-that-makes-to-go*."

[1] *Compendium*, 42.

[2] *Paṭṭhāna*, Part II., was edited by myself in 1906; Parts I., II. and III. and the Commentary I published in 1921.

(This is the mediæval 'buried-city' etymology common to Europe and Asia.) "That is to say, it is concerned with what is *not-opposed*." (More 'buried-city.') "For the phenomenon (*A*) which stands or happens in non-opposition to another phenomenon (*B*) is said to be the *paccaya* of the latter." We now become more positive again: "*Paccaya* has the essential mark of *rendering service* (literally working-up-to, *upakāraka*). *A* is *B*'s *paccaya* in so far as it renders service to *B*'s existing or becoming. *Paccaya,* condition, reason-why, source, coming-to-be, origin (*pabhăva*), etc., are one in meaning, different in verbal form." Judging by this passage, therefore, the twenty-four kinds of *paccaya* distinguished in the Book of Relations are twenty-four ways in which the happening of *A affects* the happening of *B*; or conversely, in which the happening of *B* is as it is because of the happening of *A*.

When this definition is applied to the correlation of one mental moment (*citta*) with another, we get a much less empty abstract conception than that of two terms just 'standing in relation one to the other.' We come to realize that in a continuum of momentary *citta*'s we have *not* just a number of isolated, mutually independent units, simulating by their speed a unity of substance, just as a red-hot point whirled round in the dark simulates an unbroken circle.[1] We *have* a number of units simulating unity, but they are such that each one is what it is because of the 'service-rendering' of those that have preceded it. Thus according to the Book of Relations, and the echo of it in the *Compendium*,[2] *B citta*, related to *A citta* as (1) immediately succeeding, (2) present while *A* is absent, (3) present with *A* in abeyance, that is, telling

[1] *Cf. Compendium*, p. 33, *n.* 1. [2] P. 193, § 9.

upon it, is, in consequence, so and not otherwise. Or again when *A* and *B* are in the *paccaya* of association (*sampayutta*), *A* has rendered such service to *B* that it is wrought up into *B*, and hence in *B* our past appears as present. (In the latter case reference is not made to mutually contiguous *citta*'s.)

This influence, or service-rendering, or conditioning of one momentary phenomenon (whether mental or otherwise) came to be termed *satti* (Sansk. *śakti*), that is ability, *vis*, influence, force, chiefly, it would seem, through the teaching of Ariyavaṃsa, a notable and noble-natured Burmese teacher of the fifteenth century.[1] And I mention the theory as showing that the Buddhist theory of non-soul, or of no abiding entity-who-*has*-*citta*'s, has not caused the substitution, in place of such a doctrine, of disconnected momentary monads, each one being a *tabula rasa* of anything that had gone before.

All this is insufficient to explain the 'reinstatement' of any given section of the past at any given moment, in other words, why *citta*'s *A B* . . . *call up* certain former *citta*'s *X Y* . . ., whether we add, with Locke, why *C* is the consciousness that 'we did have' *XY* . . . once, or whether we do not. But this is a matter which the hypothesis of a perduring entity does not explain either. Theories of association may state that, for instance, a man, passing some object one day and making a remark, may recollect, when passing a year later, what he said, and continue the conversation, and call it association by contiguity and similarity. But the *form* of persistence, the actual mechanism

[1] *Cf.* Mrs. Bode's *Pali Literature of Burma*, 41. I owe the information to the late S. Z. Aung's kind reply to my questions as to the earliest mention of *paccaya-satti*.

of reinstatement, that has gone on 'in' the mental continuum, the theory can no more describe than the electrician can say how wire or ether is molecularly affected during transmission of electric force. We cannot describe mental experience, which is 'much more vast than cerebral life,'[1] in terms of space, nor can we broaden into detail in terms of time.

Hence the sublimated animism of a 'psychic continuum' is really no better off as to an intelligible description of memory than is the Buddhist non-animism. If the former seem at first sight to help us out, it is because we have been surreptitiously conceiving mind in spatial dimensions, either as a storehouse,[2] and modified substance, or else as a long, long lane down which come pilgrims from the past. Such at least is, I think, the vaguely floating image of the remembering mind held, if not by psychologists, at least by the general reader. If we strip off these quasi-visible vestments of mind, and think of it only in terms of its processes experienced as results, then the upspringing of potential *citta*'s (not empty and mutually disconnected, but each fraught with the informing *satti* of this or that among former *citta-continua*) brings all our past right up to and about our present at least as much as does a real, and not a simulated unity in the *continuum*.

In putting down the *Compendium*, we note that, in the last part, which is concerned with that mental training, or 'making to become,' so as to realize, for those who were ripening for it, the final goal of life, the word *paññā* has gone, and *vipassanā*, dis-cern-

[1] Prof. Bergson, 'Presidential Address,' S.P.R., translated by the late Wildon Carr.

[2] A *boîte à souvenirs*, Prof. Bergson would say.

ment, insight, has replaced it. The twin terms, 'calm and insight,' date from the oldest books, but they come, as twin terms, to the very front rank only in mediæval works. Each now comprises a *khandha* or group of exercises. 'Calm' (*samathā*) includes all that Bgh. classed under *samādhi* (concentration), and the older books partly under training (*sikkhā*) of *citta*, partly under *paññā*. Under 'calm' is now included 'supernormal intellection,' or *abhiññā*.[1] Of its six modes the last—the spiritual 'destruction of the *āsava*'s or vicious instincts'—is suppressed, and the other five are very briefly dismissed. 'Insight' comprises the intellectual realization of certain truths.

In spite of the ample statement given to one of them, to *iddhi*, in Aung's interesting introduction, I see in these altered proportions an evolution of thought. Sixteen hundred years, perhaps, had elapsed since the wonderful age that produced the Founder and his colleagues, and then 'arahans'; over a thousand years since the earliest records were committed to writing. Even Bgh. could only refer to the marvels achieved by saints of old, while it would seem that for A.'s still later age, the sight and sound of things ineffable, and the godlike will that could say of Brahma-heaven "Be thou near to me!"[2] were become as things that were very far away.

Let me bring to a close these fragmentary inquiries into the long career of psychology in Hīnayāna thought by linking those into the *citta* and the *paññā* of the oldest books with the latest utterances from Burma.

In the late Thera Ledi Sayadaw of Mandalay were combined a desire to give of his best to those in Europe

[1] *Compendium*, p. 209, and above, pp. 126-130.
[2] *Visuddhi-Magga*. '*Iddhividhā*.'

who had ears to hear, and a culture that is quite untouched by anything that Europe might have to give him of its own thought. His diction, so far as I know it, seems to me ageless; his similes might all be in the Nikāyas, or in Buddhaghosa; his ideas belong to a machine-less world. As such he comes rightly under my 'mediæval developments.' Such a product must, even in Burmese monasteries, be soon a thing of the past. Fortunately his works, written in Pali, are numerous, and are in print. In them (I do not say in them only) we may in time learn something of modern South Asian Buddhism, undistorted by filtration through minds born and trained in European tradition. Such 'distortion' may eventually bring about an evolution in that Buddhism greater than any it has experienced—an evolution that will eventually react mightily on our own philosophic standpoints—and be ultimately acknowledged by Buddhists themselves as the cause of a great renascence. And who can say how mighty a 'distorter' the translation of the Piṭakas now going on, in Burma and Japan and S.E. India, may prove? For the present we need to record this uncontaminated, unleavened heritage, deriving without break, from the Burmo-Sinhalese Council of A.D. 1165, not to mention the cult of the preceding centuries.

"*Citta* (consciousness), *mano* (mind), *mānasa* (intelligence), *viññāṇa* (awareness)," writes Ledi Sayadaw, "all are really one in meaning: they are various modes of coming to know.[1] . . . *We know*, whether our knowing be of blue as such or not as such, or whether it be of the real, as real or as otherwise, or whether it be what we desire or do not desire. Now knowing is

[1] So Bgh.

threefold: there is knowing as being aware of, knowing as perceiving, knowing as understanding. Perceiving is a clearer knowing than awareness, and is also knowing without forgetting over a lapse of time. Understanding (*pajānana*) is knowing adequately by way of class and species. It is knowing completely all about any [given] knowable thing. For even in any one such thing there is much to be known, viz. as to its nature, conditions, correlations, effects, the evil, the good of it, its impermanence, the ill connected with it. And *pajānana, paññā*, is to have an exhaustive knowledge of all this, as it is said: 'The limit of knowledge is the knowable, the knowable is the limit of knowledge.' *Paññā* in its fullest sense is omniscience. . . . Yet even for the learner, whenever through coming to know he conquers natural failings, his knowing has become *paññā*. . . . And whenever ordinary folk by coming to know dispel what is harmful, induce what is good, their knowledge too is *paññā*."[1]

The writer refers to passages in the canonical scriptures illustrating each kind of knowledge. A little further on he launches into a disquisition, varied by dialectic, on *citta* as "the especial basis, the peculiar soil of the error of Permanence," and on the doctrine of *citta* as a phenomenon "which uprises and ceases from one moment to another." From the standpoint of popular thought and diction, he goes on, it is correct to speak of mind, person, soul, as being or persisting, or passing hence, when from the standpoint of ultimate or philosophical truth nothing of the kind is so.

We will not go into that here. But we can pick up the thread again for a moment, where his discussion is psychological.

[1] *Yamaka*, ii., Appendix, p. 264 (P.T.S. ed.).

"Knowledge (*ñāṇa*),[1] do you say, is the criterion of truth? But that knowledge is twofold: inferential or intuitive.[2] When ordinary folk are investigating abstruse, subtle, deep matters, they know by way of inference. But with proper mental training, by developing *paññā*, they may attain intuition in such matters. By intuition, they discard the concepts 'person,' 'entity,' 'self or soul,' 'living thing' (*jīva*), and know things as of purely phenomenal nature, under the concept of element (*dhātu*). Now mind, mental coefficients, matter, *nibbāna*,[3] are just such abstruse, subtle, deep matters, to be truly understood only as inferential knowing becomes, through persistent training, transformed into intuitive knowing."

Here we see intuition considered as one aspect of that *paññā*, which is thorough knowing.

It may be noticed that Dr. Ledi makes no reference to Bgh.'s frequently repeated simile of the child, the citizen, and the gold-expert (above, pp. 266), when distinguishing between the three modes of coming-to-know. Aung told me that it is given in Sumangala's commentary on the Compendium. Aung himself disapproved of consciousness (*viññāṇa*) being graded with perception and *paññā*, which belong to the philosophically different category of mental coefficients (*cetasika*'s).

Here the reader of the Nikāyas and Buddhaghosa will note that the ancient five-group distinction is passed over. Ledi Sayadaw, however, in commenting on that classification, has illustrated, by a new and ingenious parable, the functions of the five *khandha*'s,

[1] *Ibid.*, 274. This to the objector.
[2] *Paṭivedha*, lit. penetrating.
[3] The fourfold category of Bd. and the *Compendium*. See above, pp. 402 f.

in vindication of the adequacy of this ancient category to take into account all human activities in such spheres as are governed by natural desire (*taṇhā-visayesu ṭhānesu*):[1]

"It may be asked: Why did the Exalted Buddha, when classifying conditioned experience under the concept of aggregates (*khandhā*), make the number five? We reply: By these five groups of phenomena our acts, regarded as felicific, on occasions where natural desires have play, find accomplishment. This the following parable may illustrate: A wealthy man, seeking wealth, builds a ship, and equips it with a crew of fifty-two sailors. By transport of passengers he amasses money. Of the crew one is expert in all works relating to the ship, and has these carried out; and one is acquainted with the ports to be visited and the routes thither, and he from a commanding position[2] directs the steering. The owner, maintaining boat and crew, receives and enjoys the ensuing wealth.

"Now by the sea we may understand the way of life ever renewed (*saṃsāra*); by the ship-owner, a person pursuing natural and worldly desires. By the ship we may understand the material aggregate (*rūpa-kkhandha*); by the wealth it brings in, the aggregate of feeling; by the former officer, the aggregate of perception; by the crew carrying out his orders, the mental properties labelled as *sankhāra*-aggregate; and by the latter officer, who directs the ship's course, the *viññāṇa*-aggregate.

"'Feeling' covers all our enjoying, partaking of. 'Perception' includes our conversance with, our intelligence of, our competence respecting all experience in

[1] I have very slightly condensed the following.

[2] I felt that 'the bridge' was too modern for this 'ageless' prose!

the range of things human, divine, or infra-human. That which we call *sankhāra*'s covers all that we do by thought, word, or deed according to what we have perceived. And *viññāṇa*, or the aggregate of consciousnesses or cognitions, is all those sense-impressions, sense-cognitions, which act as heralds and guides wherever we happen to be, pointing out, as it were, in our daily activities, and saying: 'this is here, that is there!' Thus it is that the five aggregates cover all that is wrought within the range of natural and worldly desires."

Hence, in this our little inquiry over some twenty-three centuries or more, we are still, in these words written in this century, well within sight of our starting-point. In them we see that, with a considerable evolution in introspective and analytical and critical power, there has been and still is an unbroken current of consistently upheld tradition, and that, even for a writer credited with so much independent and progressive judgment as was the Sayadaw, the word ascribed by him unquestioningly to his 'Exalted Buddha,' adored and believed to be omniscient, has not yet passed away, but is still held to sanction a division of man's instruments which we, if we read with historical criticism, may come to judge, were by him never uttered or entertained.

Striking to me, in the parable, is the finding a place for the 'ship-owner.' Or, as to that, in seeing in *viññāṇa* the officer who directs the ship. Almost I wonder whether, when his works come to be edited (I have a typescript of one of them half-buried in a cupboard), we may find in him a reincarnation, so to speak, of the Man-worder of Vesālī, who at Patna defended his Master and the Man? I fear not (see page 425).

A LAST WORD

In this re-creation of my *Buddhist Psychology*, I have kept more closely to the story of India's young analyses of mind than I did in the supplement added to the second edition (1924). I have not introduced any independent discussion of matters philosophical or anchistological.[1] I have compelled any such discussion to come in subserviently, to make more historically true the treatment of matters psychological. Any further discussion, as put forward in that edition, must take its turn elsewhere. I have here but a final word, the more fitly to close this inquiry on that which we, at our distance of time and space, can assign as the emerging of an attitude of mental analysis in India and its development in what we have come to call Buddhism.

Had I seen signs in the latest books by Hindu and Buddhist writers of an historical treatment of both emergence and development, I should have sung a mental *Nunc dimittis* and let my 20-year-old Manual take its shortcomings into a booky grave. But I have not seen such signs.

Hindu writers are beginning to acclaim the heretic Śākyamuni as a Hindu of superlative merit, but they see in him mainly a mere reformer of abuses in Brahman ecclesiasticism, and not as yet the seer of a new, if

[1] So long as 'eschatological' is current, I prefer my term as *more true*:—of 'the next things.'

just then wilting religious clue to man's nature, life and destiny—wilting in the academic teaching of Immanence, but new to the Many—namely, that the man is not 'being,' but 'becoming.' Nor have they shown as yet discernment of the effect of the growing psychological outlook on the growth of the Buddhist movement.

Buddhist writers, if orthodox, are not *free* to see and to write, concerning that movement, with historical criticism. For them, the Founder has no need that men see him as the child of the gospel of Immanence, yet new to, and taught by, his teachers. He has been too deified for that. He is made instead the mouth-piece of his deifiers. He is shown as merely a sort of great Doctor, seeking to save the body (and with it the wielding instrument, the mind) from disease, old age and death, as summed up in the word *dukkha*; but not as a Gardener of the growing plant that the man or soul really is. He is shown as a teacher of Man-in-the-Less, that is, of man as just body and mind—he, who had from the first warned the man, he was not just and only that. He is shown teaching Becoming as merely change, or transience. That he taught Becoming as, not this, but Growth—growth not of the impermanent body and mind, but of the very Man, of whom we have no scientific right to say, he must, after growing, decay:—this is passed over. Shown as teaching this mere gospel of impermanence, he and his mates are shown teaching the great word *bhava* as a nightmare-thing, to be shunned and dreaded, instead of so many God-sent opportunities of growth, of becoming in a More towards the Most. He is made to hold out, not his own aim or goal: the *attha samparā-yika*, the thing needed and sought, of the life 'beyond,' but the monk-goal of a waning-out (*nir-vana*) into an emptiness that is not-Man. He is made to show the best men as ready here below for that consummation (?), when, as compared with the Man consummate, that is, Deity, they were but as children. He is shown, not as telling men to seek the God-in-self of his day, not to take that God-in-self and His monitions as a lamp, a refuge and nothing else, but as telling man in modern parlance to walk by his own little imperfect light and save himself, unaided by That. He is shown as the man of endless sympathy and amity, and yet is his great symbol 'the Way' torn from what it symbolized—man the wayfarer through the worlds in his 'Becoming'—and turned into a category of eight wherein is no mention of amity, pity or sympathy.

Has any great Helper of man ever been so libelled? Will this book serve to clear to any extent these libels? Will it help the thoughtful of the next generation to look on these things in a truer, because more historical perspective?

It is for us of today and tomorrow, reading these things of the past, and heeding the dying call of India's great son to us to "accomplish earnestly," to work out a truer word than they had, or than we yet truly have, of man by his will becoming what he yet may be.

APPENDIX

Among many other difficulties hindering worthy achievement in this very provisional manual, two hindrances have been outstanding: (1) The fact that I have suffered much of its first edition to survive; (2) the absence of evidence in either Pali or Sanskrit literature, showing how the 'Buddhist development' may be seen growing, in a way consciously felt and expressed, out of the current and more 'established' religious culture.

As to this second difficulty, the many conversations between Sakyans and brahmans and cultured laymen in the Suttas give some help. But in brahman literature there is nothing handed down, affording us outspoken evidence of what brahmans were thinking about the Sakyans, during the last four centuries of the pre-Christian era. Collateral evidence may aid us herein, when the oldest Jaina literature has been fully opened up and the interesting history elicited, of how the growing vogue in mind-analysis reveals a midway result between its effects on Brahmanism and on Buddhism. But at present, Buddhism is shown as either a causeless irruption in Indian culture, or as at best a reform movement in matters of ritual, birth-monopoly and popular theodicy. Neither view should be acceptable to historical criticism. I do not say, that the Buddhist movement included no such reforms. I do not say, that in the birth of Buddhism there was nothing irruptive. Sunrise is an irruption, for all the dawn that preceded it. 'Sakya' may remain more of an 'irruption' than was Christianity, when this is studied in the light of preceding Apocalyptic thought.

This difficulty might have found mention when I came to Buddhist psychology. I have instead left it to the reader to see, how far the new ways in mental terminology and outlook in the 'Middle' Upaniṣads find an echo in early Buddhist terms and outlook.

In connection with the difficulty called (1), I would here add a note called for by the trend taken in European interest in Buddhism, since my first, or indeed since my second edition appeared.

This trend lies in the growing notion, that in the practice of 'Yoga,' and in the cult of 'meditation,' supposed to be a cardinal feature in all Buddhism, may be found one of the strongest levers of propaganda for converting the 'West' to Indian outlook on religion. Possibly aiding in this persuasion is the opinion, expressed by one or two European writers, that Buddhism is largely just Yoga.

This matter is relevant in a study of Indian mind-ways, and should have been given more emphasis on p. 332, corresponding to the treatment given on earlier pages to the positive emergence of Yoga in Upaniṣadic thought.

The word, the idea of 'yoga' is seen, in Buddhism, undergoing an interesting history. But everywhere it appears as a term and an idea that is merely accessory, and in no way betraying a specific practice. On the one hand the word is used with appreciation; on the other with depreciation. The teacher is sometimes said to be engaged in *paṭisallāna*, or reflection, during which it may be an idea occurs to him of something to be done. Next, *paṭisallāna* is in one Sutta commended, *yoga* being adduced in one of its two Buddhist meanings of 'devotion,' 'concentration,' thus: *paṭisallāne yogaṃ āpajjetha* : "in meditation bring devotion to bear; the meditative monk knows *x* as it really is" (*i.e.* has become).[1] Be it noted, that *paṭisallāna* is never mixed up with musing (*jhāna*); that, as I have shown, was *not meditation*, but purged alertness for the purpose of psychic experience. Again, a disciple is, in a few Suttas, seen asking the teacher for a subject or test on which he may ruminate in solitude, so that he 'may dwell remote, earnest, ardent, beselved' (*pahitatto*).[2] This is not always for his private benefit alone. One such is found saying, he may thereby bring others along, who may afterwards be consulting (*ajjhesanti*) him. This practice came later to be called *kammaṭṭhāna* : 'occasion for work,' namely, of *mano-kamma*, work of mind; it is an exegetical term. Again, the Dhammapada, perhaps the oldest metrical compilation, at least as to parts of it, uses the term *yoga* also as just 'diligence.'

But the Dīgha categories (Sangīti) and the Abhidhamma Piṭaka see in the word one of the names for spiritual hindrances: fetters, 'yokes,' cankers, knots, floods. There is no reference, textual or exegetical, to any worthier current meaning of *yoga*. The only mention of *yoga* in Dīgha Suttas is to it as a group of cheating 'practices' (iii. 176).

The only form in which the word everywhere maintains appreciation is in the verb *anu-yuñj-*, 'devoted to': *Mā pamādaṃ anuyuñjetha* : Be not given to slackness, etc., etc.

The error of linking up Buddhism with Yoga as religious practice is the stranger, when we consider how opposite were the objects mainly sought in each.

[1] *Saṃyutta*, v, 414. [2] *Ibid*., pp. 142, 187 f.

Upaniṣadic Yoga was thought and will concentrated introversively on the One: the Man supreme Within, to whom approach in growth was in Yoga sought. In Buddhism the Divine Man was being ejected; the real human 'man' was being denied. The outlook sought was to see man as not one, but manifold. It is true that at least one canonical work, of later build, praises *ekatta* (unity), decries *nānatta* (diversity); but nowhere is this made a general principle. Hence the student, in so far as he seeks, not to construct a new eclecticism and christen it 'Buddhism,' but to get at historic truth, should be careful to avoid seeing in either 'Meditation' or 'Yoga' anything that has ever been truly and integrally Buddhist.

But there is yet another strand in the modern trend in Buddhist study which has, in the last twenty years, come to the front. This is that Buddhism is virtually, especially in the significance of the work *dhamma*, a teaching of the solution of world-problems by the fact of causation, *karma* being the term for its functioning in man.

I did let this matter slip by (p. 300). My book was, after all, not on logic, nor on natural philosophy. But in that the way in which a preoccupation with cause and effect, as against credence in the fortuitous: *adhicca-samuppanna*, was put into formula *in terms of mind-ways*, I should have perhaps been more explicit about it. Yet I would insist that the real grip of the 'law' of causation is *not* worded in terms of mind. The mind terms are only used in the *special application* of the law, of which I have duly spoken (p. 251). Namely, that by noting how birth involves (the principle of) becoming, this of life-fuel, this of desire, this of feeling (experience), this of contact, this of sense, this of name and shape, this of *viññāṇa*, the persisting man, he may see how the 'ill' dominating all sentient existence *comes to pass*.

So far the monkish, the later turning of a great vision to a monkish outlook on life, coupled with the new insight, that mind has its causal uniformities, not matter only. But the vision of cause as law is in terms which bring us to that deeper psychology which sees in man's nature not being but becoming. "This being, that becomes; from the uprising of this, that uprises. This not being, that becomes not; from the stopping of this, that is stopped." In so far as this saying may truly be Gotama's own, we may not therefrom deduce that the new quickened interest in causation was due entirely to him. But we may incline to believe that, in this current interest, he saw a way of expressing the truth in his own teaching of man, as essentially a growing, a becoming phenomenon. It was with *this* that he was primarily concerned; not with any explaining of the universe. His aftermen were interested mainly in a monastic ideal best to be conveyed in terms of the *vogue* of mind-analysis.

It is as a contribution to the emergence of that deeper psychology that I have laid these pages in student hands. Our young psychology, starting as the truant child of philosophy under the guidance of physiology has yet to find her true level. She has dealt overmuch with analysis of man as just mind 'run by' body, considered in a transverse section of what happens just now to be held as the normal mind. She reminds me of Rembrandt's surgeons inspecting a corpse. She needs, with the first Buddhism, to see in mind the instrument of the man as essentially willer wayfaring in a quest of that which for him seems a Better in this or that, nay, which seems a present Best. It is impossible rightly to understand him, so questing with his mind, as just a phenomenon of earth, or even of an earth wherein Utopia in any final sense is the measure of him. Always herein his will in the long run outruns his mind, that is, his thought. To all seeming, his questing is will carrying out the dictates of him-as-minding. Actually he is in a becoming, that is, in a sought welfare he is willing to win. His 'idea' of that welfare is his self-directing, his will, pausing to give shape to what he wills. In a semi-wordless way, the message of Buddhism, buried in a multitude of words, sought to show in man this eternally true thing.

ADDENDUM

Too late for its right placing, on p. 258, I have stumbled on a quite overlooked, quite unformularized reference to *satippaṭṭhāna* in *Saṃyutta*, v. 168 f. The Founder is made to tell of acrobat and pupil disputing, whether, in climbing a bamboo pole balanced on the former, each shall watch (lit. ward) himself or the other. Gotama's 'moral' is, that 'presence of mindfulness' is best practised by both; that in warding the self, one must ward the 'other,' and conversely. "The self, by practice, 'making-become,' repetition; the other, by patience, not-harming, amity, kindness. By guarding the self one guards the other man; by guarding the other man one guards the self."

As a scrap of contributory evidence in the fact of Sakyan mission work as yet untortured by formulas, the context has interest. But how would it not have been quoted, had it been found in Sokrates' talks, or in the Gospels! What has befallen it and us, that it has never before been told?

INDEX I

ENGLISH WORDS AND NAMES

INDEX II

PALI AND SANSKRIT

Printed by Billing and Sons Ltd., Guildford and Esher